T0178357

Communications in Computer and Information Science 1558

More information about this series at https://link.springer.com/bookseries/7899

Chunjie Cao · Yuqing Zhang · Yuan Hong ·
Ding Wang (Eds.)

Frontiers in Cyber Security

4th International Conference, FCS 2021
Haikou, China, December 17–19, 2021
Revised Selected Papers

 Springer

Editors
Chunjie Cao
Hainan University
Haikou, China

Yuan Hong 🆔
Illinois Institute of Technology
Chicago, IL, USA

Yuqing Zhang
National Computer Network Intrusion
Protection Center (NCNIPC)
Beijing, China

Ding Wang
Nankai University
Tianjin, China

ISSN 1865-0929   ISSN 1865-0937 (electronic)
Communications in Computer and Information Science
ISBN 978-981-19-0522-3   ISBN 978-981-19-0523-0 (eBook)
https://doi.org/10.1007/978-981-19-0523-0

This Springer imprint is published by the registered company Springer Nature Singapore Pte Ltd.
The registered company address is: 152 Beach Road, #21-01/04 Gateway East, Singapore 189721, Singapore

Preface

This volume contains the papers from the 4th International Conference on Frontiers in Cyber Security (FCS 2021). The event was organized by School of Cyberspace Security (School of Cryptology), Hainan University. This series, which started in 2018, brings together individuals involved in multiple disciplines of cyber security in order to foster exchange of ideas.

In recent years, cyber security threats have increased rapidly. All kinds of extremely dangerous attack behaviors expose every common user to risks including privacy leakage, property loss, etc. Cyber security has also received increasing attention from researchers. The development of cyber security requires extensive communication. In view of this situation, and the permanent theme of FCS being "Cyber Security", aiming to introduce security concepts and technology achievements from the international forefront in the field of information security, and to share insights into the latest development trends and innovative technology of cyber security, the FCS conference provides a good platform for researchers and practitioners to exchange the latest research achievements and discuss these questions of network security, system security, cryptography, trust management, privacy protection, information hiding, computer forensics, content security, and their applications, etc. keeping the pace with international security innovation concepts to provide theoretical and technical support for international cyber space development.

The FCS conference has been held four times, starting at the University of Electronic Science and Technology of China in 2018. In these four years, hundreds of researchers have exchanged ideas with each other at the FCS events, which has promoted the development of cyber security. In 2021, FCS was held in Haikou, China, and organized by Hainan University which is one of the most important research institutes in China. FCS 2021 received 58 papers and accepted 22 papers, including two short papers. Reviewers were assigned an average of 4.3 papers and the average number of reviews per paper was 2.7. A double-blind peer review process was employed to promote transparency.

The conference received great attention from all over the world, with participants from countries such as China, Japan, the Netherlands, Denmark, the USA, etc. Taking place during the COVID-19 pandemic, the conference needed to comply with the relevant prevention regulations. For the health of the participants, some overseas participants needed to participate in the conference online, which was a big challenge.

According to the accepted papers, the five topics of FCS 2021 classified by reviewers were as follows: cryptography, intelligent security, system security, network security, and multimedia security.

The proceedings editors wish to thank the dedicated Program Committee members and all the other reviewers for their contributions. We also thank Springer for their trust and for publishing the proceedings of FCS 2021.

September 2021

Chunjie Cao
Yuqing Zhang
Yuan Hong
Ding Wang

Organization

Steering Committee

Baocang Wang	Xidian University, China
Chunhua Su	University of Aizu, Japan
Fagen Li	University of Electronic Science and Technology of China, China
Guangquan Xu	Tianjin University, China
Kai Chen	Institute of Information Engineering, CAS, China
Kaitai Liang	Delft University of Technology, Netherlands
Mingwu Zhang	Hubei University of Technology, China
Robert H. Deng	Singapore Management University, Singapore
Tsuyoshi Takagi	University of Tokyo, Japan
Weizhi Meng	Technical University of Denmark, Denmark
Xiaojiang Du	Temple University, USA

General Chairs

Chunming Rong	University of Stavanger, Norway
Chunjie Cao	Hainan University, China
Yuqing Zhang	National Computer Network Intrusion Protection Center (NCNIPC), China

Program Committee Chairs

Yuan Hong	Illinois Institute of Technology, USA
Ding Wang	Nankai University, China

Program Committee

Si Chen	West Chester University, USA
Debasis Giri	Haldia Institute of Technology, India
Song Han	Zhejiang Gongshang University, China
Tao Li	Nankai University, China
Guozhu Meng	Institute of Information Engineering, CAS, China
Shanchen Pang	Tiangong University, China
Meng Shen	Beijing Institute of Technology, China
Ding Wang	Nankai University, China
Xiaofei Xie	Nanyang Technological University, Singapore

Qiuling Yue	Hainan University, China
Debiao He	Wuhan University, China
Bok-Min Goi	University Tunku Abdul Rahman (UTAR), Malaysia
Fagen Li	University of Electronic Science and Technology of China, China
Jingqiang Lin	Institute of Information Engineering, CAS, China
Weizhi Meng	Technical University of Denmark, Denmark
Hao Peng	Zhejiang Normal University, China
Gautam Srivastava	Brandon University, Canada
Wei Wang	Beijing Jiaotong University, China
Hongyu Yang	Civil Aviation University of China, China
Fangguo Zhang	Sun Yat-sen University, China
Shaojing Fu	National University of Defense Technology, China
Guangquan Xu	Tianjin University, China
Jianxin Li	Beihang University, China
Wojciech Mazurczyk	Warsaw University of Technology, Poland
Wei Ou	Hainan University, China
Honggang Qi	University of Chinese Academy of Sciences, China
Baocang Wang	Xidian University, China
Zhijun Wu	Civil Aviation University of China, China
Jun Ye	Hainan University, China
Mingwu Zhang	Hubei University of Technology, China
Chao Zhang	Tsinghua University, China
Anmin Fu	Nanjing University of Science and Technology, China
Hong Lei	Hainan University, China
Jianhui Lv	Tsinghua University, China
Wenyuan Wu	Chongqing Institute of Green and Intelligent Technology, CAS, China
David Glance	University of Western Australia, Australia
Ali Yavari	Swinburne University of Technology, Australia
Wuping Xie	Jiangxi Normal University, China
Yu Wei	Purdue University, USA
Guixin Ye	Northwestern University, USA
Zhenzhuo Hou	Peking University, China
Qiying Dong	Nankai University, China
Hao Wang	Shandong Normal University, China
Haoyu Ma	Xidian University, China
Jianfeng Wang	Xidian University, China

Saru Kumari	Chaudhary Charan Singh University, India
Yunkai Zou	Nankai University, China
Xavier de Carné de Carnavalet	Hong Kong Polytechnic University, China

Publicity Chairs

Hao Peng	Zhejiang Normal University, China
Hongyu Yang	Civil Aviation University of China, China
Weizhi Meng	Technical University of Denmark, Denmark
Yong Ding	Pengcheng Lab, China
Yuanyuan Ma	Qingdao Agricultural University, China

Organization Committee Chairs

Xiaoyi Zhou	Hainan University, China
Dian Zhang	Hainan University, China
Zifeng Xu	Hainan University, China
Qiuling Yue	Hainan University, China
Xiaoli Qin	Hainan University, China

Organization Committee

Longjuan Wang	Hainan University, China
Xuefeng Fan	Hainan University, China
Lu Zhang	Hainan University, China
Tianshuo Zhang	Hainan University, China
Bingbing Zhu	Hainan University, China

Contents

Intelligent Security

DACN: Malware Classification Based on Dynamic Analysis and Capsule
Networks 3
    Binghui Zou, Chunjie Cao, Longjuan Wang, and Fangjian Tao

Research on Automatic Analysis and Exploitation Technology of Remote
Code Execution Vulnerability for Grid System 14
    Hongwen Wu, Xiaoming Wang, Ke Zhou, Jianming Zou, Congyun Wu,
    Wenjian Wen, Zhicheng Huang, Jiezhen Deng, and Tingyu Qiu

GWDGA: An Effective Adversarial DGA 30
    Xiang Shu, Chunjie Cao, Longjuan Wang, and Fangjian Tao

Imperceptible and Reliable Adversarial Attack 49
    Jiawei Zhang, Jinwei Wang, Xiangyang Luo, Bin Ma, and Naixue Xiong

Architecture and Security Analysis of Federated Learning-Based
Automatic Modulation Classification 63
    Xianglin Wei, Chao Wang, Xiang Jiao, Qiang Duan, and Yongyang Hu

Detecting Inconsistent Vulnerable Software Version in Security
Vulnerability Reports 78
    Hansong Ren, Xuejun Li, Liao Lei, Guoliang Ou, Hongyu Sun,
    Gaofei Wu, Xiao Tian, Jinglu Hu, and Yuqing Zhang

System Security

Multi-modal Universal Embedding Representations for Language
Understanding 103
    Xi Luo, Chunjie Cao, and Longjuan Wang

New Federation Algorithm Based on End-Edge-Cloud Architecture
for Smart Grid 120
    Xin Ji, Haifeng Zhang, Juan Chu, Linxiao Dong, and Chengyue Yang

Certificateless Authentication and Consensus for the Blockchain-Based
Smart Grid 134
    Egide Nkurunziza, Gervais Mwitende, Lawrence Tandoh, and Fagen Li

Information System Security Risk Assessment Based on Entropy Weight
Method - Bayesian Network 152
   Xinjian Lv, Nan Shi, Jing Wei, Yuan Tian, Jie Li, and Jian Li

Survey of 3D Printer Security Offensive and Defensive 163
   Jiayuan Zhang, Mengyue Feng, Yuhang Huang, Tao Feng, Wenjie Wang,
   He Wang, and Han Zhang

Network Security

Requirements for Total Resistance to Pollution Attacks in HMAC-Based
Authentication Schemes for Network Coding 181
   Lawrence Tandoh, Fagen Li, Ikram Ali, Charles Roland Haruna,
   Michael Y. Kpiebaareh, and Christopher Tandoh

Network Security Situation Assessment Method Based on MHSA-FL
Model 197
   Kejun Zhang, Xinrui Jiang, Xinying Yu, and Liwen Feng

A Hybrid Network Intrusion Detection Model Based on CNN-LSTM
and Attention Mechanism 214
   Jieru Mu, Hua He, Lin Li, Shanchen Pang, and Cong Liu

System Security Analysis of Different Link Proportions Between Nodes
in the Cyber-Physical System Against Target Attack 230
   Hao Peng, Zhen Qian, Ming Zhong, Dandan Zhao, Guangquan Xu,
   Songyang Wu, and Jianming Han

Multimedia Security

A GDIoU Loss Function-Based YOLOv4 Deep Learning Network
for High-Performance Insulator Location in Field Images 245
   Bin Ma, Yongkang Fu, Jian Li, Chunpeng Wang, and Yuli Wang

Identification of Synthetic Spoofed Speech with Deep Capsule Network 257
   Terui Mao, Diqun Yan, Yongkang Gong, and Randing Wang

Privacy, Risk and Trust

Cloud-Aided Scalable Revocable Identity-Based Encryption
with Ciphertext Update from Lattices 269
   Yanhua Zhang, Ximeng Liu, Yupu Hu, and Huiwen Jia

A Privacy-Preserving Medical Image Scheme Based on Secret Sharing
and Reversible Data Hiding 288
    Ming Cheng, Yang Yang, Yingqiu Ding, and Weiming Zhang

Correlation Power Analysis and Protected Implementation on Block
Cipher RainDrop 308
    Zhixuan Gao, Shuang Wang, Yaoling Ding, An Wang, and Qingjun Yuan

Data and Application Security

Research on Security Assessment of Cross Border Data Flow 327
    Wang Na, Wu Gaofei, Yue Qiuling, Hu Jinglu, and Yuqing Zhang

A Review of Data Representation Methods for Vulnerability Mining
Using Deep Learning 342
    Ying Li, Mianxue Gu, Hongyu Sun, Yuhao Lin, Qiuling Yue, Zhen Guo,
    Jinglu Hu, He Wang, and Yuqing Zhang

Author Index 353

Intelligent Security

DACN: Malware Classification Based on Dynamic Analysis and Capsule Networks

Binghui Zou[1,2], Chunjie Cao[1,2], Longjuan Wang[1,2(✉)], and Fangjian Tao[1,2]

[1] School of Cyberspace Security, Hainan University, Haikou 570228, China
{bhzou,wanglongjuan}@hainanu.edu.cn
[2] Key Laboratory of Internet Information Retrieval of Hainan Province, Hainan University, Haikou 570228, China

Abstract. In the existing classification method of malware visualization, an individual static feature leads to an incomplete characterization of malware and affects classification accuracy, and the max-pooling layers in a convolutional neural network-based classification model disregard the spatial location relationships between features and loses valuable information. To overcome these drawbacks, we build a new malware classification system, DACN, which first maps the three dynamic features (i.e., API calls, DLL loads, and registry operations) of malware to the R, G, and B channels of an image respectively. Then, based on the capsule network, a malware classification model is proposed to capture the spatial location relationships between features. Experimental results demonstrate that using fused features instead of an individual feature improves the accuracy of malware classification by 1.3%–13.8%. DACN can achieve 97.5% classification accuracy, which is better than the model based on convolutional neural network.

Keywords: Malware classification · Dynamic analysis · Capsule network · Feature fusion

1 Introduction

Although many security vendors and researchers have been battling malware for years, it remains one of the biggest threats in cyberspace. Malware is growing rapidly and causing great harm, the AVTEST report shows [1], the number of malware is increasing year by year, and the total number has increased nearly 12 times in the past 10 years. The IBM X-Force Threat Intelligence Index report [2] points out that destructive malware attacks can cost companies a heavy price and the average cost paid after each incident is as high as $239 million.

In the face of the growing threat of malware, researching effective detection methods is a top priority for businesses and organizations. Static analysis [3] and dynamic analysis [4] are two main methods to analyze malware, since there is no need to reverse engineer files, dynamic analysis can significantly reduce the time to discover malicious code. Many current studies consider an individual feature

© Springer Nature Singapore Pte Ltd. 2022
C. Cao et al. (Eds.): FCS 2021, CCIS 1558, pp. 3–13, 2022.
https://doi.org/10.1007/978-981-19-0523-0_1

when characterizing malware [5,6], and these features are extracted based on static analysis. However, malware generates a multitude of dynamic behaviors during execution [7] and these features are very important for analyzing malware, yet few studies have mentioned such features and fused them. Deep learning is now widely used for malware classification tasks [8], however, signature-based or API-based calls alone do not characterize malware well.

In order to implement malware classification with convolutional neural networks(CNN), there have been studies on converting original binary files into grayscale images [9] or color images [10]. However, CNN with max-pooling layers disregard the spatial location relationships between features when performing feature extraction [11], which may have an impact on malware classification results. Capsule network is a new neural network, unlike traditional neural networks, which are composed of capsules instead of neurons, a capsule is a collection of compositions of a set of neurons that not only have length but also exist in direction at the same time, it can obtain spatial location relationships [12]. There have been studies [13] that have applied capsule network to the malware classification task, however, these studies used individual features and did not combine dynamic features (i.e., API calls, DLL loads, and registry operations) for fusion.

To better characterize malware and learn spatial location relationships between features, and improve malware classification performance, a malware classification system DACN (Dynamic Analysis and Capsule Networks) is constructed. Firstly, to address the problem of individual feature extraction and incomplete characterization of malware, we adopt a dynamic analysis approach where three dynamic features of malware: API calls, DLL loads, and registry operations are extracted and mapped to the RGB space of the image respectively. Secondly, to be able to learn the spatial location relationship between features, we introduced a capsule network, and after improvement, we developed a capsule network model for malware classification, and the experiments showed that DACN classified the fused feature images with an accuracy of 97.5%.

The main contributions of this work are summarized as follows:

(1) We create a new dataset that can be used for Windows malware classification tasks. Using Cuckoo Sandbox [14], 3749 malwares were completely analyzed and 3749 detailed dynamic analysis reports were obtained.
(2) We propose a feature fusion method based on dynamic analysis to transform the dynamic features of malware into images. Three malware features (i.e., API calls, DLL loads, registry modifications) are extracted, and then mapped to R, G and B spaces respectively and transformed into color images.
(3) Based on capsule network, we propose an improved malware classification model. We add a channel attention layer after the first convolution layer, the convolution layer in the Primary Capsule layer was removed. In the decoder, four transposed convolution layers are used to replace three full connection layers, the reconstruction loss is measured by JS divergence to measure the distance between the reconstructed image and the original image, and then propagates back to the total loss function formed by the edge loss.

The remainder of this paper is organized as follows. In Sect. 2, we review related work, while Sect. 3 describes our system architecture. Section 4 introduces the method of feature fusion and presents the details of the improved model. In Sect. 5, experimental results are described, and the performance of DACN is systematically evaluated. Finally, we draw concluding remarks in Sect. 6.

2 Related Work

In order to detect malware variants, Zhang et al. [15] proposed a feature mixing technique for malware variant detection based on CNN and back propagation neural network for opcode based feature embedding and API based feature embedding, which achieved 95% accuracy on malware detection task and 90% accuracy on classification task. However, these methods use static analysis, whereas malware in real environments often employs adversarial techniques, such as obfuscation, encryption. In addition, these methods consider an individual feature, and cannot fully and accurately characterize malicious software.

Nataraj et al. [9] first studied malware images and visualized malware binaries as grayscale images, Yuan et al. [16] proposed a byte-level malware classification method based on Markov images and deep learning and Naeem et al. [17] proposed a method based on color image visualization and deep CNN for malware on industrial IOT devices. These studies are based on static analysis, which is simple and versatile, but the classification effect is not ideal in practice.

Droid-Sec [18] used a deep learning-based model for malware detection, and Yoo et al. [19] proposed a hybrid decision model based on machine learning by combining random forest and deep learning model. Wadkar et al. [20] analyzed a large number of malware and applied feature ranking based on linear support vector machine weights to identify variations within a malware family. Cayir et al. [21] proposed an integrated capsule network model, RCNF, based on bootstrap aggregation technique, with F-score of 0.9661 in Malimg dataset [9]. RCNF does not use dynamic analysis and directly converts raw binaries into images, where classification performance suffers when adversarial techniques such as encryption are present.

3 System Architecture

The architecture of our proposed malware classification system, DACN, is shown in Fig. 1. It consists of the following components:

- **Data collection:** Through VirusShare [22], we obtain a malware dataset. The raw dataset provided by VirusShare includes multiple types of files, and the API provided by VirusShare can be used to screen out malicious software that can run on Windows, known as EXE executables.
- **Dynamic analysis:** This module uses Cuckoo Sandbox for dynamic analysis of malware, combined with the VirusTotal scanning service [23] for tag aggregation with avclass2 [6], and finally obtains malware analysis reports and family tags.

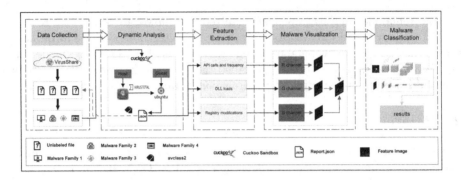

Fig. 1. System architecture of DACN

- **Feature extraction:** Based on the analysis report of the previous module, we extract the three dynamic features contained in the report: the API and the number of calls when the malware is running, the loaded DLL file, and the operations on the registry.
- **Malware visualization:** In this module, we map the API, DLL, and registry to the RGB channel of an image, and use the bilinear interpolation algorithm to zoom in or out the features, so that the size of the output feature image is 28×28.
- **Malware classification:** Based on the capsule network, we propose a malware classification model and train it with feature images. The improved capsule network model can predict the family tags of malicious software.

4 Proposed Method

4.1 Malware Visualization

To obtain more features and characterize the malware more comprehensively, we extracted the three dynamic features of the API called and the number of calls during the runtime, the loaded DLL file, and the operations on the registry. In this work, the total number of APIs called was 249, all DLL files loaded was 730, and all malware registry keys present were 5013. In order to map these three features to the R, G, and B spaces of an image. First, we convert the three features into vectors v_1, v_2, and v_3, with dimensions of 249, 730, and 5013 respectively. Then, we resized v_1, v_2, and v_3 into v_1', v_2', v_3' with two-dimensional arrays of 16×16, 28×28, 71×71. The three matrix arrays correspond to the R, G, and B channels of an image, but due to the differences in dimensions, they cannot be mapped directly. Therefore, we adopt bilinear interpolation transformation to zoom in v_1' to 28×28 and zoom out v_3' to 28×28 with the v_2' vector as the reference.

4.2 Malware Classification

Our proposed malware classification model based on capsule network is shown in Fig. 2, which consists of two parts: an encoder and a decoder. The encoder

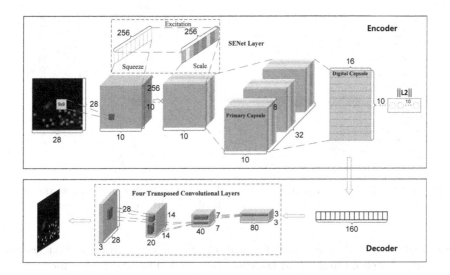

Fig. 2. The improved capsule network model

is composed of convolutional layer, SENet layer [24], Primary Capsule layer, and Digital Capsule layer. The decoder is composed of four transposed convolutional layers. For the task of malware classification, we have made the following three improvements in the classic capsule network: 1) A SENet layer is added to the encoder, while the original convolution of Primary Caps layer is reduced, and the whole network is reduced from two convolution layers to one convolution layer. 2) Three full connection layers in the encoder section are removed, and four transposed convolutional layers are used to reconstruct the image; 3) The reconstruction loss uses JS divergence to measure the distance between the reconstructed image and the original image.

SENet Layer. Squeeze-and-Excitation Networks (SENet) is a novel channel attention mechanism proposed in [24], it uses a feature recalibration strategy to learn the importance of each feature channel by learning the correlation between channels. Based on the degree of importance, useful features are promoted and useless features are suppressed to strengthen the more useful information. In this research, we introduce a SENet layer between the convolutional layer and the Primary Capsule layer of the capsule network, and enhance the feature channels extracted by the convolutional layer.

Transposed Convolution Layer. DCGAN was proposed in [25], the authors used transposed convolution in the generator part to generate real images. Inspired by this idea, we remove the fully connected layer of the capsule network decoder part and use transposed convolution to reconstruct the image. We use four transposed convolutional layers in the decoder part. In addition, in order to make the transmitted data distribution more reasonable and speed up the

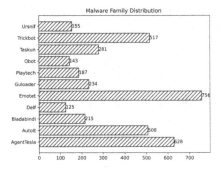

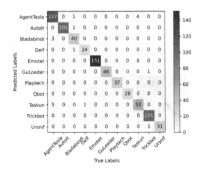

Fig. 3. Malware family distribution

Fig. 4. The confusion matrix of the ours model on the dataset

convergence speed of the model, each transposed convolutional layer passes through a batch normalization layer and is activated by the ReLU function.

Loss Function. The loss function of the capsule network consists of two parts: margin loss and reconstruction loss. The margin loss is consistent with the loss function used in the classic capsule network, as shown in Eq. 1. The output v_k of the capsule k is a discriminant vector, and the modulus length of the vector v_k represents the probability of the existence of the corresponding category. The reconstruction loss is a measure of the distance between the reconstructed image and the original distribution. We use the JS divergence instead of the Mean Square Error loss in the classic capsule network, as given in Eq. 2.

$$L_{margin} = T_k max \left(0, m^+ - \| v_k \| \right)^2 + \lambda \left(1 - T_k\right) max \left(0, \| v_k \| - m^-\right)^2 \quad (1)$$

$$L_{recon} = D_{JS}\left(P_1 \| P_2\right) = \frac{1}{2}D_{KL}\left(P_1 \| \frac{P_1 + P_2}{2}\right) + \frac{1}{2}D_{KL}\left(P_2 \| \frac{P_1 + P_2}{2}\right) \quad (2)$$

where P_1 and P_2 denote two probability distributions, D_{KL} is given in Eq. 3.

$$D_{KL}\left(P \| Q\right) = -\sum_{x \in X} P\left(x\right) log \frac{1}{P\left(x\right)} + \sum_{x \in X} P\left(x\right) log \frac{1}{Q\left(x\right)} = \sum_{x \in X} P\left(x\right) log \frac{P\left(x\right)}{Q\left(x\right)} \quad (3)$$

5   Experimental Evaluation

5.1   Malware Dataset

We obtained a dataset containing 65,536 malicious samples from VirusShare [22], which were filtered to obtain 15,872 exe executable malware. After dynamic analysis through Cukoo Sandbox, 15,872 report.json files were obtained. Cuckoo Sandbox also integrates with the VirusTotal scanning service, which allows us to obtain the virus vendor's scan results through VirusTotal. To obtain uniform malware family labels, we used avclass2 [26] for label aggregation, and finally, we obtained a malware dataset containing the complete dynamic analysis results: 11 malware families and 3749 real samples of malware, and Fig. 3 shows the distribution of the number of malware in each family.

Table 1. Performance of DACN on the test data

Family	Precision	Recall	F1 score
AgentTesla	0.95902	0.936	0.94737
Autoit	0.9902	1.0	0.99508
Bladabindi	0.93023	0.93023	0.93023
Delf	0.96	0.96	0.96
Emotet	1.0	1.0	1.0
GuLoader	0.97872	1.0	0.98925
Playtech	1.0	1.0	1.0
Qbot	1.0	1.0	1.0
Taskun	0.89655	0.92857	0.91228
Trickbot	1.0	0.98058	0.99019
Ursnif	0.96875	1.0	0.98413

Table 2. Accuracy of different features under five-fold cross-validation

Features	Five-Fold					
	1	2	3	4	5	*Mean accuracy*
API	0.936	0.92533	0.92667	0.932	0.93191	**0.93038**
DLL	0.96533	0.95867	0.95333	0.97067	0.96262	**0.96212**
REG	0.83333	0.828	0.82667	0.84533	0.8518	**0.83703**
API+DLL	0.97067	0.96267	0.96	0.97333	0.96395	**0.96612**
API+REG	0.94933	0.952	0.944	0.96133	0.96662	**0.95466**
DLL+REG	0.97333	0.964	0.96667	0.98267	0.97864	**0.97306**
API+DLL+REG	0.97467	0.96933	0.96933	0.98133	0.98131	**0.97519**

Table 3. Macro F1 Score of different features under five-fold cross-validation

Features	Five-Fold					
	1	2	3	4	5	*Mean Macro F1*
API	0.90662	0.90784	0.90786	0.90361	0.92146	**0.90948**
DLL	0.96482	0.95637	0.94806	0.97187	0.96156	**0.96054**
REG	0.7059	0.71551	0.71733	0.77111	0.73432	**0.72883**
API+DLL	0.97089	0.96319	0.9575	0.97169	0.96533	**0.96572**
API+REG	0.92501	0.93781	0.92812	0.94304	0.95678	**0.93815**
DLL+REG	0.97287	0.9585	0.96105	0.98258	0.97678	**0.97036**
API+DLL+REG	0.97483	0.96823	0.96688	0.98007	0.9798	**0.97396**

5.2 Model Training and Evaluation

We used the AdamW optimizer to update the network parameters during training, and the number of each malware family in the dataset varied widely with
uneven data distribution. To better evaluate the model, we use five-fold cross-
validation, where the entire dataset is divided into five sub-samples, one of which
is taken as the test set and the other four are used as the training set to train
the model without repeating each time. The model is trained and tested for five
cycles, and finally the average value of the model on the test set is calculated
as the final evaluation of the model. The cross-validation scores of the improved
capsule network classification model are shown in Table 1 and the specifics of
each malware family label predicted are shown in Fig. 4.

Table 4. Accuracy comparison with CNN-based models under five-fold cross-validation

Models	Five-Fold					
	1	2	3	4	5	*Mean accuracy*
AlexNet [27]	0.94267	0.90267	0.93733	0.96933	0.96395	**0.94319**
LeNet5 [30]	0.69333	0.63733	0.54933	0.73733	0.50467	**0.6244**
GoogleNet [28]	0.96133	0.95333	0.948	0.97067	0.97063	**0.96079**
ResNet18 [29]	0.972	0.97067	0.964	0.97733	0.97597	**0.97199**
DACN	0.97467	0.96933	0.96933	0.98133	0.98131	**0.97519**

5.3 Feature Selection

To determine the effects of different characteristics, we conducted seven comparative experiments. While translating malware features into images (API stands for
API calls, DLL stands for DLL loads, and REG stands for registry operations),
the three features are combined as API, DLL, REG, API+DLL, API+REG,

DLL+REG and API+DLL+REG, and then five-fold cross-validation is performed for each. We used the same hyperparameters for training each combination. Table 2 and Table 3 show the accuracy and Macro F1 score under five-fold cross-validation at different combinations of features. While characterizing malware with a feature, DLL loads can obtain the highest accuracy of 0.96212 and the highest Macro F1 Score of 0.96054, and REG get lowest accuracy and Macro F1 score.

5.4 Comparison with CNN-Based Models

To further evaluate the performance of DACN, we compared it with four CNN-based models, and the specific experimental values are presented in Table 4 and Table 5. As can be seen from Table 4, AlexNet [27], GoogLeNet [28], and ResNet18 [29] can all achieve more than 90% accuracy, which verifies the effectiveness of the extracted features. However, the CNN-based models contain maxpooling layers, they do not consider the spatial location relationship between features when extracting features, and lose some valuable information, so the classification accuracy of these models is not the highest. LeNet5 [30] performed the worst, with an accuracy of only 62.44%. ResNet18 is the best among the four CNN-based models with the accuracy of 97.199%. DACN was developed based on capsule network, different from max-pooling, capsules in capsule network can learn the spatial location relationship between features and have stronger feature extraction ability. The accuracy and Macro F1 score of DACN on the unbalanced dataset exceeded all CNN models. After five-fold cross-validation, the average accuracy was 97.519% and the average Macro F1 was 0.97396. Experiments show that DACN outperforms AlexNet, LeNet5, GoogLeNet and ResNet18 on malware classification tasks.

Table 5. Macro F1 Score comparison with CNN-based models under five-fold cross-validation

Models	Five-Fold					
	1	2	3	4	5	*Mean Macro F1*
AlexNet [27]	0.9346	0.88223	0.9296	0.96611	0.95972	**0.93445**
LeNet5 [30]	0.39469	0.31112	0.29516	0.4854	0.6244	**0.42215**
GoogLeNet [28]	0.95529	0.93989	0.93653	0.9678	0.96804	**0.95351**
ResNet18 [29]	0.97377	0.97016	0.96136	0.97292	0.97337	**0.97032**
DACN	0.97483	0.96823	0.96688	0.98007	0.9798	**0.97396**

6 Conclusion

In this work, we developed a malware classification system DACN based on dynamic analysis and capsule networks. Firstly, we extracted three dynamic features of malware (i.e., API calls, DLL loads, and registry operations) with dynamic analysis and mapped these features to the RGB channel of an image, and the more valuable features characterized the malware better. Secondly, we applied the capsule network to the problem of malware classification. Based on the classical capsule network, a channel attention mechanism is introduced, four transposed convolution layers are used to reconstruct the image and the JS divergence is used as the reconstruction loss function. DACN has stronger feature extraction ability and it can learn the spatial position relationship between features during feature extraction. The experiments show that the fused features have better classification performance compared to individual features. Compared with CNN-based classification models, DACN outperforms AlexNet, LeNet5, GoogLeNet, and ResNet18 in accuracy and F1 score.

Acknowledgement. This work was supported in part by the Natural Science Foundation of Hainan Province under Grant No.621MS017, in part by the National Natural Science Foundation of China Enterprise Innovation and Development Joint Fund under Grant No.U19B2044, and in part by the Key Research and Development Project of Hainan Province under Grant No.ZDYF2020012.

References

1. Total malware (2021). https://www.av-test.org/en/statistics/malware/
2. Ibm x-force threat intelligence index (2021). https://www.ibm.com/downloads/cas/M1X3B7QG/
3. Moser, A., Kruegel, C., Kirda, E.: Limits of static analysis for malware detection. In: Proceedings of ACSAC, pp. 421–430 (2007)
4. Afianian, A., Niksefat, S., Sadeghiyan, B., Baptiste, D.: Malware dynamic analysis evasion techniques: A survey. ACM Comput. Surv. **52**(6), 1–28 (2019)
5. Huang, N., Xu, M., Zheng, N., Qiao, T., Choo, K.K.R.: Deep android malware classification with API-based feature graph. In: Proceedings of TrustCom/BigDataSE, pp. 296–303 (2019)
6. Iwamoto, K., Wasaki, K.: Malware classification based on extracted API sequences using static analysis. In: Proceedings of AINTEC, pp. 31–38 (2012)
7. Wong, M.Y., Lie, D.: Intellidroid: A targeted input generator for the dynamic analysis of android malware. In: Proceedings of NDSS, vol. 16, pp. 21–24 (2016)
8. Zhang, Z., Qi, P., Wang, W.: Dynamic malware analysis with feature engineering and feature learning. In: Proceedings of AAAI, pp. 1210–1217 (2020)
9. Nataraj, L., Karthikeyan, S., Jacob, G., Manjunath, B.S.: Malware images: Visualization and automatic classification. In: Proceedings of VizSec, pp. 1–8. Association for Computing Machinery (2011)
10. Nguyen, K.D.T., Tuan, T.M., Le, S.H., Viet, A.P., Ogawa, M., Minh, N.L.: Comparison of three deep learning-based approaches for IOT malware detection. In: Proceedings of KSE, pp. 382–388 (2018)
11. Xiong, Y., Su, G., Ye, S., Sun, Y., Sun, Y.: Deeper capsule network for complex data. In: Proceedings of IJCNN, pp. 1–8 (2019)
12. Sabour, S., Frosst, N., Hinton, G.E.: Dynamic routing between capsules. In: Proceedings of NIPS, pp. 3859–3869 (2017)

13. Wang, Z., Han, W., Lu, Y., Xue, J.: A malware classification method based on the capsule network. In: International Conference on Machine Learning for Cyber Security, pp. 35–49. Springer (2020). https://doi.org/10.1007/978-3-030-62223-7_4
14. Cuckoo sandbox - automated malware analysis. https://cuckoosandbox.org/
15. Zhang, J., Qin, Z., Yin, H., Ou, L., Zhang, K.: A feature-hybrid malware variants detection using CNN based opcode embedding and BPNN based API embedding. Comput. Secur. **84**, 376–392 (2019)
16. Yuan, B., Wang, J., Liu, D., Guo, W., Wu, P., Bao, X.: Byte-level malware classification based on markov images and deep learning. Comput. Secur. **92**, 101740 (2020)
17. Naeem, H., et al.: Malware detection in industrial internet of things based on hybrid image visualization and deep learning model. Ad Hoc Netw. **105**, 102154 (2020)
18. Yuan, Z., Lu, Y., Wang, Z., Xue, Y.: Droid-sec: Deep learning in android malware detection. In: Proceedings of SIGCOMM, pp. 371–372 (2014)
19. Yoo, S., Kim, S., Kim, S., Kang, B.B.: Ai-hydra: Advanced hybrid approach using random forest and deep learning for malware classification. Inf. Sci. **546**, 420–435 (2021)
20. Wadkar, M., Di Troia, F., Stamp, M.: Detecting malware evolution using support vector machines. Expert Syst. Appl. **143**, 113022 (2020)
21. Çayır, A., Ünal, U., Dağ, H.: Random capsnet forest model for imbalanced malware type classification task. Comput. Secur. **102**(2), 102133 (2021)
22. Virusshare. https://virusshare.com/
23. Virustotal. https://www.virustotal.com/
24. Hu, J., Shen, L., Sun, G.: Squeeze-and-excitation networks. In: Proceedings of CVPR, pp. 7132–7141 (2018)
25. Radford, A., Metz, L., Chintala, S.: Unsupervised representation learning with deep convolutional generative adversarial networks. arXiv:1511.06434 (2015)
26. Sebastián, S., Caballero, J.: Avclass2: Massive malware tag extraction from AV labels. In: Proceedings of ACSAC, pp. 42–53 (2020)
27. Krizhevsky, A., Sutskever, I., Hinton, G.E.: Imagenet classification with deep convolutional neural networks. Adv. Neural. Inf. Process. Syst. **25**, 1097–1105 (2012)
28. Szegedy, C., et al.: Going deeper with convolutions. In: Proceedings of CVPR, pp. 1–9 (2015)
29. He, K., Zhang, X., Ren, S., Sun, J.: Deep residual learning for image recognition. In: Proceedings of CVPR, pp. 770–778 (2016)
30. LeCun, Y.: Lenet-5, convolutional neural networks. J. Vis. Commun. Image **20**(5), 14 (2015). http://yann.lecun.com/exdb/lenet

Research on Automatic Analysis and Exploitation Technology of Remote Code Execution Vulnerability for Grid System

Hongwen Wu[1], Xiaoming Wang[2(✉)], Ke Zhou[2], Jianming Zou[1], Congyun Wu[3], Wenjian Wen[1], Zhicheng Huang[1], Jiezhen Deng[1], and Tingyu Qiu[1]

[1] Dispatching Center of Wuzhou Power Supply Bureau, Wuzhou 543002, Guangxi, China
[2] Power System Institute, Guangxi Electric Power Research Institute, Nanning 530000, Guangxi, China
[3] Power Dispatch Center of Guangxi Power Grid Co. Ltd., Nanning 530000, Guangxi, China

Abstract. In the industrial network security attack and defense, remote code execution vulnerability can directly control the target power grid system, and it is one of the most harmful vulnerabilities. After an attack, relevant defense personnel often need to use network traffic and other residual traces through forensic analysis. However, it is difficult to analyze the remote code execution vulnerability of this type of memory corruption, given that randomization of the address space may be used in this type of vulnerability. We design and implement a tool to analyze and reproduce the remote code execution vulnerability of memory corruption type. Through the proposed shadow service technology and synchronous processing technology, the same shadow service as the target service environment is established in a fully controlled environment, the recorded attack traffic is processed synchronously, and the shadow service is reproduced in accordance with the sending and receiving conditions of the recorded attack traffic, and the recurrence is recorded at the same time. In the process of reproduction, address space randomization bypass is processed. The results show that defenders can use the system to quickly perform vulnerability investigations on remote codes for native services, thereby preventing re-attacks of similar vulnerabilities.

Keywords: Memory corruption · Remote code execution · Network traffic analysis · Vulnerability re-exploit · ASLR bypass

1 Introduction

The attack and defense of vulnerabilities in smart grid system is a permanent topic in the research of power grid security. In the process of software development, developers' negligence or lack of deep understanding of the underlying technology may lead to the generation of vulnerabilities, making the server device a highly valuable target for attackers.

If the client in the B/S architecture or C/S architecture of the power grid system is controlled by an attacker, the consequence is that the personal information of the user is hijacked, and the identity of the user on the network is forged or abused. However, for the equipment or software on the server side of the power grid system, the damage caused by security vulnerabilities is more serious, which may lead to the theft of the server permission. Attackers can use the server to further attack, or enhance the permission to obtain the highest permission of the server to completely obtain all the data of the power grid server. Another possibility is that the security policy of the target enterprise is broken due to the control of a server, the Intranet is exposed to the Internet and all user data and internal data of the enterprise are in crisis, as shown in Fig. 1. The consequences of the attack on the server and client are shown in Fig. 2. In comparison, the damage caused by the breach of the server is far greater than that of the client.

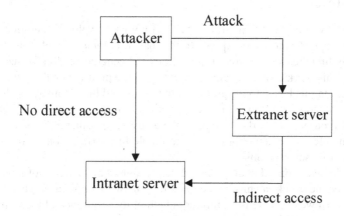

Fig. 1. Access the Intranet after the server is breached.

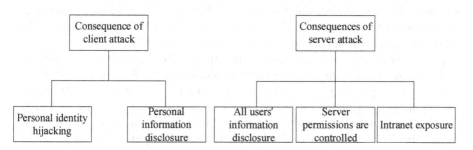

Fig. 2. Comparison of client and server being attacked.

Attacks on these targets often need to adopt a variety of forms of vulnerability. Among them, the two most powerful types of vulnerabilities are arbitrary address read/write vulnerability and remote code execution vulnerability.

According to different attack targets, remote code execution vulnerability attacks are divided into different ways. In attacks against Web servers, because the hypertext transfer protocol (HTTP) used in Web applications is presented in the form of text and has no state [1], there are relatively few cases that need to rely on the output information of the server to carry out the next attack, and the analysis is relatively simple. It is relatively easy for the defense of the attacked target to try to defend against the attack in the first time or to assess the damage to the target after the attack. The other type of target, commonly referred to as a binary target, is a native service running directly on the target machine and communicating using TCP or UDP.

If the attack traffic against the binary native service remote code execution vulnerability has been obtained, the vulnerability process can be reproduced through automated analysis. At the same time, the specific location and cause of the vulnerability used in the attack traffic can be quickly analyzed, or the attack process can be extracted as a backup weapon.

1.1 Related Work

[2] Thanassis Avgerinos et al. in 2011 at AEG: Automatic Exploit Generation puts forward the concept of automatic exploit. In this paper, automatic exploit is defined to automatically find the existence of vulnerabilities and generate exploit for security vulnerabilities. This work is mainly aimed at automatic exploit under the premise of no attack traffic. On this basis, [3, 4] proposed and optimized the automated vulnerability exploitation method based on symbolic execution and other program analysis methods. This method is also used to automate the analysis of vulnerabilities contained in binary executable files when only binary executable files exist and aim for automated exploitation of those vulnerabilities.

In 2005, [5] Newsome J et al. proposed the dynamic taint analysis of attack traffic, which detected the attacks against vulnerabilities in network traffic through the dynamic taint analysis. However, there is no further vulnerability recurrence of the same type of attack or automatic vulnerability utilization by changing the target.

In 2017, [6] T. Bao et al. proposed a method for automated migration of Shellcode in vulnerability exploitation, which is similar to the target replacement of vulnerability exploitation process faced by this research. However, this method requires vulnerability exploitation process rather than processing network attack traffic.

[7] Yan Wang et al. proposed Revery in 2018 to solve the problem that program crash could not be used on site. Based on the memory layout of abnormal objects, this scheme uses fuzzy testing technology to explore alternative paths of vulnerability, and uses key memory operation instructions to locate the vulnerability points, so that the available states can be found in alternative paths by using stain analysis technology. The splicing point is determined, and after the path splicing is completed, the path constraint, vulnerability advantage constraint and other conditions are solved by symbolic execution technology to generate vulnerability exploitation.

In this paper, we mainly study the analysis and recurrence of remote code execution vulnerability in smart grid system under the premise of network traffic. It is similar to automated vulnerability exploitation in concept, but there is no need for automated vulnerability mining, nor for automated exploitation of different vulnerability types after mining. In addition, after discovering the existence of vulnerability exploitation, our research in this paper also needs to reproduce the vulnerability, which is different from the existing work.

1.2 Our Contribution

Due to the characteristics of Web type vulnerability, the repetition process is relatively easy, so we mainly study the memory corruption vulnerability of binary native service. The vulnerability utilization technology of binary service mainly targets at the memory corruption vulnerability in binary executable files, which has extremely high complexity. Specifically, our contribution mainly includes the following aspects:

1. In our scheme, we explore the recurrence of the utilization process of the same target and the same environment under the premise of the existence of TCP attack traffic targeting the remote code execution vulnerability of memory corruption type. When brute force cracking is not used in the exploitation process, the exploit process can be used multiple times for different smart grids.
2. In the experiment, we use the binaries of three Strong Net Cup CTF subjects and the sample binaries with vulnerabilities of CVE-2013-2028 and CVE-2010-4221 as test objects. And we analyze the results after experiment.
3. We design and realizes the automatic analysis and utilization of smart grid system based on traffic. In the process of utilizing the original traffic, the system can successfully complete the analysis and reuse of the traffic of the native service attack and reproduce the attack process in the case that the bypassing method is binary form.

1.3 Organization

The following is the structure of this paper's remaining part: Sect. 2 provides our scheme's preliminaries. Section 3 offers our system model after analyzing some challenges faces in the process of vulnerability exploitation recurrence. Section 4 shows our experiment environment, specific methods, results and analysis. In Sect. 5, we present the conclusion and analyze some feasible future work of this paper.

2 Preliminaries

2.1 Memory Corruption Vulnerability

In low-level languages such as C and C++, in order to accurately control the memory allocation process, manual memory allocation is generally used for memory management. This type of memory management is more efficient and accurate than garbage collector [8]. Programmers can precisely control the time of allocation and release, thus reducing memory usage and making the overall latency of the system lower.

Although the manual management method enables the programmer to have more powerful control over the memory, it also brings certain problems. Since the allocation, use, and release of memory are controlled by the programmer, the programmer may use memory incorrectly in the process, resulting in "unexpected" results. In severe cases, it can directly lead to the attacker taking full control of the target system.

Among the attack technologies of software security, there are two main types, namely, Web application attack technology and binary attack technology. The first type of Web application attack technology attacks web application services, including SQL injection attack, XSS cross-site scripting attack [9] and other attack means. The second type of binary attack is mainly aimed at binary executable files compiled by programs written in C, C ++ and other compiled languages. This section provides a brief introduction to binary security vulnerability types.

Buffer Overflow Vulnerability. Buffer overflow vulnerability is one of the most serious security problems at present [10]. Since garbage collector free languages such as C and C++ use manual memory management, there are a variety of error conditions that can occur when using memory, leading to a variety of memory corruption vulnerabilities. One of the classic forms of memory corruption vulnerability is the buffer overflow vulnerability.

Buffer overflow vulnerability refers to that when the programmer allocates memory, the size of the allocated memory is wrongly calculated. When using the memory region, the memory space beyond the allocated memory boundary is used, resulting in the used memory space is actually invalid memory. The "invalid memory" may contain data structures needed elsewhere in the program, causing the data structure to be destroyed. After the execution process is controlled, the execution of any code can be completed through precise construction methods, so that the vulnerability is transformed into the most serious arbitrary code execution vulnerability.

The cause of this vulnerability is that the programmer uses a dangerous C language function, which leads to the user input content size is larger than the buffer size expected by the programmer, resulting in the buffer overflow vulnerability.

Buffer overflow vulnerabilities can be roughly divided into stack overflow, heap overflow, BSS and data segment overflow according to different overflow locations. According to the memory distribution diagram in Fig. 3, the stack, heap, BSS, and data segments have the possibility of user-controlled memory in the program. Stack space is usually used to store local variables of functions in a program. It is the memory managed by the program itself. In C, the memory managed by system functions malloc and free is in the heap space. The other part is BSS and data segment. The variable type when overflow occurs is different, the memory map location where overflow occurs is also different. The attacker uses different methods when facing different overflow vulnerability types.

Use-After-Free Vulnerability. Buffer overflow vulnerability is one of the most serious security problems at present [10]. Since garbage collector free languages such as C and C++ use manual memory management, there are a variety of error conditions that can occur when using memory, leading to a variety of memory corruption vulnerabilities. One of the classic forms of memory corruption vulnerability is the buffer overflow vulnerability.

In addition to buffer overflow vulnerability, another type of memory corruption vulnerability with great risk is use-after-free vulnerability [11]. Such vulnerabilities may cause user input content to be stored in the released memory. According to different heap management implementation mechanisms, the released memory and allocated memory of some implementation mechanisms are reused in memory space [13]. A read or write

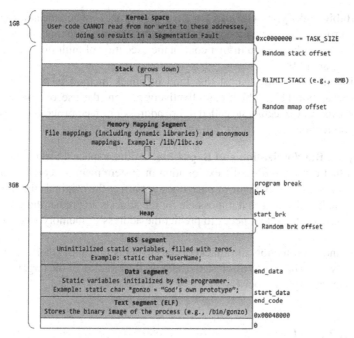

Fig. 3. Memory distribution [12].

to the released memory will cause the metadata content for heap management to be output or even changed.

Double-Free Vulnerability. The double-free vulnerability is similar to the use-after-free vulnerability, which is also caused by the programmer incorrectly using the memory allocation and release mechanism. Double-free vulnerability occurs when the programmer fails to clear the pointer after the memory is freed, and then mistakenly releases the pointer again. If the vulnerability is not recognized by the heap management mechanism, the same memory may be allocated multiple times when the next memory allocation is processed, resulting in a use-after-free effect, in which multiple pointers point to the same memory block.

Format String Vulnerability. Format string vulnerability [10] refers to that when programmers use scanf, printf and other format string functions in C language, they mistakenly input or output user input as format string, so that users can control the content of format string. In this case, the attacker can make the extra data output according to the pass-parameter rules by passing in the constructed format string.

2.2 Memory Corruption Vulnerability Mitigation and Bypass

Memory corruption vulnerability is very common in early smart grid systems. Some effective mitigation technology protection systems have been developed.

Non-executable and Bypassed Data. In the exploit process, when the attacker has the ability to control the execution process of the target program at one time, the technology called Shellcode can be used to further control the execution of multiple instructions by the target program [14].

The mitigation measure against this kind of attack method is named data non-executable protection [15], which can effectively prevent the use of Shellcode technology. However, a new technique called return address-oriented programming [16] can bypass this protection.

Address Space Randomization and Bypassing. Address space information is the key information that can be used in the exploitation of system memory corruption vulnerability. Randomization in the unit of page does not affect the original running process of the program, but also makes it impossible for the attacker to predict the random base address, so that the attack that needs to predict the address of memory space is invalid [17].

For this kind of protection, the attacker needs to cooperate with other vulnerabilities and use other vulnerabilities to disclose the address information of the target process, so as to complete the exploit process.

3   System Model

3.1   Challenges

Our purpose is to reproduce vulnerability exploitation through attack traffic. One of the simplest methods is to directly replay the attack traffic and output the attack traffic to another target. Some variable content may be involved in the process of protection bypass. A typical variable content is the address information needed in the process of address space randomization bypass, which leads to the problem of recurrence of address space randomization bypass.

Instability of TCP Traffic Records. Binary native services are often written in C, C++ and other low-level languages, using TCP protocol network communication. Compared with application layer protocols such as HTTP, TCP network communication is at a lower level, so the communication process on native services is usually at a lower level. The encapsulation is simpler, or even lack of encapsulation. Due to the lack of encapsulation of standard protocols such as HTTP at the application layer, traffic is generally captured at the TCP protocol level. As a result, the capture process is unstable and may lead to recurrence failures.

Address Space Randomization Bypass Recurrence. In the process of attack traffic analysis, random bypassing of address space will affect vulnerability recurrence. If address space randomization exists during bypass, address information needs to be leaked by exploiting vulnerabilities. It is necessary to identify the address space randomization bypass process in the traffic of the recorded remote code execution vulnerability, and to identify the recurrence, so as to achieve the goal of multiple recurrence.

3.2   Specific System Model

The system is divided into three main parts, as shown in Fig. 4. Through the network traffic preprocessing part, the system is initialized as a whole, the environment is built, and the traffic is cleaned, so as to provide conditions and data input for the subsequent analysis part. After configuration, the attack process of other remote services can be repeated to complete automatic vulnerability exploitation and recurrence.

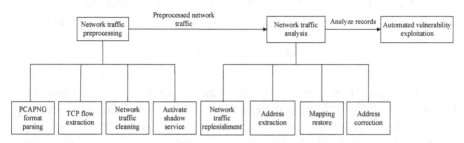

Fig. 4. System module.

Network Traffic Preprocessing. The system starts first through the network traffic pre-processing part. The main work of this part is to parse the format of the captured traffic, clean the traffic and prepare for the service. In modern traffic capture software, PCAPNG [18] is commonly used as the traffic capture record format. The PCAPNG format defines the packet structure and stores the basic information and data information of each packet in network traffic. Traffic cleaning mainly involves cleaning the parsed and processed traffic according to the flow structure based on the port number and some filtering rules to improve the processing efficiency.

Service preparation includes target service preparation and shadow service preparation. Target service refers to the target drone environment prepared locally during the analysis process, which is the same as the remote environment of the original attack traffic. Shadow service is to configure the environment as similar as possible to the attacked system, so that the local operation is almost the same as the attacked environment. At the same time, some control rights are reserved. The comparison between target service and shadow service is shown in Fig. 5.

Automatic Network Traffic Analysis. The traffic analysis part is the core module of the system, its main work is to use the shadow service to analyze the recorded traffic so as to extract the address information in the traffic and recover the address space information of the recorded traffic. In essence, the bypassing of random attack on address space is to partially recover the address space information of remote service. In the bypassing process, address information leakage attack is needed to obtain the address space information of the target process. Therefore, the address information in the attack payload can be inferred through certain analysis.

Traffic synchronization is performed on the shadow service based on the received and received traffic. The data is sent and received synchronously according to the length and number of received packets in the recorded traffic, and the specific data will be further processed.

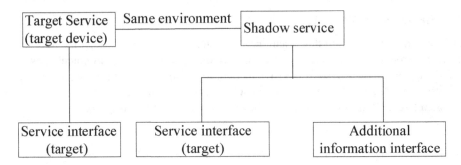

Fig. 5. Target service versus shadow service.

The traffic complement phase is to deal with the different lengths of data in the shadow service and recorded traffic in the process of sending or receiving. In the receiving process, the length of the address is inconsistent because the high address is empty in the case of the small endian order. We can adjust the address information to ensure the same length. The model of traffic complement is set to minimize the gap between the two parts of network traffic by supplementing empty bytes. This model can be solved by using the algorithm of dynamic programming. As shown in Fig. 6, empty bytes in the red part are added to make the two parts of traffic more consistent, so that byte misplacement will not be caused by incomplete address bytes in the subsequent analysis.

The address extraction phase is an attempt to extract address data from the data during the sending or receiving process. The process is shown in Fig. 7. If the data can be confirmed to be in the address space of silver service, according to the method of synchronous processing, this part of data can be corresponding to the original service data. Therefore, the location of address data in the original service can be confirmed.

After the address extraction phase has successfully extracted the address locations in the traffic received by the shadow service, the mapping recovery phase can be entered. As shown in Fig. 8, while not all of the memory mapping information can be recovered at this stage, all of the memory mapping information needed in the send can be recovered.

After the mapping is restored, to ensure the correctness of the sent traffic, it is necessary to correct the address information used in the traffic to be sent, so that the utilization process can continue. The correction method is to adopt the same sliding window method as in the address extraction stage, as shown in Fig. 9. The suitable address for the current shadow service can be obtained to complete the correction step.

In the traffic analysis module, the receiving and sending steps are mapping recovery and address correction respectively by synchronizing traffic processing. This section describes how to restore all memory mapping information in recorded traffic through the circular sending and receiving process. The necessary information is provided for the subsequent vulnerability exploitation process, as shown in Fig. 10.

Automated Vulnerability Reoccurring. During the analysis of the traffic analysis module, the location and offset of the mapped address in the receiving process and the location of the address in the sending process have been recorded, as shown in

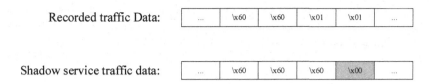

Fig. 6. Example of traffic complement.

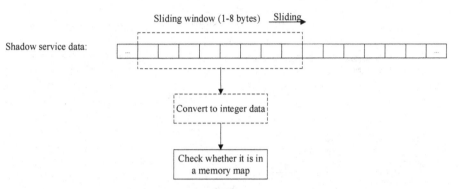

Fig. 7. Address extraction process.

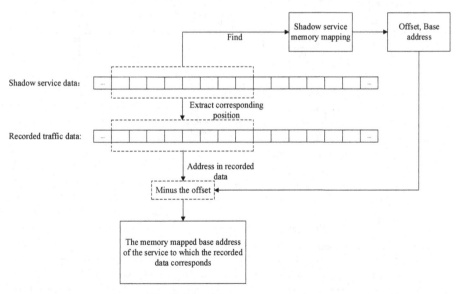

Fig. 8. Mapping recovery process.

24   H. Wu et al.

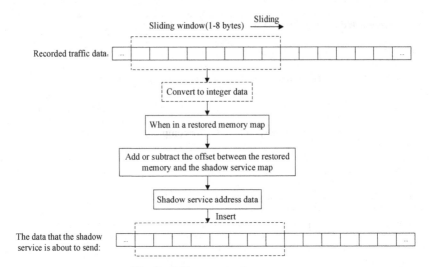

Fig. 9. Address correction process.

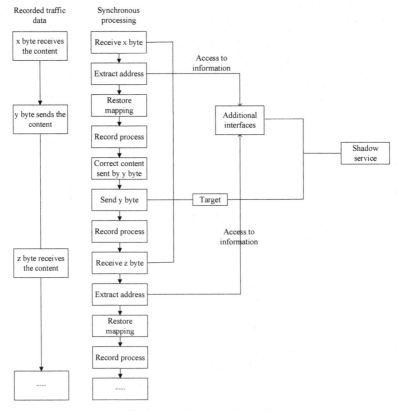

Fig. 10. Synchronous processing.

Fig. 11. In the automated utilization process, all records can be processed one by one, depending on the type of each send and receive.

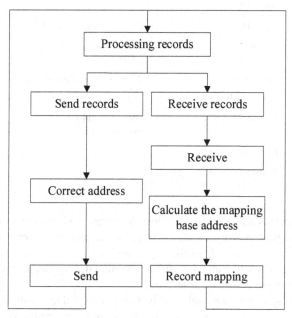

Fig. 11. Records processing.

4 Experimental Results and Analysis

4.1 Experiment Environment

Our experiment was carried out in the environment as shown in Table 1.

4.2 Experimental Method

In the experiment, we expect to use binary questions in the CTF of the Strong Net cup as targets, as well as cVE-2013-2028 and CVE-2010-4221 vulnerability samples. The vulnerabilities involved in binary topics in CTF are relatively easy to exploit and can be easily simulated when the most harmful vulnerabilities occur in the real environment. CVE-2013-2028 and CVE-2010-4221 vulnerabilities are both binary native service vulnerabilities and can reflect the vulnerabilities in the real environment. Therefore, these two types of experimental objects can simulate various situations after the occurrence of remote code execution vulnerabilities in a relatively real way. In addition, vulnerabilities in all test samples involved in the experiment need to be protected and bypassed by randomization of address space in the process of exploitation, which can reflect a more complex exploitation process.

Table 1. Experiment environment.

Hardware and software conditions	Parameters
Operating system	macOS Mojave 10.14.4
Memory	16 GB 1600 MHz DDR3
Processors	2.8 GHz Intel Core i7
Docker edition	18.09.2
Docker mirroring	ubuntu 16.04 official mirrors
Linux kernel edition	4.10
Python edition	3.6

The main experimental method is to test the target environment first and confirm the existence of remote code execution vulnerability in samples. After that, the attack is executed against the remote code of the target sample by using the constructed vulnerability. During the attack, the attack traffic is recorded through tcpdump [19] to obtain the traffic of the remote code execution attack.

After that, the system in our study is used to input the vulnerability samples and the obtained traffic of remote code execution to attack the vulnerability. By observing the system results, it can confirm whether the vulnerability has been successfully exploited. The specific effect of this research method can be judged by the vulnerability utilization. In order to ensure the consistency of the experimental environment, Docker was used to provide a consistent binary stable execution environment. The experiments were all run under the Docker basic image of Ubuntu 16.04.

4.3 Results and Analysis

In the experiment, we use the binaries of three Strong Net Cup CTF subjects and the sample binaries with vulnerabilities of CVE-2013-2028 and CVE-2010-4221 as test objects. In the Ubuntu 16.04 environment, CVE-2013-2028 and CVE-2010-4221 can both successfully complete the automated vulnerability exploitation reoccurrence process. Three CTF questions in the Strong Net Cup can complete the automated vulnerability exploitation reoccurrence process, and the experimental results are shown in Table 2.

In the experiment, the two real CVE vulnerability processes mainly adopt the attack mode of return address programming, which is used to carry out information leakage attack on address space. During the exploitation process, the read and write parts may cause continuity problems, which will affect the exploitation process of vulnerabilities. In addition, the address space randomization bypass part can be well tested for the system. After testing, the system can be used stably in this situation.

Table 2. Experiment results.

Test projects	Test results
CVE-2010-4221 recurrence	Success
CVE-2013-2028 recurrence	Success
2018 Strong Net Cup secular recurrence	Success
2018 Strong Net Cup funnyjob recurrence	Success
2018 Strong Net Cup debugvm recurrence	Success

In the Strong Net Cup CTF competition problem, because its vulnerability itself is more theoretical, the use process is more accurate. In the process, it is necessary to precisely arrange the heap space, and then complete the exploit process according to the principle of heap implementation in Libc library. Even multiple vulnerabilities are needed to be used together, and the address space randomization is bypassed by one of them. Then another vulnerability is utilized to complete the vulnerability process of the target program, and the utilization process is of high accuracy. In the reproduction process, it is necessary to ensure a high degree of consistency with the exploitation process, otherwise the exploit process cannot be completed. In addition, due to address space randomization, null characters may occur in the heap space. The utilization process may require certain processing of the leaked address, otherwise the utilization cannot be completed. This situation has been considered in the system design, and there is a strategy of address leakage information replenishment using dynamic programming.

The experiment shows that the system works stably under the experimental hypothesis. It can automatically analyze the attack traffic of remote code execution of binary memory corruption type under certain conditions, and automatically utilize and reproduce it stably.

5 Conclusion

Based on the study of binary remote code execution vulnerability, aiming at the bypassing means of address space randomization in the binary remote code execution vulnerability, we design and implement the automatic analysis and utilization of smart grid system based on traffic.

In the process of utilizing the original traffic, the system can successfully complete the analysis and reuse of the traffic of the native service attack and reproduce the attack process in the case that the bypassing method is binary form. By using this system, the defender can quickly investigate the vulnerability of remote code execution of native services to prevent the second attack of the same kind of vulnerability. It can also extract the similarity of vulnerability attacks by using samples to detect attacks, so as to expose the attack process.

In the process of this study, it is found that leaks using unconventional binary forms cannot be handled at present when randomization protection is bypassed on the address space. The main reason is that the smart grid system has not abstracted the leakage form of address space randomization bypass. The current solution is to make leaks identifiable with a small amount of human intervention. However, this method requires a certain degree of human intervention. In future work, the format of leakage information can be further studied. The system can be further enhanced by using heuristic methods and other abstract processing of the leakage form, which can be applied to a wider range of automated analysis and reason of remote code execution vulnerability utilization process traffic.

References

1. Fielding, R., Gettys, J., Mogul, J., et al.: Hypertext transfer protocol – HTTP/1.1. Comput. Sci. Commun. Dic. **7**(4), 595–599 (1999)
2. Avgerinos, T., Sang, K.C., Rebert, A., et al.: Automatic exploit generation. Commun. ACM **57**(2), 74–84 (2014)
3. Shoshitaishvili, Y., Wang, R., Salls, C., et al.: Sok:(state of) the art of war: Offensive techniques in binary analysis. In: 2016 IEEE Symposium on Security and Privacy (SP), pp. 138–157. IEEE[C], New York, U.S. (2016)
4. Sang, K.C., Avgerinos, T., Rebert, A., et al. Unleashing Mayhem on Binary Code. 2012 IEEE Symposium on Security and Privacy (SP) (2012)
5. Newsome, J., Song, D.X.: Dynamic taint analysis for automatic detection, analysis, and signatureregeneration of exploits on commodity software. In: The Network and Distributed System Security Symposium, pp. 3–4. Reston, Virginia (2005)
6. Bao, T., Wang, R., Shoshitaishvili, Y., et al.: Your exploit is mine: Automatic shellcode transplant for remote exploits. In: 2017 IEEE Symposium on Security and Privacy (SP), pp. 824–839. IEEE[C]. New York (2017)
7. Wang, Y., Zhang, C., Xiang, X., et al.: Revery: From proof-of- concept to exploitable. In: Proceedings of the 2018 ACM SIGSAC Conference on Computer and Communications Security, pp. 1914–1927 (2018)
8. Jones, R.E., Lins, R.D.: Garbage Collection: Algorithms for Automatic Dynamic Memory Management. Wiley, New York (1996)
9. Stein, L.D.: Web security. Addison-Wesley, Massachusetts **26**, 1–4 (1998)
10. Lhee, K.S., Chapin, S.J.: Buffer overflow and format string overflow vulnerabilities. Softw.: Prac. Exp. **33**(5). 423–460 (2003)
11. Szekeres, L., Payer, M., Wei, T., et al.: Sok: Eternal war in memory. In: 2013 IEEE Symposium on Security and Privacy, pp. 48–62. IEEE[C], New York, U.S. (2013)
12. Bryant, R.E., David Richard, O.H., David Richard, O.H.: Computer Systems: A Programmer's Perspective, pp. 777–848. Prentice Hall, Upper Saddle River (2003)
13. Gloger, W.: Ptmalloc [EB/OL] (2019). http://www.malloc.de/en
14. Blomgren, M.: Introduction to Shellcoding: How to exploit buffer overflows [EB/OL] (2019). http://tigerteam.se/dl/papers/intro_to_shellcoding.pdf
15. Silberman, P., Johnson, R.: A comparison of buffer overflow prevention implementations and weaknesses [EB/OL] (2019). https://www.blackhat.com/presentations/bh-usa-04/bh-us-04-silberman/bh-us-04-silberman-paper.pdf
16. Roemer, R., Buchanan, E., Shacham, H., et al.: Return-oriented programming: Systems, languages, and applications. ACM Trans. Inf. Syst. Secur. **15**(1), 2 (2012)

17. Team, P.X.: PaX address space layout randomization (ASLR)[EB/OL] (2019). https://pax.grs
ecurity.net/docs/aslr.txt
18. Tuexen, M., Risso, F., Bongertz, J., et al.: PCAP Next Generation (PCAPNG) Dump File
Format [EB/OL] (2019). http://xml2rfc.tools.ietf.org/cgi-bin/xml2rfc.cgi?url=https://raw.git
hubusercontent.com/pcapng/pcapng/master/draft-tuexen-opsawg-pcapng.xml&modeAsFor
mat=html/ascii&type=ascii
19. Jacobson, V., Leres, C., McCanne, S.: The tcpdump manual page [EB/OL] (2019). https://
www.tcpdump.org/manpages/tcpdump.1.html

GWDGA: An Effective Adversarial DGA

Xiang Shu[1,2], Chunjie Cao[1,2], Longjuan Wang[1,2(✉)], and Fangjian Tao[1,2]

[1] School of Cyberspace Security (School of Cryptology), Hainan University,
Haikou 570100, China
{19083900210009,wanglongjuan}@hainanu.edu.cn
[2] Key Laboratory of Internet Information Retrieval of Hainan Province,
Hainan University, Haikou 570228, China

Abstract. Domain name generation algorithm (DGA) is a technique that can help botnets improve their crypticity. To discover botnets, the DGA detection methods based on deep learning have been proposed, which significantly reduce the usability of DGAs. However, due to the security problems of deep learning itself, this type of DGA detection method also faces the threat of adversarial attacks. Adversarial DGAs can generate anti-detection domain names to deceive the DGA classifier so that it can help researchers discover the shortcomings of existing DGA detection methods. Meanwhile, the existing adversarial DGAs generally only generate domain names based on characters without considering word-level elements. In this paper, a new type of adversarial DGA named GWDGA was proposed. It is implemented based on the statistical language model, the gated convolutional network, and the variational auto-encoder. The core point of GWDGA is to treat domain names as a combination of commonly used n-grams and high-frequency words so that it can learn their intrinsic arrangements and generate new domain names. GWDGA was evaluated on three well-known DGA classifiers (Endgame, Invincea, MIT). The AUCs of GWDGA under the three detection methods are $0.43, 0.42$, and 0.43, respectively. The result shows that GWDGA has stronger anti-detection capabilities than similar adversarial DGA. Its performance is stable under the detection of DGA classifiers of different architectures. In addition, the ability of the classifiers to resist GWDGA can be improved by adding the adversarial domain names generated by GWDGA to the training sets of the classifiers.

Keywords: Domain generation algorithms · Deep learning · Adversarial domain names · Adversarial retraining

1 Introduction

The Botnet is one of the main threats in the field of cyberspace security. A botnet is made up of geographically dispersed Internet-connected devices (bots) whose security has been breached by bot malware so that the botnet owner (botmaster) can control these bots remotely. The botnet is generally used to carry out a range of malicious cyber-attacks, such as the distributed denial of

© Springer Nature Singapore Pte Ltd. 2022
C. Cao et al. (Eds.): FCS 2021, CCIS 1558, pp. 30–48, 2022.
https://doi.org/10.1007/978-981-19-0523-0_3

service (DDoS), spam [1], click fraud [2], etc. In addition, they may be used to theft personal information [3]. Meanwhile, due to the distributed nature of both botnets and cryptocurrency mining, botnets also tend to aggregate computing power to mine bitcoin or other virtual currencies [4]. However, the premise of these malicious acts is to ensure that the botmaster and bots can exchange information freely. To communicate covertly, botmaster manipulates the bots through a communication channel based on domain-flux instead of the address of a command and control (C&C) server that was hardcoded in the malware. Domain-flux refers to a technology for keeping a malicious botnet in operation by constantly changing the domain name of the botnet owner's C&C server [5]. The key of the domain-flux is the domain generation algorithms (DGAs).

DGAs can be used to periodically generate a large number of domain names, which are called algorithmically generated domains (AGDs). They can also be called DGA domain names. Attackers can choose some of the AGDs not yet registered, one of which will actually be registered by the botnet operator so that the domain name system (DNS) can map it to the IP address of a C&C server. On the bots' side, the malware can generate the same AGDs list by the same DGA and the same seed. Each bot then sends out DNS queries to the random domain names until one of them actually resolves to the address of the C&C server. From that moment on, communication channels have been established. When the C&C server goes offline or the domain name is blacklisted, the attacker can restart the process to reestablish communication. DGAs can make it difficult for security researchers and administrators to block instructions from a C&C server and shut a botnet down.

To identify AGDs and defend against DGAs, researchers have proposed many approaches. Initially, the detection of AGDs was done by reverse-engineering the malware samples to extract DGAs and seeds from them. Then security experts can predict the domain names in advance and take some methods to mitigate the attack. It is effective to pre-register, sinkhole these domain names, or add them to the blacklist. However, attackers can easily circumvent this approach by using new seeds. Therefore, this defence becomes increasingly difficult and costly as the rate of dynamically generated domain names increases [6]. Meanwhile, reverse-engineering of malware executables is not always feasible. With the wide application of machine learning technology, some researchers [7,8] detected the domain names generated by DGA by extracting a series of features of malicious domain names. Nonetheless, the machine learning algorithm based on feature extraction is limited to manual feature extraction and is unable to detect DGA domain names outside of feature engineering. The automatic representation learning capability of deep learning is capable of dealing with constantly changing adversaries and detecting AGDs with high precision. This approach greatly reduces the effectiveness of the DGA domain names in botnet communication. As a result, DGA domain names detection based on deep learning has been widely studied and applied.

At the same time, the emergence of adversarial samples exposed some potential security issues of deep learning models. Szegedy et al. [9] first generated the adversarial examples by adding small perturbations to the original images so that they can fool state-of-the-art deep neural networks. The added perturbations are also not easily perceived by humans. In this paper, the adversarial samples we cite are not restricted to the field of the image. Broadly speaking, an adversarial sample is an elaborate input designed to cause misclassification in a learning algorithm [10]. As far as we know, DGA classifiers based on deep learning also face the threat of adversarial attacks. Therefore, research on adversarial samples in the DGA field is of great significance to the development of DGA detection methods. To discover the shortcomings of existing DGA classifiers and improve their resistance to adversarial attacks, we design a kind of effective and stealthy DGA [11] that can generate adversarial domain names and evade detection of DGA.

The contributions of this paper are as follows.

1) We design an effective adversarial DGA named GWDGA. At the same time, it is a stealthy DGA based on the statistical language model, the gated convolutional network, and the variational auto-encoder. It is helpful for researchers to discover the shortcomings of existing DGA classifiers and improve their ability to resist adversarial attacks.
2) We creatively regard benign domain names as a combination of common n-grams (N) and high-frequency words (FW). At the same time, a new approach to domain name classification is proposed on this basis. In addition, we also come up with an adversarial DGA that synthesizes new domain names based on n-grams and word-level elements.
3) We use three well-known DGA classifiers with different structures to verify the anti-detection ability of GWDGA in the black-box attack scenario. The experimental results show that the adversarial domain names generated by GWDGA have good evasion capabilities and transferability in different deep learning models. At the same time, the comparative experiment also shows that the performance of GWDGA is better.

2   Related Work

2.1   The Detection of DGAs

Regarding the work of DGA detection, there are generally two categories. The first type of task is mainly to distinguish between AGDs and benign domain names, which can be regarded as a binary classification task. The second type of task is mainly to identify the malware family that produces AGDs, which is a multiclass classification task [12]. In this paper, we mainly focus on the first type of task. In fact, the previous work on the first type of task can also be divided into two categories: retrospective detection and real-time detection [6]. The main difference between the two types is whether you need to use contextual information from the network. The contextual information includes HTTP headers, NXDomains across a network, passive DNS [6], etc. However, it is costly to obtain contextual information from network traffic. In addition, these classifiers [13–17] based on contextual information are designed as reactionary systems, making it difficult to achieve real-time detection and prevention. As a result, real-time detection based on the domain name itself is becoming mainstream. Currently, real-time detection can be divided into two categories. One is the machine learning methods based on feature extraction [8,18]. This kind of method relies on finding the difference in character distribution between benign domain names and DGA domain names. Specifically, it extracts some manually defined features from the domain names, such as domain name length, entropy, vowel-character ratio, bigrams, etc. The purpose of classification is achieved through the differences between benign domain names and DGA domain names in the selected features. Nonetheless, feature extraction is a labor-intensive process. These features really help to detect DGA domain names. But at the same time, these features are also information that an attacker can use. When such a classifier encounters some well-designed DGA domain names that can bypass these features, its performance will become very poor. The other is the deep learning methods based on non-feature extraction [19]. The biggest advantage of this method is that features can be extracted automatically from massive data. Woodbridge et al. [6] proposed a DGA classifier named Endgame, which is based on LSTM. This is the first method of DGA detection using deep neural networks. Lison et al. [20] presented a data-driven approach to the automatic detection of AGDs using recurrent neural networks. This method demonstrated the effectiveness of deep neural networks on the million-level AGDs dataset for the first time. Yu et al. [21] put forward a CNN-based DGA detection algorithm. Their work shows that real-time DGA detection methods based on deep neural networks were significantly outperformed machine learning methods based on random forests. Yu et al. [22] discussed the effectiveness of five typical character-based text classification deep learning models in the field of DGA detection through comparative experiments. Their result shows that a model based on parallel CNN achieves the best detection accuracy. This model is called Invincea [23]. Tran et al. [24] came up with a novel LSTM. MI algorithm which robust to the problem of uneven training data of different DGA categories in multi-classification. Vosoughi et al. [25] evaluated various RNN-based DGA detection methods, CNN-based DGA detection methods, and CNN-LSTM architecture-based DGA detection methods. Their work shows that CNN and various recurrent neural networks such as LSTM are very suitable for DGA detection tasks. At the same time, the hybrid network (the first layer is CNN, and the subsequent layer is LSTM) also has good performance. Vinayakumar et al. [26] proposed a DGA detection method based on the CNN-LSTM architecture and compared it with other advanced detection methods based on deep learning. The effect is excellent.

2.2   The Adversarial DGAs

As mentioned earlier, the current real-time detection for DGA is mainly based on deep neural networks. However, the security of deep neural networks has attracted more and more attention from researchers in recent years. Escape attacks are the type of problem that has received the most attention. This type of attack is mainly to make the target model produce wrong classification results by constructing specific input samples. According to whether the internal information of the target model is needed, this kind of attack can be divided into black-box attack and white-box attack. In addition, escape attacks can also be divided into the targeted attack and the untargeted attack. The targeted attack means that the adversarial sample can not only fool the target model but also make the target model classify it into a specified category. The untargeted attack only needs to make the target model misclassify the adversarial sample. This kind of security problem was first discovered in the field of computer vision [9]. But the same problem exists in the field of DGA detection.

Anderson et al. [27] proposed DeepDGA, which is the first adversarial DGA based on a Generative Adversarial Network (GAN). It can generate adversarial domain names, and these adversarial samples are also valid for random forests with artificial engineered features. At the same time, their work proved that adding adversarial domain names generated by DeepDGA to the training set can enhance the robustness of the classification model. However, DeepDGA based on the original GAN is difficult to train and exhibits limited anti-detection capability. Peck et al. [28] came up with a simple and effective method called CharBot to evade the DGA classifier. CharBot generates adversarial domain names by modifying characters in benign domain names. In order to ensure the smallest possible disturbance, it only modifies two characters. This ensures that the generated domain name can achieve the balance between anti-detection capability and usability. But the readability of the domain name generated by CharBot needs to be improved. Spooren et al. [29] put forward a new adversarial DGA named DeceptionDGA. It made use of the knowledge of the feature set used by the FANCI [8] system so that it can evade detection. Despite the different complexity, DeceptionDGA is equivalent to Charbot in terms of anti-detection capabilities [28]. Sidi et al. [30] developed an adversarial DGA called MaskDGA based on adversarial learning. It mainly uses the Jacobian-based saliency map to perform character-level perturbation on the input domain name. MaskDGA is designed to be applied to the output of the botnet's existing DGA to turn AGD names into adversarial domain names. Yun et al. [31] presented Khaos, which is an anti-detection DGA based on the Wasserstein Generative Adversarial Network (WGAN). Compared to DeepDGA, Khaos performs better and WGAN also makes training more stable. Nonetheless, the adversarial domain name generated by Khaos does not contain word-level elements. This is one of its limitations. Fu et al. [11] presented two novel DGAs named hmm_500KL3 and pcfg_ipv4_num, which are based on hidden Markov models (HMMs) and probabilistic context-free grammars (PCFGs), respectively.

In order to discover the shortcomings of the existing DGA detection methods, research on adversarial DGAs has gradually become a hot spot. However, the existing adversarial DGAs are mainly based on generative models or adversarial algorithms. Most adversarial algorithms achieve the purpose of evading detection by modifying individual characters in existing domain names. The generative model mainly generates adversarial domain names by learning the potential characteristics between the characters of benign domain names. Few adversarial DGAs currently take word-level elements into consideration. But our work takes common n-grams and high-frequency words into consideration and achieves a good escape effect.

3 Method

3.1 Overview

In this paper, we present GWDGA, an adversarial DGA based on the gated convolutional neural network [32] and the variational auto-encoder. It is suitable for the black-box attack scenario where the attacker knows nothing about training data, parameters, and the internal structure of the targeted model. Corley I et al. [33] concluded that it is important for attackers to maintain similar n-gram characteristics between the DGA domain names and benign domain names by experiments. Only in this way can AGDs achieve effective evasion. Enlightened by this, we find that benign domain names can generally be decomposed into the commonly used n-grams representation. Furthermore, the validity of Khaos [31] also demonstrates the feasibility of this idea. On this basis, we put forward our own opinions. We notice that most benign domain names contain word-level elements for easy memory, especially long domain names. Although words can also be decomposed into n-grams, we believe that keeping words as an essential component of a domain name can improve the anti-detection ability of the generated adversarial domain name. Because this can integrate the features of different dimensional levels. Our experimental results also prove the correctness of our ideas. Consequently, after studying a large number of benign domain names, we conclude that they can be regarded as a combination of common n-grams (N) and high-frequency words (FW). If there is a way to learn the internal arrangement and distribution of these benign domain names, then we can generate adversarial samples that are highly similar to the distribution of benign domain names. In addition, based on our ideas, benign domain names can be divided into three categories according to their composition. The number of N and FW in each category is variable and the following representations show the relative position relationship: (1) N+N (e.g. msdn); (2) N+FW/FW+N/N+FW+N (e.g. aliexpress/shopify/zemanta); (3) FW+FW (e.g. windowsupdate).

So, GWDGA regards common n-grams and high-frequency words as the basic components of domain names and uses a large number of benign domain names for training to learn potential arrangements and distributions. Then, it can generate new domain names through the trained generative model. Finally, it will discard some domain names that do not meet the requirements to obtain usable AGDs. It contains four modules, namely dictionary generation module, data processing module, domain names generation module, and domain names filtering module (shown in Fig. 1). In the dictionary generation module, there are two steps. The first step is to extract n-grams from benign domain names and add the most commonly used n-grams to the dictionary. The second step is to add some high-frequency words that occur in the domain names to the dictionary to

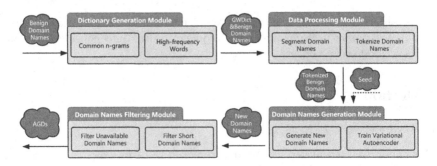

Fig. 1. Overview of GWDGA's architecture.

obtain a complete dictionary (GWDict) containing common n-grams and high-frequency words. In the data processing module, GWDGA will represent benign domain names as a combination of n-grams and words according to the GWDict. In the domain names generation module, the trained model will arrange n-grams and words according to the learned experience and combine them into domain names output. Lastly, in the domain names filtering module, some domain names that are too short or that do not meet the specifications will be removed. It should be noted that general domain names such as "A.B.com", where ".com" is called the top-level domain name, "B.com" is called the second-level domain name, and "A.B.com" is called the third-level domain name. In addition, "B" is called the second-level domain name label. Generally, the research on DGAs refers to the second-level domain name label, so the main research object in this article also defaults to the second-level domain name label.

3.2   Dictionary Generation Module

In this module, the main task of GWDGA is to construct GWDict. The first step is to obtain a list of commonly used n-grams, and the second step is to obtain a list of frequently used words in domain names. Finally, the two parts are combined into GWDict.

Actually, the n-gram is an algorithm based on statistical language models. Its basic idea is to perform a sliding window operation of size n on the content of the text, forming a sequence of fragments of length n. Commonly used are unigram (n = 1), bigram (n = 2) and trigram (n = 3). This module processes a large number of benign domain names according to n = 1, 2, 3, 4 and sorts the results according to their frequency of occurrence to obtain commonly used n-grams. In the end, the top 5000 n-grams form a list.

Meanwhile, to obtain the most frequently used words in domain name, this module uses a list of 5000 most frequently used domain name prefixes and suffixes which was generated by Lean Domain Search (LDS). It can be obtained at https://gist.github.com/cnicodeme. LDS is a well-known search engine for finding available domain names. This list counts the components of hundreds of millions of domain names and lists the most commonly used prefixes and suffixes

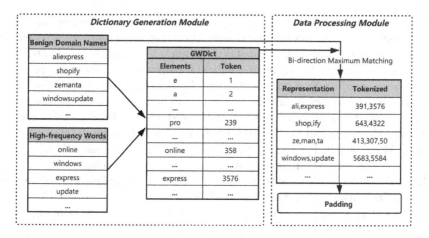

Fig. 2. Schematic diagram of dictionary generation module and data processing module. Padding means padding the data to a fixed length with padding characters.

in order of frequency. Through the analysis of this list, we find that if the number of characters in these prefixes and suffixes is greater than 4, most of them appear as words. If the number of characters in these prefixes and suffixes is less than 4, most of them appear in the form of n-grams. This is why we set the maximum value of n to 4 in the first step. In addition, this statistical list based on a huge domain name also indirectly proves the correctness of our view of treating domain names as a combination of commonly used n-grams and high-frequency words. Therefore, this list is worthy of trust and adoption. It can provide us with a list of high-frequency words.

In order to obtain GWDict, we combine the lists obtained in the two steps and remove duplicates to obtain a complete list that contains 7486 elements. Then we sort according to the frequency of these 7486 n-grams or words in the list of TRANCO benign domain names and take the serial number as their token. Finally, GWDict contains commonly used n-grams, high-frequency words, and their corresponding tokens (shown in Fig. 2).

3.3 Data Processing Module

The main task of the data processing module is to express a large number of benign domain names as a combination of commonly used n-grams and high-frequency words according to the GWDict generated by the dictionary generation module and output a list of tokenized benign domain names.

This module first needs to segment them according to GWDict so that these benign domain names can be expressed as commonly used n-grams and high-frequency words. To facilitate understanding, we can draw an analogy between domain names and Chinese sentences. Chinese sentences contain two levels of elements, namely characters and words. This is like the two levels of elements contained in the domain name we proposed, namely n-gram (n = 1, 2, 3, 4) and high-frequency words. Therefore, the method of segmenting domain names in this module is the Bi-direction Maximum Matching Algorithm (BiMM) widely used in Chinese word segmentation. The Maximum Matching Algorithm refers to matching the string to be segmented with the entries in the dictionary prepared in advance according to a certain strategy. Its principle is to match the longer entries in the dictionary as much as possible and add them to the word segmentation results. According to the direction of the start of matching, the Maximum Matching Algorithm can be divided into the Forward Maximum Matching Algorithm (FMM) and the Backward Maximum Matching Algorithm (BMM). BiMM contains FMM and BMM. It compares the segmentation results of FMM and BMM and takes the result with fewer single characters (unigram) or fewer elements as its output. Meanwhile, since GWDict contains all single characters (unigram) that appear in domain names, this ensures that all domain names can be successfully segmented.

After these benign domain names are processed by the BiMM algorithm, a tokenized list of benign domain names can be output according to the content of GWDict. In addition, zero is used as a padding character to make the length of the tokenized domain name fixed. We take a fixed length as 75. Finally, the data processing module outputs data that can be used for domain names generation model training (shown in Fig. 2).

3.4   Domain Names Generation Module

The main task of GWDGA is to generate adversarial domain names and the domain names generation module is the key to its generation ability. The main architecture of this module is based on a Variational Autoencoder (VAE). The first step of this module is to train the VAE. The second step is to use the decoder as a generative model to generate domain names. Figure 3 shows the architecture of this module.

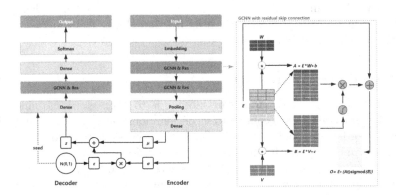

Fig. 3. The architecture of the domain names generation module.

Principle of VAE. Variational autoencoder model is an unsupervised learning framework that can use latent variables to learn the interpretable latent representation contained in the input data. It is an important type of generative model, which was proposed by Diederik P. Kingma and Max Welling in 2013 [34]. The generative model learns from the training data and approximates the true distribution of the data to generate new data. The goal is to approximate the distribution and generate data. In the probability model, the posterior probability is often not directly calculated. Variational inference constructs an approximate distribution of the required posterior probability, and then continuously optimizes the approximate distribution to make it close to the true distribution. The difference between the two distributions is measured using KL divergence. Variational autoencoders are constructed on the basis of variational inference. Suppose the input data in the variational autoencoder is x, the hidden variable is z, and the output data is x'. The idea of the variational autoencoder is to use neural networks to model two complex conditional probability density functions respectively. The first one is $q_\phi(z|x)$ which is a variational distribution parameterized by an inference network (encoder) with parameters ϕ. Meanwhile, it is generally set in the form of a normal distribution. The input of the encoder is x. The output of the encoder is $q_\phi(z|x)$, which is represented by the mean μ and the variance σ (actually $\log \sigma^2$).

$$(\mu, \log \sigma^2) = \text{encoder}_\phi(x) \tag{1}$$

$$q_\phi(z \mid x) = \mathcal{N}(z; \mu, \text{diag}(\sigma)) \tag{2}$$

The second one is $p_\theta(x|z)$ which is a conditional distribution parameterized by a generative network (decoder) with parameters θ. For any $q_\phi(z|x)$:

$$log p_\theta(x) = \mathbb{E}_{q_\phi(z|x)}\left[\log p_\theta(x)\right] = \mathcal{L}_{\theta,\phi}(x) + D_{KL}\left(q_\phi(z \mid x) \| p_\theta(z \mid x)\right) \tag{3}$$

$$\mathcal{L}_{\theta,\phi}(x) = \mathbb{E}_{q_\phi(z|x)}\left[\log\left[\frac{p_\theta(x, z)}{q_\phi(z \mid x)}\right]\right] \tag{4}$$

The Kullback-Leibler (KL) divergence is non-negative so that $\mathcal{L}_{\theta,\phi}(x)$ can be called the evidence lower bound (ELBO). From Eq. 3, we can find that increasing ELBO will cause the KL divergence between $q_\phi(z|x)$ and $p_\theta(z|x)$ to decrease and $log p_\theta(x)$ to increase. Therefore, maximizing ELBO can optimize the entire model. ELBO can also be converted into the following form:

$$\mathcal{L}_{\theta,\phi}(x) = \mathbb{E}_{q_\phi(z|x)}\left[\log p_\theta(x \mid z)\right] - D_{KL}\left(q_\phi(z \mid x) \| p_\theta(z)\right) \tag{5}$$

This ELBO consists of two parts. The first part is a reconstruction loss term that encourages the inference network to encode the information necessary to generate the data. The second part is a KL regularizer to push $q_\phi(z|x)$ towards the prior $p_\theta(z)$. For ϕ and θ in ELBO, the stochastic gradient descent method can be used to optimize the solution. However, since z is a random variable sampled from $q_\phi(z|x)$, it cannot be directly optimized using backpropagation. To solve this problem, the reparameterization trick can come in handy. Specifically, the reparameterization trick is to sample ε from the standard normal distribution outside the network and then combine it with the variational posterior parameter to indirectly obtain the hidden variable z.

$$z = \mu + \varepsilon \odot \sigma, \varepsilon \sim \mathcal{N}(0, 1) \tag{6}$$

$$x' = \text{decoder}_\theta(z) = \text{decoder}_\theta(\text{ seed }) \tag{7}$$

Then we can use backpropagation and calculate the gradient. Meanwhile, to make the model have the generative ability, it is assumed that the posterior distribution $p_\theta(z|x)$ is a standard normal distribution. So, we can deduce that the prior distribution is also a standard normal distribution. Therefore, when the model training is completed, we can sample from $\mathcal{N}(0, 1)$ to obtain a seed(a tensor of shape(128) filled with random values) and enter into the decoder so that we can get a new domain name.

Details of Model. In this module, the model based on the variational autoencoder mainly includes an encoder and a decoder. They all contain the gated convolutional neural network (GCNN) and dense layer. As far as we know, GCNN performs better than the ordinary convolutional neural network on many natural language processing tasks. Some details of our model are shown in Table 1. The task of the encoder is to learn the potential sequence characteristics and distribution of benign domain names. To facilitate training, the encoder first needs to convert the domain name into a tensor by means of an embedding layer. After that, the encoder begins to extract feature information from the embeddings by the convolutional neural network. It is worth noting that the convolutional neural network here is a gated convolutional neural network with the residual skip connection instead of a common convolutional neural network with the rectified linear unit. GCNN was proposed by Dauphin in 2016 [32]. Recurrent neural networks are known to have been the best choice for natural language processing tasks and sequence data modeling, especially LTSM. However, the research [35] shows that one-dimensional convolutional neural networks also perform well in these tasks. In addition, Dauphin et al. [32] shows that GCNN can more easily capture long-range dependencies and perform more efficiently. Because stacked convolutions allow parallelization over sequential tokens. In our work, GWDGA needs to learn the internal arrangement of n-grams or words from a large number of benign domain names. The characteristics of GCNN are in line with our needs, so we choose it. Then through the global average pooling layer and two parallel dense layers, mean and variance can be obtained. The task of the decoder is to generate new domain names that are similar to benign domain names. When generating a new domain name, it receives a seed as input and uses a dense layer to map it from a low-dimensional space to a high-dimensional space to obtain its diversity output. Thereafter, we use GCNN and the dense layer to map the previous output to the embedding space. Finally, we obtain the deterministic output through the softmax layer. According to the output of the decoder, GWDGA uses the argmax function to obtain the index with the largest embedded value. These indexes have corresponding n-grams or words. GWDGA can obtain corresponding n-grams or words according to GWDict and connect them into a new domain name.

Table 1. Some details of our model. 'OS' represents the output shape, 'S' represents the kernel size and 'L' represents the fixed domain name length.

	Layer	OS	S
Encoder	input	(L)	–
	embedding	(L,128)	–
	gcnn_1	(L,128)	3
	gcnn_2	(L,128)	3
	pooling	(128)	–
	dense_mean(pooling)	(128)	–
	dense_var(pooling)	(128)	–
Decoder	lambda	(128)	–
	dense_1	(L*128)	–
	reshape	(L,128)	–
	gcnn_1	(L,128)	3
	dense_2	(L,7487)	–
	softmax	(L,7487)	–

GCNN with Residual Skip Connection. In order to utilize the order information of benign domain names, we use the GCNN with residual skip connection in GWDGA. The process of it can be described as Eq. 8.

$$O = E + (A \otimes \sigma(B)) = E + ((E * W + b) \otimes \sigma(E * V + c)) \tag{8}$$

where both W, V, b, and c are model parameters, W and V denote convolution kernels with the same size but different weights. b and c denote the bias vector. $*$ is the symbol for convolution operation. $\otimes$ is the Hadamard product operator. σ is the sigmoid function. E is the input of GCNN. O is the output of GCNN. $O \in \mathbb{R}^{L \times M}$, $E \in \mathbb{R}^{L \times M}$, $W \in \mathbb{R}^{S \times M}$, $V \in \mathbb{R}^{S \times M}$. L is the fixed domain name length, which represents the number of components in a domain name. M is the dimension of the embedding vector. S denotes the kernel size, which represents the number of components of each convolution kernel coverage. Figure 3 contains a schematic diagram of GCNN with residual skip connection. Here, $\sigma(B)$ is equivalent to a special gating mechanism that controls what information from A is passed up to the next layer in the hierarchy. The gating mechanism also provides the layer with non-linear capabilities. To minimize the vanishing gradient problem, the residual skip connection is added to each layer so that model can contain more layers.

3.5   Domain Names Filtering Module

The main function of this module is to filter the new domain names generated by the generative model and remove some domain names that are not supported for registration. First, short domain names that are less than or equal to four in length will be filtered out. This is because most short domain names have already been registered. Next, those domain names that do not comply with the domain name naming rules will also be filtered out. For example, the hyphen (-) appears consecutively in the domain name, or the hyphen (-) appears at the beginning or end of the domain name. These domain names are unavailable. Finally, the domain names output by this module can be called AGDs.

4   Experiment

4.1   Datasets

In our work, the domain name data mainly comes from two datasets. The first is a benign domain names dataset named TRANCO [36], and the second is a malicious domain names dataset named HYDRA [37].

Table 2. The specific content of MD.

Class	Support	Class	Support	Class	Support
bamital	10,000	matsnu	10,000	ranbyus	10,000
banjori	10,000	monerominer	10,000	rovnix	10,000
ccleaner	10,000	murofet	10,000	shiotob	10,000
chinad	10,000	murofetweekly	10,000	simda	10,000
conficker	10,000	necurs	10,000	sphinx	10,000
corebot	10,000	nymaim	10,000	suppobox	10,000
cryptolocker	10,000	padcrypt	10,000	szribi	10,000
cryptowall	10,000	pandabanker	10,000	tempedreve	10,000
dircrypt	10,000	pitou	10,000	tinba	10,000
dnschanger	10,000	proslikefan	10,000	tinynuke	10,000
dyre	10,000	pushdo	10,000	torpig	10,000
emotet	10,000	pykspa	10,000	vawtrak	10,000
gameover	10,000	pykspa_v1	10,000	vidro	10,000
gozi	10,000	qadars	10,000	virut	10,000
hesperbot	10,000	qakbot	10,000	xshellghost	10,000
kraken	10,000	qsnatch	10,000	zloader	10,000
locky	10,000	ramnit	10,000	*Total*	*500,000*

The difference between TRANCO and other rankings is not only that it can resist malicious manipulation, but also that it is particularly friendly to researchers. The author of TRANCO provides an online service at https:// tranco-list.eu, in order to enhance the reproducibility of studies that rely on them [36]. Meanwhile, HYDRA dataset can be obtained at https://zenodo.org so that our malicious domain name data can also be reproduced. HYDRA contains more than 90 million domain names and more than 100 families. The main sources for the AGDs in HYDRA are DGArchive, 360 DGA and Bambenek. To facilitate the experiments, we construct four datasets based on the TRANCO dataset and the HTDRA dataset. The first is the malicious domain names dataset named MD. The second is the benign domain names dataset BD used for GWDGA training. The third is the benign domain names dataset BD1 used for training the classifier. The fourth is the benign domain names dataset BD2 used for comparison experiment. MD contains 500,000 malicious domain names. They come from 50 representative DGA families in HYDRA. 10,000 domain names were randomly selected from each family to form the MD. These families include hash-based DGAs, arithmetic-based DGAs, and wordlist-based DGAs, etc. This arrangement will make the results of our experiments more convincing. The specific content of MD is shown in Table 2. BD contains 905,436 benign domain names sourced from TRANCO. BD1 contains 500,000 benign domain names and BD2 contains 10,000 benign domain names. These benign domain names are sourced from the top 510,000 data in TRANCO. In addition, there is no duplication between BD1 and BD2.

4.2 Evaluation Metrics

In our experiment, we use some metrics to evaluate the performance of a classifier and the anti-detection ability of adversarial DGAs. (1) Area Under Curve (AUC) is defined as the area under the Receiver Operating Characteristic (ROC) curve. We can judge the performance of the classifiers by the value of AUC (larger is better for the classifiers). We can also judge the anti-detection ability of the adversarial DGA by the value of AUC (smaller is better for DGAs). (2) According to the prediction results of a series of input domain names by the classifier, we can get four indicators: True Positive (TP), True Negative (TN), False Positive (FP), and False Negative (FN). Based on these four indicators, we can get Precision (P), Recall (R), and False Positive Rate (FPR). Specifically, $P = TP/(TP+FP)$, $R = TP/(TP+FN)$ and $FPR = FP/(FP+TN)$.

4.3 Targeted Classifiers

Our experiment is based on the three most advanced DGA classifiers (Endgame [6], Invincea [20], MIT [38]), and their architectures are very representative. We reproduce them based on previous work [23]. Meanwhile, all models were trained and tested with the same number of epochs on MD and BD1. Table 3 shows the performance of the three models on the test set without adversarial attacks.

Table 3. The performance of the three models without adversarial attacks.

Target model	Architecture	P	R	AUC
Endgame	LSTM	0.95	0.94	0.99
Invincea	CNN	0.92	0.96	0.98
MIT	CNN+LSTM	0.94	0.95	0.99

4.4 Results

In this section, we show the anti-detection ability of GWDGA through experiments. As far as we know, the current adversarial DGAs based on generative models are mainly DeepDGA and Khaos. Khaos has been proven to outperform DeepDGA. To intuitively reflect the anti-detection ability of GWDGA, we compare GWDGA with Khaos [31]. It is currently one of the most advanced adversarial DGA. Specifically, we mixed 10,000 adversarial domain names generated by GWDGA and 10,000 adversarial domain names generated by Khaos with BD2 respectively and fed them into the three target classifiers already trained for detection. After that, ROC curves are drawn using the output results of the three classifiers (as shown in Fig. 4, 5 and 6).

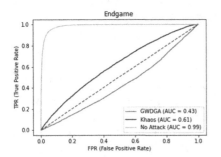

Fig. 4. ROC curves for Endgame.

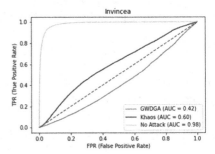

Fig. 5. ROC curves for Invincea.

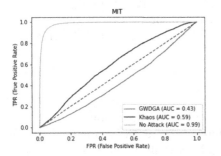

Fig. 6. ROC curves for MIT.

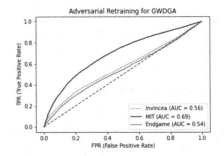

Fig. 7. ROC curves for Adv-retraining.

According to the results of the ROC curve, Khaos's performance is consistent with the results in the original text. Compared with Khaos, the AUC value of GWDGA under the detection of three classifiers is smaller. This shows that GWDGA is more likely to confuse the classifier than Khaos. In addition, our experimental results also show that GWDGA is effective and stable for DGA classifiers of different architectures. In contrast, Khaos's anti-detection ability is slightly insufficient and its FPR value will fluctuate due to different classifier architectures. There are some examples of GWDGA AGDs: mrity, grescore, thhvillierty and airablebroadinc. Table 4 shows some examples of GWDGA AGDs. Table 5 presents the details of experimental results. According to the results in the table, the Precision of the three DGA classifiers is significantly reduced after being attacked by the adversarial attack, which shows the effectiveness of the adversarial attack. Meanwhile, the Recall of the three classifiers is at a normal level, indicating that the three classifiers can work normally and identify benign domain names. A higher FPR indicates that the classifier misclassifies adversarial domain names more frequently. A low AUC indicates that the performance of the classifier is poor. Therefore, we can conclude that GWDGA can produce highly effective adversarial domain names. These adversarial domain names have strong anti-detection capabilities.

Table 4. Some examples of GWDGA AGDs.

Examples	mrity
	grescora
	thhvillierty
	airablebroadinc

Table 5. The detail of experimental results.

Metrics	Endgame				Invincea				MIT			
	P	R	FPR	AUC	P	R	FPR	AUC	P	R	FPR	AUC
GWDGA	0.50	0.94	0.96	0.43	0.50	0.96	0.97	0.42	0.50	0.95	0.96	0.43
Khaos	0.52	0.93	0.85	0.61	0.51	0.96	0.91	0.60	0.52	0.95	0.88	0.59

4.5 Adversarial Retraining

Adversarial retraining [30] is a method to enhance the robustness of the model. It can improve the model's defence ability in the face of adversarial attacks by adding adversarial samples in the training set. To understand the performance of GWDGA in the face of this defence method, 10,000 adversarial domain names were added to the MD to form a new training set denoted as MD1. Then three DGA classifiers were trained and tested with the same number of epochs on

MD1 and BD1. Finally, we use three trained DGA classifiers to detect 10,000 new GWDGA-generated domain names. The results are shown in Fig. 7. The AUC values of the three DGA classifiers have all been improved. However, this is still not the ideal state of the DGA classifiers. Therefore, the experimental results suggest that adversarial retraining does enhance the classifiers' ability to cope with GWDGA to some extent. Nonetheless, its effect is limited. In addition, this also reflects the effectiveness of GWDGA from the side.

5   Conclusion

This paper presents a new type of adversarial DGA, which we called GWDGA. GWDGA can effectively deceive advanced DGA classifiers. It is stable under the detection of classifiers of different architectures. GWDGA creatively uses commonly used N-grams and high-frequency words as the basic components of the domain name. Based on this view, the adversarial domain names generated by GWDGA reduce the AUC value of multiple advanced classifiers to below 0.45. Meanwhile, the experiment shows that adversarial retraining can enhance the classifiers' ability to cope with GWDGA to some extent. Overall, GWDGA is an effective and anti-detection adversarial DGA. Our work can provide researchers with a new method to discover the weaknesses of DGA classifiers and help them optimize detection methods.

References

1. Alauthman, M.: Botnet spam e-mail detection using deep recurrent neural network. Int. J. **8**(5), 1979–1986 (2020)
2. Alauthman, M., Aslam, N., Al-Kasassbeh, M., Khan, S., Al-Qerem, A., Choo, K.K.R.: An efficient reinforcement learning-based botnet detection approach. J. Netw. Comput. Appl. **150**, 102479 (2020)
3. Rawat, R.S., Diwakar, M., Verma, P.: Zeroaccess botnet investigation and analysis. Int. J. Inf. Technol. **13**, 1–9 (2021)
4. Zimba, A., Wang, Z., Mulenga, M., Odongo, N.H.: Crypto mining attacks in information systems: an emerging threat to cyber security. J. Comput. Inf. Syst. **60**(4), 297–308 (2020)
5. Li, X., Wang, J., Zhang, X.: Botnet detection technology based on DNS. Future Internet **9**(4), 55 (2017)
6. Woodbridge, J., Anderson, H.S., Ahuja, A., Grant, D.: Predicting domain generation algorithms with long short-term memory networks. arXiv:1611.00791 (2016)
7. Zago, M., Pérez, M.G., Pérez, G.M.: Scalable detection of botnets based on DGA. Soft. Comput. **24**(8), 5517–5537 (2020)
8. Schüppen, S., Teubert, D., Herrmann, P., Meyer, U.: Fanci: Feature-based automated nxdomain classification and intelligence. In: Proceedings of the 27th USENIX Conference on Security Symposium, pp. 1165–1181 (2018)
9. Szegedy, C., et al.: Intriguing properties of neural networks. arXiv:1312.6199 (2013)
10. Papernot, N., McDaniel, P., Jha, S., Fredrikson, M., Celik, Z.B., Swami, A.: The limitations of deep learning in adversarial settings. In: 2016 IEEE European Symposium on Security And Privacy (EuroS&P), pp. 372–387. IEEE (2016)

11. Fu, Y., et al.: Stealthy domain generation algorithms. IEEE Trans. Inf. Forensics Secur. **12**(6), 1430–1443 (2017)
12. Sivaguru, R., Choudhary, C., Yu, B., Tymchenko, V., Nascimento, A., De Cock, M.: An evaluation of DGA classifiers. In: 2018 IEEE International Conference on Big Data (Big Data), pp. 5058–5067. IEEE (2018)
13. Yadav, S., Reddy, A.K.K., Reddy, A.N., Ranjan, S.: Detecting algorithmically generated domain-flux attacks with DNS traffic analysis. IEEE/ACM Trans. Netw. **20**(5), 1663–1677 (2012)
14. Antonakakis, M., et al.: From throw-away traffic to bots: detecting the rise of DGA-based malware. In: Proceedings of the 21th USENIX Conference on Security Symposium, pp. 491–506 (2012)
15. Grill, M., Nikolaev, I., Valeros, V., Rehak, M.: Detecting dga malware using netflow. In: 2015 IFIP/IEEE International Symposium on Integrated Network Management (IM), pp. 1304–1309. IEEE (2015)
16. Wang, T., Hu, X., Jang, J., Ji, S., Stoecklin, M., Taylor, T.: Botmeter: Charting DGA-botnet landscapes in large networks. In: 2016 IEEE 36th International Conference on Distributed Computing Systems (ICDCS), pp. 334–343. IEEE (2016)
17. Shi, Y., Chen, G., Li, J.: Malicious domain name detection based on extreme machine learning. Neural Process. Lett. **48**(3), 1347–1357 (2018)
18. Schiavoni, S., Maggi, F., Cavallaro, L., Zanero, S.: Phoenix: DGA-based botnet tracking and intelligence. In: Dietrich, S. (ed.) Detection of Intrusions and Malware, and Vulnerability Assessment. DIMVA 2014. Lecture Notes in Computer Science, vol. 8550. Springer, Cham (2014). https://doi.org/10.1007/978-3-319-08509-8_11
19. Liu, W., Zhang, Z., Huang, C., Fang, Y.: Cleter: a character-level evasion technique against deep learning DGA classifiers. EAI Endorsed Trans. Secur. Safety **7**(24), e5 (2021)
20. Lison, P., Mavroeidis, V.: Automatic detection of malware-generated domains with recurrent neural models. arXiv:1709.07102 (2017)
21. Yu, B., Gray, D.L., Pan, J., De Cock, M., Nascimento, A.C.: Inline DGA detection with deep networks. In: 2017 IEEE International Conference on Data Mining Workshops (ICDMW), pp. 683–692. IEEE (2017)
22. Yu, B., Pan, J., Hu, J., Nascimento, A., De Cock, M.: Character level based detection of DGA domain names. In: 2018 International Joint Conference on Neural Networks (IJCNN), pp. 1–8. IEEE (2018)
23. Saxe, J., Berlin, K.: expose: A character-level convolutional neural network with embeddings for detecting malicious URLS, file paths and registry keys. arXiv:1702.08568 (2017)
24. Tran, D., Mac, H., Tong, V., Tran, H.A., Nguyen, L.G.: A LSTM based framework for handling multiclass imbalance in DGA botnet detection. Neurocomputing **275**, 2401–2413 (2018)
25. Vinayakumar, R., Soman, K., Poornachandran, P.: Evaluating deep learning approaches to characterize and classify malicious url's. J. Intell. Fuzzy Syst. **34**(3), 1333–1343 (2018)
26. Vinayakumar, R., Soman, K., Poornachandran, P., Alazab, M., Jolfaei, A.: DBD: deep learning DGA-based botnet detection. In: Alazab, M., Tang, M. (eds.) Deep Learning Applications for Cyber Security, pp. 127–149. Springer (2019). https://doi.org/10.1007/978-3-030-13057-2_6
27. Anderson, H.S., Woodbridge, J., Filar, B.: DeepDGA: adversarially-tuned domain generation and detection. In: Proceedings of the 2016 ACM Workshop on Artificial Intelligence and Security, pp. 13–21 (2016)

28. Peck, J., et al.: Charbot: A simple and effective method for evading DGA classifiers. IEEE Access **7**, 91759–91771 (2019)
29. Spooren, J., Preuveneers, D., Desmet, L., Janssen, P., Joosen, W.: Detection of algorithmically generated domain names used by botnets: a dual arms race. In: Proceedings of the 34th ACM/SIGAPP Symposium on Applied Computing, pp. 1916–1923 (2019)
30. Sidi, L., Nadler, A., Shabtai, A.: Maskdga: an evasion attack against DGA classifiers and adversarial defenses. IEEE Access **8**, 161580–161592 (2020)
31. Yun, X., Huang, J., Wang, Y., Zang, T., Zhou, Y., Zhang, Y.: Khaos: An adversarial neural network DGA with high anti-detection ability. IEEE Trans. Inf. Forensics Secur. **15**, 2225–2240 (2019)
32. Dauphin, Y.N., Fan, A., Auli, M., Grangier, D.: Language modeling with gated convolutional networks. In: International Conference on Machine Learning, pp. 933–941. PMLR (2017)
33. Corley, I., Lwowski, J., Hoffman, J.: Domaingan: generating adversarial examples to attack domain generation algorithm classifiers. arXiv:1911.06285 (2019)
34. Kingma, D.P., Welling, M.: Auto-encoding variational bayes. arXiv:1312.6114 (2013)
35. Zhang, X., Zhao, J., LeCun, Y.: Character-level convolutional networks for text classification. Adv. Neural. Inf. Process. Syst. **28**, 649–657 (2015)
36. Pochat, V.L., Van Goethem, T., Tajalizadehkhoob, S., Korczyński, M., Joosen, W.: Tranco: A research-oriented top sites ranking hardened against manipulation. arXiv:1806.01156 (2018)
37. Casino, F., Lykousas, N., Homoliak, I., Patsakis, C., Hernandez-Castro, J.: Intercepting hail hydra: real-time detection of algorithmically generated domains. J. Netw Comput. Appl. **190**, 103135 (2021)
38. Vosoughi, S., Vijayaraghavan, P., Roy, D.: Tweet2vec: learning tweet embeddings using character-level CNN-LSTM encoder-decoder. In: Proceedings of the 39th International ACM SIGIR Conference on Research and Development in Information Retrieval, pp. 1041–1044 (2016)

Imperceptible and Reliable Adversarial Attack

Jiawei Zhang[1], Jinwei Wang[1(✉)], Xiangyang Luo[2], Bin Ma[3],
and Naixue Xiong[4]

[1] School of Computer and Software, Engineering Research Center of Digital
Forensics, Ministry of Education, Nanjing University of Information Science
and Technology, Nanjing 210044, China
[2] State Key Laboratory of Mathematical Engineering and Advanced Computing,
Zhenzhou 450001, China
[3] Shandong Provincial Key Laboratory of Computer Networks and Qilu University
of Technology, Jinan 250353, China
[4] Department of Computer Science and Mathematics, Sul Ross State University,
Alpine, TX 79830, USA

Abstract. Deep neural networks are vulnerable to adversarial examples,
which can fool classifiers by adding small perturbations. Various adversarial attack methods have been proposed in the past several years, and
most of them add the perturbation in a "sparse" or "global" way. Since the
number of pixels perturbed by the "sparse" method and the perturbation
intensity of each pixel added by the "global" method are both small, the
adversarial property can be destroyed easily. Finally, it makes the adversarial attack and the adversarial training based on these samples unreliable. To address this issue, we present an "pixel-wise" method which is
somewhere in between the "sparse" or "global" way. First, the perception
of human eyes to the error of different image regions is different. Second,
image processing methods have different effects on the different areas of
the image. Based on these two considerations, we propose an imperceptible and reliable adversarial attack method, which projects the perturbation to the different areas differently. Extensive experiments demonstrate
our method can preserve the attack ability while maintaining good view
quality. More importantly, the proposed projection can be combined with
existing attack methods to generate a stronger generation algorithm which
improves the robustness of adversarial examples. Based on the proposed
method, the reliability of adversarial attacks can be greatly improved.

Keywords: Deep learning · Adversarial example · Human visual
system

1 Introduction

Deep Neural Networks (DNNs) have achieved state-of-the-art performance on
many artificial intelligence tasks such as object detection [19], image recognition [8,11,24], natural language processing [22]. Moreover, DNNs can combine

© Springer Nature Singapore Pte Ltd. 2022
C. Cao et al. (Eds.): FCS 2021, CCIS 1558, pp. 49–62, 2022.
https://doi.org/10.1007/978-981-19-0523-0_4

with many techniques such as Cloud Computing [5,12,18,23] to provide another solution for many realistic problems [25–27]. However, recent work [21] discovered that DNNs are vulnerable to adversarial examples, which crafted by adding small, imperceptible noise to the original clean image, but make target DNNs output wrong predictions. Since then, more and more adversarial attack methods have been proposed. Most of them aim at generating the adversarial perturbation with smaller L_p norms (e.g., L_{inf} [3,6,9], L_2 [3,16,21], L_0 [3,17]).

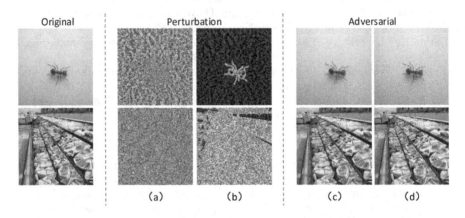

Original   Perturbation   Adversarial

(a)   (b)   (c)   (d)

Fig. 1. (a) and (c) are the perturbation and adversarial example generated by FGSM. (b) and (d) are the perturbation and adversarial example generated by our P-FGSM.

The "global" methods [6,9] focus on the L_{inf} norm of the adversarial perturbation. The adversarial example generated by this method pursues to minimize the perturbation to a single pixel rather than the number of perturbed pixels. On the contrary, the "sparse" methods proposed in [17] try to minimize the L_0 norm of the adversarial perturbation by perturbing fewer pixels with large modification.

However, the image processing methods (e.g., JEPG compression, Gaussian blur) may destroy the adversarial property of the perturbation easily because of the low intensity of modification in the "global" methods and the singularity noise in the "sparse" methods. Singularity noise means a few local pixels change dramatically, a common phenomenon in the "sparse" methods.

In this paper, we try to improve the robustness of the adversarial example by proposing a "pixel-wise" method. Firstly, various image processing methods such as JPEG compression greatly influence the smooth area of the image but have little influence on the complex texture area and edge. Secondly, human vision is a nonlinear system that is not sensitive to the modification in the texture area of the image. However, it's easy for people to perceive the singularity noise, especially when it's in the smooth area of the image.

Based on the above two considerations, we propose that the texture area of the image can be a better carrier area for adversarial perturbation. The low intensity of adversarial perturbation is the fundamental reason that various image processing techniques can easily destroy it. Therefore, we adjust the perturbation intensity selectively to improve the robustness against mainstream image processing techniques. As shown in Fig. 1, we enhance the intensity in the texture and edge area while trimming the perturbation in the smooth area.

In a one-step attack, given an input image, we first leverage the gradient-based method to calculate the perturbation according to the gradient of the input w.r.t the loss function used to train the target DNNs. Then we project the perturbation to the threshold, which is calculated according to the texture feature of the image. For iterative attacks, the perturbation can be projected to the threshold in each iteration. For simplicity and clarity, this paper mainly focuses on the one-step attack.

To our knowledge, FGSM [6] is one of the recognized benchmarks in the one-step attack. Thus, we choose FGSM as a baseline attack. For a better comparison, we also add the benchmarking iterative algorithm C&W [3], and state-of-the-art PerC-AL [28] as a competitive method.

Accordingly, for a better evaluation of the performance of adversarial examples, we introduce peak signal to noise ratio (PSNR) and structural similarity (SSIM) [29]. PSNR and SSIM are widely used in the traditional image processing field. For adversarial example generation, PSNR is used to measure the perturbation intensity while SSIM is used to measure the visual quality and imperceptibility.

The contributions of this paper can be summarized as follows:

- Base on the joint characteristic between human vision and the mainstream image process, we propose to improve the robustness of adversarial examples by adjusting the perturbation intensity selectively.
- A threshold matrix is designed to obtain the feature of the input image, which split the texture complexity into multiple levels by a non-linear function.
- Experiments have demonstrated the proposed method maintains good visual quality without huge time consumption. More importantly, the samples achieve superior robustness, which makes the attack more reliable.

2   Related Work

2.1   Method of Generating Adversarial Examples

The fast gradient sign method (FGSM) [6] is designed to generate adversarial examples at high speed. FGSM focuses on the time cost rather than the imperceptibility. It adds the perturbation according to the gradient direction of input w.r.t the loss function by a chosen step size ϵ. Let y denote the ground-truth of the input X. For a neural network with cross-entropy cost function $J(X, y)$, the adversarial example X^{adv} can be calculated as

$$X^{adv} = X + \epsilon sign(\nabla_X J(X, y)) \tag{1}$$

FGSM increases the value of the loss function by perturbing the image with a chosen step ϵ. The I-FGSM [9] limit the perturbation to a one-pixel value and calculate a new gradient in each iteration, which can be formulated as

$$X_{N+1}^{adv} = Clip_{X,\epsilon}\{X_N^{adv} + \alpha sign(\nabla_X J(X_N^{adv}, y_{true}))\} \tag{2}$$

An iterative calculation will make the perturbation more effective and accurate. However, it takes more time than the one-step method. DeepFool [16] also searches for perturbations iteratively. The perturbations added to the image in each iteration are accumulated to compute the final perturbation once the perturbed image changes its label. The minimum perturbation $r_*(x_0)$ can be calculated as

$$r_*(x_0) = \frac{|f_{\hat{i}(x_0)}(x_0) - f_{\hat{k}(x_0)}(x_0)|}{||w_{\hat{i}(x_0)} - w_{\hat{k}(x_0)}||_2^2}(w_{\hat{i}(x_0)} - w_{\hat{k}(x_0)}) \tag{3}$$

C&W [3] uses the tanh function to eliminate the box constraint and makes the generated samples achieved outstanding visual performance. The C&W can be formulated as

$$\min_w ||\tilde{x} - x||_2^2 + \lambda f(\tilde{x})$$
$$\text{where} \quad f(\tilde{x}) = \max(\max_{i \neq t}\{Z(\tilde{x})_i\} - Z(\tilde{x})_t, -\kappa) \tag{4}$$
$$\text{and} \quad \tilde{x} = \frac{1}{2}(\tanh(\text{arctanh}(x) + w) + 1)$$

where κ controls the confidence level, and $Z(\tilde{x})_i$ is the logit to the i-th class.

Zhao et al. [28] propose a state-of-the-art attack method called PerC-AL, which outperforms conventional L_p approaches in both robustness and imperceptibility. The PerC-AL optimizes adversarial perturbation directly with respect to a perceptual color distance, which is measured by CIEDE2000 [15]. The PerC-AL takes the perception ability of human eyes into consideration, which is similar to our human visual system. However, the conversion of color space of PerC-AL brings huge time costs. And, the time consumption is doubled again because of its iterative optimization. The huge time consumption makes it difficult to have practical value (e.g., performing adversarial training).

2.2   Human Visual System

The perception ability of human eyes to the error of different image regions is different. The perception of an area will be affected by its surrounding neighboring areas. Human vision is not linearly sensitive to errors, which makes it possible to hide large perturbation without the L_p constraint. Specifically, the main three properties are texture sensitivity, luminance sensitivity, and frequency sensitivity. This paper focus on the texture sensitivity [10,13,14] in RGB color space. Texture sensitivity reveals that human eyes are less sensitive to intricate textures areas of the image, which means it is difficult to perceive modifications in texture areas.

3   Proposed Method

Let x be the source image and y be the ground-truth label of x. We denote the target DNNs as $f(\cdot)$ with parameter θ. Meanwhile, the $J(\theta, x, y)$ is the loss function used to train the $f(\cdot)$. In the training stage, we want to minimize the $J(\theta, x, y)$ by gradient descent to make the DNNs achieve higher accuracy. However, adversarial example $x_{adv} = x + r$ can be obtained to fool the the target DNNs resulting $f(x_{adv}) \neq y$. The adversarial perturbation r can be calculated by various methods which are listed in Sect. 2.1.

In most cases, r is constrained to minimize the L_p norm, which leads to the different embedding styles of r. As briefly described in the introduction part, the "global" way almost perturb all pixels in the x because there are few pixels which gradient is equal to 0. However, the modification in each pixel is small to ensure the visual quality of the adversarial examples. Especially after getting the sign of gradient, there is only a sign difference between pixels. Image processing methods such as denoising can destroy the perturbation easily due to the low intensity. Similarly, the perturbation generated by the "sparse" way is not robust to the image processing techniques. As shown in Fig. 2, adversarial perturbation r is destroyed after Gaussian blur and the rounding operation. It is assumed that the adversarial perturbation will make the center of the matrix change three-pixel values. After Gaussian filtering and rounding operation, the perturbation in the center will be dispersed to the unrelated pixels so that the perturbation will lose its adversarial property.

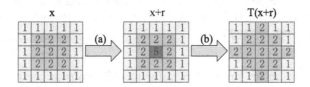

Fig. 2. x is the a smooth area of input image. (a) denote the process of adding adversarial perturbation r to the x. (b) denote the process of the Gaussian blur (kernel size $= 3 \times 3$ $\sigma = 10$) and the rounding operation.

Therefore, we propose to enhance the perturbation intensity to improve the robustness against the various image processing techniques. However, directly enhance the perturbation intensity generated by the "global" way can not achieve satisfactory results. First, this will inevitably lead to a huge decline in the visual quality of the final adversarial examples. Second, as shown in Fig. 2, enhance the perturbation intensity in the smooth region of the image can not improve the robustness effectively.

According to the texture sensitivity mentioned in Sect. 2.2, it is not easy for the human eye to perceive changes in the pixel value of the image texture area.

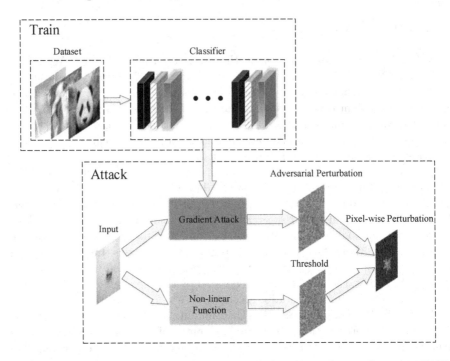

Fig. 3. The architecture of the proposed method. Classifier refers to the target DNNs trained on the corresponding data set. The specific threshold matrix of each image is calculated according to the proposed non-linear function. Combining the threshold and adversarial perturbation generated by the gradient attack, we can calculate the "pixel-wise" perturbation. By adding this perturbation to the input, we can obtain more reliable adversarial examples.

Therefore, we can make larger pixel value modifications in the texture area of the image without causing a huge degradation in visual quality.

Meanwhile, most image processing techniques have a greater influence on the modifications of the smooth area rather than the texture area. This means the large modifications made in the texture area are difficult to be erased by image processing methods (e.g., denoising).

Base on the two considerations mentioned above, we design a threshold matrix, which is adaptive to the texture feature of the image. By projecting the perturbation into this threshold, we can improve the robustness while maintaining visual quality. The structure of the entire model, a targetless white-box attack, is shown in Fig. 3.

For a 3-channel $m \times n$ color image, the threshold matrix Δ is the same size with $m \times n \times 3$ and can be calculated as

$$\Delta = (\sigma_x^2 - min(\sigma_x^2))/(max(\sigma_x^2) - min(\sigma_x^2)) \qquad (5)$$

min and max represent the operation of taking the smallest and largest value. σ_x^2 represents the variance of the area formed by the point located in (i, j, k) and its surrounding 8 neighboring pixels. For the edge pixels of the image, we clone the inner side pixels as the outer side pixels to compensate for the lack of 8 neighboring pixels. Then, the σ_x^2 can be calculated as

$$\sigma_x^2(i, j, k) = \frac{1}{9}\left(\sum_{a=i-1}^{i+1} \sum_{b=j-1}^{j+1} (x_{a,b,k} - \bar{x})^2 \right) \tag{6}$$

$\bar{x}$ represents the average pixel value of the area composed of these nine pixels.

We grab the texture feature of the image through the function designed above and normalize it to between 0 and 1. Each point (i, j, k) in the original input image x corresponds to $\Delta(i, j, k)$ in Δ, which reflects the texture intensity of the current pixel(i, j, k). When this value is closer to 1, the texture is more complex. Based on the above texture sensitivity of the human visual system and image processing characteristics, we know that this area composed of large $\Delta(i, j, k)$ is the carrier of the perturbation we are looking for. However, when the $\Delta(i, j, k)$ is closer to 0, the perturbation that this point can hold should be correspondingly smaller because the perturbation embedded at this point is easily perceptible by the human eye and erased by the image processing techniques.

The threshold gives a reasonable modification for each pixel and can be easily combined with existing attack methods. For the iterative way (e.g., I-FGSM), project the perturbation calculated in each iteration into Δ and proceed to the next iteration. For the one-step method, we set the perturbation step ϵ as the perturbation upper limit by mapping the Δ from 0-1 to 0-ϵ by

$$\Delta = (\sigma_x^2 - min(\sigma_x^2))/(max(\sigma_x^2) - min(\sigma_x^2)) \cdot \epsilon \tag{7}$$

Afterward, let $r(i, j, k)$ denote the perturbation on the pixel with coordinates (i, j, k). $r(i, j, k)$ can be calculated by mutiple the ϵ by the gradient g in the corresponding coordinates (i, j, k), which can be described as

$$r(i, j, k) = \epsilon \cdot g(i, j, k) \tag{8}$$

Finally, the "pixel-wise" perturbation $r'(i, j, k)$ can be calculated by

$$r'(i, j, k) = P_{\Delta(i,j,k)}(r(i, j, k)) \tag{9}$$

where

$$P_{\Delta x}(x) = max(min(x, \Delta x), -\Delta x), \quad \Delta x >= 0 \tag{10}$$

4 Experiment

This section evaluates the imperceptibility and the robustness of the adversarial examples generated by the proposed "pixel-wise" method. In the comparative experiment, we use the official implementation of PerC-AL [1] and follow the default settings. For C&W, we use the implementation from Torchattacks [2].

We implement all experiments on the ImageNet [4] which is widely used in related papers [3,6,7]. Inception-v3 [20] pre-trained on ImageNet was used as the target classifier. PSNR measures the perturbation intensity. SSIM [29] measures the visual quality and imperceptibility.

4.1   Imperceptibility Evaluation

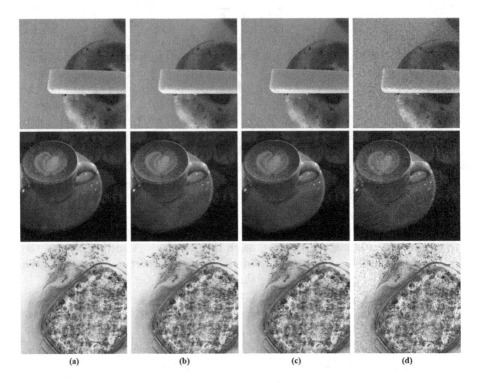

(a)   (b)   (c)   (d)

Fig. 4. Column (a) are the adversarial samples generated by the proposed P-FGSM. Columns (b), (c), and (d) are the adversarial samples generated by PerC-AL [28], C&W [3] and FGSM [6]. The samples are random selected in the condition of Table 1. ($\epsilon =$ 13 for FGSM and P-FGSM.)

Figure 4 shows some samples generated by our one-step P-FGSM, iterative C&W [3], iterative PerC-AL [28], and baseline FGSM [6]. C&W and PerC-AL are not one-step attack methods, but the adversarial samples generated by these methods have outstanding visual quality. Although they take much more time than one-step methods, we still add them to the comparison as competitive solutions. From Fig. 4, there is almost no visual difference between the proposed method and the two iterative methods. The proposed method greatly improves the visual quality and makes the samples look as good as the methods [3,28] specially optimized for visual quality.

Table 1. Time cost, PSNR, SSIM, and Attack ability of the adversarial attack methods

	Method		time (s)[a]	ϵ	PSNR (dB)	SSIM	Accuracy (%)
Natural			\	\	$+\infty$	1	93.5
Attack	One-step	FGSM [6]	<1	1	48	0.997	27.3
				2	42	0.992	19.7
				4	36	0.968	17.1
				13	26	0.770	16.2
				40	16	0.348	13.6
				60	13	0.219	9.7
		P-FGSM (our)	<1	1	70	0.999	89.3
				2	64	0.999	84.4
				4	58	0.999	75.9
				13	48	0.999	49.7
				40	39	0.997	29.5
				60	35	0.993	25.5
	Iterative	C&W [3][b]	125	\	50	0.999	0
		PerC-AL [28][c]	917	\	47	0.995	0

[a]Time for the algorithm to generate one hundred adversarial samples.
[b]c = 1, κ = 0, iterations = 1000, lr = 0.01 for C&W.
[c]α_l = 1, α_c = 0.5, 1000 iterations for PerC-AL.

Table 1 shows the time cost, PSNR, SSIM, and attack ability of the adversarial examples generated by baseline FGSM, iterative C&W, iterative PerC-AL, and the proposed method under different perturbation step ϵ. From Table 1, it can be concluded that as the ϵ increases, the perturbation intensity increases, and visual quality decreases correspondingly. Feedback can be obtained from the score of PSNR and SSIM.

Specifically, when PSNR is equal to 48, the SSIM value of the proposed method is higher than the baseline FGSM. This shows that the visual quality of the adversarial example generated by the proposed method is better when the perturbation intensity is the same.

More attractively, as the perturbation intensity (PSNR) becomes increasingly larger, the advantage of the proposed method is more apparent. As described in Sect. 3, low intensity is the fundamental reason why the perturbation is easily destroyed. This advantage allows us to solve this fundamental issue by hiding more perturbations with fewer visual quality losses. Thus, the proposed method can effectively improve the robustness of the perturbation, which is further evaluated in Sect. 4.3.

It should be noted that the PSNR of the proposed method is 39 when $\epsilon = 40$, which is smaller than PerC-AL (PSNR = 47). It means the perturbation intensity of the proposed method is bigger than the PerC-AL. However, the visual quality of the proposed method (SSIM = 0.997) is better than the PerC-AL (SSIM = 0.995). This proves that the proposed method is advanced in the optimization of visual quality.

4.2 Attack Ability Evaluation

The time and accuracy in Table 1 reflect the attack ability of the algorithm. The time describes the time consumption of the methods to generate one hundred adversarial samples. The accuracy refers to the classification accuracy of the target DNNs after being attacked. The one-step method greatly reduces the time cost (more than 100 times) owing to calculating the gradient only once. The high speed of generating adversarial examples makes it possible to implement adversarial training based on these methods. However, the increase in speed inevitably leads to the drawback of accuracy. The proposed method further limits the perturbation, resulting in a lower attack success rate than FGSM under the same ϵ.

However, The proposed method ensures that each generated adversarial sample is more robust, which makes the attack and the adversarial training more reliable. On the contrary, although C&W and PerC-AL attack can guarantee a 100% attack success rate, its perturbation is too fragile. The samples easily lose the adversarial property, which leads to the unreliability of these attacks. And, it takes too much time to perform iterative optimization of the perturbation. The two drawbacks make adversarial training base on these samples too expensive and unreliable.

In order to further compare the reliability, we tested the robustness of the adversarial samples in the following section.

4.3 Robustness Evaluation

The robust adversarial examples represent the samples can still fool the DNNs after be processed by image processing techniques. The high proportion of robust adversarial examples means that the attack algorithm is more reliable.

For a fair comparison, we select the parameters of different adversarial attack algorithms from Table 1 under the consideration of two situations, same PSNR and same SSIM. Specifically, FGSM is selected with $\epsilon = 1$ (PSNR = 48, SSIM = 0.997), the proposed method is selected with $\epsilon = 13$ (PSNR = 48, SSIM = 0.999) and $\epsilon = 40$ (PSNR = 39, SSIM = 0.997), represented by our-13 and our-40. C&W (PSNR = 50, SSIM = 0.999) and PerC-AL (PSNR = 47, SSIM = 0.995) mentioned in Table 1 is also compared.

Figure 5 shows the robustness of adversarial examples against JPEG compression, Gaussian blur, Gaussian noise, and center crop with various parameters. In addition, Table 2 shows the robustness of adversarial example against flip (along the horizontal direction), resize (to the half of image), and rotate (90°).

From Fig. 5 and Table 2, it can be seen that the performance of our-40 always achieves the best performance. Compared with the existing algorithms, the robustness of the proposed method is improved by more than 50% in the

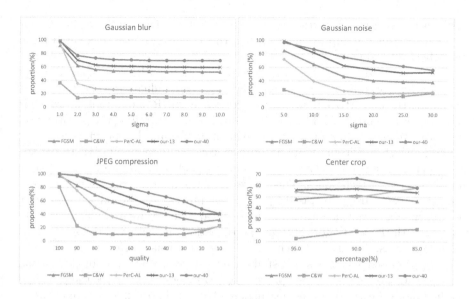

Fig. 5. The robustness of adversarial example against Gaussian blur, Gaussian noise, JPEG compression and center crop. The x-axis represents the different parameters of these image processing methods (e.g., different quality factors from 10 to 100 for JPEG compression). The y-axis represents the proportion of robust adversarial examples.

Table 2. Robustness of adversarial example against flip, resize, and rotate

Proportion (%)	FGSM [6]	C&W [3]	PerC-AL [28]	our-13	our-40
Flip	40.79	6.95	41.5	46.58	**60.78**
Resize	61.63	15.19	41.5	68.72	**77.97**
Rotate	73.11	62.25	64.3	75.8	**77.81**

best case. This shows that under the similar visual quality (SSIM = 0.997), the reliability of the proposed method is far ahead of the existing algorithms.

The improvement can be attributed to two aspects. First, from PSNR and ϵ in Table 1, the proposed method can hide larger perturbation intensity and larger modification of the pixel under the same visual quality. When the visual quality of the adversarial example is the same (e.g., SSIM = 0.997), the perturbation intensity of the proposed method (PSNR = 39) is larger than the baseline FGSM (PSNR = 48). Meanwhile, the maximum modification in pixel of the proposed methods ($\epsilon = 40$) is 40 times larger than the baseline FGSM ($\epsilon = 1$). Larger perturbations intensity and larger modification of the pixel are more difficult to be destroyed, so the robustness is improved. Second, our method focuses on disturbing specific areas in the image. The modifications in these areas are difficult to be erased by image processing techniques, which further improve the robustness.

Ablation Study. We further analyze the contributions of each part of our method towards the improvement of robustness. Thus, we introduce our-13 into the robustness evaluation.

First, our-13 disturbs the same areas as our-40 but with lower perturbation intensity. By controlling the disturbed areas, we can evaluate the effectiveness of enhancing the perturbation intensity. Second, the PSNR of our-13 is 48, which is equal to the baseline FGSM ($\epsilon = 1$, PSNR = 48). By controlling the perturbation intensity, we can evaluate the effectiveness of disturbing the specific areas.

From Fig. 5 and Table 2, our-13 outperforms the baseline FGSM. Under the same perturbation intensity, the proposed method is still more robust against image processing techniques. This proves that the area we disturb can prevent the perturbation from be erased by the image processing method. Furthermore, our-40 enhances the perturbation intensity and shows more robustness than our-13. With the joint effort of larger perturbation intensity and the selection of disturbed areas, our methods achieve the best performance in robustness.

The proposed method successfully improves the robustness of adversarial examples against various image processing techniques. This makes the proposed method more effective in implementing an adversarial attack. More importantly, it also makes the adversarial training based on the samples generated by the proposed method more reliable. By this kind of adversarial training, DNNs would show more resistance to the adversarial samples, further improving the performance on various tasks.

5 Conclusion

This paper proposed a "pixel-wise" method to generate robust and imperceptible adversarial examples. Based on the texture sensitivity and the characteristics of image processing methods, the proposed method calculates a threshold of each input image which can guide the distribution of adversarial perturbation. The experimental results proved that the proposed method greatly improves the robustness and imperceptibility of the perturbation. In future work, we will explore how to combine the human visual system with the generation of adversarial examples, further enhancing the reliability of the adversarial attack.

References

1. https://github.com/ZhengyuZhao/PerC-Adversarial.git
2. https://github.com/Harry24k/adversarial-attacks-pytorch
3. Carlini, N., Wagner, D.: Towards evaluating the robustness of neural networks (2017)
4. Deng, J., Dong, W., Socher, R., Li, L., Li, K., Li, F.-F.: Imagenet: A large-scale hierarchical image database. In: 2009 IEEE Conference on Computer Vision and Pattern Recognition, pp. 248–255 (2009). https://doi.org/10.1109/CVPR.2009.5206848

5. Fang, W., Yao, X., Zhao, X., Yin, J., Xiong, N.: A stochastic control approach to maximize profit on service provisioning for mobile cloudlet platforms. IEEE Trans. Syst. Man Cybern.: Syst. **48**(4), 522–534 (2016)
6. Goodfellow, I.J., Shlens, J., Szegedy, C.: Explaining and harnessing adversarial examples (2015)
7. Zhang, H., Yannis Avrithis, T.F., Amsaleg, L.: Smooth adversarial examples, pp. 2818–2826 (2020)
8. He, K., Zhang, X., Ren, S., Sun, J.: Deep residual learning for image recognition. In: Proceedings of the IEEE Conference on Computer Vision and Pattern Recognition, pp. 770–778 (2016)
9. Kurakin, A., Goodfellow, I., Bengio, S.: Adversarial examples in the physical world (2017)
10. Legge, G.E., Foley, J.M.: Contrast masking in human vision. Josa **70**(12), 1458–1471 (1980)
11. Li, H., Liu, J., Liu, R.W., Xiong, N., Wu, K., Kim, T.H.: A dimensionality reduction-based multi-step clustering method for robust vessel trajectory analysis. Sensors **17**(8), 1792 (2017)
12. Lin, et al.: A time-driven data placement strategy for a scientific workflow combining edge computing and cloud computing. IEEE Trans. Industr. Inf. **15**(7), 4254–4265 (2019)
13. Lin, W., Dong, L., Xue, P.: Visual distortion gauge based on discrimination of noticeable contrast changes. IEEE Trans. Circuits Syst. Video Technol. **15**(7), 900–909 (2005)
14. Liu, A., Lin, W., Paul, M., Deng, C., Zhang, F.: Just noticeable difference for images with decomposition model for separating edge and textured regions. IEEE Trans. Circuits Syst. Video Technol. **20**(11), 1648–1652 (2010)
15. Luo, M.R., Cui, G., Rigg, B.: The development of the CIE 2000 colour-difference formula: Ciede 2000. Color Research & Application: Endorsed by Inter-Society Color Council, The Colour Group (Great Britain), Canadian Society for Color, Color Science Association of Japan, Dutch Society for the Study of Color, The Swedish Colour Centre Foundation, Colour Society of Australia, Centre Français de la Couleur **26**(5), 340–350 (2001)
16. Moosavi-Dezfooli, S., Fawzi, A., Frossard, P.: Deepfool: A simple and accurate method to fool deep neural networks. In: 2016 IEEE Conference on Computer Vision and Pattern Recognition (CVPR), pp. 2574–2582 (2016). https://doi.org/10.1109/CVPR.2016.282
17. Papernot, N., McDaniel, P., Jha, S., Fredrikson, M., Celik, Z.B., Swami, A.: The limitations of deep learning in adversarial settings. In: 2016 IEEE European Symposium on Security and Privacy (EuroS P), pp. 372–387 (2016). https://doi.org/10.1109/EuroSP.2016.36
18. Qu, Y., Xiong, N.: RFH: A resilient, fault-tolerant and high-efficient replication algorithm for distributed cloud storage. In: 2012 41st International Conference on Parallel Processing, pp. 520–529. IEEE (2012)
19. Ren, S., He, K., Girshick, R., Sun, J.: Faster R-CNN: towards real-time object detection with region proposal networks. IEEE Trans. Pattern Anal. Mach. Intell. **39**(6), 1137–1149 (2016)
20. Szegedy, C., Vanhoucke, V., Ioffe, S., Shlens, J., Wojna, Z.: Rethinking the inception architecture for computer vision, pp. 2818–2826 (2016)
21. Szegedy, C., Zaremba, W., Sutskever, I., Bruna, J., Erhan, D., Goodfellow, I., Fergus, R.: Intriguing properties of neural networks (2014)

22. Vaswani, A., et al.: Attention is all you need. arXiv:1706.03762 (2017)
23. Xiong, N., et al.: A self-tuning failure detection scheme for cloud computing service. In: 2012 IEEE 26th International Parallel and Distributed Processing Symposium, pp. 668–679. IEEE (2012)
24. Yang, J., et al.: A fingerprint recognition scheme based on assembling invariant moments for cloud computing communications. IEEE Syst. J. 5(4), 574–583 (2011)
25. Yi, B., Shen, X., Liu, H., Zhang, Z., Zhang, W., Liu, S., Xiong, N.: Deep matrix factorization with implicit feedback embedding for recommendation system. IEEE Trans. Industr. Inf. 15(8), 4591–4601 (2019)
26. Yin, J., Lo, W., Deng, S., Li, Y., Wu, Z., Xiong, N.: Colbar: A collaborative location-based regularization framework for QOS prediction. Inf. Sci. 265, 68–84 (2014)
27. Zeng, Y., Xiong, N., Park, J.H., Zheng, G.: An emergency-adaptive routing scheme for wireless sensor networks for building fire hazard monitoring. Sensors 10(6), 6128–6148 (2010)
28. Zhao, Z., Liu, Z., Larson, M.: Towards large yet imperceptible adversarial image perturbations with perceptual color distance. In: Proceedings of the IEEE/CVF Conference on Computer Vision and Pattern Recognition, pp. 1039–1048 (2020)
29. Wang, Z., Bovik, A.C., Sheikh, H.R., Simoncelli, E.P.: Image quality assessment: From error visibility to structural similarity. IEEE Trans. Image Process. 13(4), 600–612 (2004). https://doi.org/10.1109/TIP.2003.819861

Architecture and Security Analysis of Federated Learning-Based Automatic Modulation Classification

Xianglin Wei[1]([✉]), Chao Wang[2], Xiang Jiao[2], Qiang Duan[1], and Yongyang Hu[1]

[1] The 63rd Research Institute, National University of Defense Technology, Nanjing 210007, China
wei_xianglin@163.com
[2] School of Computer and Software, Nanjing University of Information Science and Technology, Nanjing 210044, China

Abstract. Conducting effective deep learning for automatic modulation recognition (AMR) plays a key role in non-cooperative communication systems. Applying federated learning (FL) to train AMR-oriented deep neural networks (ADNN) models is promising in achieving high recognition accuracy while maintaining the data privacy and saving precious wireless transmission bandwidth. In this paper, a FL architecture for ADNN training is presented, and four ADNN models are implemented under the FL architecture. Moreover, to evaluate the security vulnerability of the FL architecture facing ADNN models, multiple adversarial attacks are deployed at the clients to attack the central model training. Besides, label poisoning attacks targeting the FL architecture are investigated. To evaluate the efficiency and vulnerability of the FL architecture for ADNN training, a series of experiments are conducted on an open RF dataset. Results show that ADNN models can achieve high recognition accuracy. Moreover, data or label poisoning attacks are more effective in degrading recognition accuracy than adversarial attacks under the FL architecture.

Keywords: Federated learning · Modulation · Classification · Security

1 Introduction

Realizing automatic modulation recognition (AMR) is vital for sensing, understanding, and utilizing the increasingly-crowded spectrum space in the Internet of Things (IoT) era. Traditional AMR methods developed based on maximum likelihood hypothesis or statistical pattern recognition are usually labor-intensive in feature extraction; moreover, they are usually problem-dependent and have degraded performance when being transferred to different domains. Inspired by the great success of deep neural networks (DNN) in object recognition and classification, practitioners have developed a few AMR-oriented DNN (ADNN) models in recent years.

Current ADNNs are mostly developed for identifying Single-Input-Single-Output (SISO) wireless communication systems. To be specific, the received signal at some particular time interval is usually represented as a data sample that typically contains

© Springer Nature Singapore Pte Ltd. 2022
C. Cao et al. (Eds.): FCS 2021, CCIS 1558, pp. 63–77, 2022.
https://doi.org/10.1007/978-981-19-0523-0_5

two data sequences, named the in-phase and quadrature-phase (IQ) data. Then, the sample is treated as the input of an ADNN model, and the output of the network is its modulation type. Typical ADNN models could be built based on Convolutional Neural Network (CNN), Recurrent Neural Network (RNN), or their combinations. However, existing proposals are generally developed based on an over-simplified AMR problem, in which: 1) a clear or slightly noisy signal could be utilized for classification purpose; 2) a large amount of data samples are available for each modulation type. In fact, these ideal assumptions are hard to hold in real-world transmission environments. The main challenge is brought by the hardness and overhead of data collection in harsh or even hostile environments. It is hard for a single monitor or eavesdropper to a large number of samples for each modulation type. There may exist one-shot or even zero-shot signals. Without the support of enough data, the trained model is usually biased. Moreover, the increasing highlight of data privacy [1] has hindered wireless devices from sending their raw data to a central server (e.g. an edge server) for ADNN training. To alleviate the dilemma between data privacy preserving and accurate ADNN training, federated learning (FL) is a promising framework to achieve a tradeoff between the two.

FL aims at building a collaborative training framework between a number of training entities, who possess their own training data. Typically, a central server that maintains a global model is needed to orchestrate the user authentication, communications interaction, and parameter updating with the raw data at each entity intact. Besides model accuracy promotion, FL has the built-in nature to reduce the data transmission between wireless devices, thereby saving precious transmission bandwidth and energy consumption. FL has been initially applied to signal modulation recognition and a CNN model is training with different scenario settings; an overall 70% classification accuracy is reported after 20 rounds of training. However, the security vulnerability facing the FL system is not investigated.

In this backdrop, a FL framework for ADNN training is established first. After detailing the design training server and entities, the pros and cons of the framework is analyzed. Then, the security threat the framework faces is highlighted. Afterwards, a few verification experiments are conducted on an open RF dataset to verify the analysis results. The contributions of this paper are threefold:

- An FL framework for ADNN training is established. The interaction between the central server and multiple clients is detailed in the wireless network scenarios.
- The unique efficiency issues and security threats faced by ADNN-oriented FL framework are analyzed in wireless network scenarios. Both data poisoning and label poisoning attacks are evaluated under the FL architecture.
- A series of experiments have been conducted on an open RF dataset under the presented FL framework. The results are detailed from both accuracy and security perspectives.

This rest of the paper is organized as follows. Section 2 summarizes existing efforts. Section 3 describes the FL architecture for ADNN training. Section 4 shows the experimental settings and results. Finally, we conclude our main work and further research in Sect. 5.

2   Related Work

2.1   Federated Learning

Federated learning is inherently an inter-discipline term that involves techniques not only from machine learning, but also from distributed computation, privacy protection, cryptography, statistics, etc. Several different FL paradigms were formulated with different data and features characteristics, including vertical FL, horizontal FL, federated transfer learning, etc.

A conceptual illustration of the horizontal FL is shown in Fig. 1. A central server is in charge of coordinating the training of the global model through collecting and disseminating parameter updates with clients. Each client maintains its local machine learning model, and sends its updated parameters to the central server as requested. From the perspective of the central server, different clients typically have heterogeneous data quality and volume, communication bandwidth, and trustfulness. To promote training efficiency, the activation/selection/scheduling mechanism of the clients has always been the focus of FL practitioners. Typically, the clients with the minimum transmission latency, or the minimum Age of Information (AoI), or the highest importance will be scheduled for some particular training round by the central server to achieve the best performance. To facilitate efficient client scheduling, the allocation of the resources in the wireless network, e.g. wireless channels, bandwidth, or transmission power, is usually jointly optimized with client scheduling problem. Privacy leakage during the parameter exchanging process is possible. In short, the characteristics of the raw data can be reversely obtained based on a client's uploaded model parameters.

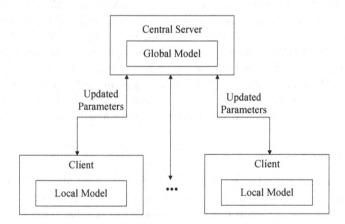

Fig. 1. A conceptual horizontally FL framework.

Besides the efficiency and privacy concerns, the decentralized-nature makes the FL framework vulnerable to a few security threats facing distributed systems. For example, the uploaded gradients by the clients may be compromised to poison the global model [2]. The data samples at a malicious client may be poisoned by the attacker, and wrong gradients will be uploaded to the central server, leading to a biased global model.

2.2 ADNN Models

In ADNN method, features are automatically extracted by selecting the appropriate neural network as the model, and the pre-processed signal data are sent to neural network for training. Finally, the trained network is used to identify the unknown signal modulation mode.

In the past three years, a few ADNN models have been put forward. CNN was the first choice for ADNN design since its powerful feature extraction ability. O'Shea et al. adopted VGG and Resnet for ADNN design, and investigated their performance with different signal-to-noise ratios (SNRs) [3]. Skip connection is utilized by MCNet, and three types of convolutional blocks with asymmetric convolution kernel are designed to ensure the extraction of rich features while reducing training time [4]. Huang et al. proposed a Contrastive Fully Convolutional Network (CFCN), which adopts the form of grid constellation matrix (GCM) after simple pre-treatment instead of directly using IQ data as the input of the network. At the same time, contrastive loss is used as the loss function [5]. Combining the features of cyclic spectrum and constellation diagram, Wu et al. established a CNN-CSCD network with two branches, which can improve the classification accuracy by feature fusion [6]. Considering that ADNN is usually deployed on lightweight devices, Lin et al. designed a VTCNN2 model, which optimized the processing speed of the network by pruning technique and omitted the convolution filter [7]. Wang et al. proposed a LightAMC algorithm suitable for deployment in considering that adnn is often deployed on lightweight devices (UAV) auxiliary system to reduce the complexity of the network by allocating scale factors to neurons and deleting redundant neurons by pruning technology [8]. Combining the advantages of CNN and LSTM, Zhang et al. proposed a bi-branch AMR algorithm based on CNN-LSTM feature interaction, and the data were input in IQ and AP forms respectively [9]. Njoku et al. put forward CGDNet, which is composed of CNN, Gated Recurrent Units (GRU), and DNN. Unlike CLDNN, CGDNet replaces LSTM with GRU which has fewer parameters and is better at learning time series data with lower computational complexity [10]. GCN, which is good at processing graph data, is also used for AMR problem. Liu et al. proposed to use two-layer graph convolutional network (GCN) to achieve modulation classification after feature extraction and data graphics [11].

2.3 Adversarial Examples

The adversarial example refers to the sample formed by artificially adding subtle disturbances that are not visible to the human eyes. Adversarial example will cause the networks predicted wrong labels with high confidence [12]. It has been confirmed that most of the current neural network classifiers are vulnerable to adversarial examples. The fundamental reason is that the training dataset cannot cover all possibilities, and the trained model cannot cover all features. Even if the effect of the trained classifier is already very well, there still exits inconsistency between the training model boundary and the actual decision boundary, and it is the inconsistency that leads to the existence of adversarial examples.

Goodfellow et al. proposed a gradient-based fast gradient sign method (*FGSM*), which generates adversarial samples by calculating the gradient of the loss function relative to the input itself [13]. Kurakin et al. proposed the Basic Iterative Method (BIM), which optimizes the single-step disturbance of FGSM by adding disturbances in multiple small steps [14]. Dezfooli et al. proposed the DeepFool algorithm, which uses the linear characteristics of the classifier to gradually generate counter disturbances and move the pixels within the classification boundary to outside the boundary [15]. Carlini and Wagner proposed the C&W attack, which uses three different evaluation distances (l_1, l_2, and l_∞) to generate disturbances [16]. Moosavi-Dezfooli et al. discovered the existence of general adversarial disturbances and realized an attack method that does not rely on samples [17].

Although ADNN design is still at its initial stage, its security vulnerabilities have already been exploited by practitioners using adversarial examples. Seo et al. presented an adversarial signal design method by integrating multiple optimization objectives into the loss function, to mislead an eavesdropper's equipped ADNN while protecting the intended receiver's correct acquisition [18]. Flowers et al. modified the design of FGSM through including the desired signal-to-perturbation ratio in the loss function [19]. In the design of the loss function, Lin et al. defined fitting difference (FD), to measure the similarity of the signal waveform before and after the attack [20, 21]. Roy et al. built a framework, called Radio Frequency Adversarial Learning (RFAL), to find out the rogue RF transmitter using generative adversarial net (GAN) [22]. Shi et al. trained a generator network using GAN to spoof an DNN-based receiver [23].

3 FL Framework for ADNN Training

3.1 FL Framework

From the perspective of ADNN training, a conceptual horizontally FL framework is illustrated in Fig. 2. In this framework, one central server and N clients are interconnected using a wireless network. Each client maintains a local ADNN model, and it can train the model independently without the introducing of FL. Under FL framework, the clients collaborate with each other and the central server to co-train a global ADNN model. Typically, clients connect to the server via wireless links, including 5G cellular networks or WiFi etc. The centralized training architecture of FL perfectly matching the wireless access network, where a star-topology is typically maintained. Under wireless edge computing paradigm, the edge server acts as the central server and is connected to the access point (AP) or the base station (BS). Wireless devices that connect to the AP or BS are the clients that can collect data and maintain local models. In ADNN scenario, each client could receive a number of signal samples with specific labels that may overlap with each other. However, none of them could train an ADNN model with satisfactory accuracy relying solely on its own data.

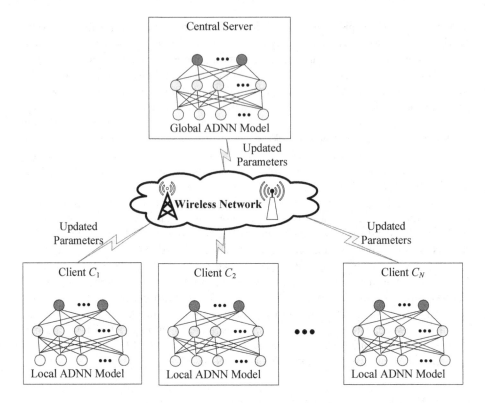

Fig. 2. FL framework for ADNN training.

3.2 FL Training Model

The set of clients is denoted as $\mathcal{C} = \{c_1, c_2, \dots, c_N\}$, and N is the number of clients. The client c_i connects to the server through wireless links, and the transmission bandwidth is B_i, $1 \leq i \leq N$. Each training round of the FL-based AMR includes 5 steps, i.e. client selection, local training, parameter aggregation, global model updating, global model dissemination.

1) Client selection. Based on the bandwidth constraint, security, and efficiency consideration, the central server selects a few clients (named activated clients) from $\mathcal{C}$ for each training round. The set of activated clients is denoted as $\mathcal{C}_A, \mathcal{C}_A \subset \mathcal{C}$. The server notifies these chosen clients to activate their local training through broadcasting messages.

2) Local training. After receiving the message, each activate client conducts local model training. A batch of local data are feed into the local ADNN model; afterwards, a loss function and the local gradient is calculated.

3) Parameter aggregation. Each activated client sends its parameter updating, in particular the gradient, after finishing its local model training. All the updated parameters from activated clients are transmitted through the wireless links to the server.

4) Global model updating. The server calculates the parameter updates based on all received gradients. For instance, the global gradient can be derived through calculating a weighted sum of all local gradients. Then, the global model is updated based on the global gradient.

5) Global model dissemination. The updated global model is broadcast to all clients for the next round of training.

3.3 Adversarial Model

As mentioned in Sect. 2.3, various security threats from both application and underlying layers can severely degrade the performance of FL frameworks.

The adversarial examples can be generated by an attacker utilizing the methods presented in Sect. 2.3. In this paper, we consider a scenario that an attacker adopted adversarial techniques (will be detailed later) at one or more clients to generate adversarial examples. Then, the generated malicious examples are fed into the ADNN model for training.

(1) L-BFGS Attack

Szegedy et al. introduced the concept of adversarial samples for the first time in 2014, and proposed the L-BFGS attack method [24]. The attack process mainly solves the following optimization problems:

$$\min_{x'} c\|\eta\| + J_\theta\left(x', l'\right)$$
$$\text{s.t. } x' \in [0, 1]. \tag{1}$$

where constant c is usually determined by linear search or binary search, so the L-BFGS attack is a very time-consuming and impractical attack method.

(2) FGSM

In order to solve the time-consuming problem, Goodfellow et al. proposed a fast method called Fast Gradient Sign Method (FGSM) [13]. The idea is to generate disturbances by calculating the gradient of the loss function relative to the sample, which can be expressed as:

$$\eta = \epsilon \, \text{sign}\left(\nabla_x J_\theta(x, l)\right) \tag{2}$$

where ϵ is the size of the perturbation, and the adversarial example is $x' = x + \eta$. Since the gradient is calculated only once, the attack speed is greatly improved.

(3) BIM

Kurakin et al. proposed the *Basic Iterative* method [14]. The idea is to optimize a large-step disturbance through the superposition of multiple small-step disturbances to conduct an adversarial attack, so as to obtain a more adversarial sample. The iterative process is as follows:

$$x_0 = x$$
$$x_{n+1} = \text{Clip}_{x,\xi}\left\{x_n + \epsilon \, \text{sign}\left(\nabla_x J\left(x_n, y\right)\right)\right\}. \tag{3}$$

where $\text{Clip}_{x,\xi}\{x'\}$ limits the changes of the generated adversarial example in each iteration.

(4) DeepFool

Moosavi-Dezfooli et al. proposed DeepFool to find the closest distance from the original input to the decision boundary of adversarial examples [15]. In order to overcome the non-linear problem in high-dimensional space, they regarded the classifier as approximately linear, and found that the perturbation that produced the adversarial example was the distance from the example to the hyperplane $\mathcal{F} = \{x : w^T x + b = 0\}$. The calculation of this disturbance is:

$$\eta^*(x) = -\frac{f(x)}{\|w\|^2} w \tag{4}$$

if f is s a binary differentiable classifier, the minimal perturbation is computed as:

$$\begin{aligned} \arg\min_{\eta_i} \ &\|\eta_i\|_2 \\ \text{s.t.} \quad &f(x_i) + \nabla f(x_i)^T \eta_i = 0. \end{aligned} \tag{5}$$

This result can also be extended to the multi-class classifier by finding the closest hyperplanes. *DeepFool* provided less perturbation compared to *FGSM* did.

(5) Universal Adversarial Perturbation

Based on *DeepFool*, Moosavi-Dezfooli et al. proposed a new method which does not rely on samples, called *Universal Adversarial Perturbation* [17]. The problem they formulated is to find a universal perturbation vector satisfying

$$\begin{aligned} &\|\eta\|_p \le \epsilon \\ &\mathcal{P}\left(x' \ne f(x)\right) \ge 1 - \delta. \end{aligned} \tag{6}$$

where ϵ is adopted to limit the size of universal perturbation, and δ controls the failure rate of the adversarial examples.

For each iteration, *DeepFool* is used to get a minimal perturbation against each input data and gather the perturbation to the total perturbation η.

3.4   Data Poisoning

From the attacker's point of view, data poisoning for federated learning can be divided into target attack and random attack. Target attack aims to force the output of FL model to be a specified label category under the control of the attacker, while random attack aims to reduce the recognition accuracy of the global ADNN model. Obviously, target attack is more difficult than random attack. For FL model, the data poisoning attack can be divided into two categories: 1) clean-label [25] and 2) dirty-label [26].

Clean-label attack assumes that the attacker cannot change the training data samples and maintain the correspondence between the correct labels and training data samples, but the data samples will be poisoned and the poisoning process will not be imperceptible i.e. adversarial example. In contrast, the attacker just adjusts the training data labels to desired miss-classification target labels in dirty-label poisoning. Label-flipping attack is one common example of dirty-label poisoning attacks. In the attack process, the labels of origin training examples of one class are flipped to another class while the examples of the dataset are kept unchanged. For example, the malicious clients in the system can poison their dataset by flipping all 1s into 7s. A successful attack produces a model that is unable to correctly classify 1s and incorrectly predicts them to be 7s.

4 Experiments and Results Analysis

4.1 Dataset

All experiments are conducted on the RML2016.10A dataset, which was collected and opened to the public by DeepSig. The dataset contains 11 modulation modes: 8 digital modulations (BPSK, QPSK, 8PSK, QAM16, QAM64, GFSK, CPFSK and PAM4) and 3 analog modulations (WBFM, AM-DSB and AM-SSB). SNR of the data samples varies from -20 dB to 18 dB, with an interval of 2 dB. The dataset simulates real-time radio communication signals using different modulations in various SNRs. During data acquisition, a number of error effects are added in channel environments, such as time-varying multi-path fading of the channel impulse response, random walk drifting of carrier frequency oscillator and sample time clock, and additive Gaussian white noise. The dataset contains 220,000 data samples; and the number of each modulation type under a single SNR is 1,000. Each data sample contains the in-phase data and quadrature-phase data with a size of 2×128.

4.2 Experimental Settings

We use TFF, a federal learning framework proposed by Google to evaluate whether it is feasible to apply the FL framework for ADNN training [27]. Therefore, four common network models: VT-CNN2 [28], VGG [29], Bi-LSTM [30] and CLDNN [31] have been adopted. In the experiment, a total of 5–10 clients were considered. The number of data samples allocated by each client remains the same. All experiments are conducted on a computer equipped with NVIDIA GeForce RTX 3080 Ti 12 GB and the programming environment is Keras.

4.3 Results Analysis

4.3.1 Recognition Accuracy of Different ADNN Models
As shown in Fig. 3, the recognition accuracy of VT-CNN2, VGG, Bi-LSTM and CLDNN with SNR of +18 dB is described. The recognition rate of the four models can reach more than 70%. Among them, Bi-LSTM and CLDNN with LSTM unit perform better due to their capability to extract the timing information contained in IQ signals. CLDNN, which combines the advantages of CNN and LSTM, performs best, and its accuracy can reach 78%.

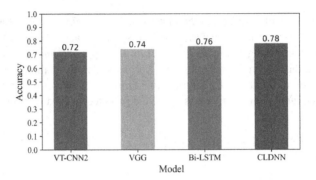

Fig. 3. Classification accuracy of four different ADNN models under the presented FL architecture.

4.3.2 Performance Under Different Training Rounds

Figure 4 shows the loss curves of VT-CNN2 training and testing data after 200 rounds of training with the SNR being 18 dB. It can be found that the loss decreases with the increase of training rounds. In the first 25 training rounds, the loss of both training and testing data decreases dramatically. Then, the downward trend gradually flattens. After 200 rounds of training, the training of the ADNN model converges, and the loss value tends to be 0. This means that the model needs to be fully trained, at least not less than 25 rounds.

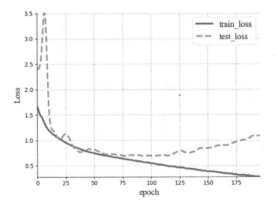

Fig. 4. Classification loss of the VT-CNN2 model under the FL architecture.

Figure 5 shows the recognition accuracy of training and test data with a 18 dB SNR. The results show that after 200 rounds of training, the recognition rate of the training set reaches 85%, while the recognition rate of the test set can be stabilized at about 72%.

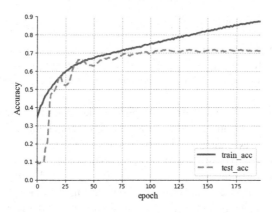

Fig. 5. Classification accuracy of the VT-CNN2 model under the FL architecture.

4.3.3   Recognition Accuracy of the Test Data with Different SNRs

The recognition accuracy of VT-CNN2 under different SNR values is shown in Fig. 6. We can see that the recognition accuracy of the model improves with the increase of SNR. When the SNR is lower than -8 dB, the recognition rate is less than 10%, which is mainly due to the large proportion of noise in the signal at low SNRs that leads to the inaccurate features extracted by the model. With the increase of SNR, the recognition rate improves significantly. When the SNR is higher than 2 dB, the recognition rate is higher than 70%.

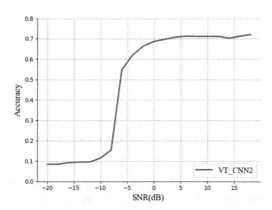

Fig. 6. Classification accuracy of the VT-CNN2 model under FL framework with different SNR values.

4.4   Data Poisoning Results

In this section, we perform data poisoning attacks on the training process of AMR-oriented FL architecture. Since VT-CNN2 has a relatively simple structure, it is more intuitive to compare various attack methods. Therefore, the ADNN model we choose to attack is VT-CNN2.

To show the effect of adversarial examples on the training of federated learning model, we compare the training accuracy of VT-CNN2 model under the FL framework with different adversarial examples. The results are shown in Fig. 7. Then, to evaluate the impact of the number of malicious clients, we compare the accuracy curves of clean-label poisoning and dirty-label poisoning attack for FL model training with different number of malicious clients. The results are shown in Fig. 8 and Fig. 9 respectively.

In Fig. 7, we can notice that the adversarial examples all make the recognition accuracy of ADNN model decline, but the descent range is slight. Specifically, FGSM reduces the ADNN model accuracy to about 60%, UAP reduces to 58%, BIM reduces to 55% and DeepFool reduces to 46%. The results show that DeepFool attack is the best. UAP, as the only universal attack method, is less powerful than some example-related attacks. FGSM performs worse than BIM since FGSM is a one-step method, which is less aggressive than an iterative attack.

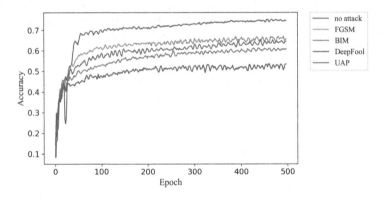

Fig. 7. Clean label poisoning with different adversarial examples.

Figure 8 shows the results of the FL model training under the clean-label poisoning attack, where BIM attack method was used to modify the training data samples. We can see that the overall process of training is stable relatively and can achieve convergence results. As intuitively expected, with the increase of malicious clients, the recognition accuracy of FL model declines.

Figure 9 displays the training results of data poisoning attacks in dirty-label circumstances. It can be observed that the dirty-label poisoning attack has a great impact on the FL model training than clean-label poisoning. Specifically, when the number of malicious clients is more than two, the training process of FL model is becoming

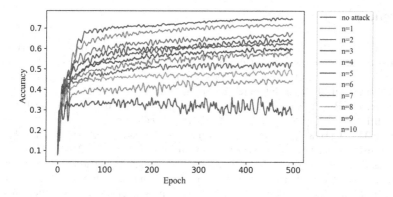

Fig. 8. Clean label data poisoning attack (n is the number of malicious clients).

unstable. The FL model collapses and cannot be trained normally when the quantity of malicious clients is more than five, and the classification accuracy of the model has been maintained at about 0.09 (i.e. random guessing).

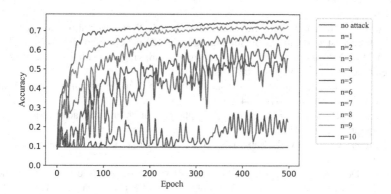

Fig. 9. Dirty label data poisoning attack (n is the number of malicious clients).

5 Conclusion

A federated learning architecture for Automatic Modulation Recognition (AMR)-oriented deep neural network (DNN) training is presented in this paper. Moreover, from the perspective of security, adversarial examples and label poisoning attacks are evaluated on the presented architecture. Results have shown that CLDNN can achieve acceptable recognition accuracy under the FL architecture. Label poisoning attacks are more effective than adversarial examples in degrading the recognition accuracy.

In the future, we will further promote the recognition accuracy of ADNN models under the FL architecture. Moreover, new attack and defense methods for the FL architecture will be developed.

References

1. Yao, Y., Xiong, N., Park, J.H., Ma, L., Liu, J.: Privacy-preserving max/min query in two-tiered wireless sensor networks. Comput. Math. Appl. **65**(9), 1318–1325 (2013)
2. Guo, X., et al.: VERIFL: communication-efficient and fast verifiable aggregation for federated learning. IEEE Trans. Inf. Forensics Secur. **16**, 1736–1751 (2021)
3. O'Shea, T.J., Roy, T., Clancy, T.C.: Over-the-air deep learning based radio signal classification. IEEE J. Sel. Top. Signal Process. **12**(1), 168–179 (2018)
4. Huynh-The, T., Hua, C.H., Pham, Q.V., Kim, D.S.: MCNet: an efficient CNN architecture for robust automatic modulation classification. IEEE Commun. Lett. **24**(4), 811–815 (2020)
5. Huang, S., Jiang, Y., Gao, Y., Feng, Z., Zhang, P.: Automatic modulation classification using contrastive fully convolutional network. IEEE Wirel. Commun. Lett. **8**(4), 1044–1047 (2019)
6. Wu, H., Li, Y., Zhou, L., Meng, J.: Convolutional neural network and multi-feature fusion for automatic modulation classification. Electron. Lett. **55**(16), 895–897 (2019)
7. Lin, Y., Tu, Y., Dou, Z.: An improved neural network pruning technology for automatic modulation classification in edge devices. IEEE Trans. Veh. Technol. **69**(5), 5703–5706 (2020)
8. Wang, Y., Yang, J., Liu, M., Gui, G.: LightAMC: lightweight automatic modulation classification via deep learning and compressive sensing. IEEE Trans. Veh. Technol. **69**(3), 3491–3495 (2020)
9. Zhang, Z., Luo, H., Wang, C., Gan, C., Xiang, Y.: Automatic modulation classification using CNN-LSTM based dual-stream structure. IEEE Trans. Veh. Technol. **69**(11), 13521–13531 (2020)
10. Njoku, J.N., Morocho-Cayamcela, M.E., Lim, W.: CGDNet: efficient hybrid deep learning model for robust automatic modulation recognition. IEEE Netw. Lett. **3**(2), 47–51 (2021)
11. Liu, Y., Liu, Y., Yang, C.: Modulation recognition with graph convolutional network. IEEE Wirel. Commun. Lett. **9**(5), 624–627 (2020)
12. Akhtar, N., Mian, A.: Threat of adversarial attacks on deep learning in computer vision: a survey. IEEE Access **6**, 14410–14430 (2018)
13. Goodfellow, I.J., Shlens, J., Szegedy, C.: Explaining and harnessing adversarial examples. arXiv preprint arXiv:1412.6572 (2014)
14. Kurakin, A., Goodfellow, I., Bengio, S., et al.: Adversarial examples in the physical world (2016)
15. Moosavi-Dezfooli, S.M., Fawzi, A., Frossard, P.: DeepFool: a simple and accurate method to fool deep neural networks. In: Proceedings of the IEEE Conference on Computer Vision and Pattern Recognition, pp. 2574–2582 (2016)
16. Carlini, N., Wagner, D.: Towards evaluating the robustness of neural networks. In: 2017 IEEE Symposium on Security and Privacy (SP), pp. 39–57. IEEE (2017)
17. Moosavi-Dezfooli, S.M., Fawzi, A., Fawzi, O., Frossard, P.: Universal adversarial perturbations. In: Proceedings of the IEEE Conference on Computer Vision and Pattern Recognition, pp. 1765–1773 (2017)
18. Seo, J., Park, S., Kang, J.: Adversarial, yet friendly signal design for secured wireless communication. In: 2021 IEEE Wireless Communications and Networking Conference (WCNC), pp. 1–7 (2021)
19. Flowers, B., Buehrer, R.M., Headley, W.C.: Evaluating adversarial evasion attacks in the context of wireless communications. IEEE Trans. Inf. Forensics Secur. **15**, 1102–1113 (2020)
20. Lin, Y., Zhao, H., Tu, Y., Mao, S., Dou, Z.: Threats of adversarial attacks in DNN-based modulation recognition. In: IEEE INFOCOM 2020 - IEEE Conference on Computer Communications, pp. 2469–2478 (2020)
21. Lin, Y., Zhao, H., Ma, X., Tu, Y., Wang, M.: Adversarial attacks in modulation recognition with convolutional neural networks. IEEE Trans. Reliab. **70**(1), 389–401 (2021)

22. Roy, D., Mukherjee, T., Chatterjee, M., Blasch, E., Pasiliao, E.: RFAL: adversarial learning for RF transmitter identification and classification. IEEE Trans. Cogn. Commun. Netw. **6**(2), 783–801 (2020)
23. Shi, Y., Davaslioglu, K., Sagduyu, Y.E.: Generative adversarial network in the air: deep adversarial learning for wireless signal spoofing. IEEE Trans. Cogn. Commun. Netw. **7**(1), 294–303 (2021)
24. Szegedy, C., et al.: Intriguing properties of neural networks. arXiv preprint arXiv:1312.6199 (2013)
25. Shafahi, A., et al.: Poison frogs! targeted clean-label poisoning attacks on neural networks. arXiv preprint arXiv:1804.00792 (2018)
26. Gu, T., Dolan-Gavitt, B., Garg, S.: BadNets: identifying vulnerabilities in the machine learning model supply chain. arXiv preprint arXiv:1708.06733 (2017)
27. Shi, J., Zhao, H., Wang, M., Tian, Q.: Signal recognition based on federated learning. In: IEEE INFOCOM 2020 - IEEE Conference on Computer Communications Workshops (INFOCOM WKSHPS), pp. 1105–1110 (2020)
28. O'Shea, T.J., Corgan, J., Clancy, T.C.: Convolutional radio modulation recognition networks. In: Jayne, C., Iliadis, L. (eds.) EANN 2016. CCIS, vol. 629, pp. 213–226. Springer, Cham (2016). https://doi.org/10.1007/978-3-319-44188-7_16
29. Long, J., Shelhamer, E., Darrell, T.: Fully convolutional networks for semantic segmentation. In: 2015 IEEE Conference on Computer Vision and Pattern Recognition (CVPR), pp. 3431–3440 (2015)
30. Ma, M.: Multimedia emergency event extraction and modeling based on object detection and Bi-LSTM network. In: 2021 IEEE International Conference on Consumer Electronics and Computer Engineering (ICCECE), pp. 574–580 (2021)
31. Sainath, T.N., Vinyals, O., Senior, A., Sak, H.: Convolutional, long short-term memory, fully connected deep neural networks. In: ICASSP 2015–2015 IEEE International Conference on Acoustics, Speech and Signal Processing (ICASSP) (2015)

Detecting Inconsistent Vulnerable Software Version in Security Vulnerability Reports

Hansong Ren[1,3], Xuejun Li[1(✉)], Liao Lei[3], Guoliang Ou[1,3], Hongyu Sun[1,3], Gaofei Wu[1,2(✉)], Xiao Tian[1,3], Jinglu Hu[4], and Yuqing Zhang[1,3,5]

[1] School of Cyber Engineering, Xidian University, Xian 710126, Shaanxi, China
aluckydd@mail.xidian.edu.cn
[2] Guangxi Key Laboratory of Cryptography and Information Security, Guilin University of Electronic Technology, Guilin 541010, Guangxi, China
[3] National Computer Network Intrusion Prevention Center, University of Chinese Academy of Sciences, Beijing 100049, China
[4] School of Information, Production and Systems, Waseda University, Tokyo 169-805, Japan
[5] College of Computer and Cyberspace Security, Hainan University, Haikou 570228, China

Abstract. At present, the vulnerability database research has mainly focused on whether the disclosed information is accurate. However, the information differences between the various vulnerability databases have received little attention.

This article proposes a WITTY (softWare versIon inconsisTency measuremenT sYstem) to detect the differences between the affected software versions of NVD and different language vulnerability databases (including English CVE, OpenWall, Chinese CNNVD, CNVD, and other eight databases). WITTY can enable Our large-scale quantitative information consistency. We introduce named entity recognition (NER) and relation extraction (RE) based on deep learning. We present custom design into named entity recognition (NER) and relation extraction (RE) based on deep learning, enabling WITTY to recognize previously invisible software names and versions based on sentence structure and context. Ground-truth shows that the system has a high accuracy rate (95.3% accuracy rate, 89.9% recall rate). We use data from 8 vulnerability databases in the past 21 years, involving 554,725 vulnerability reports. The results show that they are inconsistent. The software version is prevalent. The average exact match rate of English vulnerability databases CVE, OpenWall, and other vulnerability databases with cve is only 22.1%. The average exact match rate of Chinese CNNVD and CNVD is 49.5%, and the excat match rate of Russian vulnerability databases is 25.8% .

Keywords: Security breach · Natural language processing · Deep learning · Security vulnerability databases

This work was supported by the National Key Research and Development Program of China (2018YFB0804701), the Key Research and Development Program of Hainan Province (ZDYF202012), Guangxi Key Laboratory of Cryptography and Information Security (No. GCIS202123).

© Springer Nature Singapore Pte Ltd. 2022
C. Cao et al. (Eds.): FCS 2021, CCIS 1558, pp. 78–99, 2022.
https://doi.org/10.1007/978-981-19-0523-0_6

1 Introduction

Vulnerabilities in software and network systems pose a serious threat to individuals, organizations, and the entirecountry. For example, in September 2019, 42 core servers of the United Nations Information and Technology Office were attacked by the APT organization, and about 400 GB of files were stolen. In June 2020, the militant group Distributed Denial of Secrets (DDoSecrets) claimed to have stolen 296 GB of data files called BlueLeaks from U.S. law enforcement agencies and fusion centers. These data contained more than 200 U.S. police departments and law enforcement fusion centers (Fusion Centers). Reports, security announcements, law enforcement guidelines, etc. Presumably, some files also contain sensitive personal information [1].

The vulnerability database is the core of network security hidden danger analysis. Collecting and sorting out vulnerability information is of great significance to building a vulnerability database. A vulnerability database with a reasonable structure and complete information is conducive to providing technical and data support for security vendors based on vulnerability discovery and attack protection products [2]; it is conducive to the overall analysis of the number, type, threat elements and development trends of vulnerabilities and guidance they formulate future security strategies; it is helpful for users to confirm possible vulnerabilities in their application environment and take protective measures in time. Therefore, everyone began to pay attention to the quality of the vulnerability database. Mu et al. [3] found that the vulnerability reports of CVE and ExploitDB generally lack important information to reproduce the vulnerability, such as software version and operating system. Some studies (Nguyen and Massacci; Nappa et al.) [4] found the wrong version of NVD with vulnerabilities.

However, there are relatively few studies on the differences between different vulnerability databases. Authors in [5] conducted a large-scale measurement of the version differences between CVE/other vulnerability reports and NVD. They focused on the differences—vulnerability databases version difference of the same software name. However, we found that their handling of the software name was not meticulous enough, resulting in that the version difference that should have measured was not measured.

In this article, a WITTY system is proposed to detect the version differences of the same affected software name under the same CVE-id in different vulnerability databases. WITTY allows us to quantify information consistency on a large scale. The focus of research is on the vulnerability software version, which is one of the most important information for vulnerability replication and vulnerability repair. There are three main technical challenges in building the WITTY. First, it is difficult for natural language processing tools to extract software names and versions from unstructured vulnerability descriptions. Second, it is necessary to identify the name of the vulnerable software corresponding to its version. Third, for software names, different vulnerability databases may have different expressions (abbreviations, aliases) for the same software name. We need to let the WITTY recognize different expressions of the same software name. For software versions, It is necessary to quantify the words that express the version, that is, to convert the natural language that describes the range into a number range. Only in this way can we get more accurate differential results.

1.1 The Design of WITTY

We proposed WITTY which mainly consists of three parts: NER model, RE model, and difference measurement.

We have collected CVE [6, 7], NVD [8], ExploitDB [9], SecurityFocus [10], Openwall [11], China National Vulnerability Database of Information Security (CNNVD) [12], China National Vulnerability Database (CNVD) [13], Russian National Vulnerability Database (BDU) [14] 8 vulnerability data in the past 21 years. The data covers 140,703 cve and 789554 group software names. In order to evaluate the NER model, we manually marked the software names and versions in 22141 vulnerability descriptions as the ground-truth dataset. The experimental results show that the model accuracy can reach 99.5%, and F1 can reach 95.1%, showing that the NER model can extract the vulnerable software name and version from the unstructured vulnerability description. And we also marked 16144 pairs of software names and versions to evaluate whether the RE model can match the software name and the software version. The experimental results show that the accuracy of the RE model can reach 91.1%. Finally, we made a dictionary, respectively. Chinese, English, and Russian texts that indicate ranges are converted to the same number format.

1.2 Contributions

In this work, we mainly make the following contributions.

We have proposed a system that can extract vulnerable software versions in Chinese and English vulnerability reports and measure their differences. We can accurately extract software names and versions from vulnerability reports, making large-scale software versions differential measurement becomes possible.

The system's NER model has a correct rate of 99.5% for the software name and version, and the RE model has a correct rate of 91.1% for the software name and version. This allows us to get more real difference results.

Authors in [5] in the measurement software version is inconsistent, they did not handle the software name as strictly as we did. Therefore, some software versions that should measure the difference will be missed, and we will supplement these data on this basis.

1.3 RoadMap

The second section introduces the background and challenges of this work; the third section introduces the design principles of WITTY; the fourth section evaluates WITTY's NER model and RE; the fifth section carries out a large-scale measurement of software version differences; Section 6 discusses the reasons for differences, countermeasures and future work; Sect. 7 introduces related work; Sect. 8 serves as our conclusion.

2 Background and Challenges

2.1 Security Vulnerability Databases

Vulnerabilities are defects generated intentionally or unintentionally in the process of demand, design, implementation, configuration, and operation of information technology, information products, and information systems. These defects exist at various levels and links of the information system in different forms. The use of malicious subjects will cause damage to the security of the information system, thereby affecting the operation of regular services built on the information system and endangering the security of the information system and information.

In order to prevent these hazards, countries around the world have established national security databases to manage better and control information security vulnerabilities. The US NVD and CVE have a strong influence in this regard. CVE is based on public network security vulnerabilities. It consists of a list of entries, each entry contains an identification number, a description, and at least one public reference. CVE entries have been used in many network security products and services around the world, including NVD. The CVE list is provided to NVD, and then based on the information contained in the CVE entry, NVD provides enhanced information for each entry, such as repair information, severity score and impact level [7, 16].

CNVD and CNNVD are critical vulnerability databases in China. They combine NVD references and add several kinds of information from other forums and vendors, and generate their CNNVD and CNVD numbers for each CVE to give Some vulnerabilities without CVE numbers to generate information [12, 13]. Similarly, Russia's National Vulnerability Database (BDU) also has its BDU number and gives the status of the vulnerability and detailed remedial measures [14].

In general, different countries and organizations have established their vulnerability databases, and the description language of the vulnerability databases established by different countries is usually the native language. And hey have their own vulnerability numbers. Therefore, a well-known vulnerability may be described by these different national vulnerability databases at the same time, and the information between them is different. More specifically, the information listed in some vulnerability databases may be incomplete or out of date. This poses a challenge for researchers to reproduce the vulnerability. Specific vulnerability entries contain incorrect information to make matters worse, which may cause significant delays in the development and deployment of patches. In practice, industrial systems often use legacy software for a long time because of the high cost of updating. When related vulnerabilities are discovered, system administrators usually look up the vulnerability database to determine whether their software (and which version) needs to be patched.

While the vulnerability database accumulates many data, information quality has also received more and more attention [17]. So we developed the WITTY system to detect the differences in software versions in different vulnerability reports.

2.2 Challenge

1) *Challenge 1 Extract the software name and software version from the multilingual vulnerability description*
   The information in the vulnerability description is unstructured, and it is difficult to obtain satisfactory results using regular expressions (You et al.) [18]. At the same time, multiple languages may appear in the vulnerability report, such as CNVD Chinese and English frequently appear in the report, and Russian and English frequently appear in the Russian vulnerability database, so we have to design a model that can handle multiple languages at the same time.

2) *Challenge 2 Match the software name with the software version*
   Vulnerable software names and versions usually appear together in a report. An instinctive reaction is that software names and versions that are close in position are a pair, but this is not the case. As shown in Fig. 1, this simple judgment method is not suitable for us. If we do this, some errors will inevitably occur, so our model needs to be able to identify whether the software name and software version match.

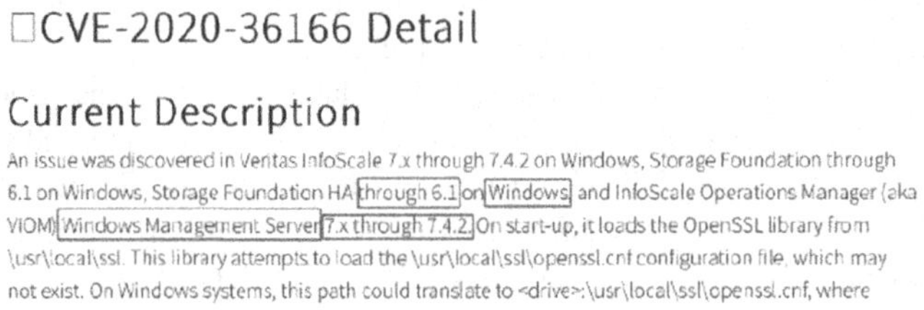

☐CVE-2020-36166 Detail

Current Description

An issue was discovered in Veritas InfoScale 7.x through 7.4.2 on Windows, Storage Foundation through 6.1 on Windows, Storage Foundation HA through 6.1 on Windows, and InfoScale Operations Manager (aka VIOM) Windows Management Server 7.x through 7.4.2. On start-up, it loads the OpenSSL library from \usr\local\ssl. This library attempts to load the \usr\local\ssl\openssl.cnf configuration file, which may not exist. On Windows systems, this path could translate to <drive>:\usr\local\ssl\openssl.cnf, where

Fig. 1. Software name and version location.

3) *Challenge 3 Quantify software name and version*
   First, the software names are complex and diverse. Researchers in the security vulnerability database often use abbreviations or aliases to edit software names for ease of use. Also, the software name is mixed with the names of manufacturers, brands, projects, etc., and different vulnerability databases may also have language differences, as shown in Fig. 2. These differences are the main obstacles to measuring the differences in software names. Secondly, the software version is not discrete data but a description in a different format. This is also the difficulty in comparing software versions of different vulnerability databases.

3 The Design of WITTY

In order to solve the above Challenges, we developed an automation tool WITTY by combining and customizing a set of the most advanced natural language processing (NLP) technologies. In this section, we will briefly introduce the design of WITTY, and then explain the NLP technology and data processing details used by WITTY.

Fig. 2. Software description of NVD and CNVD.

3.1 Overview

WITTY mainly includes three parts: extraction of software name and software version, matching of software name and software version, and measurement of differences. As shown in Fig. 3.

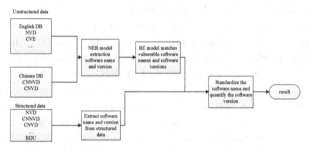

Fig. 3. System structure.

1) *Task 1 Extraction of software name and software version*

   To solve challenge 1, we train a named entity recognition model (NER) [19, 20], a model to extract entities of interest [21]. The NER model determines entities based on the structure and semantics of the input text. It can learn and distinguish the context of the vulnerable version and the non-fragile version of the software. This allows us to eliminate the non-fragile version of the software and only identify the entities we are interested in. We designed and implemented a named entity recognition model that can handle both English and Chinese vulnerability reports. This model has better scalability for processing other language vulnerability reports.

2) *Task 2 Pairing software name and software version*

   In order to solve the problem that the vulnerable software name is not closely related to the vulnerable version, the WITTY system first traverses all possible combinations between the software name and version, then uses the relation extraction (RE) model [22–24] to determine the most likely combination and treat them as the correct entity pair.

3) *Task 3 Difference measurement*

In the same CVE-id of different databases, the susceptible software versions are also different. We need to compare the sensitive versions under the same CVE-id with the same software name. So first, we Process complex and changeable software names into a unified format. Secondly, the discretization in the software version can be discretized, and the discretization that cannot be discretized in the software version should be unified. That is to compare the same CVE-id of different vulnerability databases and measure the software version's difference when the software name is the same.

3.2 Named Entity Recognition Model

The process of extracting named entities with specific characteristics from the text is called named entity recognition (NER). We develop our system based on the NER model. First, we need to segment words from the text. When dealing with English word segmentation, we use the LSTM-CRF architecture [25–27]. When dealing with Chinese, the Lattice model (a variant of the LSTM-CRF model) (Y. Zhang and Yang) [28] showed better results. The combination of the two methods allows our model to handle the Chinese and English vulnerabilities data.

In order to make full use of character information and word information, the NER model considers character embedding representation and word embedding representation. First, the NER model converts the sentence into a sequence of character vectors in character embedding and uses it as the input of the RNN. This sequence is the conversion in units of characters. Secondly, words are transformed into word vectors by word embedding as the input of a particular LSTM layer. This sequence is the conversion of words as a unit. In this way, the NER model combines character embedding and word embedding to encode text sequences into corresponding vector sequences. Because the neural network cannot directly process these texts, we need to input the text into the neural network in a vector sequence. The neural network predicts the label of each English word or Chinese character in the series, including the following labels in total: B-s (software name), B-v (software version symbol), O (other parts), As shown in Fig. 4.

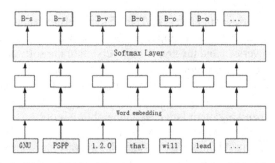

Fig. 4. ER model identifies the name and version of the software.

3.3 Relation Extraction Model

The relationship extraction model is used to extract the relationship between two entities [29]. As shown in Fig. 5, the RE model uses a three-step process to determine the correct relationship between the software name and version. In the first step, the appearance of the software name and the formation of the version information are encoded. then a set of position embeddings is generated, indicating that the current word to two specified entities (i.e., the software name and version) are in the same sentence. The second step is to encode the text and convert the text sequence into a vector sequence. Each vector can represent a possible software name-version pair. In the third step, the RE model predicts the relationship between the software name and the version, And obtains the correct software name-version pair.

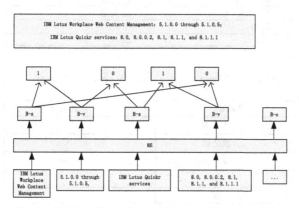

Fig. 5. RE identifies pairing software name and version.

3.4 Difference Measure

We need to do the following operations on the software name and software version to measure the difference.

To standardize the software name, we built a dictionary dict_1 to map the Chinese translation to English Table 1, then delete the redundant part of the identified software name, and then delete the vendor name uniformly. Because in the vulnerability report, the vendor name and the software name will be used as the software name, such as google chrome, and in another vulnerability report, it is Chrome. Therefore, we all go to the vendor name and only keep the software name, especially for those vendor names. In the case of the software name, we no longer remove the vendor name. Secondly, some software names have aliases. I collected these aliased software names and made a dictionary dict_2. When comparing, when a software name is an alias for another software name, our system can recognize it. Is equal. Finally, Finally, For the abbreviation of some software names, such as iPhone and ios, we need to extract all possible abbreviations of the longer word software name. compared with ios, when there is the same name as the latter, we can measure the same software the version of the name is different.

When the software names are the same, we compare the obtained software versions. First, we need to convert some words into symbols representing the scope, as shown in Table 2, change the English "before" to "<=", "after" Replaced with ">=", in Chinese, "以前" is replaced with "<=", and in Russian, "до" is replaced with <=. Secondly, we also crawled the CPE dictionary [30]. When the software name exists in the CPE, we replace the data representing the range with discrete data.

Table 1. Chinese-English software name dictionary

English	Chinese
log	日志
OS	操作系统
converter	转换器
firewall	防火墙
Tool	工具
......	......

Table 2. Chinese-English software version dictionary

Word	Range
之前的	<=
及之前	<=
及之后	>=
至	<=
до	<=
and earlier	<=
and prior	<=
through	<=
up to	<=
......	......

4 Implement and Evaluation

In this section, we introduce our dataset and evaluate the performance of WITTY and its ability to handle Chinese and English.

4.1 Dataset

We collected mainstream vulnerability database data in three countries, China, Britain, and Russia.

- English vulnerability databases: CVE, NVD, ExploitDB, SecurityFocus, Openwall.
- Chinese vulnerability databases: CNNVD and CNVD.
- Russian vulnerability database: BDU.

Table 3. Dataset

Vuln. DB	NVD	CNNVD	CNVD	RNVD	CVE	EDB	SF	OpenWall
Structured software names	140703	127,720	82,542	15,845	0	0	66,986	0
Unstructured software names	140703	128,776	77,435	0	103,118	10,752	0	6,003

We have collected 554,725 CVEs in the past 22 years, from January 1999 to March 2020. As shown in Table 3, we call the software name version involved in the vulnerability description unstructured data. After the specification, the software's name and version are structured data, as shown in Fig. 6.

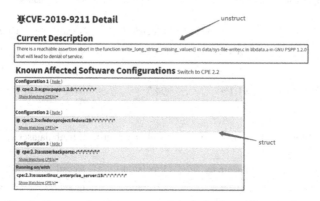

Fig. 6. Structured and unstructured data of vulnerability database.

4.2 Evaluation

We evaluated WITTY's ability to extract the software name and version by evaluating NER and RE models, and we constructed the Ground-truth dataset. The dataset includes 21,000 vulnerability reports, including 6,933 CNNVD entries and 5,995 CNVD entries in the Chinese vulnerability databases and the English vulnerability databases from [5]. (the English vulnerability databases is marked with the software name and version). Eight students in the laboratory used YEDDA [31] for two weeks to mark the software name and version on Chinese vulnerability reports, including the following labels B-s (software name entity), B-v (software version entity), pair_1, pair_2... (used to mark the same pair of software name and version), O (other).

We split the ground-truth dataset at a ratio of 8:1:1 for training, verification, and testing. First, we input the first 100 Chinese characters and English words of each sentence into the NER model. We mix the Chinese character embedding dictionary and the English word embedding dictionary and treat the English words as Chinese characters.

The extent of Chinese characters and English words is set to 50, and the dimension of Chinese words is also set to 50. The batch size and epoch are 1 and 12, respectively. We use the Adam optimization algorithm that can dynamically adjust the learning rate, and at the same time, use pruning technology to prevent the model from overfitting. As with the NER model, for RE, we also set the dimension of word embeddings to 50. The size of the embedded part is 10. The batch size is 1, and the number of epochs is 12. In fact, our performance is not sensitive to these parameters.

Train, verify and test by randomly splitting the dataset and repeat the experiment 10 times. We show the average precision, recall, and accuracy of WITTY in Table 6. It is calculated by multiplying the average accuracy, recall and accuracy of RE and NER models (The average precision, recall, and accuracy of NER and RE models are given in Table 4 and Table 5). It can be seen that the average precision of WITTY is 94.9%, the recall rate is 95.2%, and the accuracy is 95.3%. It can well extract software names and versions in different languages.

Table 4. Performance of NER model on the ground-truthd dataset

Metric	Accuracy	Precision	Recall	F1-Score
English Vuln. reports	96.4%	98.3%	92.2%	95.1%
Chinese Vuln. reports	85.8%	90.7%	77%	83.3%
Overall	91.1%	94.7	84.6	89.2

Table 5. Performance of RE model on the ground-truth dataset

Metric	Accuracy	Precision	Recall	F1-Score
English Vuln. reports	99.8%	96.4%	96.9%	96.6%
Chinese Vuln. reports	99.4%	94.6%	94.8%	94.7%
Overall	99.5%	95.0%	95.2%	95.1%

Table 6. Performance of WITTY model on the ground-truth dataset

Metric	Accuracy	Precision	Recall	F1-Score
Overall	95.3%	94.9%	89.9%	92.2%

We use an advanced word embedding dictionary, Chinese: Giga-Word, English: FastText. We respectively compared the performance difference between English as character embedding and word embedding. We found that English as a word embedding can improve English software name recognition performance without affecting the performance of Chinese software name recognition.

As shown in Fig. 7 and Fig. 8, we changed the batch size and epoch parameters' values to test whether the parameter values we obtained were the best. As a result, we found that the change of the parameter values did not significantly impact the WITTY results.

5 Measuring Inconsistencies

This section applies WITTY to the entire dataset to extract software names and versions and the different software information results. First, we classify the measurement results, measure additional software under the same cve, and classify the result. Second, we evaluate the ground-truth dataset to evaluate WITTY's deviation, then to extract the software name and version. Finally, according to the classification criteria, we get inconsistent results on the entire dataset.

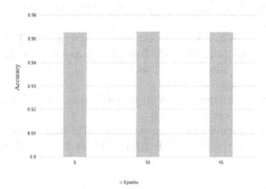

Fig. 7. Accuracy against epoch.

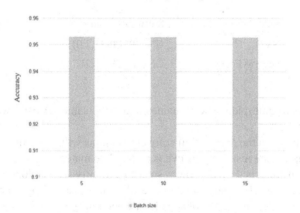

Fig. 8. Accuracy against batch size.

5.1 Measurement Results Categories

In order to obtain a more intuitive difference result, we have defined the differences. Specifically, when the two software names in the software reports of different vulnerability databases are the same, we divide the software version difference results into five categories: complete mismatch, crossing, overclaiming, underclaiming, exact matching.

Let's explain these five situations in detail. First, define the vulnerability databases D1 and D2. For one of the CVE-id, the affected software names are D1: {N1, N2, N3}, D2: {N1, N2, N3}. Among them, the version of the software name N1 in the vulnerability database D1 is Vd1, and the version of the software name N1 in the vulnerability database D2 is Vd2.

- Exact match: When V_{d1} and V_{d2} are exactly the same, or the ranges indicated by V_{d1} and V_{d2} are exactly the same, that is, $V_{d1} = V_{d2} = [v1, v2]$ such as CVE-2019-9211, as shown in Table 7
- Complete mismatch: When V_{d1} is completely different from V_{d2}, such as $V_{d1} = [v1, v2]$, $V_{d2} = [v3, v4]$, such as CVE-2018-20242, as shown in Table 8
- Overclaiming: V_{d1} is a subset of V_{d2}, such as $V_{d1} = [v1]$, $V_{d2} = [v1, v2]$, such as CVE-2019-8905, as shown in Table 9
- Underclaiming: V_{d1} is a superset of V_{d2}, such as $V_{d1} = [v1, v2]$, $V_{d2} = [v1]$, such as CVE-2018-1871, as shown in Table 10
- Crossing: V_{d1} and V_{d2} have both the same range and different ranges, such as $V_{d1} = [v1, v2]$, $V_{d2} = [v1, v3]$, such as CVE-2011-0083, as shown in Table 11.

Table 7. Example of exact matching (CVE-2019-9211)

Vuln. DB	Software version
NVD	GNU PSPP: [1.2.0]
SecurityFocus	GNU PSPP: [1.2]

When there are multiple software names under the same CVE-id, we classify the results as follows:

Exact match: When the result of all software versions with the same software name is a complete match, the result of this cve is a complete match.

completely mismatched: When the results of all software versions with the same software name are entirely mismatched, the result of this cve is altogether mismatched.

overclaiming: When the results of all software versions with the same software name are overclaiming, the result of this cve is overclaiming.

underclaim: When the results of all software versions with the same software name are reduced in underclaim, the result of this cve is underclaiming.

crossing: When the results of all software versions with the same software name include and only include the overclaiming and underclaim, the result of this cve is crossing.

Not exactly match: other circumstances.

Table 8. Example of complete mismatching (CVE-2018-20242)

Vuln. DB	Software version
NVD	JSPWiki: [1.4.0, 1.5.0, 1.5.5 beta, 1.5.7 beta, 1.6.0, 1.6.11 beta, 1.6.12 beta, 1.7.0, 1.8.0, 1.8.2]
SecurityFocus	JSPWiki: [2.10.3, 2.10.4, 2.4, 2.5.139-beta, 2.1.120, 2.1.121, 2.1.122, 2.1.123, 2.4.103, 2.4.104, 2.5.139 beta, 2.5.139]

Table 9. Example of overclaiming (CVE-2019-8905)

Vuln. DB	Software version
NVD	File: [5.35]
SecurityFocus	File: [5.29, 5.30, 5.31, 5.32, 5.33, 5.34, 5.35]

Table 10. Example of underclaiming (CVE-2018-1871)

Vuln. DB	Software version
NVD	ibm financial transaction manager: [3.0.0.0, 3.0.2.0, 3.0.5.0, 3.0.5.1]
CVE	ibm financial transaction manager: [3.0.0, 3.0.2, 3.0.5]

Table 11. Example of crossing (CVE-2011-0083)

Vuln. DB	Software version
NVD	Thunderbird: [(<, 3.1.11)]
CNNVD	Thunderbird: [0.3, 0.4, 0.5, 0.6, 2.0.0.18, 3.0.4, 3.1.8, 3.1.9, 3.1.10]

5.2 Ground-Truth Measurement

In order to measure the error caused by WITTY extracting the software name and version, we conducted a difference measurement on the ground-truth. We use WITTY to extract the software name and its corresponding software version in the ground-truth vulnerability report and measure the version difference. Then compare the measurement results with the measurement results of the software name and version marked in the ground-truth. As shown in Table 12, the deviation of the perfect match rate of the two results is in the range of 1.2%, which proves that WITTY is good enough to apply of different measurement.

Table 12. Average of the exact matching rate of vulnerability reports on the ground-truth dataset

Metric	WITTY	Ground-truth	Deviation
Relust	19.1%	20.3%	1.2%

5.3   Result Analysis

We applied WITTY to all the datasets, including the vulnerability database information in Chinese, English, and Russian, and obtained the complete match rate of other vulnerability databases with NVD. As shown in Fig. 9, we can see that most of the software version in the database vulnerability report is different from NVD, and the highest of CNNVD is less than 35%.

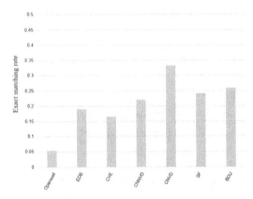

Fig. 9. The exact match rate between NVD and CVE/other vulnerability databases.

Cases that do not meet the exact matching include overclaiming, underclaim, crossing, complete mismatch, and incomplete match. As shown in Fig. 10, most vulnerability databases and NVD's complete match rate is below 50%.

1) *Measurement inside*
   We also found that the structured and unstructured data of CNNVD and CNVD are different, as shown in Fig. 11. It can be seen from the figure that, except for the perfect match, the proportion of exaggerated range is the highest.

2) *Exact matching rate over time*
   Figure 12 below shows how the complete match rate between NVD and other vulnerability databases changes over time. We performed a linear regression on the perfect match rate and found that the slope is negative. In other words, as time goes by, the perfect match rate is getting lower and lower.

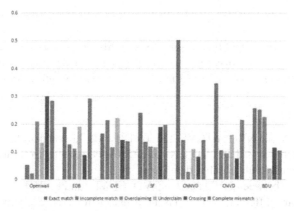

Fig. 10. Inconsistencies between NVD and CVE/other vulnerability databases

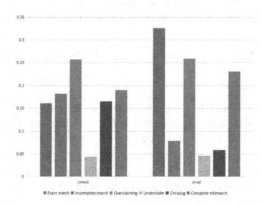

Fig. 11. Exact matching rate within the same vulnerability database

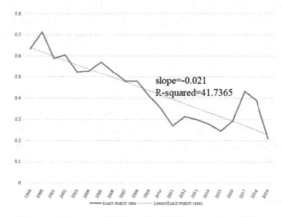

Fig. 12. Exact matching rate between NVD and CVE/other vulnerability databases over time.

6 Discuss

In this section, we discussed the reasons for the differences and gave corresponding countermeasures. Next, we discussed the development of natural language processing. And we compared our work with [5]. Finally, we discussed future work.

6.1 Key Insights

The difference between NVD and CVE, Exploit DB and other English-language security vulnerability databases is that NVD has not effectively collected information on these other English security vulnerability databases.

The difference between NVD and CNNVD, CNVD, and RNVD is that their information sources are different, which may be a reason for their differences. Although CNNVD, CNVD, and RNVD also refer to NVD information, they refer to other reliable information sources, as shown in Table 13, So this difference is caused. Of course, only by referring to as many information sources as possible and sifting out accurate information from them can the vulnerability database be built more perfectly.

Table 13. Primary information sources of vulnerability database

Vuln. DB	Information source
NVD	CVE (cve.mitre.org), ExploitDB (https://www.exploit-db.com/), SecurityFocus (https://www.securityfocus.com/ vulnerabilities), Openwall (http://www.openwall.com/), SecurityFocus Forum (https://www.securityfocus.com/archive/1)
CNNVD	NVD (https://nvd.nist.gov/), Auscert (www.auscert.org.au), SecurityFocus (https://www.securityfocus.com/ vulnerabilities), Vigilance (vigilance.fr), Github (github.com), Packetstormsecurity (packetstormsecurity.com)
CNVD	NVD (https://nvd.nist.gov/), SecurityFocus (https://www.securityfocus.com/ vulnerabilities), Secunia (secunia.com), Oracle (www.oracle.com), Github (github.com), Cisco (tools.cisco.com), Seclists (seclists.org)
RNVD	NVD (https://nvd.nist.gov/), Debian (www.debian.org), CVE (cve.mitre.org), SecurityFocus (https://www.securityfocus.com/ vulnerabilities), Redhat (rhn.redhat.com), Apple (support.apple.com), Adobe (helpx.adobe.com), Oracle (www.oracle.com)

Regarding NVD, CNNVD, CNVD, which give structured data and unstructured data simultaneously, there are differences in their data. This difference is that the vulnerability database's information management is not standardized enough, of course, the same CVE-id. The structured data and unstructured data below are not updated synchronously, which may be one reason.

6.2 Countermeasures

In the vulnerability database construction, it is necessary to consider the classification of the degree of damage to the vulnerability. According to the time environment of the vulnerability formation, the severity is rated [42, 43]. Simultaneously, it must be compatible with the information of multiple vulnerability databases, which can be used in different vulnerabilities. Sharing and circulation between databases and security tools, not only that but some also proposed a new idea of building vulnerability databases from many aspects. We propose the following suggestions:

1. Manage the vulnerability database in a standardized manner, and update the structured and unstructured data of the vulnerability database simultaneously to ensure that there will be no difference between the structured information in the same vulnerability database and the unstructured information in the vulnerability description.
2. Collect as many reliable information sources as possible so that accurate vulnerability information can be extracted from them.
3. Standardize the software name and version. Different vulnerability databases may have different interpretations of the same software name and version. This difference can only be avoided by adopting a unified format.
4. Regularly use our WITTY to perform measurements and correct any discrepancies in time.

6.3 Limitations

WITTY comprises three parts: the NER model, the RE model, and the measuring incon-sistencies. In the second step, the RE model part, the performance is reduced when processing Chinese, although the average accuracy rate (91.1%). Secondly, our dataset only contains mainstream vulnerability databases in China, Russia, and the United States and only includes three languages. In the future, we should expand the dataset to have more extensive data. According to [4, 44], it shows that the data in NVD may also be wrong. What we get is the difference between each vulnerability database and NVD, and the vulnerability database with large difference from NVD does not It is not necessarily a data error in other vulnerability databases. On the contrary, it may also be a difference caused by a NVD error. We need to manually verify some vulnerabilities.

6.4 Compare

[5] conducted a version difference measurement, Still, they ignored the software name in measuring the software version difference, which would also bring some difference, which led to the limitation of their experimental results. Specifically, their handling of software names is not as rigorous as we are. They believe that if the number of matching words of two software names is greater than or equal to the number of unmatched words, then the two software names are considered the same. On the one hand, they may miss some software names that need to be measured for version differences. On the one hand, they may miss some software names that need to be measured for version differences. On the other hand, they may also mistake two software names that are not the same as the same software name and measure the differences between the two software names' versions, which will lead to inaccurate version differences measurement results. We took

Table 14. CVE ID with different software names for software version inconsistency measurement obtained by Dong et al. and us

Vuln. DB	Different
CVE	74.0%
EDB	82.7%
OpenWall	94.7%
Sec.Forum	77.4%

out a comparison with their software name and found a big difference. As shown in the Table 14, most databases have the same software name, less than 20%.

[5] conducted a version difference In addition, we compared the internal data of the Chinese vulnerability database (internal refers to the difference between the structured and unstructured data of the vulnerability database itself) and found that there are also some version inconsistencies. As shown in Fig. 11 (Sect. 5.3).

6.5 Future Work

For the vulnerability database for which the measurement results have been obtained, we only know that the two vulnerability databases are different. Still, we don't know that the data given by the vulnerability database is more credible. We can subsequently classify the vulnerabilities in the vulnerability database by type. Compare the differences, and then manually verify these different CVE-ids to see which of the two vulnerability databases is correct. When a vulnerability database is always correct about a certain type of vulnerability information when this type of vulnerability occurs in the future, and the information described in this vulnerability database different from other vulnerability databases, we think this vulnerability database more useful. Secondly, the vulnerability information not only includes the software name and version, such as the hazard level, score, threat type, etc. are all important information about the vulnerability, and different vulnerability databases of this information are also different. Based on these differences, we can evaluate the construction of each vulnerability database. When there is a difference, it is more credible to give the information of a vulnerability database, rather than need to manually verify.

7   Related Work

7.1   The Development of NLP

From [32] proposed natural language processing, to [33] proposed an end-to-end sequence learning method to solve the problem of long sentences, (Kai Shuang et al.) [34]. solved the common polysemy and task fewer problems in NLP, (Hongyeon Yu et al.) [35] improved the general word representations method, and researchers also used NLP to analyze private information (Nan et al. [36]; Andow et al. [37]); Some researchers also use Bayesian networks to measure and mitigate cybersecurity risks [38–40], using vulnerability database data to analyze countries cyber risk [41].

7.2 The Quality of the Vulnerability Databases

[45] pointed out that the statistics in CVE are biased. [44] reflected the error of the vulnerable software version of Chrome in NVD. Mu et al. (Mu et al. 2018) found that the vulnerability reports of CVE and ExploitDB generally lack important information to reproduce the vulnerability, such as software version and operating system. [4] found missing and unrelated vulnerabilities in NVD data. [5] measured the software version differences between the CVE/CVE reference report and the NVD entry and found that only 59.82% of the CVE/CVE reference report strictly matched the NVD. Our work is based on the previous work to re-measure the software version differences and increase the data, including the differences between the eight vulnerability databases, such as CVE and NVD, and the internal differences of the two Chinese vulnerability databases.

8 Conclusion

In this paper, we design and develop an automated tool WITTY, which can deal with Chinese and English Vulnerability report. It can extract the vulnerable software names and versions in the vulnerability report in pairs and evaluate the differences of different vulnerability databases on a large scale, and accuracy rate is 95.3%, recall rate is 89.9%. Our results show that inconsistent information is pervasive. Our research reveals this difference and gives some suggestions.

References

1. Top 10 cybersecurity incidents in global government agencies. https://www.secrss.com/art icles/23835. Accessed Feb 2020
2. Munir, R., Disso, J.P., Awan, I., Mufti, M.R.: A quantitative measure of the security risk level of enterprise networks. In: 2013 Eighth International Conference on Broadband and Wireless Computing, Communication and Applications, pp. 437–442. IEEE (2013)
3. Mu, D., et al.: Understanding the reproducibility of crowd-reported security vulnerabilities. In: 27th USENIX Security Symposium (USENIX Security 2018), pp. 919–936 (2018)
4. Nappa, A., Johnson, R., Bilge, L., Caballero, J., Dumitras, T.: The attack of the clones: a study of the impact of shared code on vulnerability patching. In: 2015 IEEE Symposium on Security and Privacy, pp. 692–708. IEEE (2015)
5. Dong, Y., Guo, W., Chen, Y., Xing, X., Zhang, Y., Wang, G.: Towards the detection of inconsistencies in public security vulnerability reports. In: 28th USENIX Security Symposium (USENIX Security 2019), pp. 869–885 (2019)
6. CVE and NVD Relationship. https://cve.mitre.org/about/cve_and_nvd_relationship.html. Accessed Feb 2020
7. CVE List. https://cve.mitre.org/cve/. Accessed Feb 2020
8. NVD data feeds. https://nvd.nist.gov/vuln/data-feeds. Accessed Feb 2020
9. Exploitdb. https://www.exploit-db.com/. Accessed Feb 2020
10. Securityfocus. https://www.securityfocus.com/vulnerabilities. Accessed Feb 2020
11. Openwall. http://www.openwall.com/. Accessed Feb 2020
12. CNNVD. https://www.cnvd.org.cn/. Accessed Feb 2020
13. CNVD. http://www.cnnvd.org.cn/. Accessed Feb 2020
14. BDU. https://bdu.fstec.ru/threat. Accessed Feb 2020

15. Breu, S., Premraj, R., Sillito, J., Zimmermann, T.: Information needs in bug reports: improving cooperation between developers and users. In: Proceedings of the 2010 ACM Conference on Computer Supported Cooperative Work, pp. 301–310 (2010)
16. CVE and CVE relationship. https://cve.mitre.org/about/cve_and_nvd_relationship.html. Accessed Feb 2020
17. Chaparro, O., et al.: Detecting missing information in bug descriptions. In: Proceedings of the 2017 11th Joint Meeting on Foundations of Software Engineering, pp. 396–407 (2017)
18. You, W., et al.: SemFuzz: semantics-based automatic generation of proof-of-concept exploits. In: Proceedings of the 2017 ACM SIGSAC Conference on Computer and Communications Security, pp. 2139–2154 (2017)
19. Lample, G., Ballesteros, M., Subramanian, S., Kawakami, K., Dyer, C.: Neural architectures for named entity recognition. arXiv preprint arXiv:1603.01360 (2016)
20. Yang, Z., Salakhutdinov, R., Cohen, W.W.: Transfer learning for sequence tagging with hierarchical recurrent networks. arXivpreprint arXiv:1703.06345 (2017)
21. Are there references available for CVE entries? https://cve.mitre.org/about/faqs.html#cve_entry_references. Accessed Feb 2020
22. Lin, Y., Shen, S., Liu, Z., Luan, H., Sun, M.: Neural relation extraction with selective attention over instances. In: Proceedings of the 54th Annual Meeting of the Association for Computational Linguistics (Volume 1: Long Papers), pp. 2124–2133 (2016)
23. Zhou, P., et al.: Attention-based bidirectional long short-term memory net-works for relation classification. In: Proceedings of the 54th Annual Meeting of the Association for Computational Linguistics (volume 2: Short papers), pp. 207–212 (2016)
24. Giorgi, J., Wang, X., Sahar, N., Shin, W.Y., Bader, G.D., Wang, B.: End-to-end named entity recognition and relation extraction using pre-trained language models. arXiv preprint arXiv:1912.13415 (2019)
25. Huang, Z., Xu, W., Yu, K.: Bidirectional LSTM-CRF models for sequence tagging. arXiv preprint arXiv:1508.01991 (2015)
26. Dong, C., Zhang, J., Zong, C., Hattori, M., Di, H.: Character-based LSTM-CRF with radical-level features for Chinese named entity recognition. In: Lin, C.-Y., Xue, N., Zhao, D., Huang, X., Feng, Y. (eds.) ICCPOL/NLPCC -2016. LNCS (LNAI), vol. 10102, pp. 239–250. Springer, Cham (2016). https://doi.org/10.1007/978-3-319-50496-4_20
27. Levow, G.-A.: The third international Chinese language processing bakeoff: word segmentation and named entity recognition. In: Proceedings of the Fifth SIGHAN Workshop on Chinese Language Processing, pp. 108–117 (2006)
28. Zhang, Y., Yang, J.: Chinese NER using lattice LSTM. arXiv preprint arXiv:1805.02023 (2018)
29. Mintz, M., Bills, S., Snow, R., Jurafsky, D.: Distant supervision for relation extraction without labelled data. In: Proceedings of the Joint Conference of the 47th Annual Meeting of the ACL and the 4th International Joint Conference on Natural Language Processing of the AFNLP, pp. 1003–1011 (2009)
30. CPE dictionary. https://nvd.nist.gov/products/cpe. Accessed Feb 2020
31. YEDDA. https://github.com/QiaoShiA/YEDDA-python3.8. Accessed Feb 2020
32. Collobert, R., Weston, J., Bottou, L., Karlen, M., Kavukcuoglu, K., Kuksa, P.: Natural language processing (almost) from scratch. J. Mach. Learn. Res. **12**, 2493–2537 (2011)
33. Sutskever, I., Vinyals, O., Le, Q.V.: Sequence to sequence learning with neural networks. arXiv preprint arXiv:1409.3215 (2014)
34. Shuang, K., Zhang, Z., Loo, J., Su, S.: Convolution–deconvolution word embedding: an end-to-end multi-prototype fusion embedding method for natural language processing. Inf. Fusion **53**, 112–122 (2020)

35. Yu, H., An, J., Yoon, J., Kim, H., Ko, Y.: Simple methods to overcome the limitations of general word representations in natural language processing tasks. Comput. Speech Lang. **59**, 91–113 (2020)
36. Nan, Y., Yang, Z., Wang, X., Zhang, Y., Zhu, D., Yang, M.: Finding clues for your secrets: semantics-driven, learning-based privacy discovery in mobile apps. In: NDSS (2018)
37. Andow, B., et al.: PolicyLint: investigating internal privacy policy contradictions on google play. In: 28th USENIX Security Symposium (USENIX Security 2019), pp. 585–602 (2019)
38. Frigault, M., Wang, L., Singhal, A., Jajodia, S.: Measuring network security using dynamic Bayesian network. In: Proceedings of the 4th ACM Workshop on Quality of Protection, pp. 23–30 (2008)
39. Khosravi-Farmad, M., Rezaee, R., Harati, A., Bafghi, A.G.: Network security risk mitigation using Bayesian decision networks. In: 2014 4th International Conference on Computer and Knowledge Engineering (ICCKE), pp. 267–272. IEEE (2014)
40. Liao, X., Yuan, K., Wang, X., Li, Z., Xing, L., Beyah, R.: Acing the IOC game: toward automatic discovery and analysis of open-source cyber threat intelligence. In: Proceedings of the 2016 ACM SIGSAC Conference on Computer and Communications Security, pp. 755–766 (2016)
41. Zhang, S., Ou, X., Caragea, D.: Predicting cyber risks through national vulnerability database. Inf. Secur. J. Global Persp. **24**(4–6), 194–206 (2015)
42. Allodi, L., Massacci, F.: Comparing vulnerability severity and exploits using case-control studies. ACM Trans. Inf. Syst. Secur. (TISSEC) **17**(1), 1–20 (2014)
43. Khosravi-Farmad, M., Rezaee, R., Bafghi, A.G.: Considering temporal and environmental characteristics of vulnerabilities in network security risk assessment. In: 2014 11th International ISC Conference on Information Security and Cryptology, pp. 186–191. IEEE (2014)
44. Nguyen, V.H., Massacci, F.: The (un)reliability of NVD vulnerable versions data: an empirical experiment on google chrome vulnerabilities. In: Proceedings of the 8th ACM SIGSAC Symposium on Information, Computer and Communications Security, pp. 493–49 (2013)
45. Christey, S., Martin, B.: Buying into the bias: why vulnerability statistics suck. BlackHat, Las Vegas, USA, Technical report, vol. 1 (2013)

System Security

Multi-modal Universal Embedding Representations for Language Understanding

Xi Luo[1,2,3], Chunjie Cao[1,2,3], and Longjuan Wang[1,2,3]([✉])

[1] School of Cyberspace Security, Hainan University, Haikou 570228, China
wanglongjuan@hainanu.edu.cn
[2] School of Cryptography, Hainan University, Haikou 570228, China
[3] Key Laboratory of Internet Information Retrieval of Hainan Province,
Hainan University, Haikou 570228, China

Abstract. In recent years, machine learning has made good progress in Computer Vision (CV), Natural Language Processing (NLP), and Vision + Language (V + L). However, most existing pre-training models just focus on single-modal (i.e., using only linguistic or visual features for training) or multi-modal (i.e., using both linguistic and visual features for training) scenarios, and can only use single-modal data or limited multi-modal data. This means that models for different scenarios need to be pre-trained separately, which requires a lot of computing resources and time. In this paper, we propose a universal method to train a general pre-training model to solve the problems in different scenarios and modalities. Moreover, we find that the model pre-trained with multi-modal data performs better in the single-modal downstream tasks. We use the General Language Understanding Evaluation (GLUE) benchmark for single-modal tasks to evaluate our model, which outperforms Bidirectional Encoder Representations from Transformers (BERT) in four tasks. For Vision + Language (V + L) tasks, we test our model on downstream tasks such as Visual Question Answering (VQA) and achieve similar performance to the current top-level model.

Keywords: Single-modality · Multi-modality · Pre-training · Fine-tuning · General learning method

1 Introduction

In recent years, pre-training has drawn much attention from CV and NLP due to its strong capability of generalization and efficient usage of large-scale data.

In CV, a series of image feature extraction models were proposed and pre-trained on the large-scale ImageNet, such as ResNet [1], VGG [2], which effectively improved image recognition capability for numerous tasks.

In NLP, self-supervised pre-training models such as BERT [3], GPT [4], and RoBERTa [5], using large-scale single-modal data to train powerful semantic representation capabilities and can achieve outstanding performance in multiple downstream tasks. A series of multi-modal pre-training methods have been proposing

C. Cao et al. (Eds.): FCS 2021, CCIS 1558, pp. 103–119, 2022.
https://doi.org/10.1007/978-981-19-0523-0_7

to adapt to multi-modal scenes, and pre-training on the image-text corpus, such as ViLBERT [6], UNITER [7], has significantly improved the ability of processing multi-modal information. However, these models can only utilize the limited corpus of image-text pairs and cannot effectively adapt to single-modal scenarios. Furthermore, different models need to be pre-trained separately to handle tasks in different scenarios, which wastes a lot of time and computing resources. We argued that current techniques restrict the power of the pre-trained representations, especially for the fine-tuning approaches. The major limitation is that the model only used the pre-training tasks for a single scenario in the pre-training stage. For example, to achieve good results in NLP, BERT only did text training (though the tasks like MLM and NSP).

In the V+L scenario, the pre-training tasks proposed by UNITER are aiming at the better alignment of text and images at different levels of granularity. The single-modal models like BERT ignore the improvements of the model brought by other modal data. Moreover, the multi-modal model like UNITER ignores the model's progress obtained by training single-modal tasks. A universal model framework can improve task processing capabilities in various scenarios and reduce computing resources and time costs.

There are many single-modal data of text and images and multi-modal data of image and text pairs. A powerful and universal AI system should be able to process different modalities of information effectively. To this end, we propose a general method for learning the universal semantic representation of text and images so that the model can handle single-modal downstream tasks and multi-modal downstream tasks. At the same time, to map the representation of text and images to a universal semantic space, we propose a multi-modal universal learning method. The contributions to our paper are as follows:

- We propose a universal training method for different scenarios, which allows the model to give a universal representation for different modalities.
- Through ablation experiments and comparative frontier models, we have verified that the model parameters trained through multi-modal data can be used as the initialization parameters of tasks in different scenarios.
- We verify through ablation experiments that multi-modal data helps to improve the performance of single-modal tasks.
- Unify the model structure of tasks in different scenarios.

2   Related Work

Self-supervised learning as a commonly used machine learning method has been applied to many computer vision tasks, such as image colorization [8], solving jigsaw puzzles [9], inpainting [10], rotation prediction [11], and relative location prediction [12]. Recently, pre-trained language models such as ELMo [13], BERT, GPT2 [14], and XLNet [15] have made significant progress in NLP tasks. Most of them also used self-supervised learning methods for pre-training on large language corpora and used Transformer [16] as the context feature extractor. It has been verified that this method of self-supervised learning in a large corpus in the pre-training stage is an efficient method to solve different tasks in a scenario. Besides, there are many variants of the Bert model, such as EarlyBERT [17], InfoBERT [18], ChineseBERT [19], and RpBERT [20]. They have achieved quite good results in NLP. Recently, the multi-modal scenario also used the two-stage learning method like BERT, first through pre-training on image and text pairs and then fine-tuning specific downstream tasks. For example, VideoBERT [21] learns the bidirectional joint feature over video and textual tokens by training on video-text pairs. ViL-BERT and LXMERT [22] use the two-stream architecture. Two Transformers are applying to the Feature extraction of images and text independently, and the third Transformer will fuse in a later stage. On the other hand, VisualBERT [23], UNITER, Unicoder-VL [24], VL-BERT [25], and B2T2 [26] proposed the single-stream architecture, where a single Transformer is applying to both image and text. Specifically, LXMERT model was pre-trained on downstream tasks such as VQA [27] and GQA [28], while the others were pre-trained on image-text pairs only. Similarly, in the V + L scenario, the methods of pre-training and fine-tuning have also achieved good performance. However, whether it is a model in the CV, NLP, or V + L scenarios, they can only handle tasks in their respective scenario, like BERT and UNITER. They ignored the improvement of the model by the pre-training task in other scenarios and the data of other modes.

Our model use a single-stream architecture similar to UNITER, VL-BERT, and make further improvements on this basis. We also use the form of pre-training and fine-tuning to deal with our model. A critical difference between our model and others is that we use both V + L tasks and NLP single-modal (text-only) tasks to pre-train the model so that the model can solve not only V + L tasks but also pure for text tasks. The two kinds of pre-training models are merged into a standard model, which significantly saves the computational resources and time cost of pre-training.

3   Multi-modal Universal Embedding Representations

We introduce multi-modal universal embedding and its detailed implementation in this section. We used the usual steps: pre-training and fine-tuning. We use pre-training tasks in different scenarios to pre-train the model so that the model can be applied to downstream tasks in different scenarios.

We extend the single-stream model framework similar to UNITER, using Transformer as the core and its attention mechanism to learn the universal embedding representation of pictures and text. A distinctive feature of multi-modal universal embedded representation is to unify different tasks in different scenarios into the same architecture. When applied to specific tasks, it only needs to make corresponding changes to the model's input and add an additional layer for classification.

The model divides into two parts of the input: Image Embedder and Text Embedder. These two parts respectively encode image regions (visual features and target region features) and linguistic tokens (marks and positions) into a joint embedding space. Through different pre-training tasks, apply the Transformer to learn the context embedding of each region and word.

3.1 Model Architecture

The model frame is showing in Fig. 1. The overall architecture used a multi-layer bidirectional Transformer encoder. We will omit the detailed description of the transformer model architecture because Transformer is already a general framework, and our implementation is almost the same as the original.

Before entering the Transformer, the Image Embedder and the Text Embedder extract the embedding features of the image and text, respectively. These embeddings are then input into a multi-layer self-attention Transformer to learn the cross-modality contextualized embedding of visual regions and textual tokens. We encode the location and position as additional input to characterize the image region and tokens position because the Transformer is disordered.

Specifically, in Image Embedder, we first use fast R-CNN [29] to extract the visual features of each region. Furthermore, we use 7-dimensional vectors to encode the position features of each region. Visual and positional features are projected into the same embedded space through the full connection (FC) layer. After adding the outputs of the two FC layers together, the regional visual features are obtained by layer normalization (LN) [30]. For Text Embedder, tokenize the input sentence into WordPieces [31] and transfer the WordPices into token embeddings. And then, the position embedding, segment embedding, and token embedding are summed up before being fed into the LN. Finally, the added embedding is passed through the LN layer to obtain the final text embedding. Most V + L Models only used the task of single-sentence training during pre-training, so the segment embedding is not using. We added segment embedding to the model to distinguish different sentences. Finally, these two parts are embedding through the Transformer for feature learning and alignment.

3.2 Data Processing

We process the data into two different forms to train different scenarios of tasks. For the V + L tasks, the feature of the text part comes from the position embedding, tokens embedding, and the segment embedding. The position embedding represents the position of each token, and the segment embedding distinguishes different sentences.

The tokens embedding is converted from WordPiece embeddings with a 30,000 tokens vocabulary (like BERT), and we use the hugging face open-source interface for concrete implementation. In addition, as with BERT, the CLS and SEP tokens are jointed at the beginning and end of the text sequence, respectively. The feature of the image part is the superimposition of the regional feature and the position encoding. Finally, the two parts are jointed and sent to the Transformer. For the text-only task, the same is to joint the CLS and SEP tokens at the beginning and the end of the text sequence, and then add the word

Our Model

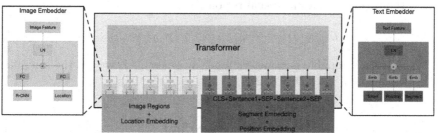

Fig. 1. The overview of our model, consisting of an Image Embedder, a Text Embedder and a multi-layer self-attention Transformer, learned through five pre-training tasks.

embedding of the text with the position encoding and the segment embedding. The visual feature vectors are replaced by all zeros.

3.3 Pre-training Tasks

Our pre-training tasks include V + L multi-modal tasks and NLP single-modal tasks. For the V + L multi-modal task, we use the three pre-training tasks proposed by UNITER (MLM, MRM, and ITM). We propose MLM2 (Masked Language Modeling without Image Regions) and RMLM (Reinforcement of Masked Language Modeling) on the single-modal tasks. Among them, MRM, MLM, MLM2, and RMLM are in analogy to BERT, where we randomly masked some words or regions from the input and learn to recover the words or regions as the output of Transformer.

Specifically, word masking realizes by replacing the token with a unique token [MASK]. In the area masking task (MRM), the region masking is implementing by adding noise to the visual feature vector. While MLM2 and RMLM replacing the visual feature vector with all zeros, aiming at completely mask one modality and then randomly masking another modality to improve the task effect of single-modal.

Multi-modal universal learning aims to train both V + L and text-only tasks simultaneously, and it can train single-modal and V + L tasks simultaneously without additional text-only datasets.

Task1: Masked Language Modeling Without Image Region (MLM2).
We completely replace the visual feature vector with all zeros, and the input word is expressing as $\mathbf{w} = \{\mathbf{w}_1, \ldots, \mathbf{w_T}\}$, and $\mathbf{m} \in \mathbb{N}^M$ refers to the mask index. In MLM2, we randomly take the probability of 15% to replace the input words $\mathbf{w_i}$ with a special token [MASK], and the masked one is described as $\mathbf{w_m}$. We use the final hidden vector corresponding to the first input token [CLS] as the aggregate representation to facilitate the classification of downstream tasks. The goal of this task is to predict these masked words by minimizing the negative

log-likelihood ($\mathcal{L}_{\mathbf{MLM}}(\theta)$), base only on the observation of the surrounding words $\mathbf{w}_{\backslash \mathbf{m}}$ without considering the visual region:

$$\mathcal{L}_{\mathrm{MLM}}(\theta) = -E_{(\mathbf{w}) \sim D} \log P_\theta \left(\mathbf{w_m} \mid \mathbf{w}_{\backslash \mathbf{m}} \right) \tag{1}$$

The θ is the trainable parameters. Each $\mathbf{w} = \{\mathbf{w}_1, \ldots, \mathbf{w}_T\}$ is the sampling of the whole training set D (Fig. 2).

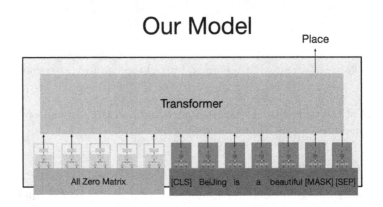

Fig. 2. Example of MLM2.

The goal of this task is to improve the comprehension of single-modal tasks. Combined with the original pre-training task of UNITER, our model can be pre-trained on single-modal tasks and multi-modal tasks at the same time without changing the model architecture. Furthermore, the downstream tasks of single-modal and multi-modal can be processed by universal architecture. At the same time, because the model uses two modal information in each batch of training, and visual features are not redundant to text, the model trained in this way can achieve better results in downstream tasks in different scenarios. Moreover, this training method helps the model handle single-modal downstream tasks. When the model is doing a single-modal task, only the input needs to be preprocessed, and the visual feature vectors are replaced by all zeros, and the input becomes [MASK]-Text Pair form. This form is consistent with the training, so there will be no over-fitting problems.

Task2: Reinforcement Masked Language Modeling (RMLM). Like MLM2, we also completely replace the visual feature vector with all zeros. And all process of RMLM is the same as MLM2 except that the RMLM joints two identical texts together through [SEP]. The two text sequences can take different masked words, joint the two text sequences together through [SEP] token and input them into the model. Similar to MLM2, The goal of this task is to predict these masked words by minimizing the negative log-likelihood $(\mathcal{L}_{\mathrm{MLM}}(\theta))$, based only on the observation of the surrounding words $w_{\backslash m}$.

$$\mathcal{L}_{\mathrm{MLM}}(\theta) = -E_{(\mathbf{w}) \sim D} \log P_\theta \left(\mathbf{w_m} \mid \mathbf{w}_{\backslash \mathbf{m}} \right) \qquad (2)$$

Similar to MLM2, the image region part is replaced with zeros, and the same loss function is used. Since the text part of the COCO dataset is short, this task helps to improve the model's ability to cope with long and double-sentence tasks (Fig. 3).

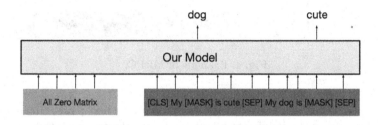

Fig. 3. Example of RMLM.

The V + L Tasks (MLM, MRM, and ITM). These tasks are proposed by UNITER, so we will not introduce them in detail in this section. Detailed descriptions of these three pre-training tasks are presenting in Appendix A.

3.4 Pre-training Dataset

The full name of MS COCO is Microsoft Common Objects in Context. It originated from the Microsoft COCO dataset that Microsoft funded and annotated in 2014. Like the ImageNet competition, it regards as one of the most popular and authoritative competitions in computer vision.

The COCO dataset is large and rich object detection, segmentation, and captioning dataset. This dataset aims at scene understanding, which is mainly intercepting from complex daily scenes. The target in the image is calibrating through precise segmentation. The image includes 91 types of targets, 328,000 images and 2,500,000 labels. There are 80 categories and more than 330,000 images, of which 200,000 are labeled. The number of individuals in the entire dataset exceeds 1.5 million.

3.5 Fine-Turning

Compared with pre-training, fine-tuning requires less computing resources and only adds the layers for classification to the original structure. The self-attention mechanism in the Transformer allows our model to model many downstream tasks-whether they involve single text, text pairs, or image-text pairs-by swapping out the appropriate inputs and outputs. The self-attention is using to encode the joint embedding of text and image features, includes bidirectional cross attention between two sentences or between pictures and texts.

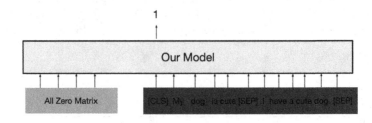

Fig. 4. Example of MRPC.

In single-modal NLP tasks, for the tasks involving text pairs, our model use the [SEP] token to distinguish two sentences, and the two sentences are joined together through the [SEP] token and then input into the model as a whole. At the same time, the image regions are replacing with all zeros as input. As shown in Fig. 4, we take MRPC as an example to show the processing of single-modal text pair tasks. For the single sentence tasks, the image part is also set to all zeros, and the text part is still in the form of [CLS] + sentence + [SEP]. As shown in Fig. 5, we take CoLA as an example to show the processing of single-modal text pair tasks.

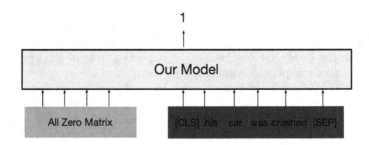

Fig. 5. Example of CoLA.

For the V + L tasks, our processing form is similar to other V + L models. The image part is the input of image features, and the text part is processing in the same way as the single-modal NLP tasks.

4   Experiment

In this section, we present our model in 6 NLP single-modal tasks and 4 V + L tasks. We use GLUE tasks to evaluate single-modal NLP tasks, and V + L multi-modal tasks use VQA, VCR, NLVR, and VE to evaluate. We use the same number of parameters as the UNITER-Base as the model's initialization to ensure the experiment's fairness.

4.1   GLUE

The General Language Understanding Evaluation(GLUE) benchmark collects diverse natural language understanding tasks. Detailed descriptions of GLUE datasets include in Appendix B.1 (Table 1).

Table 1. GLUE Test results, scored by the evaluation server (https://gluebenchmark. com/leaderboard). F1 scores are reported for QQP and MRPC, Matthews correlation coefficient is reported for CoLA, and accuracy scores are reported for the other tasks.

System	CoLA	SST-2	MRPC	QQP	QNLI	RTE
OpenAI GPT	45.4	91.3	82.3	70.3	87.4	56
Bert-base	52.1	93.5	88.9	71.2	90.5	66.4
Our model (train with MLM2)	52.31	93.74	89.57	75.88	89.86	62.45
Our model (train with RMLM)	51.39	92.18	87.87	76.7	90.19	62.82

When fine-tuning GLUE, the input sequence is processed as described in Sect. 3. Different layers need to be added for classification during fine-tuning according to the needs of different downstream tasks. We use the label of the task and the output of the classification layer to calculate the standard classification loss.

BERT and GPT are two classic models proposed in the past two years with significant comparative value. And the results show that the model trained by the multi-modal universal embedding representations method has achieved excellent results in most tasks, indicating that it is efficient to learn features of different modalities simultaneously.

The tasks has dramatically improved the model's performance, and the future trend may be to use different modal data to improve the classification efficiency of a single-modal task. At the same time, the experimental results show that the model using the MLM2 method for pre-training will perform better than RMLM on a smaller dataset and single sentence tasks. However, on large datasets and text pair tasks, the model that uses RMLM as a pre-training task will perform better than MLM2.

4.2　V + L Tasks

In the Scenario of V + L, we choose VQA, VE, NLVR, and VCR to test (Table 2).

Table 2. V + L task test results. For the VCR task, the accuracy of our answer is the evaluation standard (the original task also included the accuracy of the reason for choosing the answer. Since the training datasets are not entirely consistent, we compare the UNITER trained only on the COCO dataset to ensure the experiment's effectiveness.

System	VQA	VE	NLVR	VCR (Q-A)
VL-BERT	70.83	–	–	74.00
VisualBERT	71.00	–	67.00	71.60
UNITER-Base (train with coco)	70.87	75.08	75.35	74.67
Our model (MLM2)	71.56	76.23	75.64	74.72
Our model (RMLM)	71.03	76.67	76.35	75.98

Detailed descriptions of these four tasks are included in Appendix B.2. To fine-tune these four tasks, we represent the input sequence as described in Sect. 3. For different tasks, we need to slightly change the model's architecture, mainly through the features provided by the hidden layer corresponding to [CLS] as the classification basis.

The results show that our method achieves better results than UNITER under the same training conditions (training on COCO dataset only). Therefore, we further verify the feasibility of universal multi-modal embedding, both for single-modal and multi-modal tasks.

5　Conclusion and Future Work

In this paper, we present a multi-modal universal embedding representations method for data of different modalities. We present two new pre-training tasks and verify them through ablation experiments. Training on the COCO dataset can make our model perform at a first-class model level on V + L and NLP tasks. Furthermore, under the condition that the pre-training dataset is much smaller than BERT, we have obtained performance close to BERT and even surpassed BERT on some GLUE tasks.

We can conclude that additional image features will help to improve the model's ability to deal with text-only tasks. Therefore, we believe that a universal model that combines multiple modalities should achieve better results in every single-modal tasks in the future. Future work includes training our model on larger datasets and developing more effective pre-training tasks.

Acknowledgement. This work was supported in part by the National Natural Science Foundation of China Enterprise Innovation and Development Joint Fund (No. U19B2044), and the Key R&D Projects in Hainan Province (No. ZDYF2020012).

Appendix

We organize the appendix into two sections:

- The details of the tasks proposed by UNITER are presented in Appendix A.
- Additional details for our experiments are presented in Appendix B.

A   The Implementation of MLM, ITM, and MRM

Language Modeling (MLM). The image regions is expressing as $\mathbf{v} = \{\mathbf{v}_1, \ldots, \mathbf{v}_k\}$, and the input word is expressing as $\mathbf{w} = \{\mathbf{w}_1, \ldots, \mathbf{w}_T\}$, and $\mathbf{m} \in \mathbb{N}^M$ refers to the mask index. All the textual processing of MLM is the same to MLM2. The goal of this task is to predict these masked words $\mathbf{w_m}$ by minimizing the negative log-likelihood ($\mathcal{L}_{\mathbf{MLM}}(\theta)$), based on the observation of the surrounding words $\mathbf{w}_{\backslash \mathbf{m}}$ and all image regions v:

$$\mathcal{L}_{\mathbf{MLM}}(\theta) = -E_{(\mathbf{w},\mathbf{v}) \sim D} \log P_\theta \left(\mathbf{w_m} \mid \mathbf{w}_{\backslash \mathbf{m}}, \mathbf{v} \right) \tag{3}$$

The θ is the trainable parameters. Each pair (w, v) is the sampling of the whole training set D.

Image-Text Matching (ITM). In ITM, the special token [CLS] is used for output classification, which is the joint embedding representation of two modals. The fully connected layer follows the corresponding hidden layer. Finally, output the score on the degree of matching between the image and the text. The scoring function is denoted as $s_\theta(\mathbf{w}, \mathbf{v})$. In this task, we sampled a positive or negative pair (w, v) from dataset D at each step. The opposing pair is created by replacing the image or text in a paired sample with randomly selected from other samples. We denoted the label as $\mathbf{y} \in \{0, 1\}$, indicating if the sampled pair is a match. Then we used the binary cross-entropy loss for model optimization:

$$\mathcal{L}_{\mathbf{ITM}}(\theta) = -E_{(\mathbf{w},\mathbf{v}) \sim D} \left[y \log s_\theta(\mathbf{v}, \mathbf{w}) + (1 - y) \log (1 - s_\theta(\mathbf{v}, \mathbf{w})) \right] \tag{4}$$

Masked Region Modeling (MRM). Similar to MLM, we randomly take the probability of 15% to replace the visual features with a special token [MASK], and the masked one is described as $\mathbf{v_m}$. The model is trained to reconstruct the masked regions $\mathbf{v_m}$ based on the observation of the words w and remaining regions $\mathbf{v}_{\backslash \mathbf{m}}$. The noise is superimposed on the visual features $\mathbf{v_m}$ of the masked region. Unlike textual tokens that are represented as discrete labels, visual features are high-dimensional and continuous, thus cannot be supervised via class likelihood. Instead, there are three variants for Masked Region Modeling, which share the same objective base:

$$\mathcal{L}_{\mathbf{MRM}}(\theta) = E_{(\mathbf{w},\mathbf{v}) \sim D} f_\theta \left(\mathbf{v_m} \mid \mathbf{v}_{\backslash \mathbf{m}}, \mathbf{w} \right) \tag{5}$$

Masked Region Feature Regression (MRFR). MRFR learns to let the output of each masked region $v_m^{(i)}$ regress to its visual features. Specifically, an FC layer is applied to convert its Transformer output into a vector $h_\theta\left(v_m^{(i)}\right)$ of the same dimension as the input ROI (Region Of Interest) pooled feature $r\left(v_m^{(i)}\right)$. Then we apply L2 regression between the two:

$$f_\theta\left(\mathbf{v_m} \mid \mathbf{v_{\backslash m}}, \mathbf{w}\right) = \sum_{i=1}^{M}\left\|h_\theta\left(\mathbf{v_m^{(i)}}\right) - r\left(\mathbf{v_m^{(i)}}\right)\right\|_2^2 \tag{6}$$

Masked Region Classification (MRC). MRC learns to predict the object semantic class for each masked region. First, feeding the Transformer output of the masked region into an FC layer to predict the scores of K object classes, which further goes through a softmax function to be transformed into a normalized distribution $g_\theta\left(v_m^{(i)}\right) \in \mathbb{R}^K$. There is no ground-truth label, for the object categories are not provided. Thus, we used the object detection output from Faster R-CNN and take the detected object category (with the highest confidence score) as the label of the masked region, which will be converted into a one-hot vector $c\left(v_m^{(i)}\right) \in \mathbb{R}^k$. The final objective minimizes the cross-entropy (CE) loss:

$$f_\theta\left(\mathbf{v_m} \mid \mathbf{v_{\backslash m}}, \mathbf{w}\right) = \sum_{i=1}^{M}\text{CE}\left(c\left(\mathbf{v_m^{(i)}}\right), g_\theta\left(\mathbf{v_m^{(i)}}\right)\right) \tag{7}$$

Masked Region Classification with KL-Divergence (MRC-kl). MRC takes the most likely object class from the object detection model as the hard label (w.p. 0 or 1). We can also use its soft label as supervision signals, which is the raw output from the detector, i.e., a distribution of object classes $\tilde{c}\left(v_m^{(i)}\right)$. MRC-kl aims to distill such knowledge into UNITER, by minimizing the KL divergence between two distributions:

$$f_\theta\left(\mathbf{v_m} \mid \mathbf{v_{\backslash m}}, \mathbf{w}\right) = \sum_{i=1}^{M}D_{KL}\left(\tilde{c}\left(\mathbf{v_m^{(i)}}\right)\|g_\theta\left(\mathbf{v_m^{(i)}}\right)\right) \tag{8}$$

B   Detailed Experimental Setup

B.1   Detailed Descriptions for the GLUE Benchmark Experiments.

The GLUE benchmark includes the following datasets, the descriptions of which were originally summarized in Wang et al. (2018a):

– CoLA (The Corpus of Linguistic Acceptability) aims to predict whether an English sentence conforms to grammar, which is a binary single-sentence classification task (Warstadt et al., 2018).

- SST-2 (The Stanford Sentiment Treebank) aims to predict the sentiment contained in the sentences, which is a binary single-sentence classification task (Socher et al., 2013).
- MRPC (Microsoft Research Paraphrase Corpus) aims to predict whether the sentences in the pair are semantically equivalent, which consists of the sentence pairs extracted from online news sources (Dolan and Brockett, 2005).
- (QQP Quora Question Pairs) aims to confirm where the two questions asked on Quora are semantically equivalent, which is a binary classification task (Chen et al., 2018).
- QNLI (Question Natural Language Inference) is converted from The Stanford Question Answering Dataset (SQuAD 1.0). SQuAD 1.0 is a question and answer dataset composed of a question paragraph pair, in which the paragraph is from Wikipedia. A sentence in the paragraph contains the answer to the question. Here you can see an element, a paragraph from Wikipedia, a question, a sentence in the paragraph that contains the answer to the question. By combining each sentence in the question and context (i.e. Wikipedia paragraphs) and filtering out the sentence pairs with low lexical overlap, the sentences in qnli are obtained.
- RTE (Recognizing Textual Entailment) is a small dataset, contains an entailment classification task. RTE aims to predict whether the second sentence is an entailment, contradiction, or neutral concerning the first one.

B.2   Detailed Descriptions for the V + L Tasks Benchmark Experiments

- Visual Question Answering (VQA) task aims to output the distribution of answers for the input pictures and picture-related questions and take the answer with the highest probability as the predicted answer.
- Visual Entailment (VE) aims to determine whether the content of the text is contained in the picture, which is divided into three labels: entailment, neutral, and contradiction. Entailment refers to the content of the description that matches the picture. Neutral refers to the inability to judge whether the text description matches the picture. Furthermore contradiction means that the text description does not match the picture.
- Natural Language for Visual Reasoning (NLVR) enters two pictures and a description text at the same time to determine whether the text has a corresponding relationship with the two pictures. The label contains true and false. In this task, the model needs to be slightly modified. The text and two pictures are input into the pre-trained model twice, and then the model's output is input into a binary-Attention layer. This task proves that the pre-trained model can be applied to different tasks with slight modifications.
- Visual Commonsense Reasoning (VCR) asking questions based on pictures. Each question has four options as answers, and each answer has four options as reasons for the choice. When training, the picture, question, and the answer to an option are input into the model, a total of four times are input, and four scores are obtained, and the highest score is the answer. In the same

way, the reason for choosing the answer is to input the picture, the chosen answer, and one reason for choosing the answer four times to get four scores, with the highest score being the reason for selection.

References

1. He, K., Zhang, X., Ren, S., Sun, J.: Deep residual learning for image recognition. In: 2016 IEEE Conference on Computer Vision and Pattern Recognition, CVPR 2016, Las Vegas, NV, USA, 27–30 June 2016, pp. 770–778. IEEE Computer Society (2016). https://doi.org/10.1109/CVPR.2016.90
2. Simonyan, K., Zisserman, A.: Very deep convolutional networks for large-scale image recognition. In: Bengio, Y., LeCun, Y. (eds.) 3rd International Conference on Learning Representations, ICLR 2015, San Diego, CA, USA, 7–9 May 2015, Conference Track Proceedings (2015). http://arxiv.org/abs/1409.1556
3. Devlin, J., Chang, M., Lee, K., Toutanova, K.: BERT: pre-training of deep bidirectional transformers for language understanding. In: Burstein, J., Doran, C., Solorio, T. (eds.) Proceedings of the 2019 Conference of the North American Chapter of the Association for Computational Linguistics: Human Language Technologies, NAACL-HLT 2019, Minneapolis, MN, USA, June 2–7, 2019, Volume 1 (Long and Short Papers), pp. 4171–4186. Association for Computational Linguistics (2019). https://doi.org/10.18653/v1/n19-1423
4. Radford, A., Narasimhan, K., Salimans, T., Sutskever, I.: Improving language understanding by generative pre-training (2018)
5. Liu, Y., et al.: Roberta: a robustly optimized BERT pretraining approach. CoRR abs/1907.11692 (2019). http://arxiv.org/abs/1907.11692
6. Lu, J., Batra, D., Parikh, D., Lee, S.: ViLBERT: pretraining task-agnostic visiolinguistic representations for vision-and-language tasks. In: Wallach, H.M., Larochelle, H., Beygelzimer, A., d'Alché-Buc, F., Fox, E.B., Garnett, R. (eds.) Advances in Neural Information Processing Systems 32: Annual Conference on Neural Information Processing Systems 2019, NeurIPS 2019, Vancouver, BC, Canada, 8–14 December 2019, pp. 13–23 (2019). https://proceedings.neurips.cc/paper/2019/hash/c74d97b01eae257e44aa9d5bade97baf-Abstract.html
7. Chen, Y.-C., et al.: UNITER: UNiversal image-TExt representation learning. In: Vedaldi, A., Bischof, H., Brox, T., Frahm, J.-M. (eds.) ECCV 2020, Part XXX. LNCS, vol. 12375, pp. 104–120. Springer, Cham (2020). https://doi.org/10.1007/978-3-030-58577-8_7
8. Zhang, R., Isola, P., Efros, A.A.: Colorful image colorization. In: Leibe, B., Matas, J., Sebe, N., Welling, M. (eds.) ECCV 2016, Part III. LNCS, vol. 9907, pp. 649–666. Springer, Cham (2016). https://doi.org/10.1007/978-3-319-46487-9_40
9. Noroozi, M., Favaro, P.: Unsupervised learning of visual representations by solving Jigsaw puzzles. In: Leibe, B., Matas, J., Sebe, N., Welling, M. (eds.) ECCV 2016, Part VI. LNCS, vol. 9910, pp. 69–84. Springer, Cham (2016). https://doi.org/10.1007/978-3-319-46466-4_5
10. Pathak, D., Krähenbühl, P., Donahue, J., Darrell, T., Efros, A.A.: Context encoders: feature learning by inpainting. In: 2016 IEEE Conference on Computer Vision and Pattern Recognition, CVPR 2016, Las Vegas, NV, USA, 27–30 June 2016, pp. 2536–2544. IEEE Computer Society (2016). https://doi.org/10.1109/CVPR.2016.278

11. Gidaris, S., Singh, P., Komodakis, N.: Unsupervised representation learning by predicting image rotations. In: 6th International Conference on Learning Representations, ICLR 2018, Vancouver, BC, Canada, April 30–May 3 2018, Conference Track Proceedings. OpenReview.net (2018). https://openreview.net/forum?id=S1v4N2l0

12. Doersch, C., Gupta, A., Efros, A.A.: Unsupervised visual representation learning by context prediction. In: 2015 IEEE International Conference on Computer Vision, ICCV 2015, Santiago, Chile, 7–13 December 2015, pp. 1422–1430. IEEE Computer Society (2015). https://doi.org/10.1109/ICCV.2015.167

13. Peters, M.E., et al.: Deep contextualized word representations. In: Walker, M.A., Ji, H., Stent, A. (eds.) Proceedings of the 2018 Conference of the North American Chapter of the Association for Computational Linguistics: Human Language Technologies, NAACL-HLT 2018, New Orleans, Louisiana, USA, 1–6 June 2018, Volume 1 (Long Papers), pp. 2227–2237. Association for Computational Linguistics (2018). https://doi.org/10.18653/v1/n18-1202

14. Radford, A., et al.: Language models are unsupervised multitask learners. OpenAI blog **1**(8), 9 (2019)

15. Yang, Z., Dai, Z., Yang, Y., Carbonell, J.G., Salakhutdinov, R., Le, Q.V.: XLNet: generalized autoregressive pretraining for language understanding. In: Wallach, H.M., Larochelle, H., Beygelzimer, A., d'Alché-Buc, F., Fox, E.B., Garnett, R. (eds.) Advances in Neural Information Processing Systems 32: Annual Conference on Neural Information Processing Systems 2019, NeurIPS 2019, Vancouver, BC, Canada, 8–14 December 2019, pp. 5754–5764 (2019). https://proceedings.neurips.cc/paper/2019/hash/dc6a7e655d7e5840e66733e9ee67cc69-Abstract.html

16. Vaswani, A., et al.: Attention is all you need. In: Guyon, I., et al. (eds.) Advances in Neural Information Processing Systems 30: Annual Conference on Neural Information Processing Systems 2017, Long Beach, CA, USA, 4–9 December 2017, pp. 5998–6008 (2017). https://proceedings.neurips.cc/paper/2017/hash/3f5ee243547dee91fbd053c1c4a845aa-Abstract.html

17. Chen, X., Cheng, Y., Wang, S., Gan, Z., Wang, Z., Liu, J.: EarlyBERT: efficient BERT training via early-bird lottery tickets. In: Zong, C., Xia, F., Li, W., Navigli, R. (eds.) Proceedings of the 59th Annual Meeting of the Association for Computational Linguistics and the 11th International Joint Conference on Natural Language Processing, ACL/IJCNLP 2021, (Volume 1: Long Papers), Virtual Event, 1–6 August 2021, pp. 2195–2207. Association for Computational Linguistics (2021). https://doi.org/10.18653/v1/2021.acl-long.171

18. Wang, B., et al.: InfoBERT: improving robustness of language models from an information theoretic perspective. In: 9th International Conference on Learning Representations, ICLR 2021, Virtual Event, Austria, 3–7 May 2021. OpenReview.net (2021). https://openreview.net/forum?id=hpH98mK5Puk

19. Sun, Z., et al.: ChineseBERT: Chinese pretraining enhanced by glyph and pinyin information. In: Zong, C., Xia, F., Li, W., Navigli, R. (eds.) Proceedings of the 59th Annual Meeting of the Association for Computational Linguistics and the 11th International Joint Conference on Natural Language Processing, ACL/IJCNLP 2021, (Volume 1: Long Papers), Virtual Event, 1–6 August 2021, pp. 2065–2075. Association for Computational Linguistics (2021). https://doi.org/10.18653/v1/2021.acl-long.161

20. Sun, L., Wang, J., Zhang, K., Su, Y., Weng, F.: RPBERT: a text-image relation propagation-based BERT model for multimodal NER. In: Thirty-Fifth AAAI Conference on Artificial Intelligence, AAAI 2021, Thirty-Third Conference on Innovative Applications of Artificial Intelligence, IAAI 2021, The Eleventh Symposium on Educational Advances in Artificial Intelligence, EAAI 2021, Virtual Event, 2–9 February 2021, pp. 13860–13868. AAAI Press (2021). https://ojs.aaai.org/index. php/AAAI/article/view/17633

21. Sun, C., Myers, A., Vondrick, C., Murphy, K., Schmid, C.: VideoBERT: a joint model for video and language representation learning. In: 2019 IEEE/CVF International Conference on Computer Vision, ICCV 2019, Seoul, Korea (South), October 27–November 2 2019, pp. 7463–7472. IEEE (2019). https://doi.org/10.1109/ICCV. 2019.00756

22. Tan, H., Bansal, M.: LXMERT: learning cross-modality encoder representations from transformers. In: Inui, K., Jiang, J., Ng, V., Wan, X. (eds.) Proceedings of the 2019 Conference on Empirical Methods in Natural Language Processing and the 9th International Joint Conference on Natural Language Processing, EMNLP-IJCNLP 2019, Hong Kong, China, 3–7 November 2019, pp. 5099–5110. Association for Computational Linguistics (2019). https://doi.org/10.18653/v1/D19-1514

23. Li, L.H., Yatskar, M., Yin, D., Hsieh, C., Chang, K.: VisualBERT: a simple and performant baseline for vision and language. CoRR abs/1908.03557 (2019). http:// arxiv.org/abs/1908.03557

24. Li, G., Duan, N., Fang, Y., Gong, M., Jiang, D.: Unicoder-VL: a universal encoder for vision and language by cross-modal pre-training. In: The Thirty-Fourth AAAI Conference on Artificial Intelligence, AAAI 2020, The Thirty-Second Innovative Applications of Artificial Intelligence Conference, IAAI 2020, The Tenth AAAI Symposium on Educational Advances in Artificial Intelligence, EAAI 2020, New York, NY, USA, 7–12 February 2020, pp. 11336–11344. AAAI Press (2020). https://aaai.org/ojs/index.php/AAAI/article/view/6795

25. Su, W., et al.: VL-BERT: pre-training of generic visual-linguistic representations. In: 8th International Conference on Learning Representations, ICLR 2020, Addis Ababa, Ethiopia, 26–30 April 2020. OpenReview.net (2020). https://openreview. net/forum?id=SygXPaEYvH

26. Alberti, C., Ling, J., Collins, M., Reitter, D.: Fusion of detected objects in text for visual question answering. In: Inui, K., Jiang, J., Ng, V., Wan, X. (eds.) Proceedings of the 2019 Conference on Empirical Methods in Natural Language Processing and the 9th International Joint Conference on Natural Language Processing, EMNLP-IJCNLP 2019, Hong Kong, China, 3–7 November 2019, pp. 2131–2140. Association for Computational Linguistics (2019). https://doi.org/10.18653/v1/D19-1219

27. Antol, S., et al.: VQA: visual question answering. In: 2015 IEEE International Conference on Computer Vision, ICCV 2015, Santiago, Chile, 7–13 December 2015, pp. 2425–2433. IEEE Computer Society (2015). https://doi.org/10.1109/ICCV. 2015.279

28. Hudson, D.A., Manning, C.D.: GQA: a new dataset for real-world visual reasoning and compositional question answering. In: IEEE Conference on Computer Vision and Pattern Recognition, CVPR 2019, Long Beach, CA, USA, 16–20 June 2019, pp. 6700–6709. Computer Vision Foundation/IEEE (2019). https://doi. org/10.1109/CVPR.2019.00686. http://openaccess.thecvf.com/content_CVPR_2019/html/Hudson_GQA_A_New_Dataset_for_Real-World_Visual_Reasoning_and_Compositional_CVPR_2019_paper.html

29. Anderson, P., et al.: Bottom-up and top-down attention for image captioning and visual question answering. In: 2018 IEEE Conference on Computer Vision and Pattern Recognition, CVPR 2018, Salt Lake City, UT, USA, 18–22 June 2018, pp. 6077–6086. IEEE Computer Society (2018). https://doi.org/10.1109/CVPR.2018.00636. http://openaccess.thecvf.com/content_cvpr_2018/html/Anderson_Bottom-Up_and_Top-Down_CVPR_2018_paper.html

30. Ba, L.J., Kiros, J.R., Hinton, G.E.: Layer normalization. CoRR abs/1607.06450 (2016). http://arxiv.org/abs/1607.06450

31. Wu, Y., et al.: Google's neural machine translation system: bridging the gap between human and machine translation. CoRR abs/1609.08144 (2016). http://arxiv.org/abs/1609.08144

New Federation Algorithm Based on End-Edge-Cloud Architecture for Smart Grid

Xin Ji[✉], Haifeng Zhang, Juan Chu, Linxiao Dong, and Chengyue Yang

Big Data Center of State Grid Corporation of China, Beijing 100053, China

Abstract. In the smart grid, the underlying data often contains a large amount of private information and cannot be shared, which further limits the effect of large-scale data analysis and utilization. Federated learning, as a decentralized learning strategy with a privacy protection function, can learn a wider range of knowledge through model aggregation without touching local data and is suitable for smart grid scenarios. Considering the limited computing and storage capabilities of the underlying terminal of the grid system, this paper proposes a three-tier federation architecture of the end-side-cloud, using model segmentation technology to only retain the optimized feature extraction model on the local client. The back-end models that need to be repeatedly iteratively trained are allocated to edge servers and interact with the cloud to learn collaboratively, thereby reducing system overhead. We conducted extensive experiments to verify the superiority of the federated model compared to the independent training model and further analyzed the feasibility of edge computing.

Keywords: Smart grid · Federated learning · Edge computing · Model segmentation · LSTM

1 Introduction

With the advent of the Industry 4.0 era, the world is moving in the direction of the "Internet of Everything", and the Internet of Things is an important manifestation of this general trend. As an important part of people's production and life, the smart grid has realized the integration of energy flow and information flow with the help of a variety of intelligent technical means. Different from the traditional power grid, it continuously sends electricity-related data from all aspects through widely distributed intelligent sensors [1]. It is just because the amount of data collected is explosive, by building a data-driven model in the power physical network, the essential characteristics of the data can be analyzed, which is more conducive to upper-level decision-making. For example, [2] recently use the open-source smart grid profile to establish a complete comprehensive model for carbon emissions investigation by 2030. The most advanced machine learning models, including deep learning, reinforcement learning, and generative networks, are also widely used in smart grid load forecasting and renewable overview [3], defense against grid attacks [4], and false injection attacks [5].

© Springer Nature Singapore Pte Ltd. 2022
C. Cao et al. (Eds.): FCS 2021, CCIS 1558, pp. 120–133, 2022.
https://doi.org/10.1007/978-981-19-0523-0_8

However, the smart grid also has a general limitation in the field of big data analysis: data islands. Since different sensors, smart meters, etc. are deployed in different areas, the collected information is private, and privacy protection regulations restrict it from being widely shared. This further leads to the traditional learning method of aggregating separated data to a central server for analysis is no longer applicable. In 2016, Google first proposed the concept of federated learning, to learn user behavior across mobile devices [6]. Federated learning is a decentralized machine learning scheme that requires each device in the system to train its model separately without sharing any data. The specific steps are as follows: the server randomly initializes a pre-agreed model structure according to public data or randomly, selects some devices (clients) randomly in the system, and distributes the initial model. The client uses its local data to train the model, uploads the model parameters to the server for aggregation, and obtains the updated global model. Repeat the process until the model converges or achieves good results. Since then, federated learning has been further improved, mechanisms such as differential privacy and homomorphic encryption have been continuously introduced to strengthen the privacy protections of the parameter transmission process. And heterogeneous data training [7], computing power optimization [8], and cross-device communication [9] have also attracted more intense attention.

In this paper, we mainly apply federated learning and edge computing to the field of smart grids, build an efficient machine learning framework under the premise of ensuring terminal data privacy to analyze and mine the essential characteristics of electrical data. Considering the small storage and poor computing power of the underlying equipment of the power grid, we separate the feature extraction and training update of the model. The smart sensor terminal is used as the data source and is only responsible for data collection and feature extraction. The edge device is the client of the federated learning framework, responsible for the local training of the model, and uploads it to the central server for aggregation. Our contributions in this work can be summarized as follows:

- We integrate the federated learning architecture based on the original Long Short-Term Memory (LSTM) model and apply it to the power grid system, which can break "data islands" through multi-user collaboration without leaking terminal data privacy, and maximize knowledge benefits.
- We introduced edge devices to improve the traditional server-client architecture and constructed a new three-tier server-edge-client structure to make it more adaptable to the characteristics of the grid structure.
- With the help of edge devices and smart sensor terminals, the local training of the model is separated. The smart sensor terminal is responsible for simple data collection and feature extraction, and the edge device is responsible for large-scale model training, thereby reducing the load of the underlying equipment of the power grid system.
- The validity and feasibility of our proposed framework are verified through experiments.

The remainder of this paper is structured as follows: Sect. 2 discusses related works focusing on the LSTM model for electricity prediction. In Sect. 3, we define the proposed approach and used methods. Section 4 introduces the simulations and numerical results. Then in Sect. 5 we conclude the paper and discuss the future work.

2 Related Work

At present, machine learning methods are widely used in smart grid electricity forecasting. LSTM is the most commonly used method for forecasting. Its effect has been proved in [10, 11], but the Root Mean Square Error (RMSE) and Mean Average Percentage Error (MAPE) of the model still has shortcomings. Some studies believe that this is a problem of LSTM itself, and its structure has been improved. Authors in [12] proposed the sequence-to-sequence LSTM, which can better predict data within one minute, but the effect within one hour is not significantly improved compared with standard LSTM; Furthermore, other authors use a genetic algorithm to find the optimal parameters for LSTM to improve the prediction effect [13], but the combination of multiple parameters is still a probability problem. There is also work that believes that the intelligent prediction of power load is not only a problem of neural network architecture but also a data-driven model generalization problem [14]. When the proposed model is applied to a new data set, there will be a significant accuracy decrease [10]. Some works suggest that factors from the weather or the terminal device itself should be considered in the model training process [15, 16]. But this introduces a lot of extra work such as consumes manpower and material resources. Another way to enhance the model's capabilities is to collect diverse user data sets, and then perform group training to ensure the homogeneity of the data while increasing the total amount of data. The author in [17] combines the enhanced clustering algorithm with the existing prediction model and uses Markov chain sampling to group data with similar user characteristics to reduce the training variance. The author in [18] proposed a new deep recurrent neural network based on pooling, which batches a set of customer load profiles into an input pool to solve the problem of overfitting by increasing the diversity and quantity of data. To further enhance the security of interaction between multiple users, the author in [19] proposed a virtual ring architecture that can use symmetric or asymmetric encryption requested by customers belonging to the same group to provide a privacy protection solution. Other work focuses more on the use of data aggregation to cover up the original power consumption information [20, 21], but this violates the requirements of short-term load forecasting (STLF).

Federated learning, as a decentralized learning algorithm with a privacy protection function, can ensure that local data is not leaked while conducting collaborative learning and joint training, providing a new solution for forecasting in the power grid field. [14, 22] and [23] are a few federated learning implementations in electric load forecasting and energy demand forecasting based on electric vehicles. [22, 23] are direct applications of federal architecture. The local model makes decisions through repeated training and uploads them to the edge or central server for secondary collaborative decision-making. However, multi-level interaction and local training both increase the cost of the underlying equipment. In [23], edge devices are introduced to host local data and serve as clients for local training. Although the computing load of the underlying device can be reduced, data upload still has the risk of privacy leakage. Our work is to consider equipment computing costs and data privacy at the same time and propose an improved three-tier federation mechanism based on the characteristics of the power grid, to realize the separation of the model between the local and the edge, and to complete the power load forecasting and analysis tasks as efficiently and safely as possible.

3   System Model

We propose the network architecture shown in Fig. 1. There are three main components: the local terminal, the Multi-access Edge Computing (MEC) server [24], and the central server.

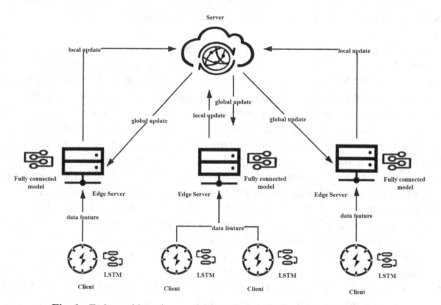

Fig. 1. Federated learning model based on end-edge-cloud architecture.

1. Local Client: Represents a series of data collection devices owned by the bottom layer of the power grid system, such as smart meters, smart sensing devices, etc. Each local device is equipped with computing and communication modules, which can transmit corresponding data to edge servers.
2. Edge server: Compared with the bottom terminal, the edge server has more storage and computing resources, and is usually deployed on the edge of the network, acting as a relay node and computing unit between the central server and edge devices.
3. Central server: As the control center, it is responsible for collecting model update parameters transmitted from all edge servers, and executing aggregation algorithms to update the global model. After the model is averaged, it distributes the shared global model to the edge terminals participating in the federated learning protocol.

Specifically, we built a multi-layer neural network based on LSTM. With the assistance of edge server computing power, the local clients use private power data to jointly complete local training, and the central server aggregates the results to obtain an efficient prediction model. In this section, we will explain in detail how to make predictions by constructing a multi-layer LSTM model and how to perform the federated learning process of model separation.

3.1 LSTM Forecasting

Time series forecasting is a regression forecasting method. On the one hand, it considers the continuity of events and uses past time series data for statistical analysis to predict the development trend of things; on the other hand, it thinks out the randomness caused by accidental factors and properly processes the original historical data to obtain accurate predictions.

In the field of machine learning, the Recurrent Neural Network (RNN) is a general term for a series of neural networks that can process sequence data. LSTM is a special kind of RNN, which is proposed to solve the common gradient disappearance and explosion problems in RNN models. The disappearance of gradient means that the gradient norm of the long-term component is smaller, which causes the weight to never change in the lower layer. The gradient explosion refers to the opposite event [25]. In the traditional RNN, the training algorithm uses BPTT. When the time is relatively long, the residual error that needs to be returned will decrease exponentially, resulting in a slow update of network weights, which cannot reflect the effect of RNN's long-term memory, so a storage unit is needed to store the memory, which is the core of LSTM. Its working principle is to choose to forget some information in the past through the forget gate, memorize some information in the present through the input gate, and merge the past and present memories to obtain the final output, as shown in Fig. 2.

In the application scenario of the smart grid system, the LSTM network can abstract key features from the historical user records, and the fully connected layer can remap the learned distributed features to the resulting space. Therefore, we combined LSTM and fully connected networks to design a multi-layer model to achieve accurate power load prediction.

3.2 Model Segmentation Technology

Intuitively speaking, model segmentation is to segment a complete multi-layer neural network model according to certain rules. Its effectiveness in the neural network model lies in the low coupling between the layers, that is, each hidden layer in the network can be executed separately by using the output of the previous layer as its input [26].

Figure 3 shows the entire model segmentation process. As we all know, the forward and backward propagation in the neural network model training process requires complicated iterative operations, which will consume a lot of terminal equipment resources. To solve this problem, this paper divides the complete prediction model mentioned above into two parts along with the last layer of LSTM: the client model and the edge model. On the client-side, only the optimized LSTM layers are deployed to extract features from the original data; the edge-side model is composed of the remaining fully connected layers, and the model parameters are updated by performing forward and backward propagation processes. Based on this multi-layer model segmentation method, the local

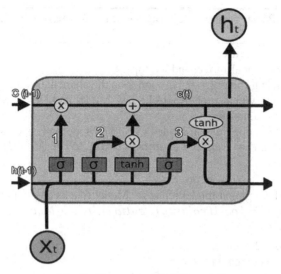

Fig. 2. The standard LSTM model.

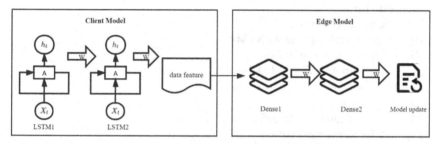

Fig. 3. Multi-layer neural network model segmentation process.

training phase of the traditional federated learning architecture is divided into two. With the help of the computing power of the edge device, the complex model update part is outsourced, which can significantly reduce the client's computing resource consumption [27].

3.3 Federated Learning Architecture

The traditional federated learning iterative process mainly includes two steps: First, the client trains the model on the local data set and uploads parameter updates to the server; the server calculates the updated global model through the averaging mechanism or other aggregation algorithms and distributes it to each client. In this paper, considering the limited computing and storage capabilities of the underlying equipment of the power grid system, we introduce the edge server on the traditional Server-Client mechanism and realize the local training of the model together with the client through model segmentation technology.

Algorithm1:	Power forecast federation algorithm based on end-edge cloud collaboration

1:	//Server executes
2:	Initialize global model and its copy
3:	Pre-training the copy global model on the share datasets
4:	Divide the global models into LSTM_Model and Dense_Model
5:	**for** c in Clients **do**
6:	send the copy global model's LSTM_Model to c as local model
7:	$Feature_i = FeatureTraining(Data_i, LSTM\_Model)$
8:	**end for**
9:	**for** e in EdgeServers **do**
10:	send the global model's Dense_Model to e as edge model
11:	$w^t_{edgei} = LocalTraining(Feature_i, Dense\_Model_i)$
12	**end for**
13:	**for** t=0,1,2,...,K **do**
14:	**for** e in EdgeServer **do**
15:	$w^t_{global} = FedAvg(w^t_{edgei})$
16:	**end for**
17:	**end for**
18:	//Clients executes:
19:	FeatureTraining(Data_i,LSTM):
20	**for** each data d in Data_i:
21:	output=LSTM_Model(d)
22:	append output into Feature_i
23:	**end for**
24:	upload Feature_i to EdgeServer encrypted
25:	//EdgeServer executes:
26:	LocalTrainging(Feature_i,Dense_Model_i):
27:	$w^t_{edgei} = w^t_{global}$
28:	**for** epoch k=1,2,...E **do**
29:	**for** each batch b={feature,y} of Feature_i **do**
30:	$w^t_{edgei} = SGD(loss, w^t_{edgei})$
31:	**end for**
32:	**end for**

For the edge-side model to achieve the best results and provide more information for the federation process, the client-side model must have efficient feature extraction capabilities. High efficiency is not only reflected in the accuracy of feature extraction but also cannot cause heavy calculation and communication overhead. For this reason, what we deploy on the client is a pre-trained frozen model whose model parameters will not be updated with the federation process [28]. When the central server initiates the federation process, two identical global models are initialized at the same time. Firstly, it is divided along with the LSTM layer. The fully connected layers are assigned to the edge server as a local model for repeated iterative updates, and the replica model is pre-trained on the shared data set. After a certain effect, the LSTM layers are assigned to the device as a local model. Among them, the shared data set can be purchased with the same distributed public data set or shared by users voluntarily without revealing privacy. The entire federation process is shown in Algorithm 1. The local client uploads the extracted data features to the edge server, then it completes local model iteration through edge computing and uploads the updates to the central server. The central server updates the global model after aggregation and sends it back to the edge server. Repeat this process until convergence.

4 Experiment and Results

4.1 Dataset and Evaluation Criteria

The data set we used comes from the ASHRAE Energy Prediction Kaggle competition. It collected data from 2,380 electricity meters in 1,448 buildings from 16 sources and records the hourly electricity consumption from 00:00 on January 1, 2016, to 23:59 on December 31, 2018, with a total of more than 20 million data points. In addition to the metadata of the electricity meter, the data set also includes the area occupied, the time of completion, and weather data provided by the weather station where the building is located. In the experiment, we structure the problem as supervised learning, and the goal is real-time electric energy data. Specifically, the model predicts the current energy consumption based on the energy consumption of the previous 12 h and other information.

The prediction problem is essentially a regression problem. Unlike classification problems, it obtains a specific value instead of a simple 0 or 1 label. Therefore, the accuracy rate cannot be used to measure it, and it is more measured by the deviation between the predicted value and the true value. In this paper, we take Root Mean Squared Error (RMSE) as the evaluation index, and its expression is shown as (1):

$$\text{RMSE} = \sqrt{\frac{1}{m} \sum_{i=1}^{m} (y_i - \widehat{y_i})^2} \tag{1}$$

Among them, m is the size of the data, y_i is the true value, and $\widehat{y_i}$ is the predicted value. The mean square error can reflect the degree to which the predicted value deviates from the true value, and the smaller the value, the higher the prediction accuracy.

4.2 Experimental Setup

As mentioned in Sect. 3, to ensure that the client has an efficient feature extraction capability, we need to pre-train the global model in the shared data set to achieve a certain effect and send the cut LSTM layer to the client. To this end, we first select 20% of the samples from the original data set as public data and train the replica global model.

Different clients and edge devices number will also have a certain impact on the experimental results. Table 1 shows the different scenarios we evaluated. We set different federated iteration times and the number of clients and edge servers to fully explore the effect of the model we proposed.

Table 1. Experimental scene-setting.

Scenarios	Clients number	Edge number	Local training epoch	Federate learning epoch
1	10	10	5	50
2	30	10	5	50
3	30	10	1	50
4	50	50	5	30
5	100	50	1	30

It is well known that the hyperparameters of deep learning models are essential for obtaining the best prediction performance. Previous work has shown that as long as a network structure with multiple layers and enough hidden nodes is used, there is no obvious difference in the effects between the models [29]. Moreover, the focus of this paper is to compare the effect of the three-tier federated architecture of end-edge-cloud collaboration we designed on the improvement of traditional distributed machine learning algorithms. Therefore, as long as we ensure that the two model structures are consistent, the specific model design will not become a key influencing factor. Considering that the complex deep network structure is prone to under-fitting and gradient disappearance problems, we only keep two layers of LSTM and two fully connected layers, and the hidden neurons are set to 64, 32, 128, 128, and use a single neutron to map the output to the predicted value.

4.3   Experimental Results

Global Model Prediction Results. After federated training, the global model maximizes the distributed knowledge from many local users and has better generalization ability and performance effect. As shown in Fig. 4, we randomly select 3 out of 5 scenarios and use the global model to predict the electricity power of 100 random records in the original data set.

Intuitively, the prediction results are almost consistent with the real data, indicating that the trained global model can analyze and predict the real-time state of the power system based on historical data. To further accurately evaluate the performance of the model, we re-run the prediction experiment of the global model on all user data sets, and count the final RMSE results, as shown in Table 2. It should be noted that we are not repeating the prediction on the training data of each user, but using the local test set divided in advance, where the training set and test set of each local data set are divided according to a ratio of 8:2.

In the comparison of scenarios 1 and 2, the average, maximum, and minimum RMSE are all reduced. This is because more local users are introduced, which provides a richer data source for model learning; The comparison of scenarios 2 and 3 further proves the influence of the local training process. The more local training, the stronger the ability to extract knowledge. In the comparison of scenarios 2 and 4, although more local clients are participating, the number of the federation round in 2 is more, and better performance

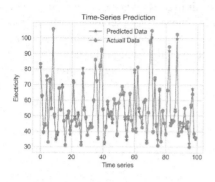 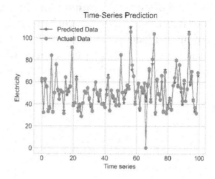

(a) global model in scenario1   (b) global model in scenario3

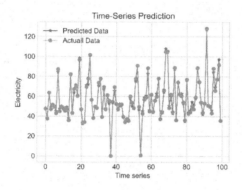

(c) global model in scenario5

Fig. 4. The predictive effect of the federated global model.

Table 2. RMSE statistical results in local datasets in different scenarios.

Scenario	RMSE		
	Min	Max	Mean
1	3.538	4.456	3.892
2	3.427	4.310	3.772
3	3.511	5.040	3.900
4	3.540	4.648	3.915
5	3.305	4.950	3.874

is achieved, which shows that the global model can indeed benefit more through more collaboration.

Comparison of Federal Training and Local Training. In this part, we performed federated training and independent local training on the user data set to prove the importance of multi-model collaboration. Specifically, independent local training uses only its private data for training by each client, while federated training is based on the local training according to the federated process in Sect. 3.3 for model aggregation.

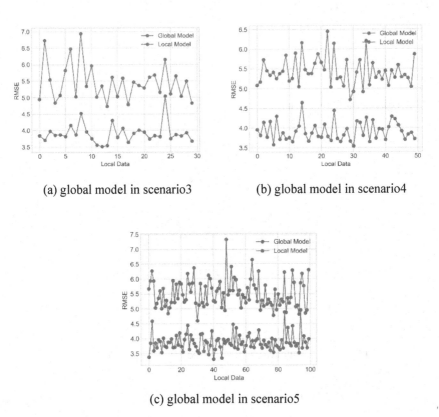

(a) global model in scenario3   (b) global model in scenario4

(c) global model in scenario5

Fig. 5. Comparison of federal training and independent training.

As shown in Fig. 5, the federated model can significantly reduce the RMSE of the local model, which means that we can improve the generalization ability through the collaborative aggregation of multiple models, and ultimately achieve more accurate prediction results.

Computational Cost Comparison. One of the innovations of this paper is to introduce edge computing to the traditional federated learning architecture, which is responsible for the heavy and complex local training process, thereby reducing the computational load of the underlying client. Therefore, in the experiment, we also compared the impact of model segmentation on the CPU state of the device, as shown in Fig. 6.

It can be seen that after edge computing, the CPU utilization of the local client has always been kept below 50%, while the traditional local training process will take a long

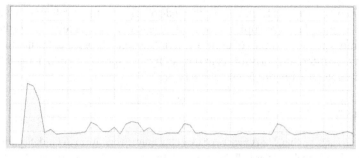

(a) Client overhead after edge computing.

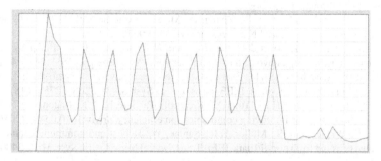

(b) Client overhead during traditional local training.

Fig. 6. CPU utilization before and after edge computing.

time and a large amount of CPU, which will inevitably affect other things such as data collection and storage. In contrast, it proves the feasibility of our proposed architecture, which can improve the efficiency of the entire grid system by reducing the load of the underlying smart meters, smart sensing devices, etc.

5 Conclusion and Future Work

With the continuous enhancement of privacy awareness in the era of big data, the isolation of the underlying data in the power grid system has become one of the challenges of energy consumption analysis and prediction. In this paper, we introduce and improve the traditional federation mechanism based on the characteristics of the grid structure, add edge computing services between the end and the cloud, and use model segmentation technology to allocate the model training process to the edge server. The bottom terminal is only responsible for data collection and feature extraction. Multi-model collaborative aggregation is carried out through the interaction between the edge and the cloud, and the learning of knowledge is maximized without touching the original private data. We conducted comprehensive experiments to verify the superiority of the global model compared to distributed training. The simulation results show that the deployment of edge computing can reduce the load of the underlying equipment of the power grid to a certain extent and improve the system efficiency.

In future work, we will further study the end-to-edge security protection technology. Even if the original data is not uploaded directly, the features extracted through the model can reveal more privacy features of users to a certain extent. At present, the homomorphic encryption and differential privacy technologies that are most used in federated learning will be our main research directions in the future.

References

1. Liu, H., Zhang, X., Sun, H.: A Federated Learning Framework in Smart Grid: Securing Power Traces in Collaborative Learning. arXiv:2103.11870 (2021)
2. Modeling a Clean Energy Future for the United States, Breakthrough Energy (2021). https://science.breakthroughenergy.org/
3. Chen, Y., Wang, Y., Kirschen, D., Zhang, B.: Model-Free Renewable Scenario Generation Using Generative Adversarial Networks. arXiv:1707.09676 (2017)
4. Wang, S., Chen, H.: A novel deep learning method for the classification of power quality disturbances using deep convolutional neural network. Appl. Energy 235, 1126–1140 (2019)
5. Chen, Y., Wang, Y., Kirschen, D., Zhang, B.: Model-free renewable scenario generation using generative adversarial networks. IEEE Trans. Power Syst. 33(3), 3265–3275 (2018)
6. Konečný, J., McMahan, H.B., Yu, F.X., Richtárik, P., Suresh, A.T., Bacon, D.: Federated learning: Strategies for improving communication efficiency. arXiv:1610.05492 (2016)
7. Sattler, F., Wiedemann, S., Müller, K.R., Samek, W.: Robust and communication-efficient federated learning from non-iid data. IEEE Trans. Neural Netw. Learn. Syst. 31(9), 3400–3413 (2019)
8. Zhan, Y., Li, P., Guo, S.: Experience-driven computational resource allocation of federated learning by deep reinforcement learning. In: 2020 IEEE International Parallel and Distributed Processing Symposium (IPDPS), pp. 234–243. IEEE, New Orleans (2020)
9. Abad, M.S.H., Ozfatura, E., Gunduz, D., Ercetin, O.: Hierarchical federated learning across heterogeneous cellular networks. In: 2020 IEEE International Conference on Acoustics. Speech and Signal Processing (ICASSP), pp. 8866–8870. IEEE. Barcelona, Spain (2020)
10. Bouktif, S., Fiaz, A., Ouni, A., Serhani, M.A.: Optimal deep learning LSTM model for electric load forecasting using feature selection and genetic algorithm: Comparison with machine learning approaches. Energies 11(7), 1636 (2018)
11. Zheng, J., Xu, C., Zhang, Z., Li, X.: Electric load forecasting in smart grids using long-short-term-memory based recurrent neural network. In: 51st Annual Conference on Information Sciences and Systems (CISS), pp. 1–6. IEEE, Baltimore, MD, USA (2017)
12. Marino, D.L., Amarasinghe, K., Manic, M.: Building energy load forecasting using deep neural networks. In: 42nd Annual Conference of the IEEE Industrial Electronics Society, pp. 7046–7051. IEEE, Florence, Italy (2016)
13. Almalaq, A., Zhang, J.J.: Evolutionary deep learning-based energy consumption prediction for buildings. IEEE Access 7, 1520–1531 (2018)
14. Taïk, A., Cherkaoui, S.: Electrical load forecasting using edge computing and federated learning. In: 2020 IEEE International Conference on Communications (ICC), pp. 1–6. IEEE, Deqing, China (2020)
15. Zhu, G., Chow, T.T., Tse, N.: Short-term load forecasting coupled with weather profile generation methodology. Build. Serv. Eng. Res. Technol. 39(3), 310–327 (2018)
16. Kong, W., Dong, Z.Y., Hill, D.J., Luo, F., Xu, Y.: Short-term residential load forecasting based on resident behaviour learning. IEEE Trans. Power Syst. 33(1), 1087–1088 (2018)
17. Stephen, B., Tang, X., Harvey, P.R., Galloway, S., Jennett, K.I.: Incorporating practice theory in sub-profile models for short term aggregated residential load forecasting. IEEE Trans. Smart Grid 8(4), 1591–1598 (2015)

18. Shi, H., Xu, M., Li, R.: Deep learning for household load forecasting—A novel pooling deep RNN. IEEE Trans. Smart Grid **9**(5), 5271–5280 (2017)

19. Badra, M., Zeadally, S.: Design and performance analysis of a virtual ring architecture for smart grid privacy. IEEE Trans. Inf. Forensics Secur. **9**(2), 321–329 (2014)

20. Gong, Y., Cai, Y., Guo, Y., Fang, Y.: A privacy-preserving scheme for incentive-based demand response in the smart grid. IEEE Trans. Smart Grid **7**(3), 1304–1313 (2015)

21. Park, H., Kim, H., Chun, K., Lee, J., Lim, S., Yie, I.: Untraceability of group signature schemes based on bilinear mapping and their improvement. In: 4th International Conference on Information Technology (ITNG'07), pp. 747–753. IEEE, Las Vegas, NV, USA (2007)

22. Taik, A., Nour, B., Cherkaoui, S.: Empowering Prosumer Communities in Smart Grid with Wireless Communications and Federated Edge Learning. arXiv:2104.03169 (2021)

23. Saputra, Y.M., Hoang, D.T., Nguyen, D.N., Dutkiewicz, E., Mueck, M.D., Srikanteswara, S.: Energy demand prediction with federated learning for electric vehicle networks. In: 2019 IEEE Global Communications Conference (GLOBECOM), pp. 1–6. IEEE, Waikoloa, HI, USA (2019)

24. Pham, Q.V., et al.: A survey of multi-access edge computing in 5G and beyond: Fundamentals, technology integration, and state-of-the-art. IEEE Access **8**, 116974–117017 (2020)

25. Hochreiter, S., Schmidhuber, J.: Long short-term memory. Neural Comput. **9**(8), 1735–1780 (1997)

26. Wang, J., Zhang, J., Bao, W., Zhu, X., Cao, B., Yu, P.S.: Not just privacy: Improving performance of private deep learning in mobile cloud. In: Proceedings of the 24th ACM SIGKDD International Conference on Knowledge Discovery & Data Mining, pp. 2407–2416 (2018)

27. Lane, N.D., Georgiev, P.: Can deep learning revolutionize mobile sensing? In: Proceedings of the 16th International Workshop on Mobile Computing Systems and Applications, pp. 117–122 (2015)

28. Zhang, J., Zhao, Y., Wang, J., Chen, B.: FedMEC: Improving efficiency of differentially private federated learning via mobile edge computing. Mobile Netw. Appl. **25**(6), 2421–2433 (2020)

29. Kong, W., Dong, Z.Y., Jia, Y., Hill, D.J., Xu, Y., Zhang, Y.: Short-term residential load forecasting based on LSTM recurrent neural network. IEEE Trans. Smart Grid **10**(1), 841–851 (2017)

Certificateless Authentication and Consensus for the Blockchain-Based Smart Grid

Egide Nkurunziza[1(✉)], Gervais Mwitende[2], Lawrence Tandoh[1], and Fagen Li[1]

[1] School of Computer Science and Engineering, University of Electronic Science
and Technology of China, Chengdu 611731, China
fagenli@uestc.edu.cn
[2] Pivot Access Ltd., Kigali, Rwanda
mwitende.gervais@pivotaccess.com

Abstract. Authentication and key agreement scheme facilitates secure
two-way communication in the smart grid (SG) and enables each entity
to verify whether the received message comes from a legitimate sender.
Also, it assists in establishing the shared key that will be used to secure
subsequent communication. Several schemes of authentication and key
agreement have been proposed over the last few years, but many of
them are not efficient in terms of communication overhead and computational overhead. In addition to that, they do not adequately adhere
to the fundamental security of the smart grid authentication, such as
forward secrecy. In this paper, we suggest a certificateless authentication
and consensus for a blockchain-based smart grid. The proposed protocol
has a lightweight communication overhead and puts less computation
cost on the smart meter. Furthermore, it satisfies the fundamental security requirements of the smart grid, plus consensus in the blockchain.
Besides, the security of the proposed protocol is rooted in the intractabil-
ity assumption of the elliptic curve discrete logarithm (ECDL) problem,
and it is proved using the random oracle model (ROM).

Keywords: Authentication · Key agreement · Blockchain · Smart
grid · Certificateless cryptography

1 Introduction

The internet of things (IoT) is a state-of-the-art internet technology that connects various kinds of objects, namely sensors, actuators, smart meters (SM),
vehicles, etc. To benefit from various features of IoT such as interconnectivity,
scalability, and autonomous process, the smart grid is one of the huge con-
sumers of IoT technology. IoT can assist in power generation, forecast customer
needed energy, and collect customer energy consumption [1]. A smart grid is
a leading-edge grid furnished with a bidirectional communication network that
enables diverse entities of SG to communicate with each other. Furthermore,
the fundamental communication infrastructure of the smart grid includes home

C. Cao et al. (Eds.): FCS 2021, CCIS 1558, pp. 134–151, 2022.
https://doi.org/10.1007/978-981-19-0523-0_9

area networks (HAN), building area networks (BAN), and neighborhood area networks (NAN). This infrastructure facilitates the smart meter installed at HAN to periodically report the consumed energy to the service provider (SP). Despite the advantage of integrating IoT in the SG, the smart grid has inherited the IoT security threat and has become a subject to malicious attacks. Attacks are regrouped in two classes, passive and active attacks. [2]. Therefore, a number of mutual authentication and key agreement schemes have been suggested to ensure safe communication between various SG entities [3–5]. Mutual authentication and key agreement protocol can be realized using three different asymmetric cryptographic settings. These are the public key infrastructure (PKI) model [6,7], identity-based public-key cryptography (ID-PKC) [8], and certificateless public-key cryptography (CL-PKC) [9]. Both ID-PKC and CL-PK are suitable for smart grid limited-resource devices since they are not as computationally expensive as PKI infrastructure. The CL-PKC features are utilized, then we design a certificateless authentication and consensus for the blockchain-based smart grid scheme. The designed scheme is lightweight and meets the computational capacity of SG devices, avoids a single point of failure, and enables blockchain consensus. Certificateless authentication and consensus for the blockchain-based smart grid built trust among communicating parties in the smart grid network. That is to say that each entity ensures that it is communicating with another legitimate entity. Furthermore, it prohibits an adversary invade the smart meter thus, avoiding collecting data exchanged within SG and preventing an adversary modify or dropping a message [10].

1.1 Why Blockchain Is Introduced in AMI Communication Architecture?

The early major breakthrough of the smart grid is the advanced metering infrastructure (AMI). It facilitates loads control, price signaling, and customer voltage measurement, to name a few. Mainly, it enabled intelligent communication between smart meters and the service provider [11]. Since data exchange is crucial in the smart grid, data management is of paramount importance in the SG. In convention AMI communication architecture, meter data management system (MDMS) is a fundamental component, and it works in centralized architecture settings. An MDMS is a database equipped with analytical tools that facilitates it to interact with other operation and management systems [12]. As illustrated in Fig. 1, conventional architecture settings comprise three main entities, smart meter, MDMS, as well as operation and management systems. The operation and management systems are outage management system (OMS), geographical information system (GIS), distribution management system (DMS), and consumer information system (CIS)/billing. Furthermore, the conventional AMI communication architecture in Fig. 1 works as follows.

- The smart meter computes energy consumed by the customer and sends the data to the MDMS. In addition, they are other numerous works done and reported by the smart meter, including time-based price, net metering, power

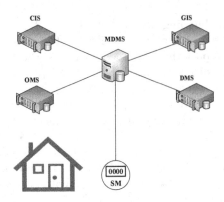

Fig. 1. Conventional AMI communication architecture.

outage (and restoration) alerting, power quality monitoring, and remote power on/power off operations.
– The MDMS collects data from smart meters, processes it, stores it, and makes it available for usage.
– The operation and management systems use the available and processed data from MDMS. The processed data is mostly utilized in outage management services through OMS, activities of geographical information services through GIS, billing operations through CIS, and in the management of power quality and load prediction through DMS.

However, the structure in Fig. 1 suffers from a single point of failure and a single point of management. For that reason, once MDMS is down, dependent services are also unavailable. Conversely, in Fig. 2, a blockchain-based architecture is shown, and it has no central management. Therefore, nodes in the blockchain cannot face issues related to a single point of failure or a single point of management. A blockchain [13] is a distributed database that relies on cryptographic technologies to ensure security. Applications that are based on blockchain communicate via the internet and form a peer-to-peer network architecture. The sender signs a transaction with a public-key cryptography signature then broadcasts it to other nodes in the blockchain. The transaction is considered valid when a correct signature is applied. According to the consensus rules, the transaction is verified separately by other nodes and get stored in the nodes' distributed ledger. Furthermore, due to the cryptographic technology (e.g., hash function), transactions cannot be altered or deleted. In this new architecture, nodes have identical privileges. Figure 2 illustrates the blockchain-based architecture, and it performs as follows. The smart meter assembles information from the customer side and delivers it to node C. Here, node C is considered as a local database where data from smart meters are assembled. This node is chosen by the rest of the nodes as a collector node depending on the proof of work results between blockchain nodes. The rest of the nodes are nodes that have a consensus on the blockchain. They are allowed to use the smart meter data collected and broadcasted by node C. In addition, node Z can be considered as a device from the billing unit at SP in charge of customer invoices and payments. Node V can be considered as a device used by field crew that is used in power restoration and outage management. Node X can be considered as a device utilized by the customer to track the advancement of power restoration during power outage incidents. Node W is considered as a device from a load management system that issues commands to a customer's appliance during emergence so that they can reduce their power load.

1.2 Motivation

As mentioned before, the combination of IoT and smart grid has exposed communicating parties to several security threats. Thus, it is essential to deploy a secure authentication and key agreement protocol among parties before they initiate conversation and transmit data to each other. Besides, existing conventional AMI centralized architecture can be susceptible to a single point of failure, for example, in case MDMS is down due to a DoS attack. This kind of attack can halt services provided by the MDMS to other systems then a huge financial loss is incurred. It is in this regard that a blockchain-based architecture is important to avoid a single point of management plus keeping nodes' ledger consistent through implementing consensus in the blockchain. Therefore, a new protocol of certificateless authentication and consensus for blockchain-based smart grid is proposed to shield the security of SG at a reduced computational cost.

1.3 Contribution

The presented paper contains two phases, and their contributions are as follows. The first two belong to the first phase, while the third belongs to the second phase.

- Mutual authentication and session key sharing between the smart meter and collector node is guaranteed.
- Fundamental security requirements such as forward secrecy, man-in-the-middle attacks, and others are achieved.
- Consensus in the blockchain nodes and the authentication between the collector node and other nodes in the blockchain are attained.
- Finally, we made a thorough security analysis under the random oracle model ROM to prove the security of the proposed protocol.

1.4 Organization of the Paper

The rest of the paper is organized as follows: We detailed related work in Sect. 2. We describe preliminaries in Sect. 3. We presented the proposed protocol of certificateless authentication and consensus for blockchain-based smart grid in Sect. 4. We presented security analysis in Sect. 5 to prove the security of our protocol. We compared the communication cost and computational cost of our protocol with the existing protocols in Sect. 6. We presented the conclusion in Sect. 7.

2   Related Work

In the past years, several authentication protocols have been proposed using different approaches to secure different parts of the smart grid at a lightweight cost of both communication and computation. Mahmood et al. [5] designed a message authentication scheme for SG, the session key used in the scheme is produced using AES and RSA. In addition, their scheme is immune to replay attacks, man-in-the-middle attacks, among others. Based on ECC, He et al. [14] designed an anonymous key distribution for SG. The developed scheme is lightweight and enables mutual authentication without the third party. Sakhnini et al. [15] presented a bibliometric survey on the security features of IoT-aided smart grids. In addition, the paper encapsulates varieties of cyber threats against smart grids as well as gaps in the area of SG security. Utilizing blockchain technology, Belhadi et al. [16] designed a privacy reinforcement learning for faults detection in SG. They managed to blend local abnormal patterns into the global complex abnormal patterns. Kaveh and Mosavi [17] pointed out that apart from passive attacks and active attacks, which targets communication paths, physical attacks can also be conducted, targeting the smart meter. Hence, they presented a lightweight mutual authentication scheme for a smart grid based on Physical Unclonable Function (PUF). Also, Kaveh et al. [18] designed a signcryption scheme to secure bidirectional communication between SM and neighborhood gateways NG based on PUF. Elkhalil et al. [19] designed an efficient signcryption scheme to enable communication between internet of vehicles (IoVs) nodes and server while they belong to different cryptographic settings. IoVs works in certificateless cryptography settings, whereas the server works from PKI settings. Moreover, other signcryption schemes [20,21] have been designed, and they implement important security features, which include confidentiality and authentication at a single logical step plus assurance of security for customer's data access. Li et al. [4] designed a scheme that provides mutual authentication and establishes key agreement. In addition, the presented scheme does not disclose the identities of the gateways. Mahmood et al. [22] proposed a lightweight authentication scheme based on ECC to secure SG communication. However, it suffers from a key escrow problem, cannot resist known session-specific temporary information attacks, cannot provide perfect forward security, and susceptible to private key leakage. Abbasinezhad-Mood and Nikooghadam [23] suggested a lightweight authentication scheme based on ECC so that they can remove security issues in [22]. Fortunately, they managed to solve most of the security problem mentioned above, except that their scheme cannot withstand a replay attack, cannot provide perfect forward security once the private keys of both entities are compromised, and there is no message integrity in the first message of authentication request since there is no signature. Chen et al. [24] came up with an identity-based authentication scheme based on a bilinear map that has solved the security issue pointed out in the protocol suggested in [22,23]. In 2021, Wu et al. [25] corrected impersonation attacks and known session-specific temporary information attacks found in the scheme in [24].

3   Preliminaries

Elliptic curve cryptography and security model are described in this section.

3.1   Elliptic Curve Cryptography (ECC)

The equation $y^2 + d_1xy + d_2y = x^3 + c_1x^2 + c_2x + c_3$ is for the elliptic curve in general. However, $y^2 = x^3 + ax + b$ with discriminant $\Delta = 4a^3 + 27b^2 \neq 0$ is the equation for E/F_p (an elliptic curve E over a prime field), where $a, b \in Z_p$. Furthermore, zero is a point at infinity, and $P \in E(F_p)$ is the generator point. Moreover, the scalar point multiplication of E/F_p can be expressed as $\omega P = P + P + P + \ldots P$ (ω times) [22, 23].

3.2   Hard Assumptions

- Discrete logarithm problem (DLP) assumptions, given a random element $Z \in G$ and generator P of G. It is hard to extract x from $Z = xP$, where $x \in Z_q^*$ is unknown value [22].
- Computation Diffie-hellman (CDH) assumption, given $Z, Q \in G$, where $Z = aP$ and $Q = bP$; $a, b \in Z_q^*$ are unknown values. It is hard to compute abP without knowing a and b values [24].

3.3   System Model

Various communication architectures [22, 24, 26] have been used in the advanced meter infrastructure (AMI). Furthermore, we adopted the architecture [27] to explain the functionality of the proposed protocol. As it is explained below, the system model contains three main entities:

- KGC generates a partial private key (PPK), public parameters $params$ and distributes them to the smart meter and Node C.
- Smart meter quantifies energy consumed in real-time, records and hoards the measurement at a predetermined time intervals. Next, it forwards the data to node C but, it can also receive data from the collector node [28, 29].
- The collector node (Node C) collects and processes data from the smart meter, then broadcasts it to the blockchain nodes after receiving a consensus message from the smart meter.

In the subsequent text, the notation of the smart meter is E_m, and the notation of the collector node is E_n.

3.4   Security Model

Every certificateless public key cryptography (CL-PKC) scheme should be secure against two types of adversaries, Type 1 and Type 2, where Type 1 adversary represents external attacker that can replace the public key of CL-PKC since it is not authenticated but does not have access to both master secret key and partial private key of the user. Furthermore, a Type 2 adversary represents a malicious KGC that possesses the system master key but cannot replace the public key [30]. However, Huang et al. [31] made a further research on the security of certificateless signature schemes and revisited their security models, and organized Type 1 adversary $\mathcal{A}_1$ and Type 2 adversary $\mathcal{A}_2$ into three types according to their attack power, normal adversary, strong adversary, and super adversary. Concerning the super adversary, he/she can obtain a right signature of a legitimate entity without providing the secret value associated with a public key replaced by super Type 1 adversary $\mathcal{A}_1$. In the subsequent part, we employ two games and demonstrate the power of adversary and provide security need for mutual authentication and key exchange protocol [32–34]. Note that the instance k of participant u is designated as Θ_u^k.

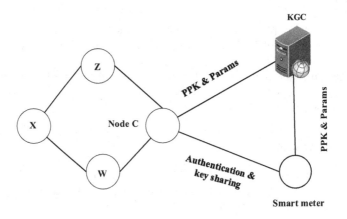

Fig. 2. System model.

Game 1

This game entails two participants, the challenger $\mathcal{C}_{h1}$ and the super Type 1 adversary $\mathcal{A}_1$. Following are different steps of interaction.

Setup. The setup algorithm receives λ as input, where λ is a security parameter. The challenger $\mathcal{C}_{h1}$ employs the algorithm and generates both the master secret key msk and system parameters $params$. Furthermore, the challenger $\mathcal{C}_{h1}$ dispatches parameters to adversary $\mathcal{A}_1$ and stays with msk the master key.

Create-User. After checking whether ID_u exists in the list of D^{list}, $\mathcal{C}_{h1}$ dispatches PK_u to adversary $\mathcal{A}_1$. Else the subsequent algorithms are executed, extract-partial-private-key, extract-private-key and request-public-key and d_u, g_u, and PK_u are obtained, separately. Furthermore, D^{list} is updated (ID_u, d_u, g_u, PK_u) then PK_u is dispatched to $\mathcal{A}_1$. N.B: (We assume that other queries succeed the create-user query).

Query. The adversary $\mathcal{A}_1$ does the following oracle queries according to his/her choice.

- **Extract-Partial-Private-Key** (ID_u): After finding the associated item to ID_u in D^{list}, $\mathcal{C}_{h1}$ dispatches the requested partial private key d_u to the $\mathcal{A}_1$ adversary, otherwise, $\perp$ is returned.
- **Extract-Private-Key** (ID_u): The challenger $\mathcal{C}_{h1}$ obtains the request from $\mathcal{A}_1$ on ID_u, then $\mathcal{C}_{h1}$ finds the associated items from D^{list} and returns the private key PR_u to the adversary $\mathcal{A}_1$.
- **Request-Public-Key** (ID_u): The adversary $\mathcal{A}_1$ forwards the request on ID_u, then the challenger $\mathcal{C}_{h1}$ retrieves the corresponding items from D^{list} and returns the public key PK_u to $\mathcal{A}_1$.
- **Replace-Public-Key** (ID_u, PK_u^*): $\mathcal{A}_1$ Adversary may choose another public key PK_u^* different from the real PK_u public key of the user.
- **Send** (Θ_u^k, M): This query demonstrates that $\mathcal{A}_1$ can forward the message M to $\mathcal{C}_{h1}$. At the time $\mathcal{C}_{h1}$ obtains M in respect to the suggested protocol, $\mathcal{C}_{h1}$ does computations and gives responses to $\mathcal{A}_1$.
- **Reveal** (Θ_u^k, M): In this query, adversary $\mathcal{A}_1$ makes an exceptional request to oracle $\mathcal{C}_{h1}$. Furthermore, $\mathcal{A}_1$ asks for session key disclosure if the oracle accepts the session key is given to $\mathcal{A}_1$, otherwise, $\perp$ is returned.
- **Corrupt** (ID_u): Adversary $\mathcal{A}_1$ forwards a request about the private key of participant u identified as ID_u, and $\mathcal{C}_{h1}$ replies with the private key of the participant.
- **Test** (Θ_u^k): The Adversary $\mathcal{A}_1$ conveys an isolated test query to $\mathcal{C}_{h1}$, $\mathcal{C}_{h1}$ flips the coin $b \in \{0, 1\}$ if $b = 1$, returns the session key sk to $\mathcal{A}_1$. Otherwise a random string is returned. Moreover, this query evaluates the semantic security of sk. The adversary $\mathcal{A}_1$ generates b^* as the assumption of the value of b in the test query. In addition to that $\mathrm{Adv}(\mathcal{A}_1) = |\Pr[b^* = b] - 1/2|$ is the probability for $\mathcal{A}_1$ to correctly predict the value of b. In this game, adversary $\mathcal{A}_1$ cannot extract the private key of ID_u at any phase. Furthermore, PK_u cannot be replaced by $\mathcal{A}_1$ before the challenger phase. However, adversary $\mathcal{A}_1$ can extracts the partial private key at some phases.

Game 2

This game entails two participants, the challenger $\mathcal{C}_{h2}$ and the super Type 2 adversary $\mathcal{A}_2$, and the following are different steps of interaction.

- **Setup:** As in game one, the challenger $\mathcal{C}_{h2}$ employs the setup algorithm and produces both the master key msk and system parameters $params$. Then, the challenger dispatches parameters $params$ and master key msk to the adversary $\mathcal{A}_2$.
- **Query:** The adversary $\mathcal{A}_2$ does the following oracle queries according to his/her choice. Create-user (ID_u), Extract-Private-Key (ID_u), Request-Public-Key (ID_u), Send (Θ_u^k, M), Reveal (Θ_u^k, M), Corrupt (ID_u) and Test (Θ_u^k) query. Note that the challenger $\mathcal{C}_{h2}$ replies the query as in game 1. The adversary can extracts the d_u itself as it owns the master key msk. Nonetheless, the adversary $\mathcal{A}_2$ is unable to make public-key replacement query.

In [32], the author simulated the interaction of two entities and demonstrated that it is existentially unforgeable against two types of super adversaries, super Type $\mathcal{A}_1$ and $\mathcal{A}_2$ adversaries. Regarding the key agreement features without authentication attribute [33], the following queries can be made by the adversary, Send, Reveal, Corrupt, and Test query. Comprehensive requirements for extra security of mutual authentication and key exchange protocol can be found in [33–35]. The adversary $\mathcal{A}_2$ generates b^* as the assumption of the value of b in the test query. In addition to that $\mathrm{Adv}(\mathcal{A}_2) = |\Pr[b^* = b] - 1/2|$ is the probability for $\mathcal{A}_2$ to correctly predict the value of b. In this game, adversary $\mathcal{A}_2$ cannot make extract partial private as well as replace public key request on the challenged identity ID_U at any phase.

4 Proposed Protocol

In this part, the proposed protocol of certificateless authentication and consensus for blockchain-based smart grid is presented in two phases. The first one ensures mutual authentication and key agreement between the smart meter and collector node. The second one ensures consensus in blockchain and authentication from the collector node to other nodes in the blockchain.

4.1 Certificateless Mutual Authentication and Key Agreement Scheme

In phase one, we utilized the signature in [32] to design pairing free mutual authentication and key agreement protocol between the smart meter and collector node. Furthermore, it is explained in three phases: Initialization, Registration, and Authentication.

Initialization

1. KGC selects G in ECC Group of order q, the value P is a generator of G, and the E/F_P is an ECC of finite field F with order P.
2. KGC chooses a master secret $x \in Z_q^*$, and generates system public key $P_{pub} = xP$.
3. KGC selects hash functions: $H_i : \{0,1\}^* \to Z_q^*$ $i = \{1,2,3,4,5\}$.
4. KGC outputs $params = (F_p, E/F_p, G, q, P, P_{pub}, H_i)$ and keeps x secret.

Registration. In this phase, each user/entity u gets its credentials via a secure channel as follows:

1. Entity u sends its identity ID_u to KGC through a reliable medium.
2. On inputting $params$, ID_u, KGC chooses $\gamma_u \in Z_q^*$ at random, and computes
   $Y_u = \gamma_u P$.
   $h_1 = H_1(ID_u, Y_u, P, P_{pub})$.
   $d_u = \gamma_u + h_1 x \pmod q$.
3. Returns d_u to entity ID_u as its partial private key.

4. Entity u chooses $g_u \in Z_q^*$ as the secret value, then the full private key is $PR_u = (d_u, g_u)$.
5. Computes $G_u = g_u P$, $PK_u = (G_u, Y_u)$ which is the entity ID_u's public key.

Authentication

To establish a shared session key between E_m and E_n entities, both do the following steps.

- $step1$: E_m sends to E_n message$_1$ $\{ID_m, R_m, t_m, \beta_m, r\}$
  The Entity E_m that has the secret value g_m and public key $PK_m = \{G_m, Y_m\}$, selects $k_m \in Z_q^*$ and sets time stamp t_m. The entity E_m computes $R_m = k_m g_m G_n$, $\beta_m = k_m P$, $h_2 = H_2(ID_m, R_m, \beta_m, t_m, PK_m, P_{pub})$ and $h_3 = H_3(ID_m, R_m, \beta_m, t_m, PK_m, P_{pub}, h_2)$ then after computes $r = k_m^{-1}(h_2 g_m + h_3 d_m) \bmod q$, at the end, entity E_m sends message$_1$ $\{ID_m, R_m, t_m, \beta_m, r\}$ to E_n through a public channel.
- $Step2$: E_n sends to E_m message$_2$ $\{ID_n, R_n, h_n\}$
  Upon receiving message$_1$, E_n checks t_m freshness, if not recent, terminates otherwise computes $h_2 = H_2(ID_m, R_m, \beta_m, t_m, PK_m, P_{pub})$, and $h_3 = H_3(ID_m, R_m, \beta_m, t_m, PK_m, P_{pub}, h_2)$ then verifies if the equation $r\beta_m = h_2 G_m + h_3(Y_m + h_1 P_{pub})$ holds, if not abort. The entity E_n selects $k_n \in Z_q^*$, sets time stamp t_n, computes $R_n = k_n g_n G_m$, $sk_n = H_4(k_n R_m)$, $Z_n = (h_2 g_n + h_3 d_n)\beta_m$. At the end, the entity E_n computes $h_n = H_5(ID_n, R_n, Z_n, sk_n, t_n)$ then sends message$_2$ $\{ID_n, R_n, h_n\}$ to entity E_m.
- $Step3$: After receiving message$_2$, entity E_m computes $Z_m = (h_2 G_n + h_3(Y_n + h_1 P_{pub}))k_m$, and $sk_m = H_4(k_m R_n)$, if $h_n = H_5(ID_n, R_n, Z_m, sk_m, t_n)$, both E_n and E_m have the same consent to the shared session key $sk_n = sk_m = sk$.

Correctness. Below is the proof of correctness of signature verification, if it is valid, entity E_n ensures that the message$_1$ is not changed and it is from entity E_m with identity ID_m and public key PK_m.

$$
\begin{aligned}
r\beta_m &= k_m^{-1}(h_2 g_m + h_3 d_m)\beta_m \\
&= k_m^{-1}(h_2 g_m + h_3 d_m)k_m P \\
&= (h_2 g_m + h_3 d_m)P \\
&= (h_2 g_m P + h_3 d_m P) \\
&= h_2 G_m + h_3(\gamma_m + h_1 x)P \\
&= h_2 G_m + h_3(\gamma_m P + h_1 x P) \\
&= h_2 G_m + h_3(Y_m + h_1 P_{pub})
\end{aligned}
$$

The following equation prove the correctness of the shared session key $sk_n = sk_m = sk$.

$$
\begin{aligned}
sk_n &= H_4(k_n R_m) \\
&= H_4(k_n k_m g_m G_n) \\
&= H_4(k_n k_m g_m g_n P) \\
&= H_4(k_m k_n g_n g_m P) \\
&= H_4(k_m k_n g_n G_m) \\
&= H_4(k_m R_n) \\
&= sk_m
\end{aligned}
$$

4.2 Blockchain Nodes Authentication and Consensus

In phase 2, we guaranteed the authentication from the collector node to other blockchain nodes. Moreover, we have ensured consensus in the blockchain nodes to keep their ledgers consistent.

Certificateless Signature for IoT. We adopted the signature in [32] and enabled blockchain nodes to verify the authenticity of the collector node that assembled data and broadcasted it to the blockchain.

Consensus in Blockchain Nodes. Blockchain nodes need an authorization message to use smart meter data. Otherwise, they cannot use it. Therefore, smart meter forwards a consent message to node C. When node C obtains the consensus message, it relays the message to the blockchain nodes. Smart meter employs the computed shared session key sk and computes $M_e = ENC_{sk}(M)$ to encrypt the consent message then dispatches it to node C. Furthermore, node C receives the encrypted consent message and utilizes sk to decrypt it, $M = DEC_{sk}(M_e)$. Hence, it obtains the consensus message M that permits the blockchain node to use smart meter data. Then, node C deletes sk. Furthermore, node C signs the consensus message and relays it to blockchain nodes. Thus, any node can verify the originality of the message.

5   Security Analysis

In this section, we conduct a formal security analysis and an informal security properties discussion to demonstrate and prove the security of our protocol.

5.1 Formal Analysis

In this section, we provided the security proof of the proposed mutual authentication and key agreement scheme under the random oracle model (ROM) [36]. Furthermore, we demonstrate that it complies with the security requirements introduced in Sect. 3.4. Besides, we followed the method in [32,34] to construct our security proof.

Entity m to Entity n Authentication. In Theorem 1, we show that under the ECDL problem, the communication between entity m and entity n cannot be impersonated by $\mathcal{A}_i \in \{i = 1, 2\}$.

Theorem 1. *Suppose $\mathcal{A}_i$ is a super adversary of probabilistic polynomial time and can snap the authentication for entity m to entity n. The advantage ε is non-negligible. There exists an algorithm $\mathcal{C}_{h1}$ to solve the elliptic curve discrete logarithm problem. The adversary can make at most q_n queries to the oracle (Θ_n^i) of the entity n, and q_m queries to the oracle (Θ_m^j) of the entity m, and q_{H_i} queries on H_i hash oracle where $i \in \{1, 2, 3, 4, 5\}$.*

Proof. Assume that A_i has a non-negligible advantage ε to break the authentication of entity m to entity n while polynomial time is given under adaptive chosen message and identity attacks. Taking reference to Lemma 1 from the work of Choon and Chen [37], for a chosen target identity, the entity m to entity n authentication of the proposed protocol is possessed by ε while polynomial time is given.

Lemma 1. *The proposed protocol can't be snapped under the ECDLP assumption by the super Type 1 adversary $\mathcal{A}_1$ in random oracle model.*

Lemma 2. *In the random oracle model, the suggested protocol is secure against super Type 2 adversary $\mathcal{A}_2$ under ECDLP hard problem.*

Proof. The algorithm $\mathcal{C}_{h2}$ replies to $\mathcal{A}_2$ adversary queries. We will demonstrate how $\mathcal{C}_{h2}$ uses the below interaction to solve random instances $(P, Q = \eta P)$ of ECDLP. Hence, Lemma 2 is proved.

This proof is left off due to page limitations. A complete version can be provided by the author on demand.

Key Agreement. Theorem 2 demonstrates that the proposed protocol guarantees the provision of key agreement security under the CDH assumption. This proof is left off due to page limitations. A complete version can be provided by the author on demand.

Theorem 2. *We assume that the Adversary $\mathcal{A}_i$ where $\{i = 1, 2\}$ has the ability to guess the correct value of b in test query with non-negligible probability advantage ε. Then, there exists a challenger $\mathcal{C}_{h1}$ algorithm to solve the CDH problem. The adversary is permitted to make at most q_n queries to the oracle Θ_n^i of the entity E_n, q_m queries to the oracle Θ_m^j of the entity E_m, and q_{H_i} queries on H_i oracle $\forall i \in \{1, 2, \ldots, 5\}$.*

6   Comparison

In this part, we describe the difference between the suggested protocol and other protocols apropos of security properties, computation cost, and communication cost.

Table 1. Security features comparison among different authentication and key agreement schemes in smart grid.

Features	[5]	[14]	[17]	[18]	[22]	[23]	[24]	Ours
Replay attack resistance	Y	N	Y	Y	Y	Y	Y	Y
Provides perfect forward secrecy	N	Y	N	N	N	Y	Y	Y
Rapid detection of illegal message	Y	N	Y	Y	N	N	Y	Y
Withstand key escrow issue	N	Y	N	N	N	Y	Y	Y
Message integrity	Y	Y	Y	Y	Y	N	Y	Y
Immutability	N	N	N	N	N	N	N	Y
Consensus	N	N	N	N	N	N	N	Y
Decentralization	N	N	N	N	N	N	N	Y
Verifiability	N	N	N	N	N	N	N	Y

6.1 Security Properties Comparison

Table 1 demonstrates the contrast between the proposed protocol with the other protocols about their functional features. Note that, **Y:** Denotes that the protocol implements the mentioned security features. **N:** Denotes that the protocol does not implement the mentioned security features.

6.2 Performance Analysis

This section focuses on the efficiency of the proposed protocol compared with other existing protocols in terms of communication and computational costs. The analysis we made follows the experiment done in [6,38], and Table 2 shows the output of the experiment. To achieve the same security standard as 1024 bits RSA algorithm, they employed supersingular elliptic curve cryptography $y^2 = x^3 + 1$ in their experiment. An operating system of Windows over 32-bit Intel®, a processor of 624 MHz, and a RAM of 128 MB were utilized to simulate the client/smart meter. On the other hand, Windows XP, 3.0 GHz of Intel®PIV processor, 512 MB of memory was deployed to simulate the server/node C. In this analysis, we disregarded operations with trivial computation costs, such as addition operations for ECC points and operations of normal hash functions. We have considered T_M operation that stands for the time to execute point multiplication, and T_{PC} the time to execute pairing computation. The following Table 2 illustrates the needed time to execute cryptographic operations.

Table 2. Time to execute cryptographic operations (ms).

Notations	Computation cost
T_{PC}	96.35
T_M	30.67

Computation Costs. In our performance analysis, we focus on the computation cost of smart meter since it has a limited resource. As shown in Table 3 and Fig. 3, we compared our scheme with other existing schemes. The computational cost for the protocol of Elkhalil et al. [19] $6T_M * 30.67 \simeq 184.02$. The computational cost for the protocol of Li et al. [20] equals to $2T_M * 30.67 + 6T_{PC} * 96.35 \simeq 639.44$. The computational cost for the protocol of Ahene et al. [21] equals to $5T_M * 30.67 + 2T_{PC} * 96.35 \simeq 346.05$. The computation cost for the protocol of Chen et al. [24] $4T_M * 30.67 + 1T_{PC}96.35 \simeq 219.03$. The computational cost for the protocol of Wu et al. [25] $4T_M * 30.67 + 2T_{PC} * 96.35 \simeq 315.38$ Whereas the computational cost of the proposed protocol equals to $5T_M * 30.67 \simeq 153.35$. As shown in Table 3 and Fig. 3, our protocol is efficient in terms of computational cost compared to the other related protocols.

Table 3. Computational costs comparison (ms).

Protocols	Computational costs
Elkhalil et al. [19]	$6T_M \simeq 184.02$
Li et al. [20]	$2T_M + 6T_{PC} \simeq 639.44$
Ahene et al. [21]	$5T_M + 2T_{PC} \simeq 346.05$
Chen et al. [24]	$4T_M + 1T_{PC} \simeq 219.03$
Wu et al. [25]	$6T_M + 2T_{PC} \simeq 376.72$
Ours	$5T_M \simeq 153.35$

Communication Costs. In this part, we compared the communication cost of our protocol with other related protocols, see Table 4. Different element has different size, the size of identity, element in G, hash function, timestamp, and modulus of the order are 32 bits, 320 bits, 160 bits, 32 bits, and 160 bits, respectively.

Table 4. Comparative communication costs (bits).

Protocols	Communication costs	Number of messages
[4]	1664	2
[22]	1760	2
[23]	1697	2
[24]	1890	3
[25]	2688	2
Ours	1376	2

The communication cost for the authentication phase in our protocol is calculated as follows. The cost for identities $32 * 2 = 64$ bits, the cost for elements

in G $320 * 3 = 960$ bits, the cost for hash function $160 * 1 = 160$ bits, the
cost for timestamp $32 * 1 = 32$ bits, the cost for order $160 * 1 = 160$ bits. The
overall communication cost for authentication phase of the proposed protocol is:
$64 + 960 + 160 + 32 + 160 = 1376$ bits. Furthermore, the protocol in [4] requires
1664 bits. The protocol in [22] requires 1760 bits of communication cost, the
protocol in [23] requires 1697 bits as communication cost and 1890 bits in [24].
Additionally, the protocol in [25] requires 2688 bits. The comparative communication cost in Table 4 shows that our protocol has less communication overhead
hence, is efficient for bandwidth usage.

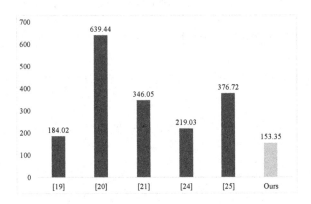

Fig. 3. Computational costs comparison.

7 Conclusion

Mutual authentication is an essential need for smart grid security. The protocol
of certificateless authentication and consensus for blockchain-based smart grid is
designed, a shared key is computed before the start of the conversation and data
exchange. Furthermore, mutual authentication is guaranteed during the session
key exchange. In addition, the integration of the blockchain and signature in
our protocol brought enhanced security features such as immutability, consensus, and verification. Moreover, the proposed protocol puts less computational
overhead on the smart meter, and it has a better communication overhead,
which optimizes the bandwidth. We used ROM to prove that our protocol is
secure and attains the security requirement for the mutual authentication protocol. The future work in this area will be anonymous mutual authentication
for blockchain-based smart grids. Actually, a smart meter in SG does a regular
collection and report of information from the customer side to SP. During the
exchange of information, an adversary can break the communication and disclose private customer information thus it is fundamentally necessary to protect
customer privacy.

Acknowledgment. This work is supported by the Sichuan Science and Technology
Program (grant no. 2021YFG0157).

References

1. Ghasempour, A.: Internet of things in smart grid: architecture, applications, services, key technologies, and challenges. Inventions 4(1), 22 (2019)
2. Komninos, N., Philippou, E., Pitsillides, A.: Survey in smart grid and smart home security: issues, challenges and countermeasures. IEEE Commun. Surv. Tutor. 16(4), 1933–1954 (2014)
3. Li, W., Li, R., Wu, K., Cheng, R., Su, L., Cui, W.: Design and implementation of an SM2-based security authentication scheme with the key agreement for smart grid communications. IEEE Access 6, 71194–71207 (2018)
4. Li, X., et al.: A provably secure and anonymous message authentication scheme for smart grids. J. Parallel Distrib. Comput. 132, 242–249 (2019)
5. Mahmood, K., Chaudhry, S.A., Naqvi, H., Shon, T., Ahmad, H.F.: A lightweight message authentication scheme for smart grid communications in power sector. Comput. Electr. Eng. 52, 114–124 (2016)
6. Mwitende, G., Ye, Y., Ali, I., Li, F.: Certificateless authenticated key agreement for blockchain-based WBANs. J. Syst. Architect. 110, 101777 (2020)
7. Kim, T., et al.: The PKI-based device authentication system for AMI
8. Shamir, A.: Identity-based cryptosystems and signature schemes. In: Blakley, G.R., Chaum, D. (eds.) CRYPTO 1984. LNCS, vol. 196, pp. 47–53. Springer, Heidelberg (1985). https://doi.org/10.1007/3-540-39568-7_5
9. Al-Riyami, S.S., Paterson, K.G.: Certificateless public key cryptography. In: Laih, C.-S. (ed.) ASIACRYPT 2003. LNCS, vol. 2894, pp. 452–473. Springer, Heidelberg (2003). https://doi.org/10.1007/978-3-540-40061-5_29
10. Agarkar, A., Agrawal, H.: A review and vision on authentication and privacy preservation schemes in smart grid network. Secur. Priv. 2(2), e62 (2019)
11. NETL Modern Grid Strategy: Advanced metering infrastructure. US Department of Energy Office of Electricity and Energy Reliability (2008)
12. Zhou, J., Hu, R.Q., Qian, Y.: Scalable distributed communication architectures to support advanced metering infrastructure in smart grid. IEEE Trans. Parallel Distrib. Syst. 23(9), 1632–1642 (2012)
13. Winter, T.: The advantages and challenges of the blockchain for smart grids (2018)
14. He, D., Wang, H., Khan, M.K., Wang, L.: Lightweight anonymous key distribution scheme for smart grid using elliptic curve cryptography. IET Commun. 10(14), 1795–1802 (2016)
15. Sakhnini, J., Karimipour, H., Dehghantanha, A., Parizi, R.M., Srivastava, G.: Security aspects of internet of things aided smart grids: a bibliometric survey. Internet Things 14, 100111 (2019)
16. Belhadi, A., Djenouri, Y., Srivastava, G., Jolfaei, A., Lin, J.C.W.: Privacy reinforcement learning for faults detection in the smart grid. Ad Hoc Netw. 119, 102541 (2021)
17. Kaveh, M., Mosavi, M.R.: A lightweight mutual authentication for smart grid neighborhood area network communications based on physically unclonable function. IEEE Syst. J. 14(3), 4535–4544 (2020)
18. Kaveh, M., Aghapour, S., Martin, D., Mosavi, M.R.: A secure lightweight signcryption scheme for smart grid communications using reliable physically unclonable function. In: 2020 IEEE International Conference on Environment and Electrical Engineering and 2020 IEEE Industrial and Commercial Power Systems Europe (EEEIC/I&CPS Europe), pp. 1–6. IEEE (2020)

19. Elkhalil, A., Elhabob, R., Eltayieb, N., et al.: An efficient signcryption of hetero-geneous systems for internet of vehicles. J. Syst. Architect. **113**, 101885 (2021)
20. Li, F., Liu, B., Hong, J.: An efficient signcryption for data access control in cloud computing. Computing **99**(5), 465–479 (2017). https://doi.org/10.1007/s00607-017-0548-7
21. Ahene, E., Qin, Z., Adusei, A.K., Li, F.: Efficient signcryption with proxy re-encryption and its application in smart grid. IEEE Internet Things J. **6**(6), 9722–9737 (2019)
22. Mahmood, K., Chaudhry, S.A., Naqvi, H., Kumari, S., Li, X., Sangaiah, A.K.: An elliptic curve cryptography based lightweight authentication scheme for smart grid communication. Futur. Gener. Comput. Syst. **81**, 557–565 (2018)
23. Abbasinezhad-Mood, D., Nikooghadam, M.: Design and hardware implementation of a security-enhanced elliptic curve cryptography based lightweight authentication scheme for smart grid communications. Futur. Gener. Comput. Syst. **84**, 47–57 (2018)
24. Chen, Y., Martínez, J.F., Castillejo, P., López, L.: A bilinear map pairing based authentication scheme for smart grid communications: PAuth. IEEE Access **7**, 22633–22643 (2019)
25. Wu, T.Y., Lee, Y.Q., Chen, C.M., Tian, Y., Al-Nabhan, N.A.: An enhanced pairing-based authentication scheme for smart grid communications. J. Ambient Intell. Hum. Comput., 1–13 (2021)
26. Fouda, M.M., Fadlullah, Z.M., Kato, N., Lu, R., Shen, X.S.: A lightweight message authentication scheme for smart grid communications. IEEE Trans. Smart grid **2**(4), 675–685 (2011)
27. Mwitende, G., Ali, I., Eltayieb, N., Wang, B., Li, F.: Authenticated key agreement for blockchain-based WBAN. Telecommun. Syst. **74**(3), 347–365 (2020)
28. Depuru, S.S.S.R., Wang, L., Devabhaktuni, V., Gudi, N.: Smart meters for power grid-challenges, issues, advantages and status. In: 2011 IEEE/PES Power Systems Conference and Exposition, pp. 1–7. IEEE (2011)
29. Siano, P.: Demand response and smart grids-a survey. Renew. Sustain. Energy Rev. **30**, 461–478 (2014)
30. Huang, X., Susilo, W., Mu, Y., Zhang, F.: On the security of certificateless sig-nature schemes from Asiacrypt 2003. In: Desmedt, Y.G., Wang, H., Mu, Y., Li, Y. (eds.) CANS 2005. LNCS, vol. 3810, pp. 13–25. Springer, Heidelberg (2005). https://doi.org/10.1007/11599371_2
31. Huang, X., Mu, Y., Susilo, W., Wong, D.S., Wu, W.: Certificateless signature revisited. In: Pieprzyk, J., Ghodosi, H., Dawson, E. (eds.) ACISP 2007. LNCS, vol. 4586, pp. 308–322. Springer, Heidelberg (2007). https://doi.org/10.1007/978-3-540-73458-1_23
32. Du, H., Wen, Q., Zhang, S., Gao, M.: A new provably secure certificateless signature scheme for internet of things. Ad Hoc Netw. **100**, 102074 (2020)
33. Jakobsson, M., Pointcheval, D.: Mutual authentication for low-power mobile devices. In: Syverson, P. (ed.) FC 2001. LNCS, vol. 2339, pp. 178–195. Springer, Heidelberg (2002). https://doi.org/10.1007/3-540-46088-8_17
34. Hassan, A., Eltayieb, N., Elhabob, R., Li, F.: An efficient certificateless user authentication and key exchange protocol for client-server environment. J. Ambi-ent. Intell. Humaniz. Comput. **9**(6), 1713–1727 (2017). https://doi.org/10.1007/s12652-017-0622-1
35. Pointcheval, D., Stern, J.: Security arguments for digital signatures and blind sig-natures. J. Cryptol. **13**(3), 361–396 (2000)

36. Bellare, M., Rogaway, P.: Random oracles are practical: a paradigm for designing efficient protocols. In: Proceedings of the 1st ACM Conference on Computer and Communications Security, pp. 62–73 (1993)
37. Choon, J.C., Hee Cheon, J.: An identity-based signature from gap Diffie-Hellman groups. In: Desmedt, Y.G. (ed.) PKC 2003. LNCS, vol. 2567, pp. 18–30. Springer, Heidelberg (2003). https://doi.org/10.1007/3-540-36288-6_2
38. Liu, J., Zhang, Z., Chen, X., Kwak, K.S.: Certificateless remote anonymous authentication schemes for wirelessbody area networks. IEEE Trans. Parallel Distrib. Syst. **25**(2), 332–342 (2013)

Information System Security Risk Assessment Based on Entropy Weight Method - Bayesian Network

Xinjian Lv[1], Nan Shi[1], Jing Wei[2], Yuan Tian[2(✉)], Jie Li[3], and Jian Li[2]

[1] Shandong Hi-speed Construction Management Group, Jinan, Shandong, China
[2] School of Artificial Intelligence, Beijing University of Posts and Telecommunications, Beijing, China
redrainiety@bupt.edu.cn
[3] School of Computer Science, Beijing University of Posts and Telecommunications, Beijing, China

Abstract. Traditional information security risk assessment models usually rely on expert analysis to obtain prior knowledge, which leads to a greater impact on the results of security risk assessment by subjective bias. To solve this problem, we added the entropy weight method to the traditional Bayesian network-based information security risk assessment model. Entropy weight method is used to compute the weight coefficients of each risk factor involved in a risk event. Compared with traditional evaluation models, weighting risk factors during risk evaluation can effectively reduce the impact of excessive reliance on expert information, that is, excessive subjective factors, and theoretically improve the accuracy of the evaluation results. Finally, an instance of the risk assessment approach on the model is analyzed, which demonstrates the rationality and feasibility of this method.

Keywords: Information system · Risk assessment · Bayesian network · Entropy weight method

1 Introduction

The popularity of the Internet and the development of information technology have changed the traditional way of information sharing. Data transmission between different devices through the network has greatly improved the efficiency of information sharing. While it is convenient for users, it also allows cyber attacks to take advantage of. Attackers will attack the security flaws in the system, which makes information security on the Internet more and more important. In order to protect the security of computer network systems and data information, various enterprises and organizations have established many preventive measures to prevent data leakage or other security problems caused by attacks, such as setting passwords to authenticate visitors, setting up firewalls, and access control mechanism. However, these information protection and management measures are not completely reliable. There will always be security vulnerabilities, and attackers will use these vulnerabilities to attack information systems. In addition, attacks from

C. Cao et al. (Eds.): FCS 2021, CCIS 1558, pp. 152–162, 2022.
https://doi.org/10.1007/978-981-19-0523-0_10

insiders cannot be avoided. Attackers use enterprise application analysis to find vulnerabilities and use them to attack systems, which poses a huge threat to information security.

The world attaches great importance to network information security issues, especially in the military. The network security management system can be used to analyze the security of the information system. The main advantage is that the accuracy of the system information is not high. Fuzzy set theory and fuzzy logic are suitable for quantitative analysis and can deal with inaccurate selections [1]. Inaccurate parameters can be represented by fuzzy sets or fuzzy numbers for subsequent analysis. The evaluation of computer network information security is generally a matter of group decision-making. Group decision-making is a process in which multiple people participate in analysis and decision-making. During the decision-making process, the opinions of multiple experts can be gathered, and various information can be fully considered to make reasonable and feasible decisions. But compared with other methods, the overall efficiency of this method is not high. So far, researchers and staff in related fields have proposed many feasible methods to solve group decision-making problems.

Bayesian algorithm is based on a simple conditional independence assumption [2]. In Bayesian networks, each node is independent of non-child nodes in the network when the state of its parent node is determined. This attribute is very important and can reduce the number of parameters required to describe variables in calculations. Because Bayesian network reasoning does not require high integrity, accuracy, and comprehensiveness of known information, and its reasoning learning results are relatively reliable, it is widely used in fault diagnosis, risk assessment and other fields. To solve the problem of information system security, an effective network information security risk assessment of the system is an indispensable step. Information security risk assessment is the application of theoretical methods of risk assessment in information systems. It mainly includes system fault tree analysis, analytic hierarchy process and fuzzy comprehensive evaluation. Information security assessment has been used in practice. Through evaluation, you can discover the risk problems and security vulnerabilities in the information system, and analyze these problems at the same time, you can get the corresponding solutions, which is very useful for preventing the occurrence of information risks. But so far, the existing evaluation models cannot effectively avoid the influence of subjective factors on the evaluation results in the evaluation process.

2 Basic Theory

2.1 Entropy Weight Method

Definition: The system has n different states: $S_1, S_2, \ldots, S_n, P_i$ represents the probability that the system is in state S_i, H indicates the degree of order of the system, and $\sum_{i=1}^{n} P_i = 1$. The entropy function of the uncertainty of the system risk state is [3]:

$$H(P_1, P_2, \ldots, P_n) = -k \sum_{i=1}^{n} l_i ln P_i \tag{1}$$

When entropy meets the following 3 conditions:

$$H(P_1, P_2, \ldots, P_n) \le H\left(\frac{1}{n}, \ldots, \frac{1}{n}\right) \tag{2}$$

$$H(P_1, P_2, \ldots, P_n) = H(P_1, P_2, \ldots, P_n, 0) \tag{3}$$

$$H(AB) = H(A)H(B|A) \tag{4}$$

Then we get:

$$H(P_1, P_2, \ldots, P_n) = -\sum_{i=1}^{n} l_i ln P_i$$

The relative importance of risk factors is reflected in the value of entropy. The formula for calculating entropy is:

$$H_i = -\sum_{j=1}^{m} P_{ij} ln P_{ij} \tag{5}$$

According to the conditions in the entropy theory:

$$H(P_1, P_2, \ldots, P_n) \leq H\left(\tfrac{1}{n}, \ldots, \tfrac{1}{n}\right) \tag{6}$$

It can be seen that the smaller the value of P_i, the larger the entropy value, which indicates the data obtained by this factor If it is not comprehensive enough, it plays a smaller role in the entire evaluation system; on the contrary, the larger P_i, the smaller the entropy value, indicating that the system is more orderly and the amount of information needed to eliminate uncertainty is also less. This factor is used in the risk assessment process. The greater the role-played in. Therefore, the weight of the risk factor can be calculated according to its degree of support for the evaluation set. When P_i is equal, the entropy is maximum, $H_{max} = \ln m$. Use H_{max} to normalize the formula, and get the formula for calculating the relative importance of the risk element entropy:

$$e_i = -\tfrac{1}{\ln m} \sum_{j=1}^{m} P_{ij} ln P_{ij} \tag{7}$$

When the values of P_{ij} are equal, the maximum value of e_i is 1. When the entropy value is the largest, the risk element plays the smallest role in the information security risk assessment. At this time, the weight of the risk element can be measured by $1 - e_i$, and the calculation formula for the weight of the risk element after normalization is:

$$\phi_i = \tfrac{1-e_i}{n-\sum_{i=1}^{n} e_i} \tag{8}$$

Where $0 \leq \phi_i \leq 1$, $\sum_{i=1}^{n} \phi_i = 1$. When e_i reaches the maximum value of 1, the entropy weight is 0. The larger the P_{ij}, the smaller the entropy value and the larger the corresponding entropy weight, the more important the risk factor is for risk assessment.

2.2 Bayesian Network

Bayesian network is a probability graph model, the theoretical basis of which is Bayesian formula, which can express and analyze uncertainty knowledge through probability reasoning, and is one of the most effective theoretical models to deal with uncertainty problem so far.

Bayesian network in the network structure is a directed ringless graph (DAG), random variables are represented by nodes in the network, observable variables, hidden variables, unknown parameters or assumptions can be used as variables; When there are no directly connected edges between the two nodes, it indicates that in some cases the two nodes are independent of each other. There is a probability function between the dependent nodes, and the observation of the state of the random variable represented by the parent node of the current node is the input of the probability function, and the output is the value of the state of the random variable represented by the node. The dependency between nodes is positively correlated with the value of the probability function.

The Bayesian formula describes the relationship between the probabilities of two conditions:

$$P(A_i|B) = \frac{P(B|A_i)P(A_i)}{\sum_{j=1}^{n} P(B|A_j)P(A_j)} \tag{9}$$

In the formula, $P(A_i)$ is the prior probability of node A_i, $P(B|A_i)$ is the conditional probability of parent node B, and $P(A_i|B)$ is the posterior probability of node A_i.

3   Information Security Risk Assessment Model

3.1   Information Security Risk Assessment Model

In the information security risk assessment model, risk calculation is mainly the process of identifying, evaluating and analyzing the three elements of asset, threat and vulnerability [5]. The information security risk assessment model is shown in Fig. 1.

Fig. 1.   Information security risk assessment model.

The key elements in the model are threats, vulnerabilities, and assets, which can be described as:

$$R = f(A, T, V) \tag{10}$$

In the formula, R represents the risk value, f is a security risk calculation function. A stands for assets; T represents threats; V indicates vulnerability. The main steps to calculate the risk value are:

1) Identify and analyze the value of assets, the likelihood of threat occurrence and the severity of vulnerability;
2) The analysis results of comprehensive threat and vulnerability, the probability of a possible security incident in the information system is analyzed and calculated;
3) The analysis results of the comprehensive asset value and vulnerability, the analysis and calculation of the losses caused by the information system in the event of a security incident;
4) Combined with the probability of the above-mentioned possible security risk event and the potential loss after the occurrence, the operation results in a risk value.

Through the above theoretical algorithm, the asset impact is calculated as R_a, the threat frequency is R_t, and the vulnerability degree is R_v. The comprehensive risk value of each element is calculated according to the weight.

$$R = f(A, T, V) = k_1 R_a + k_2 R_t + k_3 R_v \tag{11}$$

In the formula, k_1, k_2, k_3 are the relative importance of each element, and $k_1 + k_2 + k_3 = 1$.

3.2 Risk Factor Analysis

Sub-indicator classifications of assets, threats, and vulnerabilities are summarized in Table 1, Table 2 and Table 3, according to the national standard GB/T 20984–2007 [6].

Because in actual security risk events, threats are usually related only to some of the risk elements and are not determined by all risk factors. Usually in the information security risk assessment work, it is necessary for experts to analyze the actual situation of the system and determine which risk factors are specific to a security risk event based on professional knowledge. This approach is practical, but relies too much on expert knowledge.

Table 1. Asset metrics classification

Category	Evaluation indicators	Evaluation factors
Asset (A)	Confidentiality Integrity Availability	Data Software Hardware Serve Personnel

Because in actual security risk events, threats are usually related only to some of the risk elements and are not determined by all risk factors. Usually in the information security risk assessment work, it is necessary for experts to analyze the actual situation

Table 2. Threat metrics classification

Category	Evaluation indicators	Evaluation factors
Threat (T)	Frequency of threats	Hardware and software failure Physical environment failure Operational error Insufficient management Malicious code Ultra vires or abuse Cyber attack Physical attack Leak Tamper Deny

Table 3. Vulnerability indicators classification

Category	Evaluation indicators	Evaluation factors
Vulnerability (V)	Severity Difficulty of being exploited	Physical environment Network structure System software Application middleware Operating system Technology management Organizational management

of the system and determine which risk factors are specific to a security risk event based on professional knowledge. This approach is practical, but relies too much on expert knowledge.

3.3 Information Security Risk Assessment Process

The information security risk assessment process is shown in Fig. 2 [7].

Identify Risk Events and Analyze Risk Factors. For risk events present in the system, a brief analysis of risk events is made in conjunction with the risk elements listed in Table 1, Table 2 and Table 3 to establish a review set of security incidents.

Analyze and Calculate the Weight of the Risk Feature. For each risk element $S = \{S_1, S_2, \ldots, S_n\}$ involved in the risk event, analyze its contribution to the information security risk assessment through the entropy weight method, and calculate the weight k of the risk element.

Build a Bayesian Network Model. First, we determine the variable nodes in the network, which generally include information security risk R and multiple risk elements,

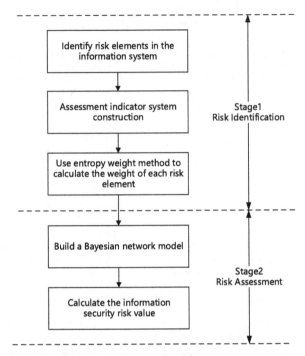

Fig. 2. The information security risk assessment process

which are independent of each other, then analyze the causal relationship between the variables to determine a topological order, and finally, according to the resulting topological order, we can determine the Bayesian network diagram, the causal relationship is represented by the directional edges in the graph. In risk assessment, security risk R is determined by risk element S, and risk elements are independent of each other, resulting in a simpler structure of bayesian network diagrams.

Determine the Conditional Probability Matrix. The conditional probability P of the network is the probability that the current node is in a state when its parent node's state observations are determined, and is the key to network reasoning. In the risk assessment, it is necessary to analyze the historical data, count the state of other variables corresponding to different levels of risk values, and calculate the conditional probability by statistical data.

Calculate the Information Security Risk Value. After constructing Bayesian network through the above steps, the information security risk value can be obtained by calculating the specific observation data according to the prior information of security events and the probability of conditions.

4 Empirical Analysis

4.1 Conditional Assumptions

Not all risks exist when risk assessments are carried out on the information systems of a large enterprise, and not all indicators are equally important. In this paper, when screening the evaluation indicators, the risk identification and simplification of the indicators, the asset risk is divided into tangible assets and data information, the threat risk is divided into vulnerability attacks and hardware and software failures, the vulnerability risk is divided into physical environment, software structure and organizational management, and the risk indicators are classified as high, middle and low [8].

Based on the selected evaluation metrics, the risk assessment model established in this article is shown in Fig. 3.

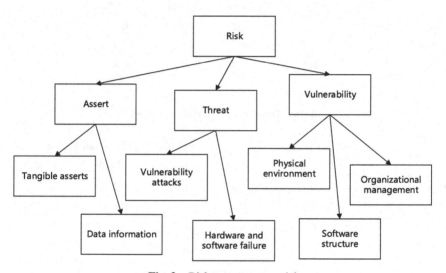

Fig. 3.   Risk assessment model

4.2 Determine the Conditional Probability Matrix

Through the statistics of historical security events and the analysis of information systems by experts, the conditional probability table is initialized. The conditional probability table is shown in Table 4, Table 5, Table 6 and Table 7.

4.3 Calculate the Risk Level

Suppose the prior information of information security risk of an information system is $\pi(R) = (0.2, 0.5, 0.3)$. Due to the evaluator's inadequate understanding of the information system, this leads to strong subjectivity of prior information. The evidence information for the child node is initialized in the same way, as shown in Table 8.

Table 4. Risk condition probability table

	Asset			Threat			Vulnerability		
	High	Middle	Low	High	Middle	Low	High	Middle	Low
High	0.8	0.1	0.1	0.7	0.2	0.1	0.8	0.1	0.1
Middle	0.2	0.6	0.2	0.2	0.7	0.1	0.3	0.6	0.1
Low	0.1	0.1	0.8	0.1	0.1	0.8	0.1	0.2	0.7

Table 5. Asset condition probability table

	Tangible assets			Data information		
	High	Middle	Low	High	Middle	Low
High	0.8	0.1	0.1	0.6	0.2	0.2
Middle	0.1	0.7	0.2	0.1	0.7	0.2
Low	0.1	0.2	0.7	0.3	0.1	0.6

Table 6. Threat condition probability table

	Vulnerability attacks			Hardware and software failure		
	High	Middle	Low	High	Middle	Low
High	0.6	0.1	0.3	0.6	0.2	0.2
Middle	0.1	0.8	0.1	0.1	0.6	0.3
Low	0.3	0.1	0.6	0.3	0.2	0.5

Table 7. Vulnerability condition probability table

	Physical environment			Software structure			Organizational management		
	High	Middle	Low	High	Middle	Low	High	Middle	Low
High	0.7	0.2	0.1	0.8	0.1	0.1	0.6	0.3	0.1
Middle	0.1	0.7	0.2	0.1	0.5	0.4	0.3	0.5	0.2
Low	0.2	0.1	0.7	0.1	0.4	0.5	0.1	0.2	0.7

Using the expert analysis method to construct the degree matrix of each risk factor, and using the entropy right method to calculate the weight, the weight vector of each risk factor can be obtained as w = (0.115, 0.223, 0.267, 0.155, 0.105, 0.056, 0.079).

Table 8. Experimental data

Serial number	1	2	3
Tangible assets	[0.1,0.5,0.4]	[0.2,0.3,0.5]	[0.4,0.5,0.1]
Data information	[0.3,0.2,0.5]	[0.1,0.3,0.6]	[0.3,0.4,0.3]
Vulnerability attacks	[0.2,0.1,0.7]	[0.3,0.1,0.6]	[0.2,0.7,0.1]
Hardware and software failure	[0.2,0.5,0.3]	[0.2,0.1,0.7]	[0.2,0.6,0.2]
Physical environment	[0.2,0.5,0.3]	[0.3,0.1,0.6]	[0.2,0.5,0.3]
Software structure	[0.1,0.1,0.8]	[0.2,0.2,0.6]	[0.1,0.7,0.2]
Organizational management	[0.4,0.4,0.2]	[0.3,0.3,0.4]	[0.4,0.4,0.2]

After initialization is completed, the information of the corresponding nodes of each risk element is updated, which triggers the network reasoning, gradually updates the probability distribution of the whole network node, and obtains the probability distribution of the parent node, that is, the final evaluation value is obtained. The simulation results are shown in Table 9.

Table 9. Simulation results

Serial number	Bel (R)
1	[0.2485, 0.3445, 0.4070]
2	[0.2659, 0.2019, 0.5322]
3	[0.2389, 0.5704, 0.1907]

4.4 Results Analysis

From the simulation result, it can be seen that when the data is not concentrated enough, the simulation results are less clear, and the probability of the evaluation results at each level is more scattered, which reflects the insufficient understanding of the security incident information. The comparison between the various sets of data shows that prior knowledge has a greater impact on the evaluation results. When the prior knowledge obtained only by expert evaluation is too subjective, it is easy to cause inaccurate inference results due to insufficient information. However, the use of entropy method in the risk assessment process fully considers the importance of each risk factor, which also makes the assessment result more reasonable. In addition, when the dynamic Bayesian network is used for evaluation, the evaluation results of the previous stage will affect the evaluation of the latter stage, and the model has the ability to accumulate information in the time dimension. In this way, the reliability of the information and evidence used in model evaluation continues to increase, and the inference results will be more reasonable and accurate.

5 Concluding Remarks

This paper briefly analyzes the process of information security risk assessment and the classification of risk elements. And based on the Bayesian network risk assessment method, we use the entropy method to provide additional information for risk assessment. Traditional information security risk assessment usually only relies on expert analysis to obtain prior knowledge, which is highly subjective. The evaluation results are greatly affected by subjective bias. Moreover, in the risk assessment process, the importance of each risk factor was not considered, and all risk factors were treated equally, which also led to a certain degree of inaccuracy in the evaluation results. To solve this problem, we use the entropy method to analyze the risk factors to obtain the weight coefficient, which can effectively reduce the impact of subjective deviation. Finally, an instance of the risk assessment approach on the model is analyzed, which demonstrates the rationality and feasibility of this method.

Acknowledgements. This work was supported by the National Natural Science Foundation of China under Grant 61472048. We also would like to thank the anonymous reviewers for their detailed review and valuable comments, which have enhanced the quality of this paper.

References

1. Zhang, X., Liu, J., Zhang, Z., Liang, H.: dynamic analysis of flight operation risk based on improved random set bayesian network. J. Wuhan Univ. Technol.(Transportation Science & Engineering) **05**, 926–929+936 (2019)
2. Dong, X., Du, J.: A risk assessment model based on evidence combination and Bayesian network reasoning. Syst. Eng.-Theory Prac. **39**(8), 2170–2178 (2019)
3. Zeng, X., et al.: Risk assessment of urban gas pipeline based on AHP and entropy weight method. J. Saf. Sci. Technol. **17**(05), 130–135 (2021)
4. Li, X.: Research on network security evaluation model based on Bayesian algorithm. Electron. Des. Eng. **29**(05), 154–158+163 (2021)
5. Xiong, W., Liu, X.: Research on computer information system evaluation standards and safety management methods. Electron. Technol. Softw. Eng. **05**, 241–242 (2021)
6. GB/T 20984–2007: Information security technology-Risk assessment specification for information security (2007)
7. Mao, Z., Mei, H., Xiao, Y., Huang, Y.: Risk assessment of smart city information security based on bayesian network. J. Mod. Inf. **40**(05), 19–26+40 (2020)
8. Guo, X.: Information Security Risk Assessment Manual vol. 1, pp. 36–37. Mechanical Industry Press, Beijing (2017)

Survey of 3D Printer Security Offensive and Defensive

Jiayuan Zhang[1,2,3], Mengyue Feng[2,3], Yuhang Huang[2,3], Tao Feng[1(✉)], Wenjie Wang[3], He Wang[4], and Han Zhang[1]

[1] Lanzhou University of Technology, Lanzhou, China
`fengt@lut.cn`
[2] National Computer Network Intrusion Protection Center, Beijing, China
[3] University of Chinese Academy of Sciences, Beijing, China
[4] Xidian University, Xi'an, China

Abstract. As a new manufacturing technology, additive manufacturing (AM, or 3D printing) is increasingly used in the production of various parts. However, with the popularization and application of 3D printers, there are also various security issues, which have seriously affected the security application of 3D printers. This article conducts an in-depth investigation and analysis on the safety of 3D printers. Firstly, it sorted out and analyzed the existing 3D printers security research related work; secondly, based on the attacker's intention as the starting point, the attack was classified and three types of attacks were summarized: theft of technical data, AM sabotage, illegal part manufacturing; then, starting from the 3D printers security framework and attack detection technology, the defense technology was analyzed and summarized; finally, the problems and challenges in this field were pointed out, and the future research direction and trend were prospected.

Keywords: Additive manufacturing · 3D printing · AM security

1 Introduction

As the application of 3D printers becomes more and more popular, more and more security issues have emerged in the field of 3D printers. At present, the attacker can even modify the products printed by the printer and restore the print job based on the residual data of the printer, so can obtain confidential technical data, which in turn brings huge losses to related enterprises. This article has extensively collected and investigated the literature on the safety of 3D printers from January 2010 to August 2021. These documents come from journals indexed in domestic and foreign databases such as IEEE Xplore, ACM Digital Library, SpringerLink, and CNKI. As well as papers included in top international security conferences (IEEE S&P, USENIX Security, CCS, NDSS, etc.). The distribution of the number of existing research work documents is shown in Fig. 1. It can be seen that the number of results in the past four years

© Springer Nature Singapore Pte Ltd. 2022
C. Cao et al. (Eds.): FCS 2021, CCIS 1558, pp. 163–178, 2022.
https://doi.org/10.1007/978-981-19-0523-0_11

from 2018 to 2021 accounted for a huge proportion, and the number of results after 2020 has increased sharply. Therefore, based on these documents, it is of great practical significance to analyze and summarize the research status and direction of 3D printer security. At the same time, the security of 3D printers will also be a direction worthy of long-term research in the future.

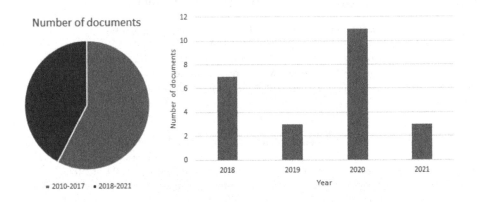

Fig. 1. Statistics of the number of 3D printers vulnerabilities over the years.

The main work and contributions of this paper are as follows:

1. Systematically combed and studied 3D printers, analyzed the safety status of 3D printers, and pointed out research hot-spots and difficulties.
2. At present, many articles have studied the attacks of 3D printers, but did not properly classify the wide variety of attacks. Starting from the attacker's intention, this article summarizes and analyzes the 3D printers attacks from three aspects: theft of technical data, sabotage attacks, and the illegal part manufacturing.
3. The security framework and attack detection technology of 3D printers in recent years were analyzed and summarized.
4. Summarized the current six major issues based on the 3D printer security field, and looked forward to the future development.

2   3D Printers Attacks

As 3D printing technology begins to surpass the speed of traditional manufacturing, malicious attackers are increasingly seeking to use this widely accessible platform to produce illegal tools for criminal activities. Network security is a key issue for 3D printers, because 3D printers rely on digital files and network connections.

This cyber-physical characteristic of the 3D printing process makes the system vulnerable to a series of unique attacks, such as side-channel attacks and attacks against STL files. However, whether an achievable operation poses a threat depends on the attacker's goals and objectives, and these goals and objectives may vary significantly in different environments. For example, an operation may be useful to counterfeiters but not useful to saboteurs. Therefore, threats come from the intersection of the achievable attack effect, the specific counter target and the attacker's intention.

Finally, we refer to the AM system attack framework proposed by LMG Graves et al. [15] of the attack target and purpose, and they determine the type of security threats from the attacker's intention as: stealing technical data, sabotage attack And illegal object manufacturing. We will analyze 3D printers attacks from these three AM security threat categories.

2.1 Theft of Technical Data

Technical data theft is the unauthorized acquisition and use of intellectual property (IP). For an attacker, IP can be the most profitable target because it forms the basis for an organization's competitive advantage. Stealing IP from a 3D printers is different from the IP of other manufacturing systems. Because, with regard to 3D printers, IP may include 3D object models, physical properties (especially functional components) and AM process specifications required by the objects [43], as well as manufacturing process specifications, which are equivalent to intellectual property rights. Zhengxiong Li et al. [22] also discussed physical watermarking technology as a means of protecting intellectual property in the additive manufacturing environment.

In addition, infringements may include the production of products beyond the original authorization or counterfeit products. Theft of technical data can also be a preparatory step for a sabotage attack. The AM deliberate sabotage attack can have several targets, which can be completed individually or in combination. Some research work on theft of technical data of 3D printers is shown in Table 1 below, in which the attack methods and effects are summarized.

Under the above circumstances, unauthorized use of relevant part of the production data is usually referred to as intellectual property (IP) theft. However, not all technical data parameters necessary for the production of high-quality products are protected by the current national intellectual property law. In the discussion of this article, technical data theft refers to the legally protectable IP and the information necessary to generate process parameters.

So far, S Belikovetsky and others have used spear phishing attacks to modify the STL file design. DO, Martini [4], and Choo [12], etc. used network sessions in a 3D printers to hijack and remotely manipulate the printer and leak sensitive data, allowing anyone on the same network to steal the model. In addition, the unique properties of 3D printing have led to other attacks. DB Miller et al. [28] demonstrated the successful retrieval and extraction of data from a specific AM device, and the data extracted from the device does contain information about the operation of the printer.

Table 1. Comparison of data theft attack methods

Paper	Methods	Describe	Effect
[4]	Malicious modification of STL files using software	Use spear phishing attack to maliciously modify the STL file and introduce the attack into G-code	Attack printing design documents to reduce the fatigue life of functional components
[12]	Remote control printer	Hijacking remote printer using network session	Manipulate the printer to disclose sensitive data
[27]	Extract data from device	Extract data from a specific 3D printers device	Retrieve the printer device and extract the remaining data information
[34]	Side-channel attack	Attack the 3D printers with the built-in sensor side-channel of the Smartphone	Steal information and infer the operation of the printer
[1, 11, 32]	Side-channel attack	The attack model is composed of digital signal processing, machine learning and context based post-processing	Refactoring G code to steal information and rebuild print objects
[9]	Side-channel attack	Change the G/M code by secretly modifying the compiler	Control printing parameters, disclose IP information, and generate printing objects

Another type of attack that exploits the features of 3D printers is to steal technical data through side-channel attacks. Song et al. [34] used the sound and magnetism of the smartphone's sensor to conduct an IP side-channel attack.

In addition to electromagnetics, thermal imaging and acoustics are the more common ways of side-channel attacks for 3D printing. In terms of thermal imaging, the literature [1] proved that thermal emission can be used as one of the side-channels to monitor the leakage of network data from 3D printers. This is an example of a physical to network domain attack, where information collected from the physical domain can be used to reveal information about the network domain.

In addition to the above, SR Chhetri et al. [9] also proposed a new attack concept, by modifying the compiler to generate G/M code, thereby controlling the parameters to leak the information of the 3D printers, while still producing the required objects, thereby hiding the real attacker. Their work proves the feasibility of using the changed tool chain to attack, which can cause huge economic losses to the manufacturing industry.

To sum up, in addition to the traditional vulnerabilities, attacks on 3D printers aimed at stealing technical vulnerabilities also exploit the physical properties of 3D printers, such as using acoustic, thermodynamic, electromagnetic and other side-channel attacks to collect data from the device. Among them, side-channel attacks do not need to directly invade and destroy 3D printers. In recent years, quite a lot of research has focused on this. However, this attack method also has certain limitations. For example, most of them are aimed at specific 3D printers and have certain requirements for sensor placement. In view of the limitations of side-channel attacks, methods such as increasing noise can be adopted to defend and protect Information security of 3D printers.

2.2   AM Sabotage

The most common manifestation of sabotage attacks is to reduce the quality of manufactured parts in the process of manipulating the 3D printers system, or to cause damage to the 3D printers system itself or its surrounding environment. Most research on the safety of 3D printers falls into this category, because the unique properties of 3D printers and 3D printed objects open up more possibilities, among which inserting gaps in printed objects is a unique attack of 3D printers. This article summarizes the attack methods of destroying 3D printers. As shown in Table 2, the common angles of sabotage attack include changing printing parameters, introducing voids, handling raw materials, and destroying the physical environment.

Table 2. Summary of sabotage attack methods.

Destruction angle	Already working
Change printing parameters	[4, 14, 29, 33, 36, 38, 41, 47, 49]
Introduce voids	[37]
Raw material handling	[47, 49]
Destroy the physical environment	[14, 38, 46, 47]

As the discussion of C. Xiao [41] and the experiment of L. Sturm [36] proved, manufactured parts can be destroyed by modifying their external shape and size, thereby affecting their quality and function. This is by modifying the object specification file or destroying The manufacturing process is realized by the network infrastructure. For example, malicious firmware can manipulate a 3D printers to implement malicious code to change the thickness of printing layer [29].

SE Zeltmann et al. [49] outlined that Attackers can change the printing direction to make objects have internal defects. L. Sturm et al. [37] also showed that introducing voids in the manufactured object or replacing the part of the manufactured object with different materials [49] will reduce the physical properties of the object; this can also change the weight and weight distribution of the object [47]. In addition, the ability to manipulate some of these parameters to destroy the quality of 3D printed parts has been experimentally proven, such as modifying the external shape [45] or combining contaminant materials [49].

S Belikovetsky et al. [4] proposed a new attack method to prove the effectiveness of reducing the fatigue life of functional components, opened up a new category of damage attacks (accelerated fatigue), and identified a new system methods for such attacks involving am options, and demonstrate the development and verification of AM specific malicious manipulation methods.

In addition, parameter attacks in the printing process can also include scanning strategy, heat source speed, AM targeting, power supply manipulation [44] and supply chain attacks [46]. The state estimation attack in the study by A. Slaughter et al. involves manipulating infrared (IR) thermal imaging sensor data. In an AM system using an IR feedback control loop, manipulating IR sensor data can be used to influence manufacturing process parameters and ultimately lead to a decrease in part quality [33]. The destruction of AM targeted functional components is aimed at reducing the mechanical strength of parts or reducing their fatigue life. The scope of sabotage attacks includes not only AM equipment, but also damage to the surrounding environment. As the Stuxnet [14] and Aurora experiments [38] proved, cyber-physical attacks that force equipment to operate outside of its designated operating range can cause physical damage. This cyber-physical attack that uses network components to control physical processes is suitable for 3D printers. Attacks that damage the 3D printing process room may also release harmful substances into the environment.

In the process of multi-material 3D printing, replacing the original operation with incorrect materials is also a feasible attack [49]. The difference between the original material and the contaminated material will affect the mechanical properties of the produced parts. The literature [47] shows that in the process of 3D printing, foreign matter can be embedded in the printed object, which causes the entire system to be contaminated. In addition, supply chain attacks also include raw material operations, such as changing the chemical composition or geometric characteristics of powders. Although raw material handling can have a direct impact on quality, they cannot be used to target specific parts [47].

The literature [14,38] shows that in the process of metal 3D printing, the mechanical parts of the 3D printing system (electron microscope, powder processing equipment, sealing and recoating system, etc.) can be excessively worn through attack scanning, thereby affecting the life of the parts. In extreme cases, it can even cause irreparable damage. At the same time, it should also be noted that in the case of using metal for 3D printing, damage to the process room may cause explosion or implosion, which will subsequently damage the manufacturing equipment environment and may cause fire [46,47]. The slow leakage of metal powder is more likely to be the result of damage to the process chamber, but implosion caused by a special attack cannot be ruled out. In addition, Mark Yampolskiy et al. [47] introduced the types of elements in the additive manufacturing workflow that can be successfully attacked and the operations that the destroyed elements can perform, as well as the weapons-like effects produced by these operations.

In summary, quite a lot of research has focused on sabotage, and sabotage attacks can have many serious consequences. Among these influences, the most obvious is the influence of quality control process on the production site, production equipment or parts acceptance. In addition, in places other than manufacturing, systems that use damaged components may also be severely affected. In addition to physical damage, destructive attacks may also affect production efficiency and the cost of each part, because the cost may be affected by parameters such as material consumption, average production time per part, and part acceptance rate. Although the impact of sabotage attacks is not the focus of this classification, it reflects the motivation of the attacker. Economically motivated attacks may focus on cost, efficiency, and acceptance rate, while military or strategic attacks may target manufacturing availability. The research of sabotage attacks on 3D printers should not only analyze the means of attack technology, but also analyze the impact of sabotage attacks more comprehensively, which involves a wider range of security, strategy, and risk assessment fields.

2.3 Illegal Part Manufacturing

Illegal component manufacturing is the creation and production of products that are prohibited by law. Different from the other two intentions mentioned above, considering the attacks of external attackers on end users, the manufacture of illegal items is not an attack in the traditional sense, but it is still an important factor that printer manufacturers need to consider. The manufacture of illegal objects happens when the attacker has the blueprint of the potentially illegal object and the necessary manufacturing equipment. Now it is becoming easier for private owners to obtain high-quality 3D printing equipment, and STL/AMF/3MF blueprint files for 3D printing are widely available.

There are several articles that discuss the abuse of components of firearms and explosive devices by 3D printers used to manufacture illegal items [35, 39]. In addition to discussing legal aspects [20, 26, 35], the research literature largely ignores the safety issues of illegal goods manufacturing. For example, with the development of 3D modeling and printing technology, 3D masks have become a more effective method of attacking face recognition systems. The literature [19] outlines the most advanced three-dimensional mask spoofing and anti-spoofing methods. Attackers can use 3D printing technology to print various types of masks and facial disguise for identity forgery, which is an advanced photo attack.

Illegal parts manufacturing is not entirely suitable for the current attack and target analysis framework. With the rapid development and widespread adoption of AM, people worry about using this technology for illegal parts manufacturing. These concerns include the manufacture of undetectable guns and nuclear components [23] and the use of 3D printing to circumvent export control regulations and the Nuclear Non-Proliferation Treaty [2]. Although the use of traditional manufacturing can achieve illegal parts manufacturing, AM can significantly simplify this process [17].

Some researchers have also investigated and proposed measures that can be used to prevent the manufacture of illegal parts. These measures include the use of image database systems to identify authorized parts manufacturing and stop unauthorized printing [21], use surface texture changes to track objects to specific printers [22], and design file watermarks [3, 7]. Once preventive measures are implemented, the attack analysis framework can be extended to identify and resolve illegal parts manufacturing targets.

3   3D Printers Security Defense Methods

Through investigating the existing research work, according to the research on attack model, we discuss the defense means and measures in the security field of 3D printers from two defense dimensions: generalized security framework, analyzing attack detection technology. For readers to further understand the defense methods of 3D printers.

3.1   Security Framework

In this paper, through the study of the construction of 3D printers security framework and system design, combined with the security risks of 3D printers discussed above. On this basis, we find that there is a great need for a design specification and security architecture, which must comply with and support the security architecture established within the organization, and it is an integral part of the organization's corporate architecture. Table 3 shows the common security defense frameworks for 3D printers summarized in this paper.

Table 3. Summary of 3D printers attack and defense security framework

Paper	Research perspective				
	Protection of print source data	Identify the origin of printed items	Policy constraint security mechanism of autonomous access control	Verify the authenticity of the printing process	Evaluate the network security of printing
[42]	✓				
[13]	✓	✓			
[24]			✓		
[5]	✓			✓	
[31]					✓
[25]					✓

At the level of defense technology, the literature [42] proposes the use of identity authentication technology to ensure the security of source data, the use of encryption technology to ensure the security of data transmission, and the use of embedded network firewalls to improve the anti-attack performance of network printers. The experimental results show that the entire network printing security system can effectively improve the security of network printing and improve the anti-attack ability of network printers.

Nawfal F. Fadhel et al. [13] proposed a framework to determine the provenance of 3D printed objects, and discussed the origin of 3D printed objects in the conversion between digital objects and physical objects. They created a unique resource identifier, 3DOI, with attributes such as accounting, authentication, and authorization, and then gathered and placed it in a secure repository. Frames and resource identifiers can evade a series of threat scenarios, and can be used to detect scenes of illegal access to 3D objects, and can also be used to detect plagiarism and counterfeiting. The future work of this research will likely provide a realistic safety benchmark for three-dimensional objects.

The literature [24] proposes to control access to printers through security permission matrices, and then these matrices can be applied to security classes, where network resources can be grouped. The goal is to achieve the best safety of 3D printers without compromising the balance between protection and usability.

Sofia Belikovetsky et al. [5] proposed a solution to verify the authenticity of the 3D printing process through the sound generated by a stepper motor to detect sabotage attacks and change the geometry of the 3D printed object. The solution adopted in this article is to use the unique noise generated by the stepper motor on the 3D printers. After using these acoustic characteristics, it can be parameterized and matched to ensure the authenticity of the manufacturing process.

Anudeep Padmanabhan et al. [31] proposed a new network security assessment framework to assess the network security vulnerability of 3D printing. Through analysis the workflow of the 3D printers, the 3D printers is divided into 6 stages: Idea, CAD tool, Slicing algorithm, tooling algorithm, Additive manufacturing unit, Finishing. For each stage of the process, different vulnerabilities are assessed and potential threats are discussed. They also proposed a new solution that uses 2D images to encrypt 3D model information. In short, the solutions they proposed enhanced the network security of 3D printers to a certain extent.

In this work, Matthew McCormack et al. [25] designed and implemented an open source network security analysis tool C3PO to systematically identify the security threats of network 3D printers. C3PO can identify computer-specific vulnerabilities on independent 3D printers and supports multiple vendors. It also takes into account how other devices in the network affect the security of 3D printers.

In summary, the existing 3D printers security architecture research describes some of the security functions required by 3D printers, as well as the security control between physical and network components, and analyzes how various security functions, mechanisms and services are coordinated. The work takes into account the impact of network equipment and physical factors on the safety of 3D printers, and provides a good foundation for the security capabilities and protection methods required by 3D printers in the future.

3.2 Attack Detection

It is essential to inspect 3D printers systems and assets to determine network security incidents and verify the effectiveness of protective measures. This includes monitoring unauthorized personnel, connections, equipment, and software. However, the traditional intrusion detection system cannot be well applied to 3D printers, because it cannot detect the increasing multi-step complex attacks of network printers, so we need to study better scheme to detect 3D printers.

In order to detect and prevent attacks on system integrity, SR Chhetri et al. [10] used electromagnetic and acoustic sensor radiation to detect dynamic network attacks on manufacturing systems, and then used machine learning methods to train predictive models, and KCAD methods to detect dynamic networks The attack achieved a high accuracy of 77.45%. This provides a good starting point and proof of concept for the attack detection method of system integrity.

Jens Müller et al. [30] implemented an open source tool called PRinter Exploitation Toolkit (PRET). They enabled attacks to use advanced cross-site printing technology from the Internet, combined with CORS technology for printer spoofing. They used PRET to evaluate printer models from 20 different manufacturers and found that printers can still be attacked by simple attacks.

The literature conducts case studies to evaluate the ability of experimenters to detect and diagnose cyber-physical attacks on STL files of test samples [37]. Based on research, the author believes that STL files are currently the most vulnerable step in the AM process chain. And the STL file reveals a method by which a gap can be automatically placed inside the part, while avoiding the detection of the usual process inspection.

Asaf Hecht et al. [16] proposed an intrusion detection method using supervised machine learning to find malicious protocol traffic and issue an alarm when malicious protocol traffic is detected, so can implemented an intrusion detection system (PIDs) to detect attacks on printing protocols. The empirical results show that PIDS is effective in detecting printing protocol attacks, providing 99.9% accuracy.

This paper [48] proposes a multi-modal damage attack detection system for 3D printers. The use of multilateral channel technology can significantly improve the system's state estimation accuracy compared to single-modal technology. In addition, they also analyzed the value of each side-channel for attack detection based on sharing information with machine control parameters, and achieved an attack detection accuracy rate of 98.15% in actual test cases.

Josh Brandman et al. [6] proposed the use of physical hashing to detect 3D printed malicious cyber-physical attacks by linking digital data to manufactured parts through a disconnected side-channel measurement system. They converted the physical hash table into the form of QR code to ensure that the IP related to the process and tool path parameters are protected, while also achieving on-site quality assurance.

Table 4. Comparison of some work of 3D printers attack detection.

Literature	Types of attacks detected	Accuracy
[10]	Dynamic cyber attack	77.45%
[16]	Attacks against printing protocols	99.9%
[48]	Multimodal destruction attack	98.15%

Table 4 summarizes the three representative existing research results that appeared above, and compares, analyzes them from two aspects: the type of attack detected and the accuracy rate. Through analysis, it is found that the attack detection technology can monitor the 3D printers system to find the above several kinds of attacks, and to understand the potential impact of the attack, and has a good performance in accuracy. And it can detect unauthorized local, network and remote connections, and protect the 3D printer's information from unauthorized access, modification and deletion. Attack detection can also monitor the system and its assets to determine network security incidents and verify the effectiveness of protective measures. In addition, it can also help people analyze the detected events to understand the target and method of the attack, collect and correlate event data from multiple sources and sensors, and determine the impact of the event.

4 Future Work

By combing and summarizing the existing research results of 3D printers security, we found that more work can be done in attack and defense, whether it is more targeted at 3D printer weaknesses, or to help 3D printers defend against the attacks mentioned in this article. Both are important directions of research. In the three types of attacks mentioned in this article, there are more details that need to be discussed and verified, and we need to think about the trend of defense technology. Based on the existing articles [37,40], our future attack and defense research directions are from six question is looked forward to for future researchers' reference.

Q1: The current research literature discussing 3D printers attacks lacks precise positioning of stealing technical data. For example, what standard of accuracy (or other attributes) does an attacker need to achieve before technical data is stolen?

A: Although the existing research has implemented a variety of attack methods to steal technical data, in the literature [1,8,34], researchers discuss how to attack 3D printers through side-channel. These studies show that side-channel attacks are affected by factors such as distance. However, it lacks a fine-grained discussion on the 3D printers stealing technical data attacks in specific scenarios. For example, when considering 3D printing in an industrial scene, when the target is an economic espionage, to what extent can these side-channel attacks achieve precise technical data theft. All these require further discussion on the fine-grained aspects of 3D printers.

Q2: At present, there is a lack of real and thorough experiments on sabotage attacks on 3D printers. How can attackers use the unique properties of 3D printers to carry out sabotage attacks that are difficult to detect, and how to deal with these challenges?

A: First of all, a possible example of a 3D printers as a weapon attack has been described in detail [47], but it lacks thorough verification experiments in the real world. Second, the feasibility of a sabotage attack depends on several factors: the ability to sabotage the environment, the effectiveness of the method to sabotage the part, and the possibility of discovering the sabotaged part [4]. So far, the detectability of attacks mainly depends on the ability to identify damaged parts after production. However, this requires a lot of time and manpower, and requires expensive specialized equipment. In addition, the ndt method used in traditional manufacturing cannot fully effectively detect the parts produced in the manufacturing process, but can only detect relatively large defects, which is far from sufficient for the current 3D printing damage attack detection. Chhetri [10] used a novel approach to reconstruct a 3D model using noise generated by a 3D printers and compare it with the original STL file. However, only 77.45% of the accuracy of damage detection has been achieved, which is not enough for the damage detection mentioned in this article. Researchers need to further develop better detection schemes for damage attacks.

Q3: What methods should be taken to prevent 3D printers from illegally manufacturing parts?

A: So far, researchers have focused on protecting users from any malicious actions by external participants. However, the problem of 3D printing technology causing harm to the external environment due to impropriety cannot be ignored. For this reason, it is necessary to enhance the safety and legal awareness of users on the one hand, and to use 3D printers correctly. On the other hand, it is necessary to strengthen the traceability of 3D printers products. Technical research. In the literature [22], the first use of fingerprint modeling in the field of 3D printing is used. They used the microstructure and physical characteristics of the printed object surface to develop fingerprint recognition technology, which is sufficient to identify the equipment used by illegal manufacturers. And researchers should further study adding watermarks to printed objects, so that they can better verify the authenticity of the product.

Q4: What is the current research status of 3D printers firmware security analysis? What are the directions for improvement in the future?

A: Firmware is a kind of software embedded in a hardware device. The firmware is installed on the 3D printers, and the embedded system is loaded and managed through the firmware to perform actual tasks (such as printing). Only by guaranteeing the security of the embedded firmware code, can we provide the most basic security guarantee for the embedded system and fundamentally solve the security problem of the embedded system. The literature [29] modifies the source code of the marlin firmware and deploys malicious code to disrupt the control flow to change the printing command. Therefore, a vulnerability detection method is needed to protect the security of the printer. Current vulnerability detection technologies, such as Fuzzy Testing, Behavior Analysis [18], etc. still have problems such as low test case coverage and low hit rate, and inaccurate classification of malicious behaviors. More research is needed in the future to improve the security of the printer.

Q5: Based on the 3D printer itself, how to better defend against cyber attacks?

A: Preventing network attacks can first improve the 3D printers system inspection, and then test the very small enclosures, because the test of these enclosures may find network attacks based on blanks. More detection of small features of non-independent housings is needed to prevent them from being printed incorrectly. Finally, improving the monitoring of the printing process is also an ongoing goal. The purpose is to better control and improve the printing process. For example, Song et al. [34] uses a smartphone's sensor for acoustic side-channel measurement, which can effectively detect the impact on the printer. Parametric network attacks, but smart attackers can make the system report false data [14]. Although feedback systems provide valuable information for the control process, using them alone is not sufficient to detect network attacks. More research is needed to build a more robust printing system and better resist network attacks.

Q6: Can 3D printers be combined with more technologies to protect the safety of 3D printers?

A: Through research and analysis, we feel that 3D printers are very suitable for the relevant combination of hashing, secure signature and blockchain. Hashing is a commonly used technique in security to ensure the validity of files. The hash value of the file is compared with the published hash value, and if the hash matches, the file can be assumed to be the same as the original file. However, the limitation of hashing is the protection and transmission of the key. If the key is leaked, the security will be threatened. The document [6] uses the hashing method to present the hash table in the form of a QR code to protect the IP information related to the printing process and path parameters.

5   Conclusions

Additive manufacturing is becoming an important tool for manufacturing. This paper sorts out and summarizes the existing research results of 3D printers offense and defense, and starts from the attacker's intentions, from the three aspects of theft of technical data, AM sabotage and illegal part manufacturing. The classification is explained, and the defense is also summarized from the 3D printing security framework and attack detection technology. Finally, the opportunities and challenges facing 3D printing offense and defense are prospected. It is hoped that it will help security personnel overcome the limitations of offense and defense of existing 3D printers and enhance the safety of 3D printers.

Acknowledgement. The author thanks Zezhong Ren, Yin Li and Jing Zhang for their information support during the writing of the paper. This work was supported by the National Key Research and Development Program of China(2018YFB0804701). And this work is supported by the National Natural Science Foundation of China (Grant No. 62162039, 61762060), Foundation for the Key Research and Development Program of Gansu Province, China (Grant No. 20YF3GA016).

References

1. Al Faruque, M.A., Chhetri, S.R., Canedo, A., Wan, J.: Forensics of thermal side-channel in additive manufacturing systems. University of California, Irvine **12**, 13 (2016)

2. Banerjee, A.: Arms and the man: strategic trade control challenges of 3D printing. Int. J. Nucl. Secur. **4**(1), 7 (2018)
3. Baumann, F.W., Roller, D.: Additive manufacturing, cloud-based 3D printing and associated services-overview. J. Manuf. Mater. Process. **1**(2), 15 (2017)
4. Belikovetsky, S., Yampolskiy, M., Toh, J., Elovici, Y.: Cyber-physical attack with additive manufacturing. In: 11th USENIX Workshop on Offensive Technologies (2017)
5. Belikovetsky, S., Solewicz, Y., Yampolskiy, M., Toh, J., Elovici, Y.: Detecting cyber-physical attacks in additive manufacturing using digital audio signing. arXiv preprint arXiv:1705.06454 (2017)
6. Brandman, J., Sturm, L., White, J., Williams, C.: A physical hash for preventing and detecting cyber-physical attacks in additive manufacturing systems. J. Manuf. Syst. **56**, 202–212 (2020)
7. Chan, H.K., Griffin, J., Lim, J.J., Zeng, F., Chiu, A.S.: The impact of 3D printing technology on the supply chain: manufacturing and legal perspectives. Int. J. Prod. Econ. **205**, 156–162 (2018)
8. Chhetri, S.R.: Novel side-channel attack model for cyber-physical additive manufacturing systems. University of California, Irvine (2016)
9. Chhetri, S.R., Barua, A., Faezi, S., Regazzoni, F., Canedo, A., Al Faruque, M.A.: Tool of spies: leaking your IP by altering the 3D printer compiler. IEEE Trans. Dependable Secure Comput. **18**(2), 667–678 (2019)
10. Chhetri, S.R., Canedo, A., Al Faruque, M.A.: KCAD: kinetic cyber-attack detection method for cyber-physical additive manufacturing systems. In: 2016 IEEE/ACM International Conference on Computer-Aided Design (ICCAD), pp. 1–8. IEEE (2016)
11. Chhetri, S.R., Canedo, A., Faruque, M.A.A.: Confidentiality breach through acoustic side-channel in cyber-physical additive manufacturing systems. ACM Trans. Cyber-Phys. Syst. **2**(1), 1–25 (2017)
12. Do, Q., Martini, B., Choo, K.K.R.: A data exfiltration and remote exploitation attack on consumer 3D printers. IEEE Trans. Inf. Forensics Secur. **11**(10), 2174–2186 (2016)
13. Fadhel, N.F., Crowder, R.M., Akeel, F., Wills, G.B.: Component for 3D printing provenance framework: security properties components for provenance framework. In: World Congress on Internet Security (WorldCIS-2014), pp. 91–96. IEEE (2014)
14. Falliere, N., Murchu, L.O., Chien, E.: W32. Stuxnet dossier. White paper, Symantec Corporation, Security Response **5**(6), 29 (2011)
15. Graves, L.M., Lubell, J., King, W., Yampolskiy, M.: Characteristic aspects of additive manufacturing security from security awareness perspectives. IEEE Access **7**, 103833–103853 (2019)
16. Hecht, A., Sagi, A., Elovici, Y.: PIDS: a behavioral framework for analysis and detection of network printer attacks, pp. 87–94, October 2018
17. Hoffman, W., Volpe, T.A.: Internet of nuclear things: managing the proliferation risks of 3-D printing technology. Bull. At. Sci. **74**(2), 102–113 (2018)
18. Hou, J.B., Li, T., Chang, C.: Research for vulnerability detection of embedded system firmware. Procedia Comput. Sci. **107**, 814–818 (2017)
19. Jia, S., Guo, G., Xu, Z.: A survey on 3D mask presentation attack detection and countermeasures. Pattern Recogn. **98**, 107032 (2020)
20. Johnson, J.J.: Print, lock, and load: 3-D printers, creation of guns, and the potential threat to fourth amendment rights. U. Ill. JL Tech. & Pol'y 337 (2013)
21. Li, Z., et al.: C3PO: database and benchmark for early-stage malicious activity detection in 3D printing. arXiv preprint arXiv:1803.07544 (2018)

22. Li, Z., Rathore, A.S., Song, C., Wei, S., Wang, Y., Xu, W.: PrinTracker: finger-printing 3D printers using commodity scanners. In: Proceedings of the 2018 ACM SIGSAC Conference on Computer and Communications Security, pp. 1306–1323 (2018)

23. Love, L.J., Nycz, A., Adediran, A.I.: An in-depth review on the scientific and policy issues associated with additive manufacturing. J. Sci. Policy Gov. **11**(1) (2017)

24. Lukusa, J.: A security model for mitigating multifunction network printers vulner-abilities. In: International Conference on the Internet, Cyber Security and Infor-mation Systems (2016)

25. McCormack, M., Chandrasekaran, S., Liu, G., Yu, T., Wolf, S.D., Sekar, V.: Secu-rity analysis of networked 3D printers. In: 2020 IEEE Security and Privacy Work-shops (SPW), pp. 118–125. IEEE (2020)

26. McMullen, K.F.: Worlds collide when 3D printers reach the public: modeling a digital gun control law after the digital millenium copyright act. Mich. St. L. Rev. 187 (2014)

27. Miller, D., Gatlin, J., Glisson, W., Yampolskiy, M., McDonald, J.: Investigating 3D printer residual data. In: HICSS (2019)

28. Miller, D.B., Gatlin, J., Glisson, W.B., Yampolskiy, M., McDonald, J.T.: Investi-gating 3D printer residual data. arXiv preprint arXiv:1901.07507 (2019)

29. Moore, S.B., Glisson, W.B., Yampolskiy, M.: Implications of malicious 3D printer firmware (2017)

30. Müller, J., Mladenov, V., Somorovsky, J., Schwenk, J.: SoK: exploiting network printers. In: 2017 IEEE Symposium on Security and Privacy (SP), pp. 213–230 (2017)

31. Padmanabhan, A., Zhang, J.: Cybersecurity risks and mitigation strategies in addi-tive manufacturing. Prog. Addit. Manuf. **3**, 87–93 (2018). https://doi.org/10.1007/s40964-017-0036-9

32. Rokka Chhetri, S.: Novel side-channel attack model for cyber-physical additive manufacturing systems. Ph.D. thesis, UC Irvine (2016)

33. Slaughter, A., Yampolskiy, M., Matthews, M., King, W.E., Guss, G., Elovici, Y.: How to ensure bad quality in metal additive manufacturing: in-situ infrared ther-mography from the security perspective. In: Proceedings of the 12th International Conference on Availability, Reliability and Security, pp. 1–10 (2017)

34. Song, C., Lin, F., Ba, Z., Ren, K., Zhou, C., Xu, W.: My smartphone knows what you print: exploring smartphone-based side-channel attacks against 3D printers. In: Proceedings of the 2016 ACM SIGSAC Conference on Computer and Commu-nications Security (2016)

35. Sternstein, A.: Things can go kaboom when a defense contractor's 3-D printer gets hacked. Nextgov, 11 September 2014

36. Sturm, L., Williams, C., Camelio, J., White, J., Parker, R.: Cyber-physical vuner-abilities in additive manufacturing systems. Context **7**(8), 951–963 (2014)

37. Sturm, L.D., Williams, C.B., Camelio, J.A., White, J., Parker, R.: Cyber-physical vulnerabilities in additive manufacturing systems: a case study attack on the .STL file with human subjects. J. Manuf. Syst. **44**, 154–164 (2017)

38. Swearingen, M., Brunasso, S., Weiss, J., Huber, D.: What you need to know (and don't) about the AURORA vulnerability. Power **157**(9), 52–52 (2013)

39. Tirone, D., Gilley, J.: 3D printing: a new threat to gun control and security policy. The Conversation (2016)

40. Venkata, R.Y., Brown, N., Ting, D., Kavi, K.: Offensive and defensive perspectives in additive manufacturing security. In: ICSEA 2020, p. 85 (2020)

41. Xiao, C.: Security attack to 3D printing. In: xFocus Information Security Conference (2013)
42. Ding, X., et al.: Security system for internal network printing. In: 2012 Eighth International Conference on Computational Intelligence and Security, pp. 596–600. IEEE (2012)
43. Yampolskiy, M., Andel, T.R., McDonald, J.T., Glisson, W.B., Yasinsac, A.: Intellectual property protection in additive layer manufacturing: requirements for secure outsourcing. In: Proceedings of the 4th Program Protection and Reverse Engineering Workshop, pp. 1–9 (2014)
44. Yampolskiy, M., King, W., Pope, G., Belikovetsky, S., Elovici, Y.: Evaluation of additive and subtractive manufacturing from the security perspective. In: ICCIP 2017. IAICT, vol. 512, pp. 23–44. Springer, Cham (2017). https://doi.org/10.1007/978-3-319-70395-4_2
45. Yampolskiy, M., et al.: Security of additive manufacturing: attack taxonomy and survey. Addit. Manuf. **21**, 431–457 (2018)
46. Yampolskiy, M., Schutzle, L., Vaidya, U., Yasinsac, A.: Security challenges of additive manufacturing with metals and alloys. In: Rice, M., Shenoi, S. (eds.) ICCIP 2015. IAICT, vol. 466, pp. 169–183. Springer, Cham (2015). https://doi.org/10.1007/978-3-319-26567-4_11
47. Yampolskiy, M., Skjellum, A., Kretzschmar, M., Overfelt, R.A., Sloan, K.R., Yasinsac, A.: Using 3D printers as weapons. Int. J. Crit. Infrastruct. Prot. **14**(C), 58–71 (2016)
48. Yu, S.Y., Malawade, A.V., Chhetri, S.R., Al Faruque, M.A.: Sabotage attack detection for additive manufacturing systems. IEEE Access **8**, 27218–27231 (2020)
49. Zeltmann, S.E., Gupta, N., Tsoutsos, N.G., Maniatakos, M., Rajendran, J., Karri, R.: Manufacturing and security challenges in 3D printing. JOM **68**(7), 1872–1881 (2016). https://doi.org/10.1007/s11837-016-1937-7

Network Security

Requirements for Total Resistance to Pollution Attacks in HMAC-Based Authentication Schemes for Network Coding

Lawrence Tandoh[1]([✉]), Fagen Li[1], Ikram Ali[2], Charles Roland Haruna[3],
Michael Y. Kpiebaareh[1], and Christopher Tandoh[4]

[1] School of Computer Science and Engineering, University of Electronic Science
and Technology of China, Chengdu 611731, China
`fagenli@uestc.edu.cn, michael.kpiebaareh@sipingsoft.com`
[2] School of Automation Engineering, University of Electronic Science
and Technology of China, Chengdu 611731, China
[3] University of Cape Coast, Cape Coast, Ghana
`charunameghan@ucc.edu.gh`
[4] Wicrecend, Wicresoft, Shanghai 200241, China

Abstract. Network coding (NC) authentication schemes based on homomorphic message authentication codes (HMACs) are usually preferred due to the low computational complexity associated with their implementation. A basic requirement of these schemes is that they should be able to resist both message and tag pollution attacks. A common approach adopted in the design of these schemes uses key vectors to generate tags that are then used to detect these attacks. Conventionally, the only constraint placed on existing key selection models is that key elements must be chosen from a predefined finite cyclic field. In this work we prove that this condition alone is not sufficient to ensure total resistance to pollution attacks. We also provide a detailed description of this security loophole as well as a proposition that defines what a scheme needs in order to achieve total resistance to pollution attacks. Based on our findings we propose a modified authentication scheme for NC that is not exposed to the security loophole and therefore provides complete resistance to pollution attacks. Our evaluation of the proposed scheme against similar state of the art schemes shows that it achieves this at no extra overhead. As a matter of fact, the proposed scheme incurs a slightly lower computational overhead at non-source nodes coupled with a slightly lower key storage overhead.

Keywords: Network coding · Complete resistance to pollution attacks · Key selection model · HMAC-based authentication

1 Introduction

NC as introduced by Ahlswede et al. [1] presented a more efficient way of routing data in networks. Unlike the traditional method of store-and-forward NC allowed

© Springer Nature Singapore Pte Ltd. 2022
C. Cao et al. (Eds.): FCS 2021, CCIS 1558, pp. 181–196, 2022.
https://doi.org/10.1007/978-981-19-0523-0_12

intermediate nodes to combine packets before re-transmitting them. By doing this, networks were able to achieve their maximum multi-cast rates as dictated by the max-flow min-cut theorem [2–5]. In addition, NC also reduced power consumption and transmission delays in networks [6–8]. Over the years, NC has been proposed for use in P2P [9], wireless [10–12], sensor [13], and the newly introduced fifth-generation communication technology (5G) [14–16] networks. Aside its traditional benefits, NC in 5G networks is also known to be an effective way of addressing the challenges that arise due to packet loss [17,18].

To ensure security, a plethora of NC authentication schemes [19–29] have been proposed by the research community over the years. Among these, the most popular authentication schemes are the ones based on the cryptographic paradigm of HMACs. In order to detect corruption, these schemes check the authenticity of HMAC tags. All existing key selection models for HMAC-based authentication schemes place a single constraint on the key selection process: keys must be chosen from a finite cyclic field. One of such schemes was introduced by Esfahani et al. [30] and serves as the error detection scheme in [14,15]. One of the most important features of this authentication scheme is the absence of a homomorphic cryptographic signature (HCS). By avoiding the use of this computationally demanding authentication parameter, Esfahani et al. presented a more efficient approach to authentication in NC. This is so far the most efficient HMAC-based, HCS-free, 100% tag pollution resistant scheme in existence. However, neither the work where the scheme was introduced nor the two other works where it serves as the error detection scheme present or discuss its key selection model.

In our attempt to come up with a concrete approach to selecting keys in the aforementioned scheme we stumbled upon an anomaly. This anomaly led us to discover that the existing constraint on key selection is insufficient and does not guarantee complete resistance to pollution attacks. The work presented was motivated by this discovery. Our contributions are outlined below:

1. We first of all analyze the security scheme proposed by Esfahani et al. [30] and explain the need to place a constraint on how the elements that make up its key vectors are selected. We generalize the results of this analysis in a proposition. In our proposition, we define the necessary condition which needs to be placed on the key selection process of HMAC-based authentication schemes to make them completely resistant to pollution attacks.

2. Secondly, based on our findings we propose a modified version of the scheme in 1 above. The major advantage of the modified scheme is that the concrete construction of its key selection model takes into consideration the security flaw of its predecessor [30]. This makes the scheme fully resistant to tag pollution attacks.

3. Finally, we compare the performance of the proposed scheme to the performance of two similar state of the art schemes [30,31]. The results of our comparison show that our scheme achieves complete resistance to pollution attacks without any overhead gains. As a matter of fact, our scheme incurs slightly lower computational overhead at non-source nodes as well as a lower key storage overhead.

The rest of this paper is organized as follows: In Sect. 2 we present the related works. Our main work which includes a discussion of the security flaw as well as the proposed scheme is presented in Sect. 3. In Sect. 4 we evaluate the performance of the proposed scheme versus similar state of the arts schemes. Section 5 concludes this paper.

2   Related Works

In order to make NC a practical solution to data routing in networks, pollution attacks had to be addressed. Schemes developed to address these attacks include but are not limited to [32–34]. In this section however we will discuss schemes based on HMACs which are usually preferred for the low computational cost associated with their implementation.

Yu et al. [24], were one of the first to propose a scheme that adapted the HMAC authentication approach to mitigate data packet pollution in NC. In their scheme, probabilistic key pre-distribution and symmetric encryption were used to provide intra-network authentication. Yu et al. suggested that the authentication parameter be made up of a vector of HMAC tags (an approach that is widely adopted these days). Linear combinations of packets received in this scheme were generated using XoR gates.

One of the first schemes to address tag pollution attacks was RIPPLE [35]. In their scheme, Li et al. used delayed key disclosure to introduce asymmetry. In this novel key distribution protocol, a new key was sent to all nodes in a particular layer in the network hierarchy with each ripple. This happened as soon as all the nodes in that layer received their packets. The scheme however had two major drawbacks. The first of them was the fact that extra communication overhead was incurred during each key transmission. Secondly, the need to synchronize nodes due to the delayed key disclosure made the scheme rather complicated.

In order to reduce the complexity associated with the delayed key disclosure approach, a new scheme was proposed by Zhang et al. [36]. In their scheme, Zhang et al. also adapted the use of a vector of HMAC tags in packet payload authentication. Some amount of asymmetry was introduced via the double random key distribution. Finally, in order to completely eliminate the possibility of a tag pollution attack, Zhang et al. proposed the use of an HCS. Unfortunately, this scheme was exposed to the following drawbacks. Primarily, the need to continuously transmit key indexes made the scheme incur extra communication overhead. Secondly, the cost of verifying the HCS was extremely high. The aforementioned drawbacks made the scheme unattractive in networks where communication and computational overheads formed a major constraint.

In an attempt to reduce the computational overhead incurred by [36], Esfahani et al. proposed an HCS-free scheme [31]. In their scheme, they replaced the HCS with a second vector of HMAC tags. Although their scheme was able to reduce the computational overhead associated with the verification of the HCS it had two major flaws. The first of them was the extra communication overhead incurred as a result of using two HMAC tag vectors. The second drawback was the fact that their scheme was widely considered to be only 50% tag pollution resistant. In order to address this security drawback, Esfahani et al. proposed a modified version of their first scheme [37]. In this scheme they appended an HCS to the two already existing HMAC tag vectors in [31]. Although this addressed the issue of the scheme being only 50% tag pollution resistant, it made the computational overhead it incurred higher.

In 2016, Esfahani et al. [30] proposed an efficient HMAC-based authentication scheme. In this scheme they addressed both of the major drawbacks associated with HMAC-based authentication schemes that were mentioned above. Firstly, they limited the number of HMAC tag vectors to one. Secondly, they were able to achieve complete tag pollution resistance without the use of an HCS. This is the most efficient HMAC-based authentication scheme as of yet. For this reason, this scheme has been used as the error detection scheme in several current authentication schemes for 5G networks [14, 15].

3   Total Resistance to Pollution Attacks in HMAC-Based Authentication

We will begin this section with an analysis of the scheme in [30]. Our analysis will point out a security loop-hole in the key selection model of the aforementioned scheme. Based on this analysis we will discuss the need for an extra constraint on the key selection models of HMAC-based authentication schemes. This discussion is summarized into Proposition 1. Following this will be a concrete construction for a proposed HMAC-based, HCS-free authentication scheme whose key selection model ensures that it is completely message and tag pollution resistant. A note on the security proof of the proposed scheme will conclude this section. Also, for the sake of clarity and simplicity we included a table of symbols in the appendix.

3.1   An Efficient Null Space-Based Homomorphic MAC Scheme Against Tag Pollution Attacks in RLNC

To begin this subsection we define the following: let l denote the total number of non-source nodes in the network and t_i (for $1 \leq i \leq l$) denote an element of an HMAC tag vector t. Also, let $k_{i,j}$ represent an element of a key vector k_i for $1 \leq i \leq l$ and $1 \leq j \leq m + n + l$. Then, the scheme in [30] can be summarized

$$
\begin{bmatrix} k_{1,1} & \cdots & k_{1,m+n} \\ \vdots & \vdots & \vdots \\ k_{l,1} & \cdots & k_{l,m+n} \end{bmatrix} \times \begin{bmatrix} \bar{x}_{i,1} \\ \vdots \\ \bar{x}_{i,m+n} \end{bmatrix}
$$
$$
+ \begin{bmatrix} k_{1,m+n+1} & \cdots & k_{1,m+n+l} \\ \vdots & \vdots & \vdots \\ k_{l,m+n+1} & \cdots & k_{l,m+n+l} \end{bmatrix} \times \begin{bmatrix} t_1 \\ \vdots \\ t_l \end{bmatrix} = 0 \tag{1}
$$

into the system presented in Eq. (1). To simplify our discussion, we break

$$
\begin{bmatrix} k_{1,1} \cdots k_{1,m+n} \\ \vdots \quad \vdots \quad \vdots \\ k_{l,1} \cdots k_{l,m+n} \end{bmatrix} \times \begin{bmatrix} \bar{x}_{i,1} \\ \vdots \\ \bar{x}_{i,m+n} \end{bmatrix} = \begin{bmatrix} t_1 \\ \vdots \\ t_l \end{bmatrix} \tag{2}
$$

Equation (1) into two smaller equations. The first equation (Eq. (2)) is used to generate the vector of HMAC tags whilst the second equation (Eq. (3)) shows how these

$$
\begin{bmatrix} t_1 \\ \vdots \\ t_l \end{bmatrix} + \begin{bmatrix} k_{1,1} \cdots k_{1,l} \\ \vdots \quad \vdots \quad \vdots \\ k_{l,1} \cdots k_{l,l} \end{bmatrix} \times \begin{bmatrix} t_1 \\ \vdots \\ t_l \end{bmatrix} = 0 \tag{3}
$$

tags are verified. Furthermore, we will henceforth refer to the matrix of keys used to generate the HMAC tags as $\boldsymbol{K}_g$ and the matrix of keys used to verify them as $\boldsymbol{K}_v$.

One possible and the most trivial solution to Eq. (3) will be to make $\boldsymbol{K}_v$ a negative identity matrix. In other words, one canonical row vector from $\boldsymbol{K}_v$ will be assigned to each of the non-source nodes in the network. This canonical vector will be used by each of the non-source nodes to verify each received HMAC tag

$$
t_j + [(0 \times t_1) + \ldots + (-1 \times t_j) + \ldots + (0 \times t_l)] = t_j - t_j = 0 \tag{4}
$$

vector. We depict an example of such a verification in Eq. (4) where a node tries to verify the HMAC tag t_j. As can be observed from Eq. (4), the HMAC tag vector passes verification and hence the received packet is authentic. This also serves as a trivial proof of the fact that the negative identity matrix is indeed a possible solution to Eq. (3).

3.2 Complete Resistance to Message and Tag Pollution Attacks

Before we proceed any further we present Proposition 1. This proposition formally defines the extra constraint that needs to be placed on the key selection models of HMAC-based authentication schemes to ensure total resistance to pollution attacks.

Proposition 1: In order for an HMAC-based, NC authentication scheme to be completely resistant to pollution attacks, its key selection model must ensure that none of its key vectors contain a zero symbol.

To understand the need for this extra constraint lets observe Eq. (5). This

$$
\begin{aligned} t_j &+ [(0 \times t_1) + \ldots + (-1 \times t_j) + \ldots + \left(0 \times t_k'\right) + \ldots \\ &+ (0 \times t_l)] = t_j - t_j = 0 \end{aligned} \tag{5}
$$

equation shows what happens if the received packet has been tampered with and the tag in position k was changed from t_k to t_k'. As can be observed, although the tag in position k has been corrupted, the current node is not able to identify the corruption. This happens because the symbol in position k of the key vector that the current node used to verify the vector of HMAC tags is 0. Hence, if the key matrix $\boldsymbol{K}_v$ is the negative identity matrix, then only the node that has a non-zero key entry in position k will be able to identify this corruption. This means that the corrupted packet is free to traverse the network and pollute other packets until it reaches that node. Therefore, for the scheme in [30], a necessary constraint on the key selection process must be placed. In its basic form, this constraint requires that the elements of $\boldsymbol{K}_v$ must be selected in such way that $\boldsymbol{K}_v$ does not form a negative identity matrix. If this constraint is not placed on the key selection process, the scheme will not be able to offer complete resistance to tag pollution attacks.

As a matter of fact, this security loophole is not limited to the scheme in [30] alone. Also, it is neither limited to tag authentication nor the case where the authentication key is a canonical vector. In a generic sense, this form of attack can be launched on any HMAC, inner product-based, NC authentication scheme where key vectors are allowed to have zero symbols as elements. As was shown in Eq. (5) the key vector fails to verify any packet/tag vector element that corresponds to any of its zero elements. As such, any node that possesses such a key vector cannot ensure complete resistance to tag pollution attacks.

3.3   Concrete Construction of the Proposed Scheme

In this sub-section we present the concrete construction of the proposed scheme. Our presentation will begin with a detailed introduction to the key selection and distribution model which will ensure that our scheme can fully resist pollution attacks. This will be followed by the tag generation, packet combination, and verification phases.

Key Selection and Distribution Model. The proposed HMAC-based authentication scheme is closely related to the scheme in [30]. However, we need the proposed scheme to be fully message and tag pollution resistant. Thus, we design its key selection model in such a way that all of its keys satisfy Proposition 1. Also, instead of using the original system of equations as proposed in [30] and depicted in Eq. (1), we use the two equations shown in Eq. (2) and Eq. (3).

To begin with, we modify Eq. (3) to form Eq. (6). From Eq. (6), we can make the following observation. Each of the ith elements in the ith row of the

$$
\begin{bmatrix} t_1 \\ t_2 \\ t_3 \\ \vdots \\ t_l \end{bmatrix} + \begin{bmatrix} \left(k_{v1,1} \times t_1\right) + \left(k_{v1,2} \times t_2\right) + \left(k_{v1,3} \times t_3\right) \\ \left(k_{v2,1} \times t_1\right) + \left(k_{v2,2} \times t_2\right) + \left(k_{v2,3} \times t_3\right) \\ \left(k_{v3,1} \times t_1\right) + \left(k_{v3,2} \times t_2\right) + \left(k_{v3,3} \times t_3\right) \\ \vdots \qquad \vdots \qquad \vdots \\ \left(k_{vl,1} \times t_1\right) + \left(k_{vl,2} \times t_2\right) + \left(k_{vl,3} \times t_3\right) \\ \begin{aligned} &+ \ldots + \left(k_{v1,l} \times t_l\right) \\ &+ \ldots + \left(k_{v2,l} \times t_l\right) \\ &+ \ldots + \left(k_{v3,l} \times t_l\right) \\ &+ \ldots + \quad \vdots \\ &+ \ldots + \left(k_{vl,l} \times t_l\right) \end{aligned} \end{bmatrix} = 0
$$

$$(6)$$

expanded sum of products consists of the principal diagonal element found in the ith row of the matrix $\boldsymbol{K}_v$ and the tag t_i. We extract these products as well

$$
\begin{bmatrix} t_1 \\ t_2 \\ t_3 \\ \vdots \\ t_l \end{bmatrix} + \begin{bmatrix} \left(k_{v_{1,1}} \times t_1\right) \\ \left(k_{v_{2,2}} \times t_2\right) \\ \left(k_{v_{3,3}} \times t_3\right) \\ \vdots \\ \left(k_{v_{l,l}} \times t_l\right) \end{bmatrix} = 0 \tag{7}
$$

as the tag vector from Eq. (6) to form Eq. (7). It is trivial to see that the solution to the system presented in Eq. (7) will consist of assigning the value of -1 to all principal diagonal elements of the key matrix $\boldsymbol{K}_v$. Although this solution is easy to obtain, its inclusion in Eq. (6) is unnecessary. This is because this verification corresponds to the verification of the packet payload performed by the corresponding non-source node. As such, there is no need to verify such an HMAC tag by the same node during tag verification. Furthermore, this verification increases the computational cost incurred during HMAC tag vector authentication by one multiplication operation.

For this reason, the tag verification stage of the proposed scheme does not include any of the elements from Eq. (7). If we remove these elements from Eq. (6) and further factor out the packet matrix, the verification at each non-source node can be seen as solving a homogeneous system of equations. In a more general sense, the constituents of the homogeneous system that correspond to the ith verification key $\boldsymbol{k}_{v_i}$ are the:

• The transpose of the sub matrix formed by removing the ith row from the matrix $\boldsymbol{K}_g$
• The transpose of the vector formed by all the remaining elements of the ith row of matrix $\boldsymbol{K}_v$ when the element in position (i, i) is removed from the matrix. We henceforth denote this matrix with $\boldsymbol{K}'_v$ and its key vectors as $\boldsymbol{k}'_{v_i}$.

Based on the above explanation, we define the following two phase key selection process for the proposed scheme:

• The KDC first forms the key generation matrix $\boldsymbol{K}_g$. The elements of this matrix are picked from the field $\mathbb{F}_q$. These elements are picked such that any $(l - 2)$ columns of the matrix are linearly independent. The remaining $(m + n) - (l - 2)$ columns are formed via linear combinations of the $(l - 2)$ linearly independent columns. Also, these elements do not include the zero symbol.
• The KDC then forms homogeneous systems using the above and finds nontrivial solutions (that do not contain the zero symbol) to each of them. If the rule defined above for the selection of elements that make up the $\boldsymbol{K}_g$ matrix is followed, such a solution will always exits. These vector solutions are then used to construct the modified verification matrix $\boldsymbol{K}'_v$.

After the KDC completes the key selection phase, it will forward matrix $\boldsymbol{K}_g$ to the source. The KDC will also distribute unique corresponding row (key) pairs from matrices $\boldsymbol{K}'_v$ and $\boldsymbol{K}_g$ among each of the non-source nodes. All of these will be communicated over secure channels. Choosing the key vectors that make up matrix $\boldsymbol{K}'_v$ as shown above has two main benefits. Primarily, the length of the key vector $\boldsymbol{k}'_{v_i}$ is reduced by one symbol when the element in position (i, i) is removed from $\boldsymbol{k}_{v_i}$. This results in a reduction of the amount of space required to store each key. Furthermore, this also reduces the number of computations that have to be performed during tag verification. Secondly, the proposed key selection process ensures that all key elements are non-zero. This eliminates the security flaw which forms the foundation for this work.

Tag Generation and Packet Combination. Due to their simplicity, we combine our introductions of the tag generation and packet combination phases.

The tag generation phase is performed by the source node. Prior to transmitting the packets of a generation over the network the source generates tags for each them. These HMAC tags are generated using a packet payload and the key matrix $\boldsymbol{K}_g$ as shown in Eq. (2). Then, the source appends these tags to the packet payloads that were used to generate them and injects these packets into the network.

The packet combination phase is performed by all non-source nodes in the network. Per the requirements of NC, received packets must be re-combined before retransmission. Packet re-combination is done as shown in Eq. (8) using randomly selected coefficients. The re-encoded/combined packets are then sent along the corresponding outgoing channels.

$$\bar{\boldsymbol{p}}_i = \sum_{i=1}^{h} \delta_1 \boldsymbol{p}_i \tag{8}$$

Verification. The verification phase of the proposed scheme consists of two stages. In the first stage, the receiving node uses the key $\boldsymbol{k}_{g_i}$ that is in its possession to verify the packet received. This verification is done as shown in

$$\begin{bmatrix} k_{g_{i,1}} & k_{g_{i,2}} & \cdots & k_{g_{i,m+n}} \end{bmatrix} \times \begin{bmatrix} \bar{x}_1 \\ \bar{x}_2 \\ \vdots \\ \bar{x}_{m+n} \end{bmatrix} = \bar{t}_i \tag{9}$$

in Eq. (9). The main objective of this verification is to compute a tag $\bar{t}_i$ and compare it to the corresponding tag t_i found in the ith position of the received HMAC tag vector. If the two tags are the same, a value of 1 is assigned to the verification parameter ω else, ω is assigned the value of 0.

In the second phase, the receiving node verifies the vector of HMAC tags. This verification is performed using the key vector $\boldsymbol{k}'_{v_i}$ assigned to the node by the KDC and the vector formed when the tag t_i is removed from the received HMAC tag vector. A mathematical summary of this verification phase is presented in Eq. (10). If the result of computing the appropriate dot product in Eq. (10) is 0, the value of 1 is assigned to the authentication parameter $\bar{\omega}$. Else, $\bar{\omega}$ is assigned the value of 0. A received packet is said to have passed verification and should be accepted by the receiving node if $\omega \times \bar{\omega} = 1$. Else, the packet has been tampered with and should be rejected.

$$
\bar{\omega} = \begin{cases}
\begin{bmatrix} k'_{v_{i,1}} & k'_{v_{i,2}} & \cdots & k'_{v_{i,l-1}} \end{bmatrix} \times \begin{bmatrix} t_2 \\ t_3 \\ \vdots \\ t_l \end{bmatrix} = 0 & \text{when } i = 1 \\[3em]
\begin{bmatrix} k'_{v_{i,1}} & k'_{v_{i,2}} & \cdots & k'_{v_{i,l-1}} \end{bmatrix} \times \begin{bmatrix} t_1 \\ \vdots \\ t_{i-1} \\ t_{i+1} \\ \vdots \\ t_l \end{bmatrix} = 0 & \text{when } 1 < i < l \\[3em]
\begin{bmatrix} k'_{v_{i,1}} & k'_{v_{i,2}} & \cdots & k'_{v_{i,l-1}} \end{bmatrix} \times \begin{bmatrix} t_1 \\ t_2 \\ \vdots \\ t_{l-1} \end{bmatrix} = 0 & \text{when } i = l
\end{cases} \tag{10}
$$

3.4   Simulation Results

In order to confirm our claims with respect to the possible damage that can be caused by the discovered security flaw as well as the effectiveness of the proposed countermeasure we carried out a simulation. The simulator was developed

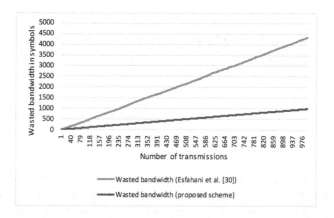

Fig. 1. Simulation results comparing wasted bandwidth during tag pollution attacks

in MATLAB 2016 and performed on a computer with an Intel 1100KF processor and 16G of RAM. The simulator generated 1000 instances of the butterfly network in which a random packet was transmitted from the source to the sink nodes. Random intermediate nodes were selected to act as rogue nodes during each instance and polluted random tags. The simulator kept track of the total number of hops polluted packets traveled before being detected. Figure 1 presents the results of this simulation. As can be observed, the proposed scheme resulted in a much lower waste of network bandwidth. This is due to the fact that the proposed key selection model allows nodes to detect tag corruption one hop away. This however is not the case with Esfahani et al.'s scheme [30] where a packet with a polluted tag can easily travel several hops without being detected.

3.5 Security

The security of our scheme is based on the condition presented in [35] which has now been widely accepted as a standard for determining the security of an HMAC based scheme. According to Li et al. [35], an HMAC scheme is said to be secure if for any probabilistic polynomial time adversary, the probability of a successful forgery is upper bound by $1/q$. Due to page limitations as well as the popularity of this proof we omit it in this work. However, for a complete proof, the reader can refer to one of our previous works [38].

4 Evaluation and Further Discussion

In this section we present a comparative evaluation of three authentication schemes: proposed scheme, ENSB HMAC [30], and the Dual HMAC [31]. In this evaluation we will be comparing their computational, communication, and key storage overheads. The schemes in [30, 31] are the two most popular current schemes in existing literature that are similar to the proposed scheme. Both of these are based on HMACs-only and are HCS-free.

Table 1. Comparison of overheads.

Schemes	CompOv at source node	CompOv at non-source node	KeStOv at source node	KeStOv at non-source node	CommOv
Proposed scheme	$l(m+n)$	$m+n+l-1$	$l(m+n)$	$m+n+l-1$	$m+n+l$
Dual HMAC [31]	$l(m+n+1)+l(l+1)$	$m+n+l+2$	$l(m+n+1)+l(l+1)$	$m+n+l+2$	$m+n+2l$
ENSB HMAC [30]	$l(m+n)$	$m+n+l$	$l(m+n)$	$m+n+l$	$m+n+l$

In Table 1, we present a general overview of the overheads incurred by the three schemes. Note that CommOv, CompOv, and KeStOv denote communication, computational, and key storage overheads respectively. Before we begin the chart comparison, we make the following observation from Table 1: at the source, the computational overhead for the three schemes is the same as the key storage overhead. The same observation can be made for the computational and key storage overheads at non-source nodes. For this reason, we shall combine our discussion of each pair. However, we make the following important note: computational overhead is measured in multiplications whilst key storage overhead is measured symbols. In our chart comparison, we evaluate how the schemes perform with respect to an increase in the number of packets in a generation. We vary the generation size from 1 to 10 whilst the payload size and number of tags per packet remain fixed at 128 and 8 symbols respectively.

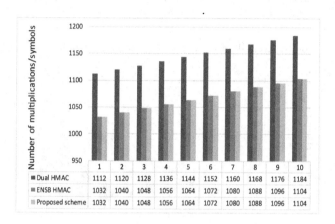

Fig. 2. Computational and key storage overheads at the source

Both Table 1 and Fig. 2 show that the proposed scheme and the ENSB HMAC incur the lowest computational and key storage overheads at the source nodes. One other interesting observation that can be made from the table of values in Fig. 2 is the slight increase in the overheads between the proposed and ENSB HMAC versus the Dual HMAC from 6.76% to 7.20%. This difference arises from the fact that the aforementioned schemes use subspace whilst the Dual HMAC scheme uses orthogonal HMAC tags.

Figure 3 presents an overview of how the three schemes perform with respect to computational and key storage overheads at non-source nodes. This time, the three schemes incur almost similar results for each generation size. As can be observed, the proposed scheme incurs overheads that are between 0.68% to 2.16% lower than the two other schemes under evaluation.

A chart comparison of the communication overheads incurred by the three schemes is presented in Fig. 4. The Dual HMAC scheme once again incurs the highest overhead. The proposed and ENSB HMAC schemes incur an overhead

192   L. Tandoh et al.

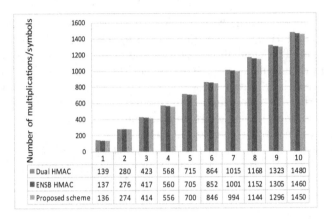

Fig. 3. Computational and key storage overheads at non-source nodes

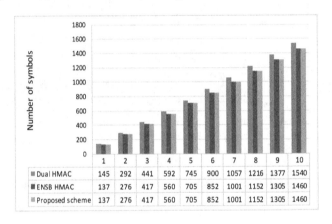

Fig. 4. Communication overhead

that is roughly 5% less than the overhead incurred by the Dual HMAC for different generation sizes.

Overall, the ENSB HMAC and the proposed scheme incur lower overheads in all scenarios. Also, the proposed scheme outperforms the ENSB HMAC in terms of computational and key storage overheads at non source nodes. However, there is still the following to consider before the most efficient and secure scheme can be determined. The key selection model of the Dual HMAC scheme can easily be adjusted to eliminate the zero symbol security loophole. However, this scheme incurs higher implementation and execution overheads. As such, even if its key selection model is adjusted, the proposed scheme will still be a better option. Furthermore, this scheme only provides 50% resistance to tag pollution attacks. With respect to the ENSB HMAC scheme, the proposed scheme bears the following advantages: First of all, the proposed scheme has a concrete key selection model which ensures that it is not prone to the security flaw introduced in this work. There has been no such model given for the ENSB HMAC. Secondly, due to the modifications made to the tag verification stage, the proposed scheme shows a slight performance improvement in the areas of computational and key storage overheads at non-source nodes. From the above, it is clear that the proposed scheme completely outperforms the remaining two schemes and offers a more practical and secure solution to authentication in network coding.

5 Conclusion

In this work we unravel an otherwise ignored vital constraint that must be considered during the selection of key vectors for HMAC-based NC authentication schemes. Ignoring this requirement reduces the resistance of these schemes to pollution attacks. With this requirement in mind, we proposed a modified NC authentication scheme that is based on the HMAC paradigm. Our authentication scheme provides full message and tag pollution attack resistance. The results of our evaluation show that the proposed scheme achieves the aforementioned resistance without any extra computational, communication, and key storage overheads. As a matter of fact, in some cases, the proposed scheme incurs computational and key storage overheads that are slightly lower than the two state of the art schemes to which it was compared.

Acknowledgments. This work is supported by the Sichuan Science and Technology Program (grant no. 2021YFG0157)

A   Description of Symbols

This appendix presents a tabulated description of all the symbols that were used in this work. Please that the symbols are listed in order of appearance (Table 2).

Table 2. List of symbols used

Symbol	Description
t_i	HMAC tag
t	An HMAC tag vector of length l
$k_{i,j}$	Element of the $i^t h$ key vector $\boldsymbol{k}_i$
$\boldsymbol{k}_i$	A key vector of length l
$\boldsymbol{K}_g$	Matrix of key vectors used to generate the HMAC tag vector for a packet in [30]
$\boldsymbol{K}_v$	Matrix of key vectors used to verify the vector of HMAC tags generated by $\boldsymbol{K}_g$ in [30]
$\boldsymbol{k}_{v_i}$	A single key vector of length l that forms the ith row of the verification matrix $\boldsymbol{K}_v$ in [30]
$\boldsymbol{K}'_v$	Matrix of key vectors used to verify the vector of HMAC tags generated by $\boldsymbol{K}_g$ in the proposed scheme
$\boldsymbol{k}'_{v_i}$	A single key vector of length $l-1$ that forms the ith row of the verification matrix $\boldsymbol{K}'_v$ in the proposed scheme
$\boldsymbol{p}_i$	Packet vector received by a node along an incoming channel i
$\overline{\boldsymbol{p}}_i$	Packet vector leaving a node along an outgoing channel i
δ_i	Local encoding coefficient
h	Number of edges incident on a node
$\boldsymbol{k}_{g_i}$	A single key vector of length $m+n$ that forms the ith row of the tag generation matrix $\boldsymbol{K}_g$ in [30]
ω and $\overline{\omega}$	Verification parameters used to denote if the received packet payload and HMAC tag vector passed verification
Rnk	Denotes the rank of the matrix formed by packet vectors in the security proof of the proposed scheme

References

1. Ahlswede, R., Ning, C., Li, S.R., Yeung, R.W.: Network information flow. IEEE Trans. Inf. Theory **46**(4), 1204–1216 (2000)
2. Menger, K.: Zur allgemeinen kurventheorie. Fundam. Math. **10**(1), 96–115 (1927)
3. Elias, P., Feinstein, A., Shannon, C.: A note on the maximum flow through a network. IRE Trans. Inf. Theory **2**(4), 117–119 (1956)
4. Ford, L., Fulkerson, D.: Maximal flow through a network. Can. J. Math. **8**, 399–404 (1956)
5. Cover, T.M., Thomas, J.A.: Elements of Information Theory. Wiley Series in Telecommunications and Signal Processing (2006)
6. Iqbal, M.A., Dai, B., Huang, B., Hassan, A., Yu, S.: Survey of network coding-aware routing protocols in wireless networks. J. Netw. Comput. Appl. **34**(6), 1956–1970 (2011)
7. Gkantsidis, C., Rodriguez, P.R.: Network coding for large scale content distribution. In: Proceedings IEEE 24th Annual Joint Conference of the IEEE Computer and Communications Societies, vol. 4, pp. 2235–2245. IEEE (2005)

8. Chachulski, S., Jennings, M., Katti, S., Katabi, D.: Trading structure for randomness in wireless opportunistic routing. SIGCOMM Comput. Commun. Rev. **37**(4), 169–180 (2007). https://doi.org/10.1145/1282427.1282400
9. Gkantsidis, C., Goldberg, M.: Avalanche: file swarming with network coding. Microsoft Research (2005)
10. Katti, S., Katabi, D., Hu, W., Rahul, H., Medard, M.: The importance of being opportunistic: practical network coding for wireless environments. Newsl. ACM SIGCOMM Comput. Commun. Rev. **36**(4), 243–254 (2006)
11. Wu, Y., Chou, P.A., Kung, S.Y.: Information exchange in wireless networks with network coding and physical-layer broadcast. Report, MSR-TR-2004 (2005)
12. Widmer, J., Fragouli, C., Le Boudec, J.Y.: Low-complexity energy-efficient broadcasting in wireless ad-hoc networks using network coding. In: Proceedings (2005)
13. Dimakis, A.G., Prabhakaran, V., Ramchandran, K.: Ubiquitous access to distributed data in large-scale sensor networks through decentralized erasure codes. In: IPSN 2005. Fourth International Symposium on Information Processing in Sensor Networks 2005, pp. 111–117. IEEE (2005)
14. Parsamehr, R., Mantas, G., Rodriguez, J., Martinez-Ortega, J.F.: IDLP: an efficient intrusion detection and location-aware prevention mechanism for network coding-enabled mobile small cells. IEEE Access **8**, 43863–43875 (2020)
15. Parsamehr, R., Esfahani, A., Mantas, G., Rodriguez, J., Martínez-Ortega, J.F.: A location-aware IDPS scheme for network coding-enabled mobile small cells. In: 2019 IEEE 2nd 5G World Forum (5GWF), pp. 91–96. IEEE (2019)
16. Adat, V., Parsamehr, R., Politis, I., Tselios, C., Kotsopoulos, S.: Malicious user identification scheme for network coding enabled small cell environment. In: ICC 2020–2020 IEEE International Conference on Communications (ICC), pp. 1–6. IEEE (2020)
17. Katti, S., Rahul, H., Hu, W., Katabi, D., Médard, M., Crowcroft, J.: XORs in the air: practical wireless network coding. In: Proceedings of the 2006 Conference on Applications, Technologies, Architectures, and Protocols for Computer Communications, pp. 243–254 (2006)
18. Chen, Y.J., Wang, L.C., Wang, K., Ho, W.L.: Topology-aware network coding for wireless multicast. IEEE Syst. J. **12**(4), 3683–3692 (2018)
19. Gkantsidis, C., Rodriguez, P.: Cooperative security for network coding file distribution. In: INFOCOM, vol. 3, p. 5 (2006)
20. Yu, Z., Wei, Y., Ramkumar, B., Guan, Y.: An efficient signature-based scheme for securing network coding against pollution attacks. In: IEEE INFOCOM 2008-The 27th Conference on Computer Communications, pp. 1409–1417. IEEE (2008)
21. Dai, B., Zhang, S., Qu, Y., Yang, J., Wang, F.: Orthogonal vector based network coding against pollution attacks in n-layer combination networks. In: 2010 5th International ICST Conference on Communications and Networking in China, pp. 1–5. IEEE (2010)
22. Charles, D., Jain, K., Lauter, K.: Signatures for network coding. Int. J. Inf. Coding Theory **1**(1), 3–14 (2009)
23. Jaggi, S., Langberg, M., Katti, S., Ho, T., Katabi, D., Médard, M.: Resilient network coding in the presence of byzantine adversaries. In: IEEE INFOCOM 2007–26th IEEE International Conference on Computer Communications, pp. 616–624. IEEE (2007)
24. Yu, Z., Wei, Y., Ramkumar, B., Guan, Y.: An efficient scheme for securing XOR network coding against pollution attacks. In: IEEE INFOCOM 2009, pp. 406–414. IEEE (2009)

25. Kehdi, E., Li, B.: Null keys: limiting malicious attacks via null space properties of network coding. In: IEEE INFOCOM 2009, pp. 1224–1232. IEEE (2009)
26. Zhao, F., Kalker, T., Médard, M., Han, K.J.: Signatures for content distribution with network coding. In: 2007 IEEE International Symposium on Information Theory, pp. 556–560. IEEE (2007)
27. Agrawal, S., Boneh, D.: Homomorphic MACs: MAC-based integrity for network coding. In: Abdalla, M., Pointcheval, D., Fouque, P.-A., Vergnaud, D. (eds.) ACNS 2009. LNCS, vol. 5536, pp. 292–305. Springer, Heidelberg (2009). https://doi.org/10.1007/978-3-642-01957-9_18
28. Krohn, M.N., Freedman, M.J., Mazieres, D.: On-the-fly verification of rateless erasure codes for efficient content distribution. In: IEEE Symposium on Security and Privacy 2004, Proceedings 2004, pp. 226–240. IEEE (2004)
29. Ho, T., Leong, B., Koetter, R., Médard, M., Effros, M., Karger, D.R.: Byzantine modification detection in multicast networks with random network coding. IEEE Trans. Inf. Theory 54(6), 2798–2803 (2008)
30. Esfahani, A., Mantas, G., Rodriguez, J.: An efficient null space-based homomorphic MAC scheme against tag pollution attacks in RLNC. IEEE Commun. Lett. 20(5), 918–921 (2016)
31. Esfahani, A., Yang, D., Mantas, G., Nascimento, A., Rodriguez, J.: Dual-homomorphic message authentication code scheme for network coding-enabled wireless sensor networks. Int. J. Distrib. Sens. Netw. 11(7), 510251 (2015)
32. Kim, M., et al.: On counteracting byzantine attacks in network coded peer-to-peer networks. IEEE J. Sel. Areas Commun. 28(5), 692–702 (2010)
33. Cai, N., Yeung, R.W.: Secure network coding. In: Proceedings IEEE International Symposium on Information Theory, p. 323. IEEE (2002)
34. Zhang, P., Jiang, Y., Lin, C., Fan, Y., Shen, X.: P-coding: secure network coding against eavesdropping attacks. In: 2010 Proceedings IEEE INFOCOM, pp. 1–9. IEEE (2010)
35. Li, Y., Yao, H., Chen, M., Jaggi, S., Rosen, A.: Ripple authentication for network coding. In: 2010 Proceedings IEEE INFOCOM, pp. 1–9. IEEE (2010)
36. Zhang, P., Jiang, Y., Lin, C., Yao, H., Wasef, A., Shenz, X.: Padding for orthogonality: efficient subspace authentication for network coding. In: 2011 Proceedings IEEE INFOCOM, pp. 1026–1034. IEEE (2011)
37. Esfahani, A., Mantas, G., Rodriguez, J., Neves, J.C.: An efficient homomorphic MAC-based scheme against data and tag pollution attacks in network coding-enabled wireless networks. Int. J. Inf. Secur. 16(6), 627–639 (2017). https://doi.org/10.1007/s10207-016-0351-z
38. Lawrence, T., Li, F., Ali, I., Haruna, C.R., Kpiebaareh, M.Y., Christopher, T.: A computationally efficient HMAC-based authentication scheme for network coding. Telecommun. Syst. 79, 47–69 (2022). https://doi.org/10.1007/s11235-021-00842-6

Network Security Situation Assessment Method Based on MHSA-FL Model

Kejun Zhang[1,2] ⓘ, Xinrui Jiang[1](✉) ⓘ, Xinying Yu[2](✉) ⓘ, and Liwen Feng[1] ⓘ

[1] Beijing Electronic Science and Technology Institute, Beijing, China
zkj@besti.edu.cn
[2] School of Cyberspace Security, Beijing University of Posts
and Telecommunications, Beijing, China

Abstract. Confront the evaluation quality problems caused by high data dimension and imbalance between positive and negative samples in the network security situation, this paper proposes a new situation assessment method based on the MHSA-FL model. Firstly, the model references multiple self-attention weight matrices to learn data information in different subspaces, which promotes the ability to extract key features of the global context. Secondly, the model introduces the Focal Loss function to reduce the weight of natural flow samples in training, which effectively mines attack samples that account for a small proportion of network data. Finally, a situation quantification method based on the network attack influence factor is proposed, which calculates the network security situation value in a period through a sliding time window, and realizes the quantitative evaluation of the network security situation. This paper conducts a situation assessment experiment on the MHSA-FL model on the open network security data set CIC-IDS2018. Experimental results show that the MHSA-FL model improves the $F1$ value by 2%–5% compared with other models.

Keywords: Network security situation assessment · MHSA-FL model · Multi-head self-attention · Focal loss function · Sliding time window

1 Introduction

With the development of mobile cloud computing [12], distributed cloud storage [18], Internet of Things [13] and other technologies, the whole society is gradually moving towards informatization. While the information society brings convenience to people's lives, it also brings many potential risks for cybersecurity. Due to the continuous expansion of network scale, extensive security loopholes are exploited by hackers, resulting in various network security incidents

Supported by organization Advanced Discipline Construction Project of Beijing Universities.

emerge endlessly. The hackers' attack means are no longer limited to the traditional ways, becoming increasingly sophisticated, which have the characteristics of long-term latency, strong persistence, strong concealment, etc. In recent years, organized and powerful hackers from abroad have launched attacks on China's Internet, targeting computers, email, mobile intelligent terminals, momentous information systems, and critical information infrastructure. Domestic lawless elements conduct network destruction activities through phishing, ransomware, and other ways. These attacks seriously affect the social order and people's property security and bring colossal menaces to China's network security. Therefore, dynamic risk assessment [25] and network situation awareness [6] play a crucial role in cybersecurity.

Network security situation awareness (NSSA) is a network security defense technology that analyzes user behavior data and determines whether user behavior is offensive. Network security situational awareness originated from the military confrontation thought in 1999 and was initially applied in the aviation field. However, the development of NSSA is slow due to backward technology and low demand. With the continuous development of Internet technology and the continuous expansion of network scale, network security situational awareness technology has become a crucial means of network security defense. NSSA helps network administrators understand the past, present, and future network status and prepare for defense in advance. NSSA platform obtains all kinds of security event data from security devices, operation, maintenance processes, external attacks, and IDS, and preprocesses heterogeneous data to improve the value density of data. Then according to the established index system, extract index data, and use data analysis and machine learning technology to conduct qualitative and quantitative analysis of the fused information, analyze the current network security state, and give the corresponding measures. At the same time, predict the security situation of the network in the future. In the current complex network society, the study of NSSA has essential practical significance.

1.1 Related Work

In 1988, Endsley [11] proposed the concept of situation awareness for the first time, and designed the conceptual model of situation awareness into three stages of situation element extraction, situation understanding and situation prediction. So far, most research in the field of network situational awareness has been based on the three-layer situational awareness model proposed by Endsley. In 2000, Bass proposed the Tim Bass intrusion detection framework based on multi-sensor data fusion [2], and applied this framework to the next generation intrusion detection system and NSAS, realizing the functions of intrusion behavior detection, intrusion rate calculation, intruder identity and intruder behavior identification situation assessment, threat assessment and so on. In 2012, Stephen E. Smith [20] proposed the comprehensive use of existing network security tools, including traffic analysis tools, vulnerability scanning tools and intrusion detection systems, and designed a system to integrate existing tools to comprehensively assess and protect network security. In 2015, Xi et al. [24]

proposed an improved quantitative assessment method for network security situation. Through experimental comparison, it was proved that the value of risk generated based on the improved algorithm was more reasonable to quantify the network security situation. In 2018, Mohammad Hossein Bazrafkan [3] proposed the concept of a national situation awareness from the perspective of national strategic decision-making, with a hierarchical structure to in-crease the efficiency of situation identification and reduce the interference of wrong information. In 2019, Matthias Eckhart et al. [10] proposed the establishment of a virtual copy of the system to comprehensively perceive the network situation in a parallel environment. In the same year, Thibault Debatty [7] proposed to provide more accurate support for decision-making by using more realistic simulation of security events at the network shooting range. In 2020, Shi et al. [15] summarized the related work of network security situation awareness, detailed the key technologies of situation awareness from multiple levels, and proposed that network security situation awareness still needs to solve the problems of anti-situation awareness, human-computer interaction and automatic response.

In 2017, Google published Attention Is All You Need [21] and put forward the Transformer model for the first time. The Multi-head self-attention mechanism as the core of Transformer, deeply welcomed by researchers. Subsequently, Wang et al. [22] enhanced the collaboration between multiple heads in multiple attention in a simple and effective way, optimizing the weight matrix parameters of each head, and improving the performance in NLP tasks. Wang et al. [23] added an additional temperature hyperparameter for each head in multihead attention to better time aggregate variable length input speech and improve the performance of end-to-end neural network for speaker recognition. Cheng et al. [5] used graph attention network and multi-head self-attention mechanism to extract the characteristics of drugs and proteins, obtain the long dependent context relationship of amino acid sequences, and effectively predict drug-target interactions (DTIs). An et al. [1] proposed a new and non-text speaker recognition method, which extends VGG and ResNet convolutional neural network through a structured self-attention mechanism, which can gather relevant information from different locations of input languages of different lengths.

Focal loss was proposed by Lin et al. [16] in 2017 to solve the problem of low accuracy caused by data imbalance in classification by reshaping standard cross entropy loss. Later, Doi et al. [9] used focal loss in the semantic segmentation task of high-resolution remote sensing images, and the accuracy of ISPRS 2D semantic labeling was improved. Kuang et al. [14] applied focal loss to pixel-level text/non-text classification task, balancing the weight loss of easy and difficult samples in the training process and improving the classification efficiency. Mayar et al. [17] introduced focal loss to solve the problem of 2D image classification, which showed good performance in fracture detection. Chang et al. [4] introduced focal loss into the MR image segmentation task of brain tumor, which solved the imbalance problem of multiple types of different brain tissues and effectively improved the segmentation accuracy.

1.2   Contribution

Situation assessment is a key part of network security situation awareness. It can dynamically reflect the security status of the network by extracting, calculating and evaluating the security data generated by network security devices. However, network security data is often characterized by high dimension and unbalanced positive and negative samples. Therefore, this paper proposes a network security situation assessment method based on MHSA-FL (Multi-Head Self-Attention Model based on Focal Loss). The contributions of this paper are as follows:

(1) The model introduces several self-attention weight matrices to learn the information of different subspaces of network data to improve the ability of extracting key features of global context and reduce data noise.
(2) Focal loss function is introduced into the model to balance positive and negative samples in network traffic and reduce the weight of normal traffic samples in training, so as to better mine attack samples which occupy a relatively small proportion in network data.
(3) Through the classification and identification of network attack, the influence degree of different network attack on different target aircraft is analyzed, and a situation quantification method based on the influence factor of network attack is proposed. The method calculates the value of network security situation in a period of time through sliding time window, and realizes the quantitative evaluation of network security situation.

2   Preliminaries

2.1   Self-attentional Mechanism

Self-attention mechanism (SA) is an improvement based on attention mechanism, which has been successfully applied in natural language processing (NLP), question answering system (QAS) and speech recognition (SR), especially in machine translation and text generation. The self-attention mechanism back-propagates the learned parameters through the network, correlates different positions in the sequence, and automatically calculates the importance of different positions in the sequence. The detailed process of self-attention mechanism is shown in Fig. 1.

Where a_i represents the input sequence data. After dimension transformation (optional), Query (q_i), key (k_i), and Value (v_i) are obtained by multiplying the mapping matrices W^Q, W^K, and W^V that are the same as the three dimensions, as shown in Formula (1), (2) and (3).

$$q_i = W^Q a_i, i = 1, 2, \cdots, n \tag{1}$$

$$k_i = W^K a_i, i = 1, 2, \cdots, n \tag{2}$$

$$v_i = W^V a_i, i = 1, 2, \cdots, n \tag{3}$$

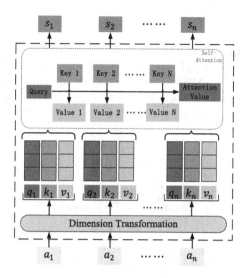

Fig. 1. Detailed process of self-attention mechanism.

The self-attention mechanism maps the output of each location to a query and a set of key-value pairs to obtain a weighted sum of different locations in the context, with the weight assigned to each value (v_i) calculated based on the query (q_i) and the corresponding key (k_i). The inner product of vectors is calculated by q_i and $k_1, k_2, \cdots, k_n$ respectively. Since the calculated result may not be between 0 and 1, it needs to be processed by softmax function. When the dimension d is too large, the dot product will greatly increase. In order to alleviate its influence, the scaling factor $\frac{1}{\sqrt{d}}$ is introduced from the attention mechanism to scale the dot product, as shown in Formula (4). Then multiply the processed results with the corresponding positions $v_1, v_2, \cdots, v_n$ to obtain the output s_i, as shown in Formula (5).

$$Attention(q_i, K, V) = softmax(\frac{q_i k_i^T}{\sqrt{d}}), i = 1, 2, \cdots, n \qquad (4)$$

$$s_i = \sum_{i=1}^{n} Attention(q_i, K, V) \cdot v_i, i = 1, 2, \cdots, n \qquad (5)$$

Fully connected self-attention module and transformer encoder structure are used to learn the characteristic information of network security data sequence. Combined with the effectiveness and robustness of multi-head self-attention mechanism, this structure solves the problem that traditional neural networks cannot obtain context information in sequences. Compared with the RNN/LSTM model, the model in this paper not only overcomes the disadvantage that the long-dependent information cannot be obtained when the sequence is long, but also ensures the parallel computation of data while learning the context information.

2.2   Multi-headed Self-attention Mechanism

Figure 2 is a schematic diagram of the multi-headed self-attention mechanism. The key technology of BERT [8] and Transformer model is the multi-head self-attention mechanism (MHSA), which can use multiple self-attention weight matrices to learn various semantic information of different spatial features.

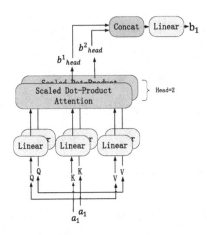

Fig. 2. Schematic diagram of multi-head self-attention mechanism.

In the self-attention mechanism, if q_i, k_i and v_i are regarded as a head as a whole, the multi-headed self-attention mechanism is to multiply multiple sets of mapping matrices W^Q, W^K, and W^V with specific sequence data a_i to obtain multiple sets of q_i, k_i, and v_i. Then the results are spliced (vector heads are connected) and output, as shown in Formula (6). Finally, a single-layer fully connected neural network (Linear) is used for Linear transformation to obtain b_1, as shown in Formula (7).

$$head_i = Attention(QW_i{}^Q, KW_i{}^K, VW_i{}^V), i = 1, 2, \cdots, n \qquad (6)$$

$$MultiHead(Q, K, V) = Concat(head_1, head_2, \cdots, head_n)W^O \qquad (7)$$

2.3   Focal Loss Function

Most of the security data collected in the real network environment are normal samples, and the proportion of abnormal data is often very small, so the positive and negative samples in the classification task are extremely unbalanced, which has a great impact on the classification accuracy. In this paper, focal loss was used as the loss function of multi-head self-attention model, which reduced the weight of a large number of normal flow samples in training and better mined the attack samples which accounted for a relatively small proportion in network data.

Focal loss function [16] is an improvement based on the traditional cross entropy loss function. Bisection cross entropy Loss function is denoted as:

$$CE(p,y) = \begin{cases} -log(p), & if \quad y = 1 \\ -log(1-p), & otherwise \end{cases} \tag{8}$$

For the sake of simplicity below, let:

$$p_t = \begin{cases} p, & if \quad y = 1 \\ 1-p, & otherwise \end{cases} \tag{9}$$

y of the above formula is the predicted output (positive and negative samples). As can be seen from Formula (9), for positive samples, the larger the output probability P of this loss function is, the smaller the loss value will be; while for negative samples, the smaller the output probability is, the smaller the loss value will be. If there are a large number of negative samples at this time, the loss function may be slow in the iterative process of a large number of simple samples and may not be optimized to the best. In other words, this loss function is equal to all kinds of samples, and is not suitable for the case of extremely unbalanced positive and negative samples. To solve the problem of unbalanced positive and negative samples, α coefficient is introduced to reduce the influence degree of a large number of positive (negative) samples. The size of α is inversely proportional to the number of positive (negative) samples. The larger the sample size, the smaller the α coefficient will be, denoted as $CE(p_t) = -\alpha_t log(p_t)$.

Focal loss function not only considers the number of positive and negative samples, but also considers the imbalance between simple samples and complex samples. Modulation factor $(1 - p_t)^\gamma$ is added into the original cross entropy function, which reduces the attention of simple samples and increases the training intensity of complex samples. Focal loss function is denoted as:

$$CE(p_t) = -\alpha_t(1 - p_t)^\gamma log(p_t) \tag{10}$$

3 Network Security Situation Assessment Method Based on MHSA-FL Model

In this paper, after the original network security data is processed by data cleaning and standardization (normalization), the standard data set is input into the MHSA-FL model for training test, and then the network situation assessment is completed according to the situation quantification and other operations, as shown in Fig. 3.

3.1 Input Data Processing

Firstly, the original network security data is preprocessed and the non-numerical features of the data set are transformed into numerical features. The second is

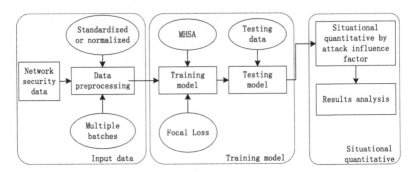

Fig. 3. Network situation assessment process based on MHSA-FL model.

to clean the data, remove the null and useless values of the data row. In order to eliminate the influence of unit and scale differences between features, the convergence rate of the model was optimized and the data set was normalized. Due to the large capacity of network security data, this paper uses Batch operation to divide the data into multiple Batch training, thus reducing equipment requirements and effectively reducing model training time.

3.2   MHSA-FL Model

As shown in Fig. 4, in the training process of MHSA-FL model, the convolution layer with convolution kernel of $1 \times 1 \times n$ is first used for dimensionality reduction of data. The convolution layer realizes cross-channel information interaction through linear combination changes of information between channels, and achieves efficient dimensionality reduction while reducing a large number of parameters.

In order to enhance the model's generalization ability and prevent model overfit-ting, multiple Dropout layers are added during training to reduce the number of intermediate features and reduce redundancy. In order to ensure the stability of data feature distribution and accelerate the convergence of the model, several layers of layer-normalization are added during the training process to transform data from different channels into data with mean value of 0 and variance of 1. In order to further avoid the gradient disappearance problem of traditional RNN, the gradient can be propagated from back to front across layers. In this paper, residual connection is made to MHSA calculation results, which effectively improves network performance.

Finally, the output probabilities of all kinds are calculated by SoftMax function, and the classification results are compared with Focal Loss function (training data labels with input data) until the Loss is reduced to the control range, and the training ends. After the initial training results are obtained, the model is fine-tuned by reducing the learning rate to obtain the optimal parameters of the model.

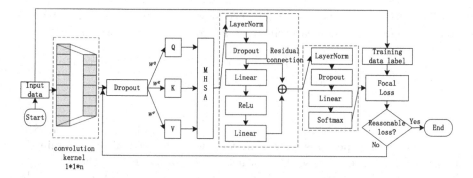

Fig. 4. MHSA-FL model training flowchart.

3.3 Quantification of Situation Assessment

Situation Quantification Method Based on Network Attack Influence Factors. Without accurate metrics, effective security awareness cannot be formed. In the real world network, the network security state cannot be directly observed, so it is necessary to construct a set of appropriate situation indicators to comprehensively and accurately express the network security situation. In combination with the construction principle of the situation assessment index system and previous research results [26], this paper proposes a situation quantification method based on network attack impact factors, including attack threat factor, attack quantity factor, attack frequency factor, attack probability factor and equipment importance factor. The relevant definitions are as follows.

Attack threat factor: indicates the impact of different attacks on the network system. It is abbreviated as I_i (i indicates different attack types and is obtained by CSVV scoring standard).

Attack number factor: reflects the total number of attacks in a period of time, abbreviated as K.

Attack frequency factor: reflects the attack frequency of each attack type within a period of time, and is abbreviated as C_i (i indicates different attack types).

Attack probability factor: reflects the total proportion of all kinds of attacks in a period of time, abbreviated as P.

Device importance factor: reflects the importance of the attacked device, which is abbreviated as H_i (i represents different attack types and is obtained from data providers), as shown in Formula (11):

$$H_i = \frac{M_i}{\sum_{i=1}^{n} M_i} \tag{11}$$

Where M_i represents the importance score of information saved by the attacked device, and the measurement standard is shown in Formula (12).

$$M_i = \begin{cases} 1.0, & confidential \\ 0.8, & important \\ 0.4, & ordinary \end{cases} \tag{12}$$

In order to effectively reflect the security situation of each time period in the network, this paper uses the sliding time window mechanism to obtain the observation sequence of the security situation, as shown in Fig. 5. The time series $T = (t_1, t_2, \cdots, t_{s-1}, t_s)$ is defined as the time window, $t_s - t_1$ is the width of the time window, and $t_i - t_{i-1}$ is the sub-time window. Define slide step length The number of steps that slide forward for multiple sub-time Windows. In order to better meet the requirements of online and real-time evaluation, smaller sub-time window and sliding step size should be set.

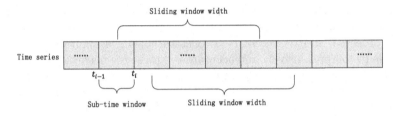

Fig. 5. Schematic diagram of sliding time window.

The influence degree of network attack on the entire network system in a sliding time window is quantified, as shown in Formula (13).

$$S = \frac{\frac{1}{e^{1-p}} \left(\sum_{i=1}^{n} C_i \cdot I_i \cdot H_i \right)}{K} \tag{13}$$

Where, the attack probability factor $p = \frac{K}{N}$, N represents the size of the sliding time window, n represents the total attack types contained in a time slice, and S represents the network security situation value within this period of time.

Classification of Network Security Assessment Levels. This paper refers to the national emergency response plan, combined with the characteristics of network hazard elements, the network space is divided into five levels of safety, light danger, danger, medium danger, high danger. In order to observe the situation assessment results more intuitively and clearly, this paper uses the interval $[0, 1]$ to represent the weight of indicators at all levels, as shown in Table 1.

Table 1. Security situation classification.

Situational value	Dangerous levels	Instructions
0.0–0.15	Security	The network runs normally and no intrusion occurs
0.15–0.40	Low risk	The network is slightly invaded and the loss is small
0.40–0.65	Risk	The network is invaded, which is usually serious
0.65–0.80	Medium risk	The network is heavily invaded
0.80–1.00	Higher risk	There are a lot of intrusions and it's very dangerous

4   Experimental Analysis

4.1   Experimental Environment and Parameters

The experimental environment information set up in this paper is shown in Table 2. The model experimental parameters of this paper are as follows: $epoch = 30, batch processing size = 24, feature length of each traffic = 78, learning\_rate = 5e - 5, convolution kernel size = (1, 1, 64), Head = 2, dropout = 0.1$, and the optimizer is $Adam$. In the quantization of situation assessment, set the sliding time window size to 20 min, the sub-time window to 1 min, and the sliding step size to 10.

Table 2. Experimental environment information.

Species	Parameter
Operating system	Windows 10
Processor	i7-8750H CPU @ 2.20 GHz 2.21 GHz
RAM	16 GB
Development of language	Python3.7.6
IDE	PyCharm2019 @ Jupyter Notebook
Related library	Numpy, Pandas, Torch, Functools···

4.2   Dataset

Due to the rapid development of network technology and the continuous update of terminal equipment, most of the classic data sets (such as KDDCUP99, NSLKDD, etc.) have been outdated and unreliable. Some of them lack traffic diversity and capacity to cover a variety of known attacks. Others anonymize packet payload data and do not reflect current trends. The experimental data CSE-CIC-IDS2018 [19] selected in this paper is from a cooperative project between the Communications Security Agency (CSE) and the Canadian Network Security Research Institute (CIC). The project uses the network traffic generator CICFlowmeter-V3 to extract more than 70 network traffic characteristics from the captured traffic CSV files, which provides good materials for the study of network situation. The CSE-CIC-IDS2018 dataset contains seven different attack types, each of which adopts a variety of attack modes. The specific information of the attack and the quantified value of threat assessment for each attack by using the general vulnerability scoring system CVSS are shown in Table 3.

Table 3. Attack types.

Attack types	Attack methods	Attack threat factor
DoS	Hulk SlowHTTPTest GoldenEye Slowloris	0.3
Heartbleed	Heartbleed Port 444	0.7
DDOS	DDOS attack-HOIC DDOS attack-LOIC-UDP	0.6
Brute force	FTP-Patator SSH-Patator	0.2
Web attack	Damn Vulnerable Web App In-house selenium framework	0.5
Botnet attack	Ares Screenshots and key logging	0.4
Infiltration attack	Dropbox download in a windows machine Nmap and portscan	0.7

Due to the different dimensionalities of multiple features in the CIC-IDS2018 dataset, the value ranges differ greatly and cannot follow the Gaussian normal distribution, which should be processed before training. In this paper, we compare the effects of data normalization and normalization on the model convergence and find that the model can be better converged by using standardized data. In the normalization process, the mean value is subtracted from the data according to its characteristics and then divided by its variance to obtain the final result, as shown in Formula (14):

$$X' = \frac{X - X_{mean}}{X_{std}} \tag{14}$$

4.3 Experimental Results

Evaluation Index. In order to objectively and accurately measure the classification performance of the model in a small number of categories, $F1 - score$ is mainly used as the comprehensive index of performance evaluation because the labels of the CIC-IDS2018 data set are irregular and unbalanced. A (accuracy), P (precision) and R (recall) were used as reference indexes. The specific calculation announcement is as follows:

$$A = \frac{TP + TN}{TP + FN + FP + FN} \tag{15}$$

$$P = \frac{TP}{TP + FP} \tag{16}$$

$$R = \frac{TP}{TP + FN} \tag{17}$$

$$F1 - score = \frac{2PR}{P + R} \tag{18}$$

TP represents the number of correctly classified normal samples. FP represents the number of normal samples incorrectly classified as attack samples; TN represents the number of attack samples correctly classified. Number of attack samples that FN was misclassified as normal samples. A large value of $F1-score$ indicates that the model has a good classification effect.

Comparative Experiment of Attack Identification. In order to further evaluate the performance of this model, other classical models are introduced for experimental comparison, including support vector machine (SVM), K-nearest Neighbor algorithm (KNN), decision tree algorithm (DT). The experimental data in this paper includes 7 categories. To facilitate comparison, the mean values of each category are calculated. The specific experimental results are shown in Table 4.

Table 4. Comparison of experimental results of each model.

Model types	Accuracy	Precidion	Recall	F1-score
SVM	95.5%	91.5%	89.3%	90.4%
KNN	96.4%	93.6%	92.1%	92.8%
DT	97.5%	95.4%	92.7%	94.0%
MHSA-CE	97.7%	95.8%	90.6%	93.1%
MHSA-FL*	96.9%	95.6%	93.2%	94.3%
MHSA-FL	97.8%	96.2%	94.2%	95.2%

As can be seen from Table 4, the accuracy, precidion, recall and $F1-score$ of the model in this paper are all higher than other models. MHSA-FL* is a common model without the addition of $1 \times 1 \times N$ convolution kernel and dropout operation. Compared with MHSA-FL* model, the proposed model has improved in all indicators. It can be seen that the application of multi-head self-attention mechanism, channel dimension reduction of $1 \times 1 \times N$ convolution kernel and dropout operation play an important role in classification performance. Compared with MHSA-CE model, the *accuracy, recall* and $F1 - score$ of MHSA-FL model were improved, indicating that focal loss function improved the classification and recognition ability of various attack categories. It is found that MHSA-FL model has good generalization ability and has good effect on network attack identification task.

Comparative Experiment of Attack Identification. The time stamp of each traffic is provided in the CIC-IDS2018 dataset. Based on the time stamp, this paper calculates the security situation value according to the situation quantization method in Sect. 3.3. Then, situation quantization results of different models were obtained through the above comparison experiments, and 20 groups of network security situation values were randomly selected in chronological order for comparison, as shown in Fig. 6.

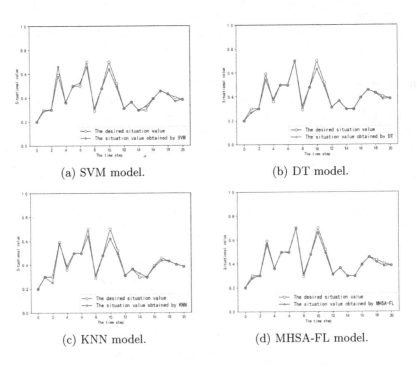

(a) SVM model.

(b) DT model.

(c) KNN model.

(d) MHSA-FL model.

Fig. 6. Quantitative comparison diagram of different model evaluations.

5 Conclusion

Given the evaluation quality problems caused by the high data dimension and the imbalance of positive and negative samples in the network security situation, we propose a network situation assessment method based on the MHSA-FL model. Firstly, the MHSA-FL model utilizes a multi-head self-attention mechanism to learn the dependency among features, which improves the ability to extract key features of global context and reduces data noise. Secondly, the MHSA-FL model introduces the Focal Loss function to balance positive and negative samples in network traffic, which reduced the weight of normal traffic samples in training and better-mined attack samples that accounted for a relatively small proportion in network data. Finally, we analyze the influence degree of different network attacks on different target aircraft through classifying and identifying the network attacks and propose a situation quantification method based on the influence factor of network attacks. The method calculates the value of network security situation in a period through a sliding time window and realizes the quantitative evaluation of the network security situation. Experimental results of this paper on the open dataset CIC-IDS2018 show that the MHSA-FL model has a good effect on network situation assessment tasks.

Although the model in this paper has improved the efficiency of attack identification, it also has some shortcomings. First, the computational characteristics of the multi-head self-attention mechanism lead to a high cost of the training process. Second, artificial parameter adjustment makes the experimental results unstable. Therefore, future research work will improve the above deficiencies and design a more stable model.

References

1. An, N.N., Thanh, N.Q., Liu, Y.: Deep CNNs with self-attention for speaker identification. IEEE Access **7**, 85327–85337 (2019)
2. Bass, T.: Intrusion detection systems and multisensor data fusion. Commun. ACM **43**(4), 99–105 (2000)
3. Bazrafkan, M.H., Gharaee, H., Enayati, A.: National cyber situation awareness model. In: 2018 9th International Symposium on Telecommunications (IST), pp. 216–220. IEEE (2018)
4. Chang, J., Zhang, X., Ye, M., Huang, D., Wang, P., Yao, C.: Brain tumor segmentation based on 3D Unet with multi-class focal loss. In: 2018 11th International Congress on Image and Signal Processing, BioMedical Engineering and Informatics (CISP-BMEI), pp. 1–5. IEEE (2018). https://doi.org/10.1109/CISP-BMEI.2018.8633056
5. Cheng, Z., Yan, C., Wu, F., Wang, J.: Drug-target interaction prediction using multi-head self-attention and graph attention network. IEEE/ACM Trans. Comput. Biol. Bioinform. 1 (2021). https://doi.org/10.1109/TCBB.2021.3077905
6. Cinque, M., Della Corte, R., Pecchia, A.: Contextual filtering and prioritization of computer application logs for security situational awareness. Future Gener. Comput. Syst. **111**, 668–680 (2020)

7. Debatty, T., Mees, W.: Building a cyber range for training cyberdefense situation awareness. In: 2019 International Conference on Military Communications and Information Systems (ICMCIS), pp. 1–6. IEEE (2019)

8. Devlin, J., Chang, M.W., Lee, K., Toutanova, K.: BERT: pre-training of deep bidirectional transformers for language understanding. arXiv preprint arXiv:1810.04805 (2018)

9. Doi, K., Iwasaki, A.: The effect of focal loss in semantic segmentation of high resolution aerial image. In: IGARSS 2018–2018 IEEE International Geoscience and Remote Sensing Symposium, pp. 6919–6922. IEEE (2018). https://doi.org/10.1109/IGARSS.2018.8519409

10. Eckhart, M., Ekelhart, A., Weippl, E.: Enhancing cyber situational awareness for cyber-physical systems through digital twins. In: 2019 24th IEEE International Conference on Emerging Technologies and Factory Automation (ETFA), pp. 1222–1225. IEEE (2019)

11. Endsley, M.R.: Design and evaluation for situation awareness enhancement. In: Proceedings of the Human Factors Society Annual Meeting, vol. 32, pp. 97–101. Sage Publications, Los Angeles (1988)

12. Fang, W., Yao, X., Zhao, X., Yin, J., Xiong, N.: A stochastic control approach to maximize profit on service provisioning for mobile cloudlet platforms. IEEE Trans. Syst. Man Cybern. Syst. **48**(4), 522–534 (2016)

13. Huang, S., Liu, A., Zhang, S., Wang, T., Xiong, N.: BD-VTE: a novel baseline data based verifiable trust evaluation scheme for smart network systems. IEEE Trans. Netw. Sci. Eng. **8**(3), 2087–2105 (2020)

14. Kuang, H., Li, Z., Ma, X., Liu, X.: Location sensitive regression algorithm for multi-oriented scene text detection with focal loss. In: 2019 11th International Conference on Measuring Technology and Mechatronics Automation (ICMTMA), pp. 462–466. IEEE (2019). https://doi.org/10.1109/ICMTMA.2019.00108

15. Le-yi, S., Jia, L., Yi-hao, L., Hong-qiang, Z., Peng-fei, D.: Survey of research on network security situation awareness. Comput. Eng. Appl. **055**(024), 1–9 (2019)

16. Lin, T.Y., Goyal, P., Girshick, R., He, K., Dollár, P.: Focal loss for dense object detection. In: Proceedings of the IEEE International Conference on Computer Vision, pp. 2980–2988 (2017)

17. Lotfy, M., Shubair, R.M., Navab, N., Albarqouni, S.: Investigation of focal loss in deep learning models for femur fractures classification. In: 2019 International Conference on Electrical and Computing Technologies and Applications (ICECTA), pp. 1–4. IEEE (2019). https://doi.org/10.1109/ICECTA48151.2019.8959770

18. Qu, Y., Xiong, N.: RFH: a resilient, fault-tolerant and high-efficient replication algorithm for distributed cloud storage. In: 2012 41st International Conference on Parallel Processing, pp. 520–529. IEEE (2012)

19. Sharafaldin, I., Lashkari, A.H., Ghorbani, A.A.: Toward generating a new intrusion detection dataset and intrusion traffic characterization, vol. 1, pp. 108–116 (2018)

20. Smith, S.E.: Tightening the net: examining and demonstrating commonly available network security tools. Ph.D. thesis, Submitted to the Faculty of the Department of Computing and Mathematical (2012)

21. Vaswani, A., et al.: Attention is all you need. In: Advances in Neural Information Processing Systems, pp. 5998–6008 (2017)

22. Wang, H., Tu, M.: Enhancing attention models via multi-head collaboration. In: 2020 International Conference on Asian Language Processing (IALP), pp. 19–23. IEEE (2020). https://doi.org/10.1109/IALP51396.2020.9310460

23. Wang, Z., Yao, K., Li, X., Fang, S.: Multi-resolution multi-head attention in deep speaker embedding. In: ICASSP 2020–2020 IEEE International Conference on Acoustics, Speech and Signal Processing (ICASSP), pp. 6464–6468. IEEE (2020). https://doi.org/10.1109/ICASSP40776.2020.9053217
24. Xi, R.R., Yun, X.C., Zhang, Y.Z., Hao, Z.Y.: An improved quantitative evaluation method for network security. Chin. J. Comput. **38**(4), 749–758 (2015)
25. Zhang, Q., Zhou, C., Tian, Y.C., Xiong, N., Qin, Y., Hu, B.: A fuzzy probability Bayesian network approach for dynamic cybersecurity risk assessment in industrial control systems. IEEE Trans. Ind. Inform. **14**(6), 2497–2506 (2017)
26. Zhao, L.: Research on network security situation assessment and prediction based on neural network. Ph.D. thesis, Northwest University (2020)

A Hybrid Network Intrusion Detection Model Based on CNN-LSTM and Attention Mechanism

Jieru Mu[1], Hua He[1,2(✉)], Lin Li[1], Shanchen Pang[2], and Cong Liu[1]

[1] Shandong University of Technology, Zibo, Shandong, China
huahe@sdut.edu.cn
[2] China University of Petroleum, Qingdao, Shandong, China

Abstract. The Internet of Things (IoT) is vulnerable to network attacks due to the real-time, open and interactive characteristics, thus causing network security risks. This makes the intrusion detection technology face new challenges of high precision and low latency. In this paper, we propose a hybrid network intrusion detection model (ACNNBN-LSTM) based on CNN-LSTM and attention mechanism to classify network intrusions in real-time. The model consists of ACNNBN and LSTM modules. In the ACNNBN module, we introduce the convolution block attention module (CBAM) and batch normalization to recognize spatial features of two-dimensional images. The LSTM module learns the temporal features of feature vectors through time series to realize real-time detection. We use the CIRA-CIC-DoHBrw-2020 unbalanced dataset to evaluate model performance. Six machine learning algorithms are selected to compare in evaluation indexes of F1 score, recall ratio, precision ratio and accuracy. Experimental results demonstrate that the ACNNBN-LSTM model is preferable than the other six models in indicators of F1 score, recall rate and accuracy. And the accuracy of our model reached 99.41%.

Keywords: Network intrusion detection · Deep learning · Attentional mechanism · Long short-term memory · Spatial and temporal feature

1 Introduction

The Internet of Things (IoT) provides us a more convenient way of life, but also brings great security risks to our lives. As network attacks become more frequent and more varied, network security has become the focus of social concern. In order to prevent virus invasion and hacker attack, intrusion detection technology sustainedly develops and has become a solid barrier to protect network security. Meanwhile, the requirement of real-time and high precision puts

This work was supported in part by National Natural Science Foundation of China under Grant 61902222, Grant 61702307, and the Taishan Scholars Program of Shandong Province under Grant tsqn201909109.

© Springer Nature Singapore Pte Ltd. 2022
C. Cao et al. (Eds.): FCS 2021, CCIS 1558, pp. 214–229, 2022.
https://doi.org/10.1007/978-981-19-0523-0_14

forward higher requirement for intrusion detection technology. In the past few years, many specialists have introduced machine learning to network intrusion detection because of its high robustness and high adaptability, such as DT [1], SVM [2], XGBoost [3] and LightGBM [4].

However, with the upgrading of computer network technology, the types of network attacks become more complex. The traditional network intrusion detection model cannot accurately identify new attacks because of its low generalization performance. These reduce model accuracy and increase false positives. Therefore, to research a classification model with high generalization capability has significant implications for network intrusion detection. Deep learning can better adapt to the diversity and complexity of network intrusion in dynamic changes of network. Wu et al. proposed a novel network intrusion detection model based on Convolutional Neural Networks (CNNs) to select traffic features automatically [5]. Potluri et al. evaluated the efficiency of CNN model for multi-class problem in network intrusion detection [6]. Nonetheless, CNNs cannot meet the requirements of high accuracy of intrusion detection.

To accommodate the diversification of cyber attacks and improve detection accuracy, we propose a hybrid network intrusion detection model (ACNNBN-LSTM) based on CNN-LSTM and attention mechanism. The feature vectors are converted to 2-dimensional images as the input of the model to realize weight sharing among data. Spatial and temporal features are extracted to learn the critical attributes of different network traffic. In the end, detecting network traffic attacks, and giving classification results. The main contributions of ACNNBN-LSTM are as follows.

- We propose a hybrid model to classify network traffic attacks. For distinguishing different network traffic features purposefully, we improve an attention-based CNN with batch normalization (ACNNBN) module to learn their spatial features. The ACNNBN module introduces the convolution block attention module (CBAM) to prevent losing the shallow feature information and batch normalization module to accelerate model convergence.
- Consider that network attacks may have a strong correlation with time, we append Long Short-Term Memory (LSTM) model after the ACNNBN module to prevent losing associated information of network traffic in adjacent time periods. The LSTM module is applied to study the temporal features of feature vectors to make real-time detection come true.

The rest of the article is structured as follows. Section 2 introduces the current research progress and achievements of network intrusion detection technology. Section 3 detailedly describes the process of the whole intrusion detection and the architecture of ACNNBN-LSTM model. Section 4 explains the characteristic attributes of CIRA-CIC-DoHBrw-2020 dataset and some data preprocessing methods we used. In Sect. 5, we compare and analyze the performance of seven models, and give the experimental results of the evaluation indexes of each model. And the paper is summarized in Sect. 6.

2   Related Work

Network information security has attracted much attention. Rule-based intrusion detection technology is gradually replaced by machine learning algorithms in recent decades due to its limitations in scalability and adaptability [7]. However, feature engineering in machine learning presents new challenges for researchers. In addition, traditional machine learning methods have obvious defects in dealing with multi-dimensional nonlinearity and network data redundancy. Thus, many experts and scholars have began to research network intrusion detection technology based on deep learning. Andresini et al. converted network traffic into 2D images and introduced nearest cluster training 2D CNN network to intrusion detection research [8]. Hinton et al. proposed a fast training method called Deep Belief Nets (DBN) algorithm [9]. Salama et al. applied it to network intrusion detection for the first time and verified the effectiveness of the DBN algorithm [10]. Vinayakumar et al. studied the deep neural network to detect different network attack classifications [11].

In recent years, attention mechanism is introduced into deep learning makes outstanding contributions to image processing in sequential processing, region proposal, and control gate [12–15]. However, there are few studies that introduce attention mechanism into convolutional neural network and successfully apply it to intrusion detection. Moreover, as the emergence of recursive neural network, a new round of reform and innovation has been carried out in the field of artificial intelligence. Yin et al. used recursive neural network to classify network attacks for the first time and achieved good results [16]. Some scientists used the recurrent neural network with attention mechanism to detect system log line anomalies and intrusion attacks [17–19]. Zhang et al. combined multi-scale convolutional neural network with LSTM model to enhance the accuracy of attack detection [20].

3   Proposed Method

In traditional CNN, the deep layers may lose some significant features from the shallow layers. Furthermore, the CNN network easily ignores the internal correlation information among the sample datasets. To deal with these problems, we propose an ACNNBN-LSTM model to specify the classification of network intrusion. This section mainly demonstrates learning process and the architecture of the ACNNBN-LSTM model.

3.1   ACNNBN-LSTM Learning Process

The process of network intrusion detection based on the ACNNBN-LSTM model is described in Fig. 1. The original datasets are preprocessed according to their different feature attributes. Low variance filter removes attributes with variance of 0. The collinear attributes with high correlation is identified by Pearson correlation coefficient matrix. It is worth noting that if category attributes are present in the dataset, one-hot encoding or numerical conversion is necessary. At the same time, the dataset introduces the normalize method to avoid the difference of feature dimensions which may affect the training precision and convergence rate. In addition, we also need to convert the label through one-hot encoding in the classification problem.

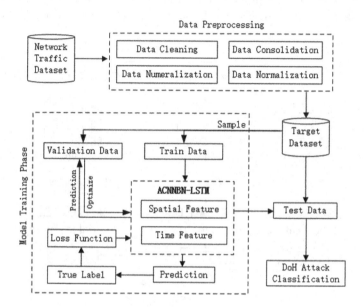

Fig. 1. Network intrusion detection learning process of ACNNBN-LSTM model

After data preprocessing, the target dataset obtained is proportionally divided into train set, validation set and test set. Where, the train set is used to learn and train the ACNNBN-LSTM model, the validation set takes advantage of the loss function to find the model optimal parameters, and the test set is applied to evaluate the ACNNBN-LSTM model training effectiveness according to different evaluation indexes.

Transforming the processed sample features into 2-dimensional images as the input to share data weight. Each training data is an image-label pair. The label represents the category of attack that corresponding sample. We take cross validation to prevent model overfitting. The model parameters are updated by the error between the true label and the prediction which obtained by model training. Finally, the optimized model is substituted into the test set for prediction, and then obtains the result of Denial of Service (DOH) attack classification.

3.2 ACNNBN-LSTM Architecture

The structure of the proposed ACNNBN-LSTM model is described in Fig. 2. By observing Fig. 2, it can be concluded that the processed dataset are transform into 2-dimensional images as the model input. In addition, the ACNNBN-LSTM model is divided into the ACNNBN module and the LSTM module, and there is a sequence between the two modules. The converted feature images are transmitted into the ACNNBN module firstly, which is used to learn the spatial features of sample features. Then, images processed by the ACNNBN module are passed into the LSTM model through a full connection layer to learn the temporal features between different images [21]. Finally, DoH labels are output by Softmax function.

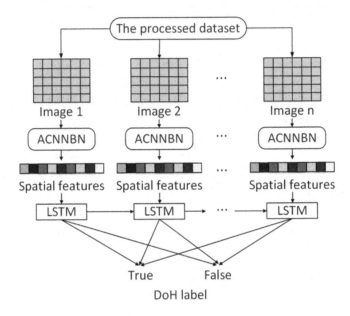

Fig. 2. The architecture of ACNNBN-LSTM model.

The spatial features belong to internal features, and are critical features that affecting network traffic classification. Network attack types can be identified accurately and quickly by extracting spatial features. The temporal features belong to external features, and are the external relation between different network traffic. Network attack is correlated with temporal attribute, so temporal attribute is also an momentous factor to improve the accuracy of network traffic classification. In addition, the introduction of LSTM model can support ACNNBN-LSTM model to detect network attacks online and in real time.

The detailed architecture of ACNNBN-LSTM is described in Fig. 3. Where the symbol $\otimes$ denotes Hadamard product, and $\oplus$ signifies element-wise summation. The network architecture consists of 3 convolutional layers, 3 batch norm layers, 2 attention mechanism blocks, 1 max-pooling layer, 1 LSTM layer and 2 full connected layers. In the ACNNBN module, we introduce two CBAMs to increase representation power and improve classification precision [22]. Meanwhile, we subjoin the batch norm layer after each convolutional layer to prevent gradient disappearing. The LSTM model cannot be computed in parallel, which results in a long training time. We append a full connect layer in front of the LSTM layer to reduce the parameter calculation and shorten the training time.

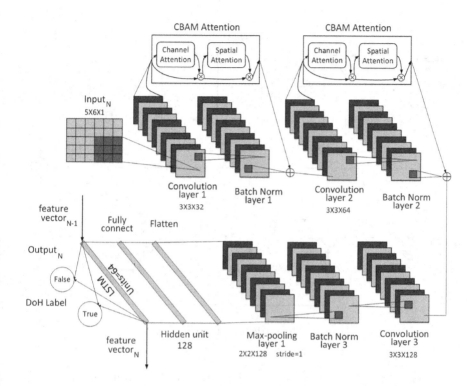

Fig. 3. The detailed architecture of ACNNBN-LSTM model.

Using the voxel matrix of 2-dimensional image as the input of the ACNNBN-LSTM model. The proposed model contains three convolution layers, and the number of convolution kernels of the three convolution layers gradually increases to prevent losing shallow feature. The size of the convolution kernel for each convolution layer is $3 \times 3 \times 32$, $3 \times 3 \times 64$ and $3 \times 3 \times 128$ respectively. Setting the parameter of the padding is 'same' and the step length is 1. After each convolution layer, a Batch Norm layer is added to prevent vanishing gradient and accelerate model convergence. Note that, each of the first two convolution layers have a CBAM for cross-channel operation to retain information about superficial features. The third convolutional layer has more comprehensively extracted the feature information of the image by increasing the number of convolution kernels.

CBAM is put forward by Sanghyun et al. to further enhance effective features and inhibit the invalid features of feature map through space and channel dimensions, which consists of channel attention module and spatial attention module [22]. Figure 4 displays the specific details of the attention module, where the symbol Ⓢ represents the softmax function [23]. Among them, the channel block focuses on what the features are, and the space block focuses on the location of features.

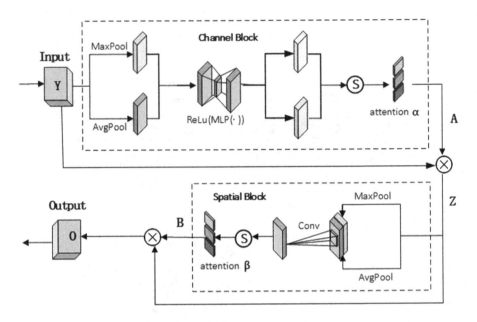

Fig. 4. The model of attention module

Suppose that the feature matrix of an intermediate convolution layer is $Y_{H \times W \times 1}$, which the meaning of H is the height and W denote the width of the feature map. In channel attention block, average pooling and max pooling are handled for the input feature matrix Y respectively. Then, the obtained feature matrices are added as the input of multilayer perceptron (MLP) function. Finally, adding the output results of MLP, and the final channel attention feature map is obtained by sigmoid activation function. The channel attention matrix $A_{H \times W \times 1}$ is calculated by Eq. 1. Where $MaxPool(\cdot)$ and $AvgPool(\cdot)$ respectively signify the max-pooling and average-pooling calculation, and $MLP(\cdot)$ expresses the multilayer perceptron (MLP) function.

$$F' = MLP(MaxPool(Y)) + MLP(AvgPool(Y))$$
$$A = (a_{i,j}) = Softmax\,(F')$$
$$\text{s.t.} \sum_{i=0}^{H-1} \sum_{j=0}^{W-1} a_{i,j} = 1 \tag{1}$$

We multiply the input matrix Y by channel attention matrix A as the input of spatial attention matrix module. Average pooling and max pooling are carried out for the feature matrix $Z = A \cdot Y$ respectively from the channel dimension. The results of the two pooling layers are added and then convolved through a convolution layer. Finally, using sigmoid activation function get the final spatial attention feature map B by calculation. Given $Conv(\cdot)$ expresses the convolution function, F denotes the convolutional filter. The spatial attention matrix $B_{H \times W \times 1}$ is calculated by Eq. 2:

$$F'' = Conv([MaxPool(Z); AvgPool(Z)], F)$$
$$B = (b_{i,j}) = Softmax\,(F'')$$
$$\text{s.t.} \sum_{i=0}^{H-1} \sum_{j=0}^{W-1} b_{i,j} = 1 \tag{2}$$

The results of the spatial attention module V are multiplied by the feature matrix Z is the output of CBAM. A batch norm layer and a max pooling layer follow the third convolution layer to accelerate model training. The convolution kernel size of the max pooling layer is 2×2 and the step is 1. The pooled feature maps is flattened 1-dimensional array to learn the temporal features of different feature maps as the input of the LSTM model. Due to the model has many parameters, we add a full connection layer in front of the LSTM model to reduce the training time. Finally, the model uses the loss function to adjust the parameters through reverse error propagation.

LSTM is a especial recurrent neural network for solving the problem of gradient disappearance and gradient explosion in the training process of long sequence [21]. The LSTM network is made up of three parts. The first part is to forget unimportant information. It outputs the information retained through sigmod activation function. The second part updates memory information at the current moment. According to the information retained at the last moment, determining the current state memory information. The reserved information output by sigmod function is multiplied by the output of the second part processed by tanh function to gain the output of the network model.

4 Dataset Description

The CIRA-CIC-DoHBrw-2020 dataset from Canadian Institute for Cybersecurity (CIC) [25], which is captured by a two-layered approach of statistical features classifier and time-series classifier. The dataset consists of 34 feature attributes and 1 label attribute. We divide the 34 statistical traffic characteristics into three categories, which are Packet-level feature, Flow-level feature and Stream-level feature. The categories of data label are split into Malicious-DoH traffic and non-Malicious-DoH traffic, where non-Malicious-DoH traffic contains Benign-DoH traffic and non-DoH traffic.

4.1 Data Cleaning

Through preliminary observating of the dataset, we find that there is no duplicate data, but some attributes exist the situation of data missing. According to statistics, the missing data account for 0.688%. The proportion of missing data for each attribute are shown in Table 1. The missing data only exists in attribute ResponseTimeTimeMedian and attribute ResponseTimeTimeSkewFromMedian, which is presentation in Table 1. By analyzing missing data, we find that two attributes exist missing condition together. Under circumstance of attribute ResponseTimeTimeMedian and attribute ResponseTimeTimeSkewFromMedian are missing, their attributes of PacketTimeCoefficientofVariation, Response-TimeTimeVariance, and ResponseTimeTimeStandardDeviation have the same value, which are −1, ResponseTimeTimeSkewFromMode has the same value, which are −0.0, and ResponseTimeTimeCoefficientofVariation has the same value, which are 1. Comprehensive of the above, we finally consider ResponseTimeTimeMedian attribute missing value filling to −1 and ResponseTimeTimeSkewFromMedian attribute missing value filling to 0.

Table 1. The proportion of missing features in CIRA-CIC-DoHBrw-2020 dataset

Data source	Missing features	Number of missing
Google Chrome	ResponseTimeTimeMedian	0.96%
	ResponseTimeTimeSkewFromMedian	0.96%
Mozilla Firefox	ResponseTimeTimeMedian	0.67%
	ResponseTimeTimeSkewFromMedian	0.67%
dns2tcp	ResponseTimeTimeMedian	0.12%
	ResponseTimeTimeSkewFromMedian	0.12%
DNSCat2	ResponseTimeTimeMedian	0.08%
	ResponseTimeTimeSkewFromMedian	0.08%
Iodine	ResponseTimeTimeMedian	0.12%
	ResponseTimeTimeSkewFromMedian	0.12%

4.2 Data Numeralization

The CIRA-CIC-DohBRW-2020 dataset contains 4 symbolic features and 31 numerical features. In the process of training and prediction, we need to transform the data samples into grayscale images as the input of the model. In reality, the values of SourceIP, DestinationIP, SourcePort, DestinationPort, and TimeStamp are varied over time. These five attributes would affect the extensibility of the model prediction, so need to be removed. The labels contain two categories: True and False. The data labeled True include Benign-DoH traffic and non-DoH traffic, and the data labeled False are all Malicious-DoH traffic. It is necessary for the labels to convert numerication. That is True is labeled by 1, and False is labeled by 0.

4.3   Data Normalization

After data cleaning and data numerical transformation, there are still dimensional differences between different features in the data, which will affect the training precision and convergence rate of the model. We perform linear transformation on the sample data according to Eq. 3 so as to avoid model ignoring the low-amplitude characteristic information, and map it into the interval $[0, 1]$.

$$f(x) = \begin{cases} \frac{x - x_{\min}}{x_{\max} - x_{\min}}, & x_{\max} \neq x_{\min} \\ 0, & x_{\max} = x_{\min} \end{cases} \tag{3}$$

5   Experiment and Results

For proving the validity of the model, we introduce the detailed calculation process of ACNNBN-LSTM based on the CIRA-CIC-DoHBrw-2020 dataset, and give the model prediction results. The performance of ACNNBN-LSTM model was evaluated by comparing six machine learning algorithms.

5.1   Model Result

After data preprocessing, we obtain the sample information with 29 features. For convenience, the data add a column with all zeros to transform into $5 \times 6 \times 1$ two-dimensional images. The transformed data is used as input to the ACNNBN-LSTM model. The network structure parameters are shown in Table 2.

Table 2. The parameters of ACNNBN-LSTM model

Layer	Type	Size	Stride	Padding	ActFunc
L1-1.1	Conv2D	$3 \times 3 \times 32$	1	Same	Relu
L1-1.2	BatchNormalization				
L1-2	CBAM				
L2-1.1	Conv2D	$3 \times 3 \times 64$	1	Same	Relu
L2-1.2	BatchNormalization				
L2-2	CBAM				
L3	Conv2D	$3 \times 3 \times 128$	1	Same	Relu
L4	BatchNormalization				
L5	MaxPooling2D	2×2	1	Same	Relu
L6	FC	0.25; 128			Drop+Sigmoid
L7	LSTM	64			tanh
L8	FC	0.25; 2			Drop+Sigmoid

To avoid model overfitting, a dropout function with parameter 0.25 is adopted after the max pooling layer, fully connected layer and LSTM layer respectively.

The feature map which is outputed by the LSTM model is further processed by sigmoid activation function to get the DoH label category. The ACNNBN-LSTM model contains 606, 471 params, and uses the loss function to adjust the parameters through reverse error propagation.

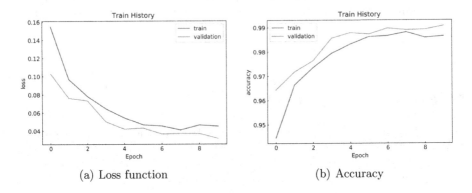

(a) Loss function   (b) Accuracy

Fig. 5. ACNNBN-LSTM model learning curve.

Figure 5 demonstrates the learning rate curve of the ACNNBN-LSTM model, which shows the effect of the model iteratively training 10 epochs. As shown in Fig. 5(a), after 10 iterations, the loss function of the validation set is reduced to about 0.0234. And Fig. 5(b) displays that when the quantity of iterations reaches 10, the accuracy rate of the validation set reaches about 99.35%. We substitute the optimized model into the test set for predicting, and experimental result gives the confusion matrix in Table 3.

Table 3. The confusion matrix of the ACNNBN-LSTM model

Actual	Predicted	
	True	False
True	179160	**365**
False	**991**	52938

Table 3 demonstrates that most of the data is classified correctly, but some data is still misclassified. There are 365 non-malicious DoH attacks classified in the positive sample, and 991 malicious DoH attacks that are not correctly identified in the negative sample. The misclassified samples account for a relatively small proportion, which is 0.58%. It is calculated by the confusion matrix that the F1 score of the ACCNBN-LSTM model is 99.18%, the accuracy is 99.41%, the precision is 99.38%, and the recall is 98.98%. Overall, the performance of the model is well.

5.2   Model Contrast

For evaluating performance of ACNNBN-LSTM model, six machine learning algorithms are choosed for comparison, that are Random Forest (RF), Logical Regression (LR), Gaussian Bayes Classifier (GBC), Convolutional Neural Network (CNN), Convolutional Neural Network with Batch Normal (CNNBN) and Convolutional Neural Network with Batch Normal based on Attentional mechanism (ACNNBN). Among the six models, there are three traditional machine learning models RF, LR and GBC, and three deep learning models CNN, CNNBN, and ACNNBN.

Three deep learning models adopt the same network structure, which is described in Fig. 6. CNN network structure adopts the combination of three groups of convolution and maximum pooling. The size of the convolutional kernel is set to $3 \times 3 \times 32$, $3 \times 3 \times 64$ and $3 \times 3 \times 128$ respectively. The padding parameter is same. The step size of both convolution and pooling are 1. Finally, the DoH classification results are obtained by a full connection layer and a Softmax activation function successively. The CNNBN model has similar structure and parameters to the CNN model, except that a Batch Normalization layer is appended in between each convolution layer and the pooling layer. ACNNBN model combines the CNNBN model and the CBAM model, but removes the maximum pooling layer after the first two convolution layers.

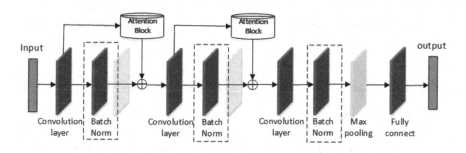

Fig. 6. Three deep learning algorithm architectures.

We compared the accuracy, recall, precision and F1 score of these models. The forecast results of each model is demonstrated in Table 4. With the purpose of better comparing the model experimental results, we use the same random seed and proportion of stratified sampling to divide the processed data sets. As shown in Table 4, among traditional machine learning algorithms, random forest algorithm gains the highest in accuracy, recall rate, precision rate and F1 score, which all reach around 99%.

In addition, the experimental results also indicated that the performance of four deep learning algorithms is generally higher than LR and GBC algorithms. However, the performance of ACNNBN model with attention mechanism is lower than random forest. To further improve the accuracy, the LSTM model is introduced in the ACNNBN model to learn the spatial features of image mapping.

Table 4. Comparison of evaluation results of different models

Algorithms	F1-score	Precision	Recall	Accuracy
RF	0.9912	0.9949	0.9876	0.9938
LR	0.8341	0.8157	0.8621	0.8730
GBC	0.8252	0.8148	0.8379	0.8711
CNN	0.9845	0.9884	0.9807	0.9890
CNNBN	0.9894	0.9939	0.9851	0.9925
ACNNBN	0.9910	0.9924	0.9896	0.9936
ACNNBN-LSTM	0.9918	0.9938	0.9898	0.9941

According to Table 4, the accuracy of ACNNBN-LSTM model is not only 0.05% higher than the ACNNBN model, but also 0.03% higher than the random forest model. The confusion matrix of the remaining six models as shown in Tables 5, 6, 7, 8, 9 and 10 to intuitively compare the performance of these model.

Table 5. The confusion matrix of RF

Actual	Predicted	
	True	False
True	179368	**157**
False	**1295**	52634

Table 6. The confusion matrix of LR

Actual	Predicted	
	True	False
True	158399	**21126**
False	**8527**	45402

Table 7. The confusion matrix of GBC

Actual	Predicted	
	True	False
True	161492	**18033**
False	**12064**	41865

Table 8. The confusion matrix of CNN

Actual	Predicted	
	True	False
True	178662	**863**
False	**1783**	52146

Table 9. The confusion matrix of CNNBN

Actual	Predicted	
	True	False
True	179330	**195**
False	**1550**	52379

Table 10. The confusion matrix of ACNNBN

Actual	Predicted	
	True	False
True	179002	**523**
False	**969**	52960

The CIRA-CIC-DoHBrw-2020 dataset is unbalanced sample, and its positive sample proportion is only about 0.231. By comparing the seven confusion matrices, the FN value of RF model is the smallest, the second is CNNBN model. The ACNNBN-LSTM model ranks third. The ACNNBN model has the lowest FP value, and the ACNNBN-LSTM model in the second place. In general, the result of ACNNBN-LSTM model is better than the other six algorithms on unbalanced CIRA-CIC-DoHBrw-2020 dataset.

Because network traffic is generally influenced by important features and time attributes, ACNNBN-LSTM model extracts crucial information influencing network attack classification from both spatial and temporal features. In addition, ACNNBN-LSTM model can output classification results in real time, which can meet the real-time requirements of network attack detection. Thus, the model proposed in this paper has general usability.

6 Conclusions

In response to the increasing frequency of malicious attacks on the status quo, we propose a hybrid network intrusion detection model based on CNN-LSTM and attention mechanism (ACNNBN-LSTM) to specify the classification of network intrusion. The model is divided into the ACNNBN and the LSTM modules, which are applied to learn the spatial and temporal features of image features respectively. For evaluating the performance of our model, we select CIRA-CIC-DoHBrw-2020 dataset for comparing the results. Experimental results show that our model performs well on unbalanced datasets. Moreover, the ACNNBN-LSTM model is compared with other six algorithms such as CNN and CNNBN, and the consequence demonstrates our model effectively enhances the detection accuracy. In the test set, the detection accuracy reached 99.41%. Because of introducing the LSTM model increases the training time, we will consider further optimizing the model architecture to improve detection efficiency and enhance the generalization ability in the future.

References

1. Farid, D.-M., Harbi, N., Rahman, M.-Z.: Combining Naive Bayes and decision tree for adaptive intrusion detection, pp. 12–25. arXiv preprint arXiv:1005.4496 (2010)
2. Aslahi-Shahri, B.-M., Rahmani, R., Chizari, M., et al.: A hybrid method consisting of GA and SVM for intrusion detection system. Neural Comput. Appl. 27(6), 1669–1676 (2015). https://doi.org/10.1007/s00521-015-1964-2
3. Dhaliwal, S.-S., Nahid, A.-A., Abbas, R.: Effective intrusion detection system using XGBoost. Information 9(7), 149 (2018)
4. Jin, D., Lu, Y., Qin, J., et al.: SwiftIDS: real-time intrusion detection system based on LightGBM and parallel intrusion detection mechanism. Comput. Secur. 97, 101984 (2020)
5. Wu, K., Chen, Z., Li, W.: A novel intrusion detection model for a massive network using convolutional neural networks. IEEE Access 6, 50850–50859 (2018)

6. Potluri, S., Ahmed, S., Diedrich, C.: Convolutional neural networks for multi-class intrusion detection system. In: Groza, A., Prasath, R. (eds.) MIKE 2018. LNCS (LNAI), vol. 11308, pp. 225–238. Springer, Cham (2018). https://doi.org/10.1007/978-3-030-05918-7_20

7. Tan, M., Iacovazzi, A., et al.: A neural attention model for real-time network intrusion detection. In: Local Computer Networks (2019)

8. Andresini, G., Appice, A., Malerba, D.: Nearest cluster-based intrusion detection through convolutional neural networks. Knowl. Based Syst. **216**, 106798 (2021)

9. Hinton, G.-E., Osindero, S., et al.: A fast learning algorithm for deep belief nets. Neural Comput. **18**(7), 1527–1554 (2006)

10. Salama, M.A., Eid, H.F., Ramadan, R.A., Darwish, A., Hassanien, A.E.: Hybrid intelligent intrusion detection scheme. In: Gaspar-Cunha, A., Takahashi, R., Schaefer, G., Costa, L. (eds.) Soft Computing in Industrial Applications. AINSC, vol. 96, pp. 293–303. Springer, Heidelberg (2011). https://doi.org/10.1007/978-3-642-20505-7_26

11. Vinayakumar, R., Alazab, M., Soman, K.-P., et al.: Deep learning approach for intelligent intrusion detection system. IEEE Access **7**, 41525–41550 (2019)

12. Gregor, K., et al.: Draw: A recurrent neural network for image generation. In: International Conference on Machine Learning, pp. 1462–1471. PMLR (2015)

13. Dai, J., He, K., et al.: Convolutional feature masking for joint object and stuff segmentation. In: 2015 IEEE Conference on Computer Vision and Pattern Recognition (CVPR), Boston (2015)

14. Cao, C., Liu, X., et al.: Look and think twice: capturing top-down visual attention with feedback convolutional neural networks. In: 2015 IEEE International Conference on Computer Vision (ICCV). Santiago, Chile (2015)

15. Wang, F., Jiang, M., et al.: Residual attention network for image classification. In: 2017 IEEE Conference on Computer Vision and Pattern Recognition (CVPR). IEEE Computer Society 2017, Honolulu (2017)

16. Yin, C., Zhu, Y., et al.: A deep learning approach for intrusion detection using recurrent neural networks. IEEE Access **5**(99), 21954–21961 (2017)

17. Brown, A., Tuor, A., Hutchinson, B., et al.: Recurrent neural network attention mechanisms for interpretable system log anomaly detection. In: Proceedings of the First Workshop on Machine Learning for Computing Systems, pp. 1–8 (2018)

18. Qin, Z.-Q., Ma, X.-K., Wang, Y.-J.: Attentional payload anomaly detector for web applications. In: Cheng, L., Leung, A.C.S., Ozawa, S. (eds.) ICONIP 2018. LNCS, vol. 11304, pp. 588–599. Springer, Cham (2018). https://doi.org/10.1007/978-3-030-04212-7_52

19. Zhu, M., Ye, K., Wang, Y., Xu, C.-Z.: A deep learning approach for network anomaly detection based on AMF-LSTM. In: Zhang, F., Zhai, J., Snir, M., Jin, H., Kasahara, H., Valero, M. (eds.) NPC 2018. LNCS, vol. 11276, pp. 137–141. Springer, Cham (2018). https://doi.org/10.1007/978-3-030-05677-3_13

20. Zhang, J., Ling, Y., Fu, X., et al.: Model of the intrusion detection system based on the integration of spatial-temporal features. Comput. Secur. **89**, 101681 (2020)

21. Greff, K., Srivastava, R.-K., Koutník, J., et al.: LSTM: a search space odyssey. IEEE Trans. Neural Networks Learn. Syst. **28**(10), 2222–2232 (2016)

22. Woo, S., Park, J., Lee, J.-Y., Kweon, I.S.: CBAM: convolutional block attention module. In: Ferrari, V., Hebert, M., Sminchisescu, C., Weiss, Y. (eds.) ECCV 2018. LNCS, vol. 11211, pp. 3–19. Springer, Cham (2018). https://doi.org/10.1007/978-3-030-01234-2_1

23. Ma, B., Wang, X., Zhang, H., Li, F., Dan, J.: CBAM-GAN: generative adversarial networks based on convolutional block attention module. In: Sun, X., Pan, Z., Bertino, E. (eds.) ICAIS 2019. LNCS, vol. 11632, pp. 227–236. Springer, Cham (2019). https://doi.org/10.1007/978-3-030-24274-9_20

24. Yakura, H., Shinozaki, S., et al.: Neural malware analysis with attention mechanism. Comput. Secur. **87**, 101592 (2019)

25. MontazeriShatoori, M., Davidson, L., Kaur, G., et al.: Detection of DOH tunnels using time-series classification of encrypted traffic. In: 2020 IEEE International Conference on Dependable, Autonomic and Secure Computing, International Conference on Pervasive Intelligence and Computing, International Conference on Cloud and Big Data Computing, International Conference on Cyber Science and Technology Congress (DASC/PiCom/CBDCom/CyberSciTech). IEEE (2020)

System Security Analysis of Different Link Proportions Between Nodes in the Cyber-Physical System Against Target Attack

Hao Peng[1], Zhen Qian[1], Ming Zhong[1], Dandan Zhao[1], Guangquan Xu[3],
Songyang Wu[2(✉)], and Jianming Han[1]

[1] Department of Computer Science and Engineering, Zhejiang Normal University,
Jinhua 321004, China
[2] The Third Research Institute of Ministry of Public Security,
Shanghai 201204, China
wusongyang@stars.org.cn
[3] Tianjin Key Laboratory of Advanced Networking (TANK),
College of Intelligence and Computing, Tianjin University, Tianjin 300072, China

Abstract. With the rapid development of Industry 4.0, Cyber-Physical System (CPS) has promoted the deep integration of the physical world and cyberspace. The close combination of virtual cyberspace and real physical space has not only brought great opportunities but also great challenges to the development of the industrial Internet. Attackers can attack cyberspace through physical space, or attack physical space through cyberspace, and cause a cascading failure. Given this target attack on the cyber-physical fusion system, how to evaluate and prevent it becomes very important. Firstly, this paper analyzes and models the CPS with different proportions of links. Then, we use the percolation theory to analyze the cascade failure process progressively and obtain the critical threshold of network collapse. Finally, we further validate the correctness of the theoretical value through simulation case study and construe the parameters impacting the system's reliability. The experimental results show that the network presents a first-order phase transition near the critical value. The power-law exponent of SF network has little effect on system reliability.

Keywords: Cyber-Physical System · Target attack · Cascading failure · System reliability

1 Introduction

Since Industry 4.0 was first proposed, it has become a top priority in industrial development [4,14]. As Industry 4.0 brings many opportunities for future technology and development [26], many countries have also planned strategies for this [2,14]. The key concept of Industry 4.0 is cyber-physical system [7,11].

© Springer Nature Singapore Pte Ltd. 2022
C. Cao et al. (Eds.): FCS 2021, CCIS 1558, pp. 230–242, 2022.
https://doi.org/10.1007/978-981-19-0523-0_15

CPS provides perception, dynamic control, and information services for modern systems through computing, communication, and control [12,13,21]. It is widely used in smart grid, transportation, medical and other industries [3,6]. CPS is usually composed of two interdependent networks, namely physical resource network and computing resource network [21]. This highly coupled characteristic brings many risks and challenges, such as cascade failure [8,20,25]. Attackers can attack cyberspace through physical space to achieve their goals [23]. The failure of the physical network triggers the failure of the nodes dependent on the information network, which in turn affects the nodes of the physical network [10]. This cascade failure phenomenon will bring great harm to modern systems [22]. Therefore, how to analyze and evaluate the risk and reliability of this system is very necessary.

Focusing on the above problems, people have gradually changed from the study of cascade failure of single network [1,24] to coupling network in recent years. Starting from the one-to-one interdependence model of Buldyrev [5], people began to use this seepage theory method to widely study the cascade failure of CPS [17,18]. The one-to-one dependent model is no longer applicable to the ever-changing CPS system, and the one-to-many model has gradually been studied by scholars. Huang [10] proposed a one-to-many model in 2015. Nodes in a computing resource network can be connected to nodes in multiple physical resource networks. It is found that if the proportion of faulty nodes exceeds the threshold, the system will crash. This paper only considers the one to many situation and does not consider the mixing proportion and more harmful target attacks. Ref. [9] proposes a method to convert target attacks into random attacks, but the connection between networks is still a simple one-to-one connection. Peng [19] studied the cascading failure of interdependent networks under one-to-many model when they were deliberately attacked, but did not consider the mixed proportion. To solve the above problems, we model the CPS system as an interdependent network model with mixed node proportion and study the reliability of the system under the target attack strategy based on node degree.

The chapters of this paper are organized as follows: Sect. 1 introduces the background and related research directions of the article. The construction of the system model and a transformation method is described in Sect. 2. For the cascading failure process, we use mathematical methods to analyze each stage in detail in Sect. 3. The solution of the theoretical value equation is solved in Sect. 4, and we have carried out a large number of simulation experiments to verify the correctness of the theoretical solution and analyze the factors affecting system reliability. The fifth section is our conclusion and outlook for the future.

2   Model and Methods

In this section, we will first build the model of the system. Then, we transform target attacks into random attacks through certain mathematical analyses. In this way, after transformation, we can study the security of the CPS system under target attack strategy in the way of a random attack.

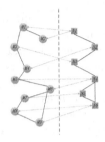

Fig. 1. The connection between networks.

2.1   Model Construction

We construct a CPS system composed of two interdependent networks. The two networks are represented by M and N respectively. Both types of networks are the most extensive scale-free networks in real life. The degree distribution of scale-free network is $P_{SF}(k) = k^{-\lambda}$. λ represents power-law exponent. From the previous analysis, we can know that the connection modes of the two networks in the network physical system include one-to-one, one-to-many and many-to-many. In practice, many-to-many situations are common. Moreover, the coupling network system composed of a variety of connection ratios also accounts for the vast majority. Therefore, we establish a coupled CPS system composed of two connection ratios. As shown in Fig. 1, the two proportions are 2:1 and 1:1 respectively. We assume that the probability of both connection ratios is 0.5. Then, the ratio of nodes of network M and N is 3:2.

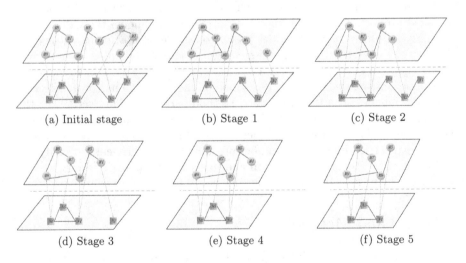

(a) Initial stage   (b) Stage 1   (c) Stage 2

(d) Stage 3   (e) Stage 4   (f) Stage 5

Fig. 2. The process of cascading failure.

After the system is deliberately attacked, the attacked node will no longer have a function and fail. The target attack method we adopt is to attack the node with the largest node degree in the network first. When a node in a network is attacked and fails, the corresponding node in another network will also fail due to interdependence. This process is called cascading failure, as shown in Fig. 2. The node in the coupled network will not fail and maintain its function only if it satisfies the following two requirements:

- The node pertains to the largest connected component;
- The node has interdependent edges.

Only functional nodes in the network can continue to survive. When there are no functional nodes in the whole network, it means that the network has completely crashed. As shown in Fig. 2, node $M1$ $M3$ loses its function after being attacked in initial stage. $M2$ also fails because it does not belong to the largest connected cluster in Stage 1. $N1$ $N3$, which has lost its dependent edge, is no longer functional in Stage 2. $N2$ does not belong to the largest connected cluster and fails in Stage 3. Node $M4$ dependents on $N2$ lose their interdependent edges and then fails in Stage 4. In Stage 5, the nodes in the network no longer invalid and reach stability. This is the whole process of network cascading failure.

2.2   Methods of Converting Target Attack

According to Ref. [15, 16], the generation function of network degree distribution is expressed as

$$G_{M0}(x) = \sum_k P_M(k)x^k, \tag{1}$$

where $P_M(k)$ is the degree distribution function of network M. The degree distribution functions of scale-free network and ER random network are $P_{ER}(k) = < k >^k \cdot e^{-<k>}/k!$ and $P_{SF}(k) = k^{-\lambda}$ respectively. Where $<k>$ is the average degree of ER network, λ is the power law exponent of scale-free network.

Furthermore, the generating function of the underlying branching processes is

$$G_{M1}(x) = G'_{M0}(x)/G'_{M0}(1). \tag{2}$$

According to Sergey's paper [5], when the network is subjected to random attacks, the proportion of remaining functional nodes in the network can be expressed by

$$g_M(p) = 1 - G_{M0}\left[1 - p\left(1 - f_M\right)\right], \tag{3}$$

where fM satisfies the transcendental equation $f_M = G_{M1}\left[1 - p\left(1 - f_M\right)\right]$.

Because target attack and random attack are different only at the first step, the principle of cascading failure is the same. Therefore, we can convert target attacks into random attacks through mathematical derivation. After the transformation, we can analyze the target attack according to the analysis method of a random attack. In Ref. [9], the probability of node failure is expressed by an equation:

$$Q_\alpha(k_i) = \frac{(k_i + 1)^\alpha}{\sum_{i=0}^{N}(k_i + 1)^\alpha}. \tag{4}$$

$Q_\alpha(k_i)$ implies the probability that node i is attacked at the first time. The larger α is, the more vulnerable the node with high node degree is to attack.

Mapping target attacks to random attacks can solve the problem of target attacks. Through mathematical formula analysis and transformation, the newly obtained node survival proportion function is

$$g_M(p) = 1 - \tilde{G}_{M0}[1 - p(1 - f_M)] \tag{5}$$

And $f_M = \tilde{G}_{M1}[1 - p(1 - f_M)]$.

$G_{M0}(x)$ can be solved by the following equations:

$$\begin{cases} \tilde{G}_{M0}(x) = G_{Mb}\left(1 + \frac{\tilde{p}}{p}(x - 1)\right) \\ G_{Mb}(x) = \frac{1}{p}\sum_k P(k)t^{k^\alpha}x^k. \end{cases} \tag{6}$$

So far, the transformation of target attack has been completed. Next, we will deduce the critical formula of network collapse after cascade failure.

3   Mathematical Analysis of Cascading Failures

We will further construe the cascading failure process of CPS systems composed of the coupled network after target attack through mathematical theory in this section. Through the analysis, we can get the quantity of remaining functional nodes in each step after the network cascade failure. Table 1 shows the meaning of some symbols.

Table 1. Symbol definitions

Symbol	Explanation
N_M, N_N	The number of initial nodes
N'_{Mi}, N'_{Ni}	Number of nodes which have supporting inter link in the network M and N
N_{Mi}, N_{Ni}	The largest connected components that remain functional in N'_{Mi} and N'_{Ni}
μ_i, μ_j	The fraction corresponding to N_{Mi} and N_{Nj}
μ'_i, μ'_j	The fraction corresponding to N'_{Mi} and N'_{Nj}
λ_M, λ_N	Power-law distribution index of network M and N

3.1   Failure in Network M

After deleting the nodes with $(1-p)$ ratio in network M, the quantity of remaining nodes is:

$$N'_{M1} = p \cdot N_M = \mu'_1 \cdot N_M, \tag{7}$$

Among them, the number of nodes with functions is:

$$N_{M1} = g_M\left(\mu'_1\right) \cdot N'_{M1} = \mu'_1 \cdot g_M\left(\mu'_1\right) \cdot N_M = \mu_1 \cdot N_M. \tag{8}$$

Therefore, the ratio of functional nodes in the first step is:

$$\mu_1 = \mu'_1 \cdot g_M\left(\mu'_1\right). \tag{9}$$

3.2   Failure in Network N Due to M

Due to the interdependence of network N and network M. The failure of nodes in network M will lead to the failure of corresponding nodes in network N. From the perspective of model construction, the number of nodes with a ratio of 2:1 accounts for 2/3, and the number of nodes with a ratio of 1:1 accounts for 1/3 in network M. Therefore, the quantity of nodes with dependencies in network N is:

$$N'_{N2} = \frac{2/3 \cdot N_M}{2} \cdot \left(\mu_1^2 + 2 \cdot \mu_1 \cdot (1 - \mu_1)\right) + \frac{1}{3} \cdot N_M \cdot \mu_1 = \frac{1}{2} \cdot \left(3 \cdot \mu_1 - \mu_1^2\right) \cdot N_N, \tag{10}$$

$$\mu'_2 = \frac{1}{2} \cdot \mu_1 \cdot (3 - \mu_1) = \frac{1}{2} \cdot \mu'_1 \cdot g_M\left(\mu'_1\right) \cdot (3 - \mu_1). \tag{11}$$

Among them, the number of nodes with functions is:

$$N_{N2} = g_N\left(\mu'_2\right) \cdot N'_{N2} = \mu'_2 \cdot g_N\left(\mu'_2\right) \cdot N_N = \mu_2 \cdot N_N. \tag{12}$$

$$\mu_2 = \mu'_2 \cdot g_N\left(\mu'_2\right). \tag{13}$$

3.3   Further Fragment of Network M

According to the initial connection relationship of the network, we can conclude that the number of nodes with connection ratio of 2:1 and 1:1 in network N is $\mu_1^2/2$ and $\left(3 \cdot \mu_1 - \mu_1^2\right)/2$ respectively.

Thus we can calculate the quantity of nodes with dependencies in network M is

$$N'_{M3} = \left(\frac{3 - 2 \cdot \mu_1}{3 - \mu_1} + \frac{\mu_1 \cdot 2}{3 - \mu_1}\right) \cdot \mu_2 \cdot N_N = \frac{2 \cdot \mu_2}{3 - \mu_1} \cdot N_M. \tag{14}$$

Owing to the nodes be eliminated in the first step do not belong to N_N, N_{M1}, and N'_{M3}, the fraction of nodes be removed from N_{M1} is equal to the same fraction of nodes removed from N'_{M1}, so

$$N_{M1} - N'_{M3} = \left(1 - \frac{2 \cdot \mu_2}{(3 - \mu_1) \cdot \mu_1}\right) \cdot N_{M1} = \left(1 - \frac{2 \cdot \mu_2}{(3 - \mu_1) \cdot \mu_1}\right) \cdot N'_{M1}. \quad (15)$$

Then the ratio of the quantity of nodes removed to the quantity of nodes in the original network is

$$1 - \mu'_1 + \left(1 - \frac{2 \cdot \mu_2}{(3 - \mu_1) \cdot \mu_1}\right) \cdot \mu'_1 = 1 - p \cdot g_N(\mu'_2). \quad (16)$$

So

$$\mu'_3 = p \cdot g_N(\mu'_2). \quad (17)$$

The number of nodes that belong to the giant component is

$$N_{M3} = \mu'_3 \cdot g_M(\mu'_3) \cdot N_M = \mu_3 \cdot N_M, \quad (18)$$

$$\mu_3 = \mu'_3 \cdot g_M(\mu'_3). \quad (19)$$

3.4 Cascading Failure in Network N Again

In the third step, node failure will further lead to the loss of function of nodes in network N. Similar to the previous calculation, the number of dependent nodes in network N is:

$$N'_{N4} = \frac{2/3 \cdot N_M}{2} \cdot (\mu_3^2 + 2 \cdot \mu_3 \cdot (1 - \mu_3)) + \frac{1}{3} \cdot N_M \cdot \mu_3 = \frac{1}{2} \cdot (3 \cdot \mu_3 + \mu_3^2) \cdot N_N. \quad (20)$$

From N_{N2} to N'_{N4}, we know

$$N_{N2} - N'_{N4} = \left[1 - \frac{(3 \cdot \mu_3 + \mu_3^2)}{2} / \mu_2\right] \cdot N_{N2} = \left[1 - \frac{(3 \cdot \mu_3 + \mu_3^2)}{2} / \mu_2\right] \cdot N'_{N2}. \quad (21)$$

Then the ratio of the quantity of nodes removed to the quantity of nodes in the original network is

$$1 - \mu'_2 + \mu'_2 \cdot \left[1 - \frac{(3 \cdot \mu_3 + \mu_3^2)}{2} / \mu_2\right] = 1 - \frac{1}{2} \cdot \mu'_1 \cdot (3 - \mu_3) \cdot g_M(\mu'_3). \quad (22)$$

So

$$\mu'_4 = \frac{1}{2} \cdot p \cdot (3 - \mu_3) \cdot g_M (\mu'_3). \tag{23}$$

Mfter analysis, we can deduce the following iterative equation:

$$\begin{cases} \mu'_{2i} = \frac{1}{2} \cdot p \cdot (3 - \mu_{2i-1}) \cdot g_M (\mu'_{2i-1}) \\ \mu'_{2i+1} = p \cdot g_N (\mu'_{2i}) \end{cases}. \tag{24}$$

4   Theoretical Solution and Simulation Results

We calculate the critical value of network collapse by image fitting firstly in this section. Then, we further verify the correctness of the theoretical value through simulation case study. Finally, the conditions impacting the robustness of the network are analyzed by changing the relevant parameters.

4.1   Theoretical Solution

When the cascading failure of the network stops, the proportion of remaining functional nodes will not change. At this time, the ratio of remaining functional nodes meets the following equations:

$$\begin{cases} \mu'_{2i} = \mu'_{2i-2} = \mu'_{2i+2} \\ \mu'_{2i+1} = \mu'_{2i-1} = \mu'_{2i+3} \end{cases}. \tag{25}$$

We define new variables x and y to meet:

$$\begin{cases} y = \mu'_{2i} = \mu'_{2i-2} = \mu'_{2i+2} \\ x = \mu'_{2i+1} = \mu'_{2i-1} = \mu'_{2i+3} \end{cases} (0 \leq x, y \leq 1) \tag{26}$$

So Eq. (24) will change by

$$\begin{cases} y = \frac{1}{2} \cdot p \cdot (3 - x \cdot g_M(x)) \cdot g_M(x) \\ x = p \cdot g_N(y) \end{cases}. \tag{27}$$

Excluding y, Eq. (27) will becomes

$$x = p \cdot g_N \left[\left(\frac{1}{2} \cdot p \cdot (3 - x \cdot g_M(x)) \cdot g_M(x) \right) \right]. \tag{28}$$

It is difficult to find an analytical solution to this equation. Therefore, we get the numerical solution by image fitting. The following equations are used to represent Eq. (28):

$$\begin{cases} z = x \\ z = p \cdot g_N \left[\left(\frac{1}{2} \cdot p \cdot (3 - x \cdot g_M(x)) \cdot g_M(x) \right) \right] \end{cases}. \tag{29}$$

As shown in Fig. 3, we draw two lines of the system of equations. The point where they are tangent is the numerical solution of the equation. We take the power-law exponent λ of SF network as 2.6. The two figures represent $\alpha = 1$ and

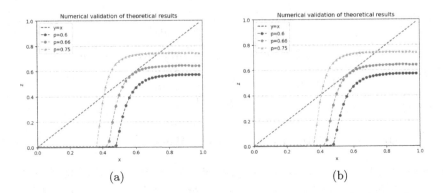

Fig. 3. The change of percolation threshold in different parameters.

$\alpha = 2$ respectively, and the rest are the same. We take three different p values to represent different situations. As can be seen from Fig. 3a, when $p > 0.575$, there are two intersections between the curve and the straight line. When $p < 0.575$, there is no intersection. $p = 0.575$ is the critical threshold pc when the network crashes. The same analysis method is used in Fig. 3b.

4.2   Simulation Results

Then, we verify the results of theoretical derivation by experiments. First, we establish two SF networks in the program. Then, the two networks are connected according to the method in the model construction. Finally, we attack the $(1-p)$ proportion of nodes in network M according to the value of attack parameter α. At each stage of network cascading failure, we will save the quantity of remaining functional nodes in the two networks. In the experiment, we carried out 50 experiments on each p value and took the average value. This ensures the accuracy of the experiment to a certain extent.

As shown in Fig. 4, the abscissa p represents the proportion of nodes retained in the network, and the ordinate represents the proportion of nodes that survive in the two networks. We take the value between the interval $[0,1]$ at the interval of 0.05, and then save the number of functional nodes that will not have cascading failure. We can observe that when p is less than the critical threshold pc, the network will collapse completely. When p is greater than pc, there are surviving functional nodes in the network. Moreover, near the critical threshold, the network presents a first-order phase transition. This is different from the second-order phase transition of a single network. Observing the figure, we can know that the number of remaining functional nodes of network M is always less than that of network N. This is because the node is attacked for the first time in network M. Furthermore, the nodes in network N have more dependent edges. This is equivalent to protecting the nodes in network N. Even if the node of one dependent edge fails and the node of the other dependent edge does not

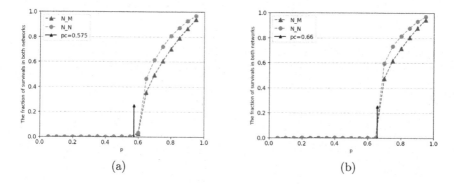

Fig. 4. Verify theoretical value.

fail, the node in the corresponding network N will not fail. This result verifies our theoretical value.

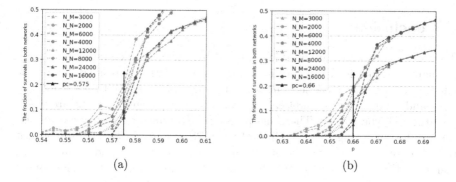

Fig. 5. Verify theoretical value.

Next, we take points near the theoretical threshold at an interval of 0.005 and calculate the number of remaining functional nodes corresponding to each point. To study the impact of different network sizes, we also selected four groups of network values with different sizes. With the increase of network scale, the image is closer and closer to the critical threshold in Fig. 5. So when the number of networks reaches a certain scale, the drawn image will approximate the critical threshold. This further validates our theoretical results.

Finally, we only change the power-law exponent of SF network under the same other conditions. From Fig. 6a, we find that when λ increases, the network percolation threshold decreases accordingly. This indicates that the robustness of the network is increased. At the same time, we also find that the power-law index has little influence on the robustness of the network. From different attack

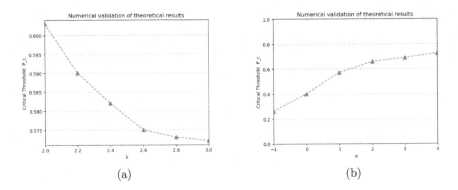

Fig. 6. Network seepage threshold under different parameters.

parameters, the network percolation threshold increases with the increase of α. Although the value of a is less than 0, it will still lead to network collapse. This is different from a single network. This is of great significance for us to learn and improve the reliability of the CPS system.

5   Conclusion

This paper constructs an interdependent physical network system in detail. Through the analysis of seepage theory, we get the critical threshold of network collapse. Moreover, we carried out several groups of simulation case studies to verify and analyze the theoretical values. The experimental results prove the correctness of the theory. These methods and experimental results are of significance for analyzing the reliability of the CPS system. However, we have not studied more types of network attacks and the proportion of node connections. Therefore, the next research plan may optimize the model and consider more different types of connection proportions. Moreover, attacks against node load will also be an interesting research direction. In future research, we will consider adding this situation to study the influence of interdependent networks.

Acknowledgments. This work was supported in part by the National Natural Science Foundation of China under grant No. 62072412, No. 61902359, No. 61702148, and No. 61672468, in part by the Opening Project of Shanghai Key Laboratory of Integrated Administration Technologies for Information Security under grant AGK2018001 and Key Lab of Information Network Security, Ministry of Public Security (Grant No. C20607).

References

1. Tan, F., Wang, Y., Wang, Q., Bu, L., Suri, N.: A lease based hybrid design pattern for proper-temporal-embedding of wireless CPS interlocking. IEEE Trans. Parallel Distrib. Syst. **26**(10), 2630–2642 (2015)

2. Posada, J., et al.: Visual computing as a key enabling technology for Industrie 4.0 and industrial internet. IEEE Comput. Graph. Appl. **35**(2), 26–40 (2015)
3. Abidi, M.H., Alkhalefah, H., Umer, U.: Fuzzy harmony search based optimal control strategy for wireless cyber physical system with industry 4.0. J. Intell. Manuf. 1–18 (2021). https://doi.org/10.1007/s10845-021-01757-4
4. Bagheri, B., Yang, S., Kao, H.A., Lee, J.: Cyber-physical systems architecture for self-aware machines in industry 4.0 environment. IFAC PapersOnLine **48**(3), 1622–1627 (2015)
5. Buldyrev, S.V., Parshani, R., Paul, G., Stanley, H.E., Havlin, S.: Catastrophic cascade of failures in interdependent networks. Nature **464**(7291), 1025–1028 (2010)
6. Chang, Y.H., Hu, Q., Tomlin, C.J.: Secure estimation based Kalman filter for cyber-physical systems against sensor attacks. Automatica J. IFAC Int. Fed. Autom. Control **95**, 399–412 (2018)
7. Cicconi, P., Russo, A.C., Germani, M., Prist, M., Monteriu, A.: Cyber-physical system integration for industry 4.0: modelling and simulation of an induction heating process for aluminium-steel molds in footwear soles manufacturing. In: IEEE International Forum on Research and Technologies for Society and Industry (2017)
8. Gao, X., Li, X., Yang, X.: Robustness assessment of the cyber-physical system against cascading failure in a virtual power plant based on complex network theory. Int. Trans. Electr. Energy Syst. **31**(11), e13039 (2021)
9. Huang, X., Gao, J., Buldyrev, S.V., Havlin, S., Stanley, H.E.: Robustness of interdependent networks under targeted attack. Phys. Rev. E **83**(6), 065101 (2011)
10. Huang, Z., Wang, C., Stojmenovic, M., Nayak, A.: Characterization of cascading failures in interdependent cyber-physical systems. IEEE Trans. Comput. **64**(8), 2158–2168 (2015)
11. Jazdi, N.: Cyber physical systems in the context of industry 4.0. In: IEEE International Conference on Automation (2014)
12. Jha, A.V., et al.: Smart grid cyber-physical systems: communication technologies, standards and challenges. Wirel. Networks **27**(4), 2595–2613 (2021). https://doi.org/10.1007/s11276-021-02579-1
13. Jirkovsky, V., Obitko, M., Kadera, P., Marik, V.: Towards plug&play cyber-physical system components. IEEE Trans. Ind. Inform. **14**(6), 1 (2018)
14. Mueller, E., Chen, X.L., Riedel, R.: Challenges and requirements for the application of industry 4.0: a special insight with the usage of cyber-physical system. Chin. J. Mech. Eng. **30**(5), 1050–1057 (2017)
15. Newman, M.: The spread of epidemic disease on networks. Phys. Rev. E Stat. Nonlinear Soft Matter Phys. **66**(1 Pt 2), 016128 (2002)
16. Newman, M., Strogatz, S.H., Watts, D.J.: Random graphs with arbitrary degree distributions and their applications (2000)
17. Parshani, R., Buldyrev, S.V., Havlin, S.: Interdependent networks: reducing the coupling strength leads to a change from a first to second order percolation transition. Phys. Rev. Lett. **105**(4), 048701 (2010)
18. Peng, H., Liu, C., Zhao, D., Hu, Z., Han, J.: Security evaluation under different exchange strategies based on heterogeneous cps model in interdependent sensor networks. Sensors **20**(21), 6123 (2020)
19. Peng, H., Qian, Z., Kan, Z., Zhao, D., Yu, J., Han, J.: Cascading failure dynamics against intentional attack for interdependent industrial Internet of Things. Complexity **2021** (2021)
20. Wang, T., Zhang, Z., Shao, F.: Survivability analysis on a cyber-physical system. Machines **5**(3), 17 (2017)

21. Wang, T., Shao, F., Zhu, K.: Structural health analysis on cyber physical system based on reliability. J. Supercomputing **77**(1), 445–470 (2020). https://doi.org/10.1007/s11227-020-03280-4
22. Wang, W., Chen, J., Lin, L., Liu, X., Nie, Q.: Vulnerability assessment method of electrical cyber-physical interdependent network considering node heterogeneity. In: 2020 IEEE 4th Conference on Energy Internet and Energy System Integration (EI2) (2020)
23. Xu, L., Guo, Q., Yang, T., Sun, H.: Robust routing optimization for smart grids considering cyber-physical interdependence. In: 2020 IEEE Power and Energy Society General Meeting (PESGM) (2020)
24. Zhang, Y., Yağan, O.: Optimizing the robustness of electrical power systems against cascading failures. Sci. Rep. **6**(1), 1–15 (2016)
25. Zhao, T., Dong, W., Lu, D., Yuan, Z., Liu, Y.: A risk assessment method for cascading failure caused by electric cyber-physical system (ECPS). In: International Conference on Electric Utility Deregulation and Restructuring and Power Technologies (2016)
26. Zhou, K., Liu, T., Zhou, L.: Industry 4.0: towards future industrial opportunities and challenges. In: International Conference on Fuzzy Systems and Knowledge Discovery (2016)

Multimedia Security

A GDIoU Loss Function-Based YOLOv4 Deep Learning Network for High-Performance Insulator Location in Field Images

Bin Ma, Yongkang Fu, Jian Li, Chunpeng Wang, and Yuli Wang[✉]

Qilu University of Technology, No. 3501, University Road, Changqing District, Jinan, Shandong, China
wyl@qlu.edu.cn

Abstract. Aiming at the slow and low accuracy of insulator positioning in the process of power line health inspection, a YOLOv4 deep learning framework based on the Gaussian Distance Intersection over Union (GDIoU) loss function is proposed in this paper. In the scheme, A GDIoU loss function is designed to accelerate the convergence speed of the YOLOv4 deep learning network, through which the performance of the YOLOv4 network is enhanced and the insulator's location speed and accuracy are accordingly improved. A large number of field insulator images are collected as training and test samples to enhance and evaluate the performance of the program. The experimental results show that the GDIoU based YOLOv4 deep learning network combined with the adaptive tilt correction method accelerates the insulator location speed by four times compared with the other state-of-the-art schemes, and the average precision is increased by 7.37% compared with naive YOLOv4 scheme. The performance can meet the requirement of online insulator location adequately.

Keywords: Insulator location · YOLO · Location · Loss function

1 Introduction

With the continuous rise of the voltage level in power systems, the performance of outdoor insulator detection under various environmental conditions is becoming increasingly important. As one of the indispensable key components in the power transmission line, the insulator strings play a significant role in electrical insulation and power line conjunction. Except for the high electric-field effects, the running environments, involved contamination, raining, icing, fog, and so on are also liable to cause damages to the power insulator. The insulator safety operation directly influences the stability of the electrical power system. Insulator inspection based on images obtained from an Unmanned Aerial Vehicle (UAV) is usually considered as the most economical and sustainable technical measure, which is especially true for power transmission networks with high rated voltage levels (shown in Fig. 1). However, as the running environment of the insulators is always very difficult, considerable attentions have been directed by researchers from

© Springer Nature Singapore Pte Ltd. 2022
C. Cao et al. (Eds.): FCS 2021, CCIS 1558, pp. 245–256, 2022.
https://doi.org/10.1007/978-981-19-0523-0_16

Fig. 1. Insulator images captured by UAV

universities and industrial research centers towards the location and diagnosis of the power insulators.

Recently, image-based insulator location and diagnosis technology has developed rapidly. Yan et al. [1] combined the gradient features and the local binary patterns to form fusion features for insulator detection. As the method is greatly affected by the background, the insulators cannot be positioned accurately in a complex environment. Zhou et al. [2] located the insulator in an infrared image with Scale Invariant Feature Transform (SIFT) feature matching method, in which the insulator temperature is achieved by simulating the distribution of the pixels, and thus the accuracy of insulator location and fault prediction is enhanced. Fang et al. [3] determined the shape of an insulator based on the method of linear fitting and template matching; however, the insulator still cannot be located accurately in an image with a complex background. Reddy et al. [4] monitored the condition of insulators with the Support Vector Machine (SVM) and the Discrete Orthogonal S-Transform (DOST) algorithm. Considering this method needs to transform the raw image to the frequency domain, its computation complexity is increased greatly.

At the same time, with the rapid development of deep learning technology [5], many object location and recognition algorithms have been presented, and their performances greatly exceed the traditional target detection methods. Insulator detection algorithms based on different deep learning frames have sprung up in recent years. Zhao et al. [6] proposed a method of insulator identification algorithm based on Deep Convolutional Neural Network (DCNN) and located the insulator in an infrared image with AlexNet model according to its middle-level features. The performance of the scheme was far better than those manually extracted features. Besides, Liao et al. [7] proposed a robust insulator detection algorithm based on local features and spatial orders for aerial images. Prates et al. [8] identified the faults of insulators in an image with Convolutional Neural Network (CNN) and applied the multitask machine learning algorithm for fault type prediction to improve the performance of the fault detection scheme. The Visual Geometry Group (VGG) 19 network is adopted in their scheme and the insulator recognition accuracy is improved significantly. Simultaneously, Lei et al. [9] put forward the Faster R-CNN based method to locate the broken insulators. Zhao et al. [10] obtained higher fault detection precision by improving the anchor generation method with Faster R-CNN. Tao et al. [11] applied the data enhancement technology for insulators location and detection with DCNN and achieved high insulator location and identification accuracy in laboratory.

High insulator location is the basis of accurate insulator identification and diagnosis. Although much research has been carried out to study optimal insulator location and identification method in the laboratory, the influence of different field conditions, such as pollution, various chemical materials, and severe weather, are difficult to simulate in laboratory. As the insulators are always installed in the harsh environment, the quality of insulator images is usually greatly influenced by certain environmental factors, such as light, clouds, fog, and wind. In most cases, the technicians first achieve insulator images through a UAV, and then, locate the insulators and diagnosis their health offline, which prevents the development of the outside insulator health detection to a great extent. Therefore, it is highly desired to locate and identify the insulator in a real-time field image. Although some specialists have studied to decrease the influence of complex environments on insulator detection, it is still difficult for the location speed and accuracy to meet the requirements of field insulator detection, especially when the image background is complex [12]. In this paper, a Gaussian Distance Intersection over Union (GDIoU) loss function based YOLOv4 deep learning network frame is proposed to accelerate the network converge speed. At the same time, an adaptive tilt correction algorithm is presented to improve the location accuracy of inclined insulators. Experimental comparisons showed that the proposed scheme could extract the deep characteristics of the insulator image and achieve high speed and accurate location of the insulators in an image even with complex background.

2 YOLOv4 Deep Learning Network Based Insulator Location

YOLO is a deep neural network-based object location and identification scheme proposed by Redmon et al. [13, 14] in 2016. The advantages of this network are that it runs very fast, and it is suitable for real-time object detection. It has been developed to the fourth generation now. Different from the previous versions of YOLO network,

YOLOv4 adopts the most optimal strategies in the CNN section. It retains the head part of YOLOv3 and upgrades the backbone network to Cross Stage Partial (CSP) Darknet 53 [15], at the same time, the idea of spatial pyramid pooling [16] is adopted to expand the receptive field. The network structure of YOLOv4 is shown in Fig. 2.

As shown in Fig. 2, YOLOv4 deep learning network adopts Complete Intersection-over-Union (CIoU) [17] as the loss function and employs the data enhancement scheme to increase the diversity ability of training samples; thereby, the robustness of the network is enhanced. Simultaneously, it takes advantage of the mish activation function, attention mechanism and optimal hyper-parameters to achieve accuracy objection detection. Compared with YOLOv3 [18], its mean Average Precision (mAP) and Frames Per Second (FPS) have increased by 10% and 12%, respectively. It can be observed from Table 1, YOLOv4 network achieves a good balance between accuracy and speed in the process of object detection. Therefore, we adopted the improved YOLOv4 network in this study to achieve high speed and accuracy location of insulators in real-time field images.

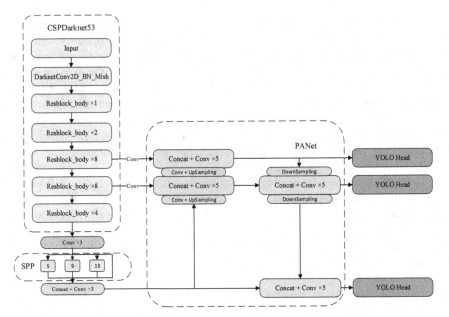

Fig. 2. Structural diagram of YOLOv4 deep learning network

Table 1. Comparison of different object detection methods on the MS COCO dataset

Algorithm	FPS	AP
YOLOv4	38	41.2%
LRF [19]	38.5	36.2%
SSD [20]	22	28.8%
RetinaNet [21]	5.1	37.8%
YOLOv3	35	31.0%
EfficientDet (D2) [22]	18	41.5%

2.1 Different IoU Loss Function of YOLOv4 Deep Learning Network

Unlike YOLOv3, YOLOv4 deep learning network employs CIoU as a new loss function to solve the problem of slow convergence speed in the process of object detection, which separately adds two penalty items, namely, the distance and aspect ratio, to the IoU loss function, enabling stable regression of the prediction box; thus, the problem of convergence failure during the training process is avoided.

Intersection over Union(IoU) is the most commonly used index in object detection, and it is often employed to evaluate the relationship between the ground truth and the prediction box (shown as Eq. (1)).

$$\text{IoU} = \frac{|B \cap B_{gt}|}{|B \cup B_{gt}|} \tag{1}$$

Here, B is the prediction box, and B_{gt} is the ground truth. If the two boxes have no overlapping areas, then, the value of IoU is 0. In this case, if IoU is employed as a loss function, the gradient would be 0, and thus the deep learning process could not be optimized. To solve this problem, a penalty item was added to the IoU loss function. thereby, the Generalized Intersection over Union (GIoU) loss [23] was proposed (shown in Eq. (2) and (3)).

$$L_{\text{GIoU}} = 1 - IoU + \frac{|A - U|}{|A|} \tag{2}$$

$$U = B \cup B_{gt} \tag{3}$$

Here, A is the area of the smallest bounding rectangle between the ground truth and the prediction box. With Eq. (2), the problem of the two frames non-overlapping is solved. However, the horizontal and vertical prediction boxes still converge slowly in this situation. Aiming at this problem, the loss function of DIoU and CIoU were proposed in two ways to accelerate the convergence speed of the prediction box.

$$L_{CIoU} = 1 - IoU + \frac{\rho^2(b, b_{gt})}{s^2} + \alpha v \tag{4}$$

$$v = \frac{4}{\pi^2} \left(\arctan \frac{w_{gt}}{h_{gt}} - \arctan \frac{w}{h} \right)^2 \tag{5}$$

$$\alpha = \frac{v}{(1 - IoU) + v} \tag{6}$$

In the front equations, b and b_{gt} represent the center point of the prediction box and the ground truth, respectively; ρ is the Euclidean distance between two points; s is the diagonal length of the smallest bounding rectangle between the prediction box and the ground truth; v is the similarity of the aspect ratio of two boxes; w_{gt} and h_{gt} are the width and height of the ground truth, respectively; w and h are the width and height of the prediction box; and α denotes the weight function. Similar to the GIoU Loss function, the DIoU Loss function can provide the direction of regression when the prediction box and the ground truth are completely non-overlapping. Moreover, the DIoU loss function can also minimize the distance between the prediction box and the ground truth, and enable the YOLOv4 network converges faster than the GIoU Loss function based one. Furthermore, the CIoU loss function involved three important factors in the process of deep learning regression, namely, the area of the overlap area, the distance between the two boxes, and the length-width ratio, which ensure that the prediction box convergence stable. Nevertheless, its convergence is still less quickly.

2.2 GDIoU Loss Function Based YOLOv4 Deep Learning Algorithm

It can be concluded through the above analysis that the CIoU based YOLOv4 network converges according to three important factors in the process of object detection, which results in a slower convergence speed. However, as to the case of insulator location and identification, the length-width ratio of an insulator in an image is similar, and the convergence speed is mainly decided by the distance between the prediction box and the ground truth. To improve the convergence speed of a YOLOv4 network employed for insulator location, a two-dimensional Gaussian model is proposed to simulate the relationship between the prediction box and the ground truth in this paper, namely, GDIoU.

In the proposed scheme, two groups of corner points of the prediction box and the ground truth are employed to measure the distance between the two frames. The distance of the two frames is represented by the distance between the predicted and the real box corners. If the two group corners are close to each other, then, the distance between the prediction box and the ground truth is supposed to be very short. As shown in Eqs. (7)–(9).

$$GD_1 = e^{-\frac{\left(x_1'-x_1\right)^2+\left(y_1'-y_1\right)^2}{2c^2}}, \ GD_2 = e^{-\frac{\left(x_2'-x_2\right)^2+\left(y_2'-y_2\right)^2}{2c^2}} \tag{7}$$

$$\overline{GD} = \frac{GD_1 + GD_2}{2} \tag{8}$$

$$L_{GDIoU} = 1 - IoU + (1 - \overline{GD}) + \alpha v \tag{9}$$

Here, (x_1', y_1') and (x_1, y_1) are the upper left corner points of the prediction box and the ground truth; (x_2', y_2') and (x_2, y_2) are the lower right corner points of the prediction box and the ground truth, respectively; GD_1 represents the Gaussian distance between (x_1', y_1') and (x_1, y_1); and GD_2 represents the Gaussian distance between (x_2', y_2') and (x_2, y_2). The closer the two points are, the nearer the Gaussian distance is to 1; on the contrary, the larger the distance is, the nearer the Gaussian distance is to 0. Here, $\overline{GD}$ is the average value of GD_1 and GD_2, it represents the distance between the prediction box and the ground truth, and the value of indicates the overlapping degree of the two boxes. In a GDIoU loss function based YOLOv4 deep learning network, the convergence speed can be controlled by adjusting parameter C. On the one hand, if the distance between the prediction box and the ground truth is large, we increase the value of C, the prediction box will move quickly to the ground truth; on the other hand, if the distance between them is small, we reduce the value of C, the prediction box would move slowly to close to the object. Finally, the prediction box will coincide with the ground truth. The parameter C is adaptively adjusted according to the training process to achieve optimal performance.

2.3 Influence of Parameter C

To study the influence of parameter C on the convergence speed of the GDIoU based YOLOv4 deep learning network, the derivative of X and Y in Eq. (8) is calculated, and the change rate of X and Y directions is obtained. The larger the change rate is, the faster the convergence speed would be achieved. In the case that only the influence of C on the convergence speed of YOLOv4 network is considered, we let d be a fixed value firstly, and then the gradient δ would changes with the parameter C. Figure 3 shows the change curve of δ versus C, and it indicates that a special parameter C can be obtained to enable the curve to attain the maximum value, namely, the fastest convergence rate. The closer the parameter C is to the special value η, the faster the convergence speed would be achieved. We can also conclude from the Fig. 3 that, when the value of parameter C is less than η, the convergence speed of YOLOv4 network drops rapidly with the decrease of C, and finally it approaches 0; however, when the value of parameter C is greater than η, it drops slowly with the increase of parameter C.

$$GD'(x) = \frac{x - x_0}{C^2} e^{-\frac{(x-x_0)^2+(y-y_0)^2}{2C^2}} \tag{10}$$

$$GD'(y) = \frac{y - y_0}{C^2} e^{-\frac{(x-x_0)^2+(y-y_0)^2}{2C^2}} \tag{11}$$

$$\delta = \sqrt{GD'(x)^2 + GD'(y)^2} = \frac{\sqrt{(x - x_0)^2 + (y - y_0)^2}}{C^2} e^{-\frac{(x-x_0)^2+(y-y_0)^2}{2C^2}} \tag{12}$$

$$\delta = \frac{d}{c^2} e^{\frac{d^2}{2c^2}} \tag{13}$$

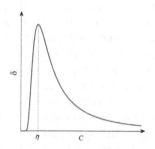

Fig. 3. The diagram of δ changes with C

3 Experimental Design

Since there is currently no public dataset of insulator strings, the images of the insulators were collected by UAVs in the experiment. The size of raw images was resized to 512 × 512 due to computational resource limits. In the experiment, we collected 2570 field insulator images with different backgrounds. Among which, 2313 (i.e. 90%) images are set for training and 257 (i.e. 10%) images for testing. The insulator string is labeled with confidence scores by a box determined by four coordinates. The details of the training and testing for different IoU based YOLOv4 networks are presented in the following. The insulator location speed and accuracy of the proposed network were evaluated and compared with other high performance object detection networks. Moreover, some results of the proposed method are shown intuitively with figures to indicate the advantage of the proposed scheme. All the experiments were run on a computer with Intel E5-2690 v4@2.60 GHz CPU and 128 G memory, NVIDIA Tesla P4 with 8 GB of GPU memory.

In the experiment, the performance of the proposed GDIoU based YOLOv4 network was evaluated by the average precision (AP) values. AP is defined as

$$AP = \frac{1}{11} \sum_{r \in [0,0,1,...,1]]} \hat{p}(r) \tag{14}$$

$$\hat{p}(r) = \max_{\bar{r} > r} p(\bar{r}) \tag{15}$$

where, r is the threshold of the recall rate; $\bar{r}$ is the current recall rate; $\hat{P}$ is the maximum accuracy rate that can be achieved when the current recall rate is greater than the threshold; and P is the corresponding accuracy rate under the current recall rate, respectively. The IoU threshold for determining positive and negative samples was set to 0.5. The convergence speed is the average time of insulator location for each image.

4   Experimental Results and Discussion

4.1   Results of GDIoU Loss Function Based YOLOv4 Deep Learning Network

In the experiment, the location of the insulator strings was achieved with the GDIoU based YOLOv4 deep learning network, and the value of parameter C was set to 15. The experimental results are shown in Fig. 4. In the image, the identified insulator strings are bounded by rectangle boxes associated with the confidence scores. The results show that the proposed scheme was fairly effective in detecting insulator strings even in an image with complex background. Generally, if the overlapping portion of the result and the ground truth is greater than 0.5, the location is considered to be successful. In the experiment, the AP was 0.902, the average recall value was 0.835, and the average insulator location and identification speed was only 135 ms. The results suggested that the proposed method could achieve high speed and accurate insulator location in a field image, which is satisfactory for the requirement of insulator string identification and the location even in a complex environment.

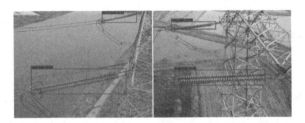

Fig. 4. Examples of insulator string location

4.2 Influence of Different Parameter C Values

In the experiment, the parameter C is adjusted from 8 to 35, to verify the influence of parameter c on the performance of a GDIoU loss based YOLOv4 deep learning network. Figure 5 shows that the AP of our proposed scheme changes with different parameter C. For an insulator images, the length-width ratio of insulators is fixed, so, the distance of the corresponding corner points are changes in a same way. The experiments results indicate that the changes of indicator AP are consistent with the theoretical analysis. When the value of parameter C is 15, AP achieves the maximum value. The value of AP drops rapidly when the parameter C decreases, however, it decreases slowly with the increase of the parameter c. when the value of parameter C is 7, the AP value drops rapidly to 21.43, but its value still up to 28.26 when the parameter C reached 25. In sum, On the left side of the peak point N, AP drops quickly with C, but on the right side of peak point, AP decreases slowly, AP achieves only 1 peak point in the whole range of the parameter C.

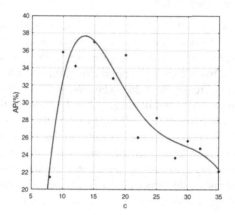

Fig. 5. The influence of parameter *C* on AP

4.3 Influence of Different Loss Functions

To compare the influence of the GDIoU and the CIoU loss functions on YOLOv4 deep learning network performance, the YOLOv4 networks with different loss functions were built for insulator location and identification test. Figure 6 shows the curves of the loss changes with the increases of iterations in the model training stage. It can be observed that the difference between the prediction box and the ground truth of the GDIoU based YOLOv4 network dropped more quickly than that of the CIoU based one in epochs 0 to 45. Although, after 45 epochs, both the GDIoU and the CIoU loss functions stabilized, but the difference between the prediction box and the ground truth of the GDIoU based YOLOv4 deep learning network was still much smaller than that based on the CIoU loss function.

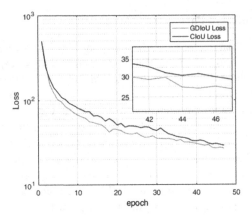

Fig. 6. The curves of the loss changes with the iteration increases

4.4 Comparison with Other Schemes

To evaluate the performance of the GDIoU based YOLOv4 deep learning network, we compared the proposed scheme with other state-of-the-art object detection schemes. The experimental results show that the AP of the proposed scheme was significantly higher than that of naive YOLOv4 at the same computational time. When the input size was 320 × 320, the AP was increased by 1.2%; when the size was 416 × 416, the AP was increased by 6.47%; and the AP was still increased by 7.37% when the input size was 512 × 512. The AP was nearly twice of that achieved with YOLOv3 at the same image size. Although the AP of the proposed scheme is similar to that of the EfficientDet scheme, its convergence speed is much lower than the counterpart. Moreover, it should be noted that, in practical engineering applications, an ultrafast insulator location is not always needed. As the insulator is a stable object, the aerial inspection aims to locate insulators in an image and then diagnosis their health conditions (Fig. 7).

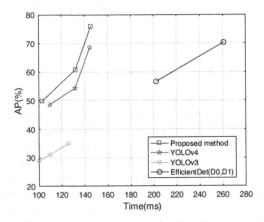

Fig. 7. Performance of insulator location with different deep learning networks

Table 2. Insulator location performance comparison with different methods

Method	AP	Inference time
GDIoU based YOLOv4	75.95%	145.5 ms
Faster RCNN + U-Net [24]	75.34%	685.3 ms
Deep CNN cascading [11]	83.61%	1421.6 ms

To further evaluate the performance of GDIoU based YOLOv4 for insulator location, we compared the proposed scheme with other two excellent methods. One is based on the Faster RCNN + U-Net architecture, and the other is based on the Deep CNN cascading scheme. The training and testing dataset of the comparative experiments were the same as that used in Sect. 3. Experimental result comparisons of the three methods are shown in Table 2. It can be observed that the proposed method achieved the fastest location convergence speed. Although the three methods had similar object location precision, the convergence speed of our proposed scheme was three times that of the Faster RCNN + U-Net scheme, and ten times that of the Deep CNN Cascading scheme. The results demonstrate the superiority of the GDIoU based YOLOv4 deep learning network for insulator location.

5 Conclusions

This paper proposed a GDIoU based YOLOv4 deep learning network for insulator location and identification. The insulator location speed and accuracy are improved significantly with the proposed GDIoU loss function based YOLOv4 network. The experimental results show that the GDIoU loss function based YOLOv4 deep learning network combined with the adaptive tilt correction method could effectively improve the accuracy and efficiency of insulator location and identification in a real-time field image. The proposed scheme has great application and popularization value in the field of real-time insulator health detection.

References

1. Tiantian, Y., Guodong, Y., Junzhi, Y.: Feature fusion based insulator detection for aerial inspection. In: 2017 36th Chinese Control Conference (CCC), IEEE (2017)
2. Zhou, S.P., et al.: Research on insulator fault diagnosis and remote monitoring system based on infrared images. In: Shakshuki, E. (ed.) 8th International Conference on Ambient Systems, Networks and Technologies, pp. 1194–1199. Elsevier Science Bv, Amster-dam (2017)
3. Ting, F., et al.: A Fast Insulator-Contour-Detection-Algorithm on Power Transmission Lines Images. In: Applied mechanics and materials pp. 337–343
4. Reddy, M.J.B., Chandra, B.K., Mohanta, D.K.: Condition monitoring of 11 kV distribution system insulators incorporating complex imagery using combined DOST-SVM approach. IEEE Trans. Dielectr. Electr. Insul. **20**(2), 664–674 (2013)
5. Zou, Z., et al.: Object detection in 20 years: a survey (2019)

6. Zhao, Z.B., et al.: Multi-patch deep features for power line insulator status classification from aerial images. In: 2016 International Joint Conference on Neural Networks (IJCNN), pp. 3187–3194 (2016)
7. Liao, S.L., An, J.B.: A robust insulator detection algorithm based on local features and spatial orders for aerial images. IEEE Geosci. Remote Sens. Lett. **12**(5), 963–967 (2015)
8. Prates, R.M., et al.: Insulator visual non-conformity detection in overhead power distribution lines using deep learning. Comput. Electr. Eng. **78**, 343–355 (2019)
9. Lei, X.S., Sui, Z.H.: Intelligent fault detection of high voltage line based on the faster R-CNN. Measurement **138**, 379–385 (2019)
10. Zhao, Z.B., et al.: Insulator detection method in inspection image based on improved faster R-CNN. Energies **12**(7), 1204 (2019)
11. Tao, X., et al.: Detection of power line insulator defects using aerial images analyzed with convolutional neural networks. IEEE Trans. Syst. Man Cyber.Syst. **50**(4), 1486–1498 (2020)
12. Bochkovskiy, A., Wang, C.Y., Liao, H.Y.M.: YOLOv4: optimal speed and accuracy of object detection (2020)
13. Redmon, J., et al.: You only look once: unified, real-time object detection. In: 2016 IEEE Conference on Computer Vision and Pattern Recognition (CVPR), p. 779–788 (2016)
14. Redmon, J., Farhadi, A.: YOLO9000: better, faster, stronger. In: Proceedings of the IEEE conference on computer vision and pattern recognition (2017)
15. Wang, C.Y., et al.: CSPNet: a new backbone that can enhance learning capability of CNN. In: Proceedings of the IEEE/CVF Conference on Computer Vision and Pattern Recognition Workshops (2020)
16. He, K., Zhang, X., Ren, S., Sun, J.: Spatial pyramid pooling in deep convolutional networks for visual recognition. In: Fleet, D., Pajdla, T., Schiele, B., Tuytelaars, T. (eds.) ECCV 2014. LNCS, vol. 8691, pp. 346–361. Springer, Cham (2014). https://doi.org/10.1007/978-3-319-10578-9_23
17. Zheng, Z., et al.: Distance-IoU loss: faster and better learning for bounding box regression arXiv (2019)
18. Redmon, J., Farhadi, A.: Yolov3: An incremental improvement (2018)
19. Wang, T., et al.: Learning rich features at high-speed for single-shot object detection. In: 2019 IEEE/CVF International Conference on Computer Vision (ICCV) (2020)
20. Liu, W., Anguelov, D., Erhan, D., Szegedy, C., Reed, S., Fu, C.-Y., Berg, A.C.: SSD: Single Shot MultiBox Detector. In: Leibe, B., Matas, J., Sebe, N., Welling, M. (eds.) ECCV 2016. LNCS, vol. 9905, pp. 21–37. Springer, Cham (2016). https://doi.org/10.1007/978-3-319-464 48-0_2
21. Lin, T.Y., et al.: Focal Loss for Dense Object Detection. IEEE Trans. Pattern Anal. Mach. Intell. **99**, 2999–3007 (2017)
22. Tan, M., Pang, R., Le, Q.V.: EfficientDet: scalable and efficient object detection. In: 2020 IEEE/CVF Conference on Computer Vision and Pattern Recognition (CVPR) (2020)
23. Rezatofighi, H., et al.: Generalized intersection over union: a metric and a loss for bounding box regression. In: 2019 IEEE/CVF Conference on Computer Vision and Pattern Recognition (CVPR) (2020)
24. Ling, Z.N., et al.: An accurate and real-time method of self-blast glass insulator location based on faster R-CNN and U-net with aerial images. CSEE J. Power Energy Syst. **5**(4), 474–482 (2019)

Identification of Synthetic Spoofed Speech with Deep Capsule Network

Terui Mao, Diqun Yan$^{(\boxtimes)}$, Yongkang Gong, and Randing Wang

Ningbo University, Zhejiang 315000, China
{yandiqun,wangrangding}@nbu.edu.cn

Abstract. The state-of-the-art models for speech synthesis and voice conversion have caused a great threat to automatic speech verification (ASV) system. In fact, it is difficult for human beings to perceive the subtle difference between the bonafide speech and spoofed speech from these models. The ASVspoof 2019 challenge, jointly launched by several world-leading research institutions, is the largest and most comprehensive challenge for spoofed speech identification. In this work, a countermeasure system for ASVspoof 2019 is proposed based on cepstrum features and deep capsule network. MFCC and CQCC features are extracted as the input of the proposed network. The convolutional layer and routing strategy of the capsule network are specifically designed to distinguish bonafide speech from spoofed ones. The experimental results on ASVspoof 2019 LA evaluation set show that the proposed deep capsule network can improve the baseline algorithms t-DCF and EER scores by 31% and 37%, respectively.

Keywords: ASVspoof 2019 · Capsule network · Deepfake

1 Introduction

The aim of automatic speaker verification (ASV) is to confirm wthether a given utterance is pronounced by a specified speaker or not. Recent years, ASV systems have achieved considerable performance improvement. Advances in voice conversion (VC) [1,2], text-to-speech (TTS) [3–5], however, have made ASV systems extremely vulnerable. There is a strong requirement to distinguish between spoofed speech and bonafide ones for improving the security of the ASV system.

Some academic organizers initiated ASVspoof Challenge on spoofing detection developments, which has been held for three times. ASVspoof 2015 focused on logical attack (LA) scenarios using TTS and VC algorithms. ASVspoof 2017 focuses on physical attack (PA), which attackers use to record bonafide speech and play it back to the ASV system. ASVspoof 2019 extends the previous two versions. First, it considers all forms of attacks. Second, the most advanced and strongest spoofing algorithms are applied. Hence, the spoofed sp eech is more difficult to distinguish. On the other hand, ASVspoof 2019 adopts Tandem detection cost function (t-DCF) [6] as the main metric and Equal error rate (EER) as the secondary metric.

© Springer Nature Singapore Pte Ltd. 2022
C. Cao et al. (Eds.): FCS 2021, CCIS 1558, pp. 257–265, 2022.
https://doi.org/10.1007/978-981-19-0523-0_17

In this paper, we focus on logical attack. The logical attack is to use TTS and VC technology to produce Spooed Speech to attack the ASV system. For logical attack, high time-frequency resolution features have become popular solutions, as they identify crucial voice-print cues using binary classifiers [7,8]. Cochlear filter cepstral coefficients (CFCC) and the change in instantaneous frequency (CFCCIF) are proposed for training two Gaussian mixture model (GMM) classifiers to detect bonafide and spoofed speech, respectively [8]. Constant Q cepstral coefficients (CQCCs) [9], which use constant Q transform (CQT) instead of the short-time Fourier transform (STFT), perform better than Mel-frequency cepstral coefficients (MFCCs).

Convolutional Neural Network (CNN) have achieved state-of-the-art performance in many research fields. In recent years, some identification methods based on CNN have been proposed. Inspired by the success of residual convolutional neural networks in other tasks, Alzantot et al. [10] proposed three various deep residual works for spoofing detection. It reached the best performance of t-DCF (0.1569) and EER (6.02). In [11], squeeze-excitation and residual network are proposed to establish within DNN models which reached the t-DCF is 0.155, EER is 6.7.

More recently, capsule network (CapsNet) as a powerful alternative to CNNs is introduced in [12], which can learn a more equivariant representation. Capsule network uses capsules instead of neurons, so that the attributes of samples can be reflected at the same time as the classification results come out. It means that the capsule network can retain the structural characteristics of samples. In this work, capsule network is applied on the forensics of synthetic spoofed speech. In this work, the depth of the capsule network is deepened to make it more suitable for identification and the number of dynamic routes is specifically designed. The experimental results on ASVspoof 2019 LA database show that the proposed capsule network can achieve better performance compared with the baseline algorithms.

The rest of this paper is organized as follows. Section 2 describes the feature extraction of the system and our model architecture design. Section 3 includes our experiment results. Finally, the paper is concluded in Sect. 4.

2   Proposed Capsule Network Model

In this section, we first briefly describe the feature extraction of MFCC and CQCC. Next, we propose a deep model based on convolutional and capsule neural net-works for identifying spoofed speech.

2.1   Feature Extraction

MFCC [13] is a feature widely used in automatic speech and speaker recognition. It is acquired by computing the short-time-Fourier-transform (STFT), then mapping the spectrum into Mel-Spectrum through a filter bank, and finally calculating a discrete cosine transform (DCT). In our work, the features consist of the first 24 coefficients. The first and second derivatives of each coefficient are concatenated with the original features to result in a 72-dimensional feature vector.

CQCC [14] is a magnitude-based feature which provides a time-frequency analysis method. Short-term-Fourier-transform provides fixed time-frequency resolution, whereas CQCC provides a higher fit tends to capture more acoustic information at lower frequencies and more time information at higher frequencies. These features utilize CQT which is originally presented for tasks related to music processing and later it was employed in speaker verification tasks. The extraction of CQCC is as follows. For a given speech signal, CQT is applied to obtain the spectrum. Then it will calculate the power spectrum and its logarithmic version. Next, uniform resampling is employed. Finally, DCT is applied as the inverse transformation to obtain the cepstrum. More details of CQCC can be found in [14].

2.2 CNN Architecture

CNN architecture, is a collection of parameters and components that we need to design a network, based on superimposing many hidden layers on top of one another. This has proven to be very effective in extracting hierarchical features. That is, they can learn features from a set of previously learned features. In a CNN architecture, the first layer is a set of convolutional feature extractors, using a set of learnable filters applied in parallel with the two-dimensional matrix extracted from audio. These filters work like a sliding window, convolving with all areas of the input matrix to an overlapping distance called stride, and producing an output called the feature map.

Table 1. CNN architecture.

	Filter	Depth	Stide	Padding
Conv1	3×3	32	1	2
Conv2	3×3	64	1	2
MaxPool3	3×3	64	3	0
Conv4	3×3	128	1	2
Conv5	3×3	128	1	2
MaxPool6	3×3	128	3	0
Conv7	3×3	256	1	2
MaxPool8	3×3	256	3	0

Figure 1 shows the proposed architecture of CNN model. The extracted MFCC or CQCC which is a 2D matrix is passed through a 2D convolution layer with 32 filters, which filter size is 3×3, stride is 1, padding is 1. The output of the first convolution layer has 32 channels and is fed into a 2D convolution layer with 64 filters. The number of channels in the subsequent convolutional layers is 128, 128 and 256, respectively. We use LeakyRelu as the activation function followed by each convolution layer. For compression purposes, three maxpooling layers, are placed behind the 2nd, 4th and 5th convolution blocks, respectively, and the number of output channels is equal to the number of input channels. The maxpooling kernel is used with size of 3 × 3, stride = 3, size of 2 × 2, stride = 2, size of 2 × 2, stride =1 in order. The detailed architecture is described in Table 1.

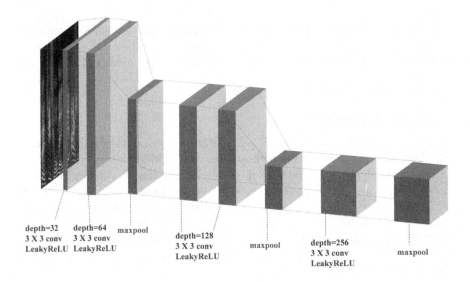

depth=32   depth=64   maxpool
3 X 3 conv 3 X 3 conv
LeakyReLU   LeakyReLU   depth=128
                              3 X 3 conv   maxpool
                              LeakyReLU   depth=256
                                                             3 X 3 conv   maxpool
                                                             LeakyReLU

Fig. 1. Architecture of CNN. CNN has 8 layers. The input is the spectrum feature, and the output of the last maxpooling is the input of the CapsNet.

2.3   Capsule Architecture

The proposed CapsNet is shown in Fig. 2, which consists of two capsule layers. In the first layer, we use eight different and parallel Conv2d (32 filters, filter size = 3 × 3, stride = 1, padding = 1) convolute the output of CNN that we introduced in the last section to make eight primary capsules. The primary capsule needs to be squeezed from a 3D matrix to a 1D vector. The second layer consists of two-digit capsules, one for bonafide and one for spoofing. Unlike the primarily capsule, the length of the digit capsule is limited from 0 to 1. The closer the digit capsule length is to 1, the more likely it is to be a bonafide speech.

Dynamic routing is used to connect the above-mentioned two layers. The non-linear computation is constructed in an iterative manner. The routing number can increase or decrease the connection strength by dynamic routing. The algorithm of routing algorithm is shown in Fig. 3 and Algorithm 1.

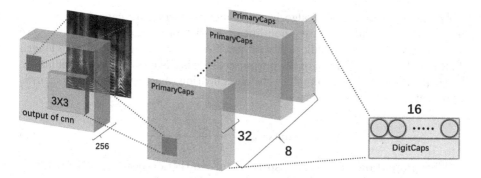

Fig. 2. CapsNet with 2 layers. The length of digitCaps indicates of presence instance of spoofed and bonafide speech.

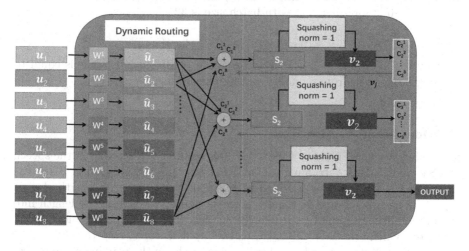

Fig. 3. CapsNet with 2 layers. The length of digitCaps indicates of presence instance of spoofed and bonafide speech.

Algorithm 1. Dynamic routing between capsules

procedure ROUTING $\left(\boldsymbol{u}_{j|i}, W, r\right)$

$\widehat{w} \leftarrow w + \mathrm{rand}(\mathrm{size}(w))$

$\widehat{\boldsymbol{u}}_{j|i} \leftarrow \widehat{w}_i \, \mathrm{squash}\left(\boldsymbol{u}_{j|i}\right) \quad w_i \in \mathrm{R}^{mn}$

for all input capsule $\boldsymbol{i}$ and all output capsule $\boldsymbol{j}$ do

for r iterations do

    for all input capsules i do $c_i \leftarrow \mathrm{softmax}\left(b_i\right)$

    for all output capsules j do $\boldsymbol{s}_j \leftarrow \sum_i c_{ij}\widehat{\boldsymbol{u}}_{j|i}$

    for all output capsules j do $\boldsymbol{v}_j \leftarrow \mathrm{softmax}\left(\boldsymbol{s}_j\right)$

    for all input capsules i and output capsules j do

$b_{ij} \leftarrow b_{ij} + \widehat{\boldsymbol{u}}_{j|i}\boldsymbol{v}_j$

return $\boldsymbol{v}_j$

In the dynamic routing algorithm, u denotes primarily capsule, and v_2 is last two-digit capsule. We use a non-linear "squashing" function as (1) to ensure that short vectors get shrunk to almost zero length and long vectors to a length slightly below 1. The length of the output capsule is the probability of prediction. The capsule can be used to replace the classification of a single neuron to express more features of the structure.

$$v_j = \text{softmax}\,(s_i) = \frac{\|s_j\|^2}{1 + \|s_j\|^2}\frac{s_j}{\|s_j\|} \tag{1}$$

The proportion of bonafide speech and synthetic speech is about 1:9 in ASVspoof 2019 LA database. The weight ratio assigned to bonafide and spoofed speech is 1:9 to balance the distribution of the training dataset. Loss function is minimizing a weight Cross Entropy as (2) using Adam optimizer with learning rate $= 5 \times 10^{-5}$ for 70 epochs with batch size is 32.

$$L = -(9 * y \log(\hat{y}) + (1 - y)\log(1 - \hat{y})) \tag{2}$$

where y is the ground truth label and $\hat{y}$ is the predicted label that is equal to the length of vector from dynamic routing algorithm.

2.4   Identification Algorithm

In training stage, MFCC and CQCC features are first extracted from the speech of ASVspoof 2019 LA training set, and fed into the CNN network. Then the output of CNN network is classified by two CapsNet layers. The length of digit capsule is be-tween 0 and 1. Finally, softmax is used to convert the length into the probability. We build two different models (MFCC-CapsNet and CQCC-CapsNet) which take MFCC, CQCC as the input features, respectively.

In testing stage, we used the classification model in the training stage to test various spoofing algorithms provided by the ASVspoof 2019 evaluation set. The final output probability is converted into the official recommended log-likelihood ratio (LLR) form as the final countermeasure (CM) score of the testing speech. Similar to the former two editions of ASVspoof, high detection score indicates bonafide and low score indicates spoofing attack.

3   Experimental Results

3.1   Experimental Setup

Dataset and Baseline Models. ASVspoof 2019 LA database is divided into three parts: training set, development set and evaluation set. There are 17 synthesis algorithms used in the LA database, and 6 algorithms of them are included in the training set and development set. The remaining 11 are upgraded versions of the above 6 algorithms or completely unknown data generation methods to make evaluation set. Evaluation set is used to more comprehensively evaluate unknown and known attacks.

Table 2. Experimental results. t-DCF and EER scores for the different models as measured on the development and evaluation sets for logical access scenarios.

Model	Development		Evaluation	
	t-DCF	EER	t-DCF	EER
Baseline LFCC-GMM	0.0633	2.71	0.2116	8.09
Baseline CQCC-GMM	0.0123	0.43	0.2366	9.57
MFCC-Capsule	0.1367	4.19	0.2001	9.21
CQCC-Capsule	0	0	0.1458	5.09

Evaluation Metrics. Tandem Detection Cost Function (t-DCF) as (3) is the newly released index of ASVspoof challenge as the main index. This metric combines the ASV system with the CM system, where the ASV system is provided by the organization. Equal Error Rate (EER) is a secondary metric, which represents the value obtained when false acceptance rate and false rejection rate are equal as the threshold changes.

$$t - DCF(s) = C_1 P_{miss}^{cm}(s) + C_2 P_{fa}^{cm}(s) \tag{3}$$

where $P_{miss}^{cm}(s)$ and $P_{fa}^{cm}(s)$ are, respectively, the false rejection rate and false acceptance rate of the capsule network at threshold s. The constants C_1 and C_1 are dictated by t-DCF costs. More details of t-DCF can be found in [6].

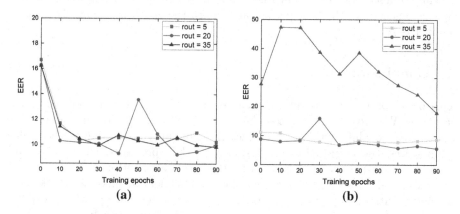

Fig. 4. EER result. (a) left is MFCC-capsule (b) right is CQCC-Capsule.

3.2   Results

Table 2 shows the performance of our proposed models on the evaluation dataset. The proposed MFCC-Capsule model shows t-DCF is 0.2001 and EER is 9.21 which are slightly smaller than baseline algorithms on evaluation set (including

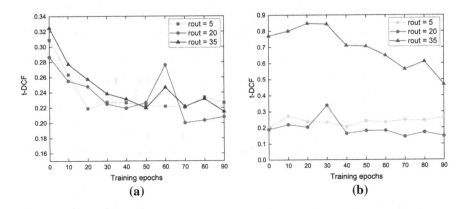

Fig. 5. t-DCF result. (a) is MFCC-capsule (b) is CQCC-Capsule.

un-known and known attacks), and our CQCC-Capsule model achieves a perfect score of zero EER and t-DCF on the development set (known attacks) and have a significantly smaller t-DCF and EER scores than the baseline algorithms on the evaluation set. CQCC-Capsule shows t-DCF is 0.1458 and EER is 5.09 which are improved t-DCF by 31% and EER by 37% respectively.

The routing number can increase or decrease the connection strength by dynamic routing [12]. In order to better analyse network performance, we try to adjust the number of the dynamic routing. EER and t-DCF with various routing numbers are present in Figs. 4 and 5. It can be seen that the proposed two models achieve the best performance when the epoch is 70 and the routing number is 20.

4   Conclusions

This paper proposes a speech spoofing identification method for logical access scenarios. We provide comparisons between the performance of our model combined with two different feature extraction algorithms. According to the evaluation scores, the proposed deep capsule network improves t-DCF by 31% and EER by 37% respectively compared with the baseline algorithm. Our future work on how to improve the generalization of our model against unknow attacks, one possible solution is to combine the dynamic routing mechanism with the RNN which used to generate synthetic speech to build a deep network.

References

1. Toda, T., et al.: The voice conversion challenge. In: Interspeech, 1632–1636 (2016)
2. Huang, W.C., Lo, C.C., Hwang, H.T., Tsao, Y., Wang, H.M.: Wavenet vocoder and its applications in voice conversion. In: The 30th ROCLING Conference on Computational Linguistics and Speech Processing (ROCLING) (2018)

3. Oord, A.V.D., et al.: A generative model for raw audio. arXiv preprint arXiv:1609.03499 (2016)
4. Wu, Z., Watts, O., King, S.: Merlin: an open source neural network speech synthesis system. In: 9th ISCA Speech Synthesis Workshop, pp. 202–207 (2016)
5. Juvela, L., et al.: Speech waveform synthesis from MFCC sequences with generative adversarial networks. In: IEEE International Conference on Acoustics, Speech and Signal Processing (ICASSP), pp. 5679–5683 (2018)
6. Kinnunen, T., et al.: t-DCF: a detection cost function for the tandem assessment of spoofing countermeasures and automatic speaker verification. arXiv preprint arXiv:1804.09618 (2018)
7. Sahidullah, M., Kinnunen, T., Hanilci, C.: A comparison of features for synthetic speech detection. In: The International Speech Communication Association (ISCA) (2015)
8. Patel, T.B., Patil, H.A.: Combining evidences from Mel cepstral, cochlear filter cepstral and instantaneous frequency features for detection of natural vs. spoofed speech. In: Sixteenth Annual Conference of the International Speech Communication Association (2015)
9. Todisco, M., Delgado, H., Evans, N: A new feature for automatic speaker verification anti-spoofing: constant Q cepstral coefficients. Odyssey: The Speaker and Language Recognition Workshop, pp. 283–290 (2016)
10. Alzantot, M., Wang, Z., Srivastava, M.S.: Deep residual neural networks for audio spoofing detection: deep residual neural networks for audio spoofing detection. In: Interspeech, pp. 1078–1082 (2019)
11. Lai, C.I., Chen, N., Villalba, J., et al.: ASSERT: anti-spoofing with squeeze-excitation and residual networks: deep residual neural networks for audio spoofing detection. In: Interspeech, pp. 1013–1017 (2019)
12. Sabour, S., Frosst, N., Hinton, G.E.: Dynamic routing between capsules: advances. In: Neural Information Processing Systems, pp. 3856–3886 (2017)
13. Tiwari, V.: MFCC and its applications in speaker recognition: Int. J. Emerg. Technol. 1, 19–22 (2010)
14. Todisco, M., Delgado, H., Evans, N.: Constant Q cepstral coefficients: a spoofing counter-measure for automatic speaker verification. Comput. Speech Lang. 45, 516–535 (2017)
15. Reynolds, D.A., Rose, R.C.: Robust text-independent speaker identification using Gaussian mixture speaker models: IEEE Trans. Speech Audio Process. 3, 72–83 (1995)
16. Reynolds, D.A., Quatieri, T.F., Dunn, R.S.: Speaker verification using adapted Gaussian mixture models. Digit. Sig. Process. 10, 19–41 (2000)
17. Jaiswal, A., AbdAlmageed, W., Wu, Y., Natarajan, P.: CapsuleGAN: generative adversarial capsule network. In: Proceedings of the European Conference on Computer Vision (ECCV) (2018)

Privacy, Risk and Trust

Cloud-Aided Scalable Revocable Identity-Based Encryption with Ciphertext Update from Lattices

Yanhua Zhang[1(✉)], Ximeng Liu[2], Yupu Hu[3], and Huiwen Jia[4]

[1] Zhengzhou University of Light Industry, Zhengzhou 450002, China
yhzhang@email.zzuli.edu.cn
[2] Fuzhou University, Fuzhou 350108, China
[3] Xidian University, Xi'an 710071, China
yphu@mail.xidian.edu.cn
[4] Guangzhou University, Guangzhou 510006, China
hwjia@gzhu.edu.cn

Abstract. Cloud-aided scalable revocable identity-based encryption with ciphertext update (CA-RIBE-CU), introduced by Wang et al. in 2017 and revocable identity-based encryption with server-aided ciphertext evolution (RIBE-CE), proposed by Sun et al. in 2020, both offer significant advantages over previous identity revocation mechanisms when considering the scenario of a secure data sharing in the cloud setting. In these two primitives, the user (i.e., receiver) can utilize the short-term decryption keys to decrypt all encrypted data (i.e., ciphertexts) sent to him or her, meanwhile, the ciphertexts stored in the cloud will update to new ones with the aided of the cloud service provider (CSP) and without any interaction with data owners, and the old ones are completely deleted, and thus, the revoked users cannot access to both the previously and subsequently shared data, i.e., to achieve both identity revocation and ciphertext update simultaneously for IBE.

In this paper, inspired by Wang et al.'s work and the current first constructions of lattice-based RIBE-CE by Zhang et al. in Inscrypt 2021, we propose the first lattice-based CA-RIBE-CU scheme. Our scheme is more efficient and secure than existing constructions of lattice-based RIBE. At the heart of our new design are two tools called "hybrid ciphertexts" and "hybrid short-term decryption keys" that enables constant ciphertexts and simplified ciphertexts update, not linear in the length of identities and without burdensome double encryption mechanism, which serves as one startlingly solution to the challenges proposed by Zhang et al., and based on the hardness of learning with errors (LWE) problem, we prove that our scheme is selectively secure in the standard model.

Keywords: Identity-based encryption · Lattices · Identity revocation · Ciphertext update · Hybrid ciphertexts

© Springer Nature Singapore Pte Ltd. 2022
C. Cao et al. (Eds.): FCS 2021, CCIS 1558, pp. 269–287, 2022.
https://doi.org/10.1007/978-981-19-0523-0_18

1   Introduction

Identity-based encryption (IBE) was a seminal notion introduced by Shamir [25] in Crypto 1984, which is an advanced form of conventional public-key cryptosystems eliminating a need for public-key infrastructure. The fundamental issue of identity revocation in IBE was firstly discussed by Boneh and Franklin [4], and a naive solution that the private key generator (PKG) periodically issues a new private key for each non-revoked user in each time period was suggested. Unfortunately, this solution is very impractical for a large-scale IBE system, as the PKG's workload grows linearly in the number of system users N.

The scalable IBE with identity revocation, or simply revocable IBE (RIBE) was set forth by Boldyreva et al. [5] in CCS 2008, in which the binary tree (BT) based revocation method [19] is adopted and the PKG's workload is only logarithmic in N. In particular, the time key update is exactly executed for all the non-revoked users over a public channel. However, when considering a practical application of RIBE, there is a serious problem that ciphertexts generated for a user, but prior to the user's revocation, remain available to the revoked user who owns the old short-term decryption keys which are enough to decrypt those ciphertexts. Thus, this problem may be undesirable for some multi-user applications, such as the scenario of a secure data sharing in the cloud setting.

To solve both the aforementioned identity revocation and ciphertexts update problems simultaneously in a practical manner, Wang et al. [30] firstly introduced cloud-aided scalable RIBE with ciphertext update (CA-RIBE-CU) in 2017 and Sun et al. [27] recently introduced RIBE with server-aided ciphertext evolution (RIBE-CE) in 2020 - two new but similar revocation methods in which the user (i.e., receiver) can utilize the short-term decryption keys to decrypt all encrypted data sent to him or her, meanwhile, ciphertexts stored in the cloud will update to new ones with the aided of the cloud service provider (CSP) and without any interaction with data owners, and the old ones are completely deleted, and thus, the revoked users cannot access to both the previously and subsequently shared data. To be more specific, a CA-RIBE-CU (or an RIBE-CE) primitive is carried out as follows: once the system is set up, the PKG issues a long-term private key to the user. A time update key is generated by the PKG and sent to CSP and all users (in the CA-RIBE-CU primitive, the CSP will re-encrypt all ciphertexts for the user at the end of each time period no matter he or she is revoked or not, thus, no time update key is involved in ciphertexts update and the time update key is only sent to users) via a public channel at each time period. The CSP does ciphertexts update on the encrypted data which may be just uploaded by a data owner or have been stored in CSP for some time to new ones, and the old ciphertexts are completely deleted. Because only a non-revoked user can obtain the valid short-term decryption keys and no revoked user can decrypt the new ciphertexts (including the former, the current and the latter ciphertexts) sent to him or her. In [27,30], apart from introducing these two new primitives, Wang et al. and Sun et al. described the pairing-based constructions of CA-RIBE-CU and RIBE-CE. It is worth mentioning that both schemes will be insecure once quantum computers become a reality [26]. Encouragingly, the first lattice-based

RIBE-CE schemes were currently introduced by Zhang et al. [32] in Inscrypt 2021. In particular, the second scheme of Zhang et al. achieves decryption key exposure resistance (DKER), a default security requirement for RIBE since it was firstly introduced by Seo and Emura [24] in PKC 2013, which is not considered by Sun et al. [27]. However, the significant shortcoming of lattice-based RIBE-CE schemes of Zhang et al. [32] is a rather low efficiency, that is, the encryptions and the ciphertexts update processing are considerably sophisticated and the bit-size of final ciphertext is linear in the length of user identity, because both the sender and the CSP utilize a double encryption mechanism which has to re-encrypt the same temporary ciphertext (i.e., an encryption of original message) for all nodes on path(id), the path from a leaf node (a user with identity id is assigned to this node) to the root node root of BT.

In this paper, inspired by the clear advantages of CA-RIBE-CU that support identity revocation and ciphertexts update simultaneously, we also bring it into the world of lattices, and design the first lattice-based CA-RIBE-CU scheme.

RELATED WORKS. The first scalable RIBE was introduced by Boldyreva et al. [5] in 2008, whose scheme is creatively designed by combining a fuzzy IBE [23] and a complete subset (CS) methodology [19]. Subsequently, an adaptively secure RIBE and an RIBE with DKER, based on pairings, were proposed by Libert and Vergnaud [14] and Seo and Emura [24], respectively. To resist quantum attacks and follow the primitive of [5], the first lattice-based RIBE without DKER, the first lattice-based RIBE with bounded (and unbounded) DKER and an adaptively secure scheme in the quantum random oracle model were constructed by Chen et al. [7], Takayasu and Watanabe [29], Katsumata et al. [10] and Takayasu [28], respectively.

The study of outsourcing RIBE (O-RIBE) was initiated by Li et al. [12] in 2015, in which a semi-trusted CSP is adopted to update each non-revoked user's time key. Subsequently, Liang et al. [13] attempted to solve these same problems introduced in this work with proxy re-encryption technique, however, exactly as it was shown in [30], the design of [13] cannot resist the re-encryption key forgery attack and collusion attack. To overcome the main decryption challenges for non-revoked users only with a limited resource, Qin et al. [21] introduced a new system model called server-aided RIBE (SA-RIBE), in their model almost all of the workloads on users are delegated to an untrusted CSP. Inspired by the former two primitives, Nguyen et al. [20] and Dong et al. [8] designed the first lattice-based SA-RIBE and lattice-based O-RIBE, respectively. Recently, the generic constructions of RIBE with CS and subset difference (SD) techniques and server-aided revocable hierarchical IBE were respectively proposed by Ma and Lin [16], Lee [11] and Liu and Sun [15].

OUR CONTRIBUTIONS AND TECHNIQUES. In this paper, we introduce the first construction of lattice-based CA-RIBE-CU. We inherit and extend the main security and efficiency advantages of Wang et al.'s model and Zhang et al.'s lattice-based RIBE-CE scheme: the ciphertexts can update to new ones with the aided of CSP and without any interaction with data owners or PKG, meanwhile, the revoked users cannot access to all the former, the current, and the latter shared data in the CSP. Furthermore, the final ciphertexts enjoys constant size and the encryptions and ciphertexts update processing are simpler, not linear in the length of identities and without a burdensome double encryption mechanism in Zhang et al. [32]. In addition, with a new treatment of the identity and time period spaces, our scheme has fewer items in the public parameters and master secret key. In particular, our scheme is provable secure under the learning with errors (LWE) hardness assumption. A detailed comparison among the lattice-based RIBE schemes [7,8,10,20,28,29,32] and ours is shown in Table 1.

Table 1. Comparison of lattice-based RIBE schemes.

Schemes	$|pp|$	$|sk_{id}|$	$|uk_t|$	$|dk_{id,t}|$	$|ct_{id,t}|$	CU	DKER	Model
[7]	$\tilde{O}(n^2)$	$\tilde{O}(n^2)$	$O(r\log\frac{N}{r})\cdot\tilde{O}(n)$	$\tilde{O}(n)$	$\tilde{O}(n)$	no	no	Standard
[20]	$\tilde{O}(n^2)$	$\tilde{O}(n^2)$	$O(r\log\frac{N}{r})\cdot\tilde{O}(n)$	$\tilde{O}(n)$	$\tilde{O}(n)$	no	Unbounded	Standard
[29]	$\tilde{O}(n^2)$	$d\cdot\tilde{O}(n^2)$	$O(r\log\frac{N}{r})\cdot\tilde{O}(n)$	$\tilde{O}(n)$	$\tilde{O}(n)$	no	Bounded	Standard
[8]	$\tilde{O}(n^2)$	$\tilde{O}(n^3)$	$O(r\log\frac{N}{r})\cdot\tilde{O}(n^2)$	$\tilde{O}(n^2)$	$\tilde{O}(n)$	no	no	Standard
[10]	$\tilde{O}(n^2)$	$\tilde{O}(n^2)$	$O(r\log\frac{N}{r})\cdot\tilde{O}(n)$	$\tilde{O}(n)$	$\tilde{O}(n)$	no	Unbounded	Standard
[28]	$\tilde{O}(n^2)$	$d\cdot\tilde{O}(n^2)$	$O(r\log\frac{N}{r})\cdot\tilde{O}(n)$	$\tilde{O}(n)$	$\tilde{O}(n)$	no	Bounded	Quantum ROM
[32]	$\tilde{O}(n^2)$	$\tilde{O}(n^2)$	$O(r\log\frac{N}{r})\cdot\tilde{O}(n)$	$\tilde{O}(n)$	$\tilde{O}(n^2)$	yes	Unbounded	Standard
Ours	$\tilde{O}(n^2)$	$\tilde{O}(n^2)$	$O(r\log\frac{N}{r})\cdot\tilde{O}(n)$	$\tilde{O}(n)$	$\tilde{O}(n)$	yes	Unbounded	Standard

Note: n is a security parameter, $N = 2^n$ is the maximum numbers of system users, r is the number of revoked users, d is the number of private keys stored in each node over path(id); $|\cdot|$ denotes the bit-size, pp is public parameters, sk_{id} is long-term private key, uk_t is time update key, $dk_{id,t}$ is short-term decryption key, and $ct_{id,t}$ is ciphertext; CU denotes ciphertext update and ROM denotes random oracle model.

As a high level, the design method of our lattice-based CA-RIBE-CU scheme is similar to the pairing-based instantiation of Wang et al. in the sense that we also utilize a lattice-based RIBE scheme [7] and a lattice-based two-level hierarchical IBE (HIBE) scheme [1] as the basic building blocks. However, looking into the details of our lattice-based CA-RIBE-CU, it is not so straightforward to make these two basic building blocks operate together. Wang et al. [30] addressed this problem by using a key re-randomization technique (i.e., both parts of a short-term decryption key are completely re-randomized) which currently seems not available in the lattice setting. To solve this problem, Zhang et al. [32] adopted a single HIBE trapdoor and a double encryption mechanism firstly employed in SA-RIBE by Nguyen et al. [20], which involves the sophisticated encryptions and ciphertexts update processing and suffers from a large ciphertext. Instead, we adopt two new tools called "hybrid ciphertexts" and "hybrid short-term decryption keys", recently introduced by Katsumata et al. [10] in the context of lattice-based RIBE with DKER, which work as follows: the system users are firstly issued by the PKG a hybrid long-term private key including a series of short vectors and a short HIBE trapdoor matrix, $sk_{id} = ((e_{id,\theta})_{\theta\in path(id)}, \mathbf{R}_{\mathbf{A}_{id}})$, which could be partially re-randomized (i.e., $\mathbf{R}_{\mathbf{A}_{id}}$ is used to sample a short vector $e_{id,t}$, the second part of the short-term decryption key $dk_{id,t} = (e_{\theta\in(path(id)\cap KUNodes(BT,RL,t))}, e_{id,t})$, for each time period independently from the previous time periods). The sender encrypts the message $m \in \{0,1\}$ under the HIBE and RIBE to obtain the hybrid ciphertexts of the form $ct_{id,t=t_0} = (id, t_0, c_0, c_{00}, c_{01})$, where c_0 is an element of

$\mathbb{Z}_q$ (for a prime modulus $q > 2$) and is the ciphertext component carrying m. The hybrid ciphertexts $ct_{id,t}$ is sent to CSP where the later can update it to a new one $ct_{id,t'=t_k} = (id, t_0, t_k, c_k, \mathbf{c}_{00}, \mathbf{c}_{01}, \mathbf{c}_{k0}, \mathbf{c}_{k1})$. Once receiving $ct_{id,t'}$ from the CSP, the non-revoked user should be able to recover the massage m $\in \{0,1\}$.

In addition, in the constructions of our scheme, we adopt a new treatment of the identity space $\mathcal{I}$ and the time period space $\mathcal{T}$, recently introduced by Wang et al. [31] in the context of simplified lattice-based RHIBE, which work as follows: both the identity space $\mathcal{I}$ and time period space $\mathcal{T}$ are treated as a subset of $\mathbb{Z}_q^n \backslash \{\mathbf{0}_n\}$, and by introducing a new space $\widetilde{\mathcal{I}}$ satisfying $\mathcal{I} \cap \widetilde{\mathcal{I}} = \emptyset$ and $|\mathcal{I}| = |\widetilde{\mathcal{I}}|$, there is a one-to-one correspondence between a real identity id $\in \mathcal{I}$ and a virtual identity $\widetilde{id} \in \widetilde{\mathcal{I}}$ (the detailed description is shown in Sect. 3). This strategy startlingly allows us to remove some items in the public parameters of Zhang et al. [32], and there is only one short trapdoor matrix in the master secret key.

ORGANIZATION. The organization of the paper is as follows. In Sect. 2, we review the definition of CA-RIBE-CU and some background knowledge on lattices. A lattice-based CA-RIBE-CU scheme in the standard model is described and analyzed in Sect. 3. In the final Sect. 4, we conclude our whole paper.

2 Definition and Security Model

Table 2 refers to the notations used in this paper.

Table 2. Notations of this paper.

Notation	Definition
$\xleftarrow{\$}$	Sampling uniformly at random
$\| \cdot \|, \| \cdot \|_\infty$	Euclidean norm ℓ_2, infinity norm ℓ_∞
mod q	$(-(q-1)/2, (q-1)/2]$
$\mathcal{O}, \widetilde{\mathcal{O}}, \omega$	Standard asymptotic notations
$\log e$	Logarithm of e with base 2
ppt	Probabilistic polynomial-time

2.1 Cloud-Aided Scalable Revocable Identity-Based Encryption with Ciphertext Update

We review the definition and security model of CA-RIBE-CU firstly introduced by Wang et al. [30]. A CA-RIBE-CU is an extension of RIBE that supports identity revocation, and additionally, it delegates the ciphertexts update to a semi-trusted CSP which is normally assumed not to collude with other entities and should perform correct operations and return correct results. A trusted center firstly issues a master secret key (msk) and a public parameters (pp). The PKG issues a long-term private key sk_{id} for each user with an identity id and a time update key uk_t with a time period t by using msk, meanwhile, uk_t is sent to all users (this is different from the RIBE-CE primitive of Sun et al. [27] and Zhang et al. [32], where uk_t is involved in ciphertexts update) and the PKG maintains a revocation list (RL) to record the state information on revoked users. The CSP periodically transforms a ciphertext (it may be just uploaded by a data owner or has been stored in the CSP for some time) for id with t into a new one for $t' > t$ no matter id is revoked or not. To decrypt a ciphertext which specifies an identity id and a time t (if it is a re-encrypted ciphertext, an original encryption time t_0 is also given), the non-revoked receiver id combines the long-term private key sk_{id} and the update key uk_t (and uk_{t_0}) to derive a short-term decryption key $dk_{id,t}$ (and dk_{id,t_0}). The system model of CA-RIBE-CU is shown in Fig. 1.

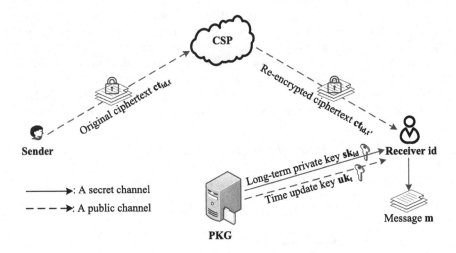

Fig. 1. System model of CA-RIBE-CU.

Definition 1. *A CA-RIBE-CU scheme involves four distinct entities:* PKG, CSP, *and users (sender and receiver), associated with an identity space* $\mathcal{I}$, *a time space* $\mathcal{T}$, *a message space* $\mathcal{M}$, *and consists of eight polynomial-time (*pt*) algorithms which are described as follows:*

- Setup(1^n, N): *This is the setup algorithm run by the* PKG. *On input a system security parameter n and the maximal number of users N, it outputs a master secret key* msk, *the public parameters* pp, *a user revocation list* RL *(initially empty), and a state* st. *Note:* msk *is kept in secret by the* PKG, *and* pp *is made public and as an implicit input of all other algorithms.*
- PriKeyGen(msk, id, st): *This is the key generation algorithm run by the* PKG. *On input an identity* id, *the master secret key* msk, *and a state* st, *it outputs a long-term private key* sk_{id} *and an updated state* st. *Note:* sk_{id} *is sent to the receiver via a secret channel.*
- KeyUpd(RL, t, msk, st): *This is the key update algorithm run by the* PKG. *On input the current revocation list* RL, *the time period* t, *the master secret key* msk, *and a state* st, *it outputs a time update key* uk_t. *Note:* uk_t *is sent to all users (no need to send it to* CSP*) via a public channel.*

- DecKeyGen($\mathsf{sk_{id}}, \mathsf{uk_t}, t$): *This is the decryption key generation algorithm run by the receiver* id. *On input a long-term private key* $\mathsf{sk_{id}}$, *a corresponding time update key* $\mathsf{uk_t}$ *(or $\perp$), and the current time* t, *it outputs a short-term decryption key* $\mathsf{dk_{id,t}}$ *(or $\perp$ indicating that* id *has been revoked). Note: to decrypt a re-encrypted ciphertext, an original encryption time* t_0 *and the time update key* $\mathsf{uk_{t_0}}$ *is also needed to compute the short-term decryption key* $\mathsf{dk_{id,t_0}}$.
- Encrypt(id, t, m): *This is the encryption algorithm run by the sender. On input a receiver's identity* id, *the encryption time period* t, *and a message* m. *It outputs a ciphertext* $\mathsf{ct_{id,t}}$.
- Update($\mathsf{ct_{id,t}}, t'$): *This is the ciphertext update algorithm run by the CSP. On input a ciphertext* $\mathsf{ct_{id,t}}$ *(no matter it is an original ciphertext or a re-encrypted ciphertext) with identity* id *and time* t, *and a new time period* $t' > t$, *it outputs a re-encrypted ciphertext* $\mathsf{ct_{id,t'}}$.
- Decrypt($\mathsf{dk_{id',t'}}, \mathsf{ct_{id,t}}$): *This is the decryption algorithm run by the receiver. On input a ciphertext* $\mathsf{ct_{id,t}}$ *and a decryption key* $\mathsf{dk_{id',t'}}$ *(the short-term decryption key* $\mathsf{dk_{id',t_0}}$ *is needed to decrypt a re-encrypted ciphertext). It outputs a message* $m \in \mathcal{M}$, *or a symbol $\perp$.*
- Revoke($\mathsf{id}, t, \mathsf{RL}, \mathsf{st}$): *This is the revocation algorithm run by the PKG. On input the current revocation list* RL, *an identity* id, *a revoked time* t, *and a state* st, *it outputs an updated* $\mathsf{RL} = \mathsf{RL} \cup \{(\mathsf{id}, t)\}$.

The correctness of a CA-RIBE-CU scheme is described as follows: for all pp, msk, RL, and st generated by Setup($1^n, N$), $\mathsf{sk_{id}}$ generated by PriKeyGen(msk, id, st) for $\mathsf{id} \in \mathcal{I}$, $\mathsf{uk_t}$ generated by KeyUpd(RL, t, msk, st) for $t \in \mathcal{T}$ and RL, $\mathsf{ct_{id,t}}$ generated by Encrypt(id, t, m) for $\mathsf{id} \in \mathcal{I}$, $t \in \mathcal{T}$ and $m \in \mathcal{M}$, and $\mathsf{ct_{id,t''}}$ generated by Update($\mathsf{ct_{id,t}}, t''$) for $t'' > t$, then it is required that:

- If $(\mathsf{id}, t) \notin \mathsf{RL}$ for all $t \leq t'$, then DecKeyGen($\mathsf{sk_{id}}, \mathsf{uk_t}, t$) = $\mathsf{dk_{id,t}}$.
- If $(\mathsf{id} = \mathsf{id}') \wedge (t = t')$, then Decrypt($\mathsf{dk_{id',t'}}, \mathsf{ct_{id,t}}$) = m (for original ciphertext).
- If $(\mathsf{id} = \mathsf{id}') \wedge (t'' = t' > t)$, then Decrypt($\mathsf{dk_{id',t'}}, \mathsf{dk_{id',t}}, \mathsf{ct_{id,t''}}$) = m (for re-encrypted ciphertext).

A CA-RIBE-CU scheme is an extension of RIBE, thus, the indistinguishability under the chosen-plaintext attack (ind-cpa) security of RIBE must be satisfied to guarantee the message hiding security against an attacker $\mathcal{A}$ who may own a long-term private key (e.g., a revoked user). Wang et al. [30] defined semantic security against adaptive-revocable-identity-time and chosen-plaintext attacks for CA-RIBE-CU. Here, we consider selective-revocable-identity-time security (a weaker notion initially was suggested in RIBE by Boldyreva et al. [5], subsequently by Chen et al. [7], Nguyen et al. [20], Katsumata et al. [10] and Zhang et al. [32], in which $\mathcal{A}$ sends a challenge identity and time pair (id^*, t^*) (for an original challenge ciphertext, t^* is a single time period, and for a re-encrypted challenge ciphertext, $t^* = (t_0^*, t_k^*)$ is a time period vector) to the challenger $\mathcal{C}$ before the execution of Setup($1^n, N$).

In our ind-cpa security model of CA-RIBE-CU, an attacker $\mathcal{A}$ can request the long-term private key, time update key, revocation, short-term decryption key, ciphertext update queries. One of the most restrictions is that if $\mathcal{A}$ has requested the long-term private key for a challenge identity id^*, then id^* must be revoked before (or at) the time update key query of challenge time t^*. Finally, $\mathcal{A}$'s goal is to determine that the challenge ciphertxet is completely random, or correctly encrypted on a challenge message m^* corresponding to $(\mathrm{id}^*, \mathrm{t}^*)$. The detailed definition is described as follows:

Definition 2. *The* ind-cpa *security of* CA-RIBE-CU *is described as the following game between* $\mathcal{C}$ *and* $\mathcal{A}$:

- Intial: *The adversary* $\mathcal{A}$ *declares a challenge identity and time pair* $(\mathrm{id}^*, \mathrm{t}^*)$.
- Setup: *The challenger* $\mathcal{C}$ *runs* Setup$(1^n, N)$ *to obtain* $(\mathsf{msk}, \mathsf{pp}, \mathsf{RL}, \mathsf{st})$. *Note:* RL *is initially empty,* $\mathcal{C}$ *keeps* msk *in secret by himself and provides* pp *to* $\mathcal{A}$.
- Query phase 1: *The query-answer between* $\mathcal{A}$ *and* $\mathcal{C}$ *is described in Table 3:*

Table 3. The Query-Answer between $\mathcal{A}$ and $\mathcal{C}$.

	PriKenGen($\cdot$)	KeyUpd($\cdot$)	Revoke($\cdot$)	DecKeyGen($\cdot$)	Update
$\mathcal{A}$	id	RL, t	RL, id, t	id, t	$\mathsf{ct}_{\mathrm{id},\mathrm{t}}, \mathrm{t}'$
$\mathcal{C}$	$\mathsf{sk}_{\mathrm{id}}$	uk_{t}	RL = RL $\cup \{(\mathrm{id},\mathrm{t})\}$	$\mathsf{dk}_{\mathrm{id},\mathrm{t}}$	$\mathsf{ct}_{\mathrm{id},\mathrm{t}'}$

Note: PriKenGen($\cdot$), KeyUpd($\cdot$), Revoke($\cdot$), DecKeyGen($\cdot$) and Update share st and the queries should be with some restrictions defined later.

- Challenge: $\mathcal{A}$ *submits a challenge* $\mathsf{m}^* \in \mathcal{M}$. $\mathcal{C}$ *firstly samples a bit* $b \xleftarrow{\$} \{0,1\}$. *If* $b = 0$, $\mathcal{C}$ *returns a challenge ciphertext* $\mathsf{ct}^*_{\mathrm{id}^*,\mathrm{t}^*}$ *by running* Encrypt$(\mathrm{id}^*, \mathrm{t}^*, \mathsf{m}^*)$ *or* Update(Encrypt$(\mathrm{id}^*, \mathrm{t}^*_0, \mathsf{m}^*), \mathrm{t}^*_k)$, *otherwise, a random* $\mathsf{ct}^*_{\mathrm{id}^*,\mathrm{t}^*} \xleftarrow{\$} \mathcal{U}$.
- Query phase 2: $\mathcal{A}$ *continues to make additional queries as before with the same restrictions.*
- Guess: $\mathcal{A}$ *outputs a bit* $b^* \in \{0,1\}$, *and wins if* $b^* = b$.

  In the above game, the following restrictions should be satisfied:
  - KeyUpd($\cdot$) *and* Revoke($\cdot$) *must be queried in a non-decreasing order of time.*
  - Revoke($\cdot$) *cannot be queried at* t *if* KeyUpd($\cdot$) *has been queried at* t.
  - Revoke($\cdot$) *must be queried on* $(\mathrm{id}^*, \mathrm{t})$ *for* $\mathrm{t} \leq \mathrm{t}^*$ *(or* $\mathrm{t} \leq \mathrm{t}^*_0$*) if* PriKenGen($\cdot$) *has been queried on* id^*.
  - DecKeyGen($\cdot$) *cannot be queried at* t *if* KeyUpd($\cdot$) *was not queried at* t.
  - DecKeyGen($\cdot$) *cannot be queried on* $(\mathrm{id}^*, \mathrm{t}^*)$ *(or* $(\mathrm{id}^*, \mathrm{t}^*_0)$*), and in* Update *query,* $\mathrm{t} < \mathrm{t}'$.

The advantage of $\mathcal{A}$ is defined as $\mathsf{Adv}^{\text{ind-cpa}}_{\text{CA-RIBE-CU},\mathcal{A}}(n) = |\Pr[b^* = b] - 1/2|$, and a CA-RIBE-CU scheme is ind-cpa secure if $\mathsf{Adv}^{\text{ind-cpa}}_{\text{CA-RIBE-CU},\mathcal{A}}(n)$ is negligible in the security parameter n.

2.2   Lattices

In this subsection, we recall the knowledge on integer lattices.

Definition 3. *Given* n, m, $q \geq 2$, *a random* $\mathbf{A} \in \mathbb{Z}_q^{n \times m}$, *and* $\mathbf{u} \in \mathbb{Z}_q^n$, *the* m-*dimensional* q-*ary orthogonal lattice* $\Lambda_q^{\perp}(\mathbf{A})$ *is defined as:* $\Lambda_q^{\perp}(\mathbf{A}) = \{\mathbf{e} \in \mathbb{Z}^m \mid \mathbf{A}\mathbf{e} = \mathbf{0} \bmod q\}$.

The discrete Gaussian over Λ with center $\mathbf{c} \in \mathbb{Z}^m$ and a parameter $s > 0$ is denoted as $\mathcal{D}_{\Lambda,s,\mathbf{c}}$, and we omit the subscript and denote it as $\mathcal{D}_{\Lambda,s}$ if $\mathbf{c} = \mathbf{0}$.

Lemma 1 ([9]). *For* $q \geq 2$, $m \geq 2n\lceil \log q \rceil$, *assume that the columns of* $\mathbf{A} \in \mathbb{Z}_q^{n \times m}$ *generate* $\mathbb{Z}_q^n$, *let* $\epsilon \in (0, 1/2)$, $s \geq \eta_\epsilon(\Lambda^{\perp}(\mathbf{A}))$, *then the followings hold:*

1. *For* $\mathbf{e} \xleftarrow{\$} \mathcal{D}_{\mathbb{Z}^m,s}$, *the statistical distance between* $\mathbf{u} = \mathbf{A}\mathbf{e} \bmod q$ *and* $\mathbf{u}' \xleftarrow{\$} \mathbb{Z}_q^n$ *is at most* 2ϵ.

2. *For* $\mathbf{e} \xleftarrow{\$} \mathcal{D}_{\mathbb{Z}^m,s}$, *then* $\Pr[\|\mathbf{e}\|_\infty \leq \lceil s \cdot \log m \rceil]$ *holds with a larger probability.*

A ppt trapdoor generation algorithm returning a statistically close to uniform $\mathbf{A} \in \mathbb{Z}_q^{n \times m}$ together with a low Gram-Schmidt norm basis for $\Lambda_q^{\perp}(\mathbf{A})$ plays a key role in lattice-based cryptography.

Lemma 2 ([2,3,18]). *Let* $n \geq 1$, $q \geq 2$, $m = 2n\lceil \log q \rceil$, *there is a* ppt *algorithm* TrapGen(q, n, m) *that returns* $\mathbf{A} \in \mathbb{Z}_q^{n \times m}$ *statistically close to an uniform matrix in* $\mathbb{Z}_q^{n \times m}$ *and a trapdoor* $\mathbf{R_A}$ *for* $\Lambda_q^{\perp}(\mathbf{A})$.

Gentry et al. [9] showed an algorithm to sample shorter vectors (or matrices) from a discrete Gaussian distribution, and an improvement was given in [18]. Meanwhile, to delegate a trapdoor for a super-lattice was given in [6].

Lemma 3 ([9,18]). *Let* $n \geq 1$, $q \geq 2$, $m = 2n\lceil \log q \rceil$, *given* $\mathbf{A} \in \mathbb{Z}_q^{n \times m}$, *a trapdoor* $\mathbf{R_A}$ *for* $\Lambda_q^{\perp}(\mathbf{A})$, *a parameter* $s = \omega(\sqrt{n \log q \log n})$, *and a vector* $\mathbf{u} \in \mathbb{Z}_q^n$, *there is a* ppt *algorithm* SamplePre$(\mathbf{A}, \mathbf{R_A}, \mathbf{u}, s)$ *returning a shorter vector* $\mathbf{e} \in \Lambda_q^{\mathbf{u}}(\mathbf{A})$ *sampled from a distribution statistically close to* $\mathcal{D}_{\Lambda_q^{\mathbf{u}}(\mathbf{A}),s}$.

Lemma 4 ([6]). *Let* $q \geq 2$, $m = 2n\lceil \log q \rceil$, *given* $\mathbf{A} \in \mathbb{Z}_q^{n \times m}$ *who can generate* $\mathbb{Z}_q^n$, *a basis* $\mathbf{R_A} \in \mathbb{Z}^{m \times m}$ *for* $\Lambda_q^{\perp}(\mathbf{A})$, *a random* $\mathbf{A}' \in \mathbb{Z}_q^{n \times m'}$, *there is a deterministic algorithm* ExtBasis$(\mathbf{R_A}, \mathbf{A}^* = \mathbf{A}|\mathbf{A}')$ *returning a basis* $\mathbf{R}_{\mathbf{A}^*} \in \mathbb{Z}^{(m+m') \times (m+m')}$ *for* $\Lambda_q^{\perp}(\mathbf{A}^*)$, *especially,* $\mathbf{R_A}$, $\mathbf{R}_{\mathbf{A}^*}$ *are with equal Gram-Schmidt norm. Note: the result holds for any given permutation of all columns of* $\mathbf{A}^*$.

Lemma 5 ([6]). *Let* $n \geq 1$, $q \geq 2$, $m = 2n\lceil \log q \rceil$, $s \geq \|\widetilde{\mathbf{R_A}}\| \cdot \omega(\sqrt{\log n})$, $\mathbf{R_A} \in \mathbb{Z}^{m \times m}$ *is a basis for* $\Lambda_q^{\perp}(\mathbf{A})$, *there is a* ppt *algorithm* RandBasis$(\mathbf{R_A}, s)$ *returning a new basis* $\mathbf{R}_{\mathbf{A}}' \in \mathbb{Z}^{m \times m}$ *and* $\|\mathbf{R}_{\mathbf{A}}'\| \leq s \cdot \sqrt{m}$. *In particular, for two basis matrices* $\mathbf{R}_{\mathbf{A}}^{(1)}$ *and* $\mathbf{R}_{\mathbf{A}}^{(2)}$ *for* $\Lambda_q^{\perp}(\mathbf{A})$, *and* $s \geq max\{\|\widetilde{\mathbf{R}_{\mathbf{A}}^{(1)}}\|, \|\widetilde{\mathbf{R}_{\mathbf{A}}^{(2)}}\|\} \cdot \omega(\sqrt{\log n})$, RandBasis$(\mathbf{R}_{\mathbf{A}}^{(1)}, s)$ *is statistically close to* RandBasis$(\mathbf{R}_{\mathbf{A}}^{(2)}, s)$.

Lemma 6 ([1]). *Let* $q > 2$, $m > n$, $\mathbf{A} \in \mathbb{Z}_q^{n \times m}$, $\mathbf{A}' \in \mathbb{Z}_q^{n \times m'}$, *and* $s > \|\widetilde{\mathbf{R_A}}\| \cdot \omega(\sqrt{\log(m + m')})$, *given a trapdoor* $\mathbf{R_A}$ *for* $\Lambda_q^\perp(\mathbf{A})$ *and* $\mathbf{u} \in \mathbb{Z}_q^n$, *there is a* ppt *algorithm* SampleLeft$(\mathbf{A}|\mathbf{A}', \mathbf{R_A}, \mathbf{u}, s)$ *returning a shorter* $\mathbf{e} \in \mathbb{Z}^{2m}$ *sampled from a distribution statistically close to* $\mathcal{D}_{\Lambda_q^{\mathbf{u}}(\mathbf{A}|\mathbf{A}'),s}$.

Lemma 7 ([1]). *Let* $q > 2$, $m > n$, $\mathbf{A}$, $\mathbf{B} \in \mathbb{Z}_q^{n \times m}$, $s > \|\widetilde{\mathbf{R_B}}\| \cdot \mathcal{O}(\sqrt{m}) \cdot \omega(\sqrt{\log m})$, *given a trapdoor* $\mathbf{R_B}$, *a low-norm* $\mathbf{R} \in \{-1, 1\}^{m \times m}$, *and* $\mathbf{u} \in \mathbb{Z}_q^n$, *there is a* ppt *algorithm* SampleRight$(\mathbf{A}, \mathbf{B}, \mathbf{R}, \mathbf{R_B}, \mathbf{u}, s)$ *returning a shorter* $\mathbf{e} \in \mathbb{Z}^{2m}$ *distributed statistically close to* $\mathcal{D}_{\Lambda_q^{\mathbf{u}}(\mathbf{F}),s}$, *where* $\mathbf{F} = [\mathbf{A}|\mathbf{AR} + \mathbf{B}]$.

The learning with errors (LWE) problem was firstly introduced by Regev [22].

Definition 4. *The* LWE *problem is defined as follows: given a random* $\mathbf{s} \xleftarrow{\$} \mathbb{Z}_q^n$, *a distribution* χ *over* $\mathbb{Z}$, *let* $\mathcal{A}_{\mathbf{s},\chi}$ *be the distribution* $(\mathbf{A}, \mathbf{A}^\top \mathbf{s} + \mathbf{e})$ *where* $\mathbf{A} \xleftarrow{\$} \mathbb{Z}_q^{n \times m}$, $\mathbf{e} \xleftarrow{\$} \chi^m$, *and to make distinguish between* $\mathcal{A}_{\mathbf{s},\chi}$ *and* $\mathcal{U} \xleftarrow{\$} \mathbb{Z}_q^{n \times m} \times \mathbb{Z}_q^m$. *Let* $\beta \geq \sqrt{n} \cdot \omega(\log n)$, *for a prime power* q, *given a* β-*bounded* χ, *the* LWE *problem is as least as hard as the shortest independent vectors problem* SIVP$_{\widetilde{\mathcal{O}}(nq/\beta)}$.

An injective encoding function $\mathcal{H} : \mathbb{Z}_q^n \to \mathbb{Z}_q^{n \times n}$ is adopted for our CA-RIBE-CU schemes. An explicit design called encoding with full-rank differences (FRD) was proposed by Agrawal et al. [1].

Definition 5. *Let* $n > 1$, *prime* $q \geq 2$, *an injective encoding function* $\mathcal{H} : \mathbb{Z}_q^n \to \mathbb{Z}_q^{n \times n}$ *is called* FRD *if:*

1. *For* $\forall \mathbf{e}_1, \mathbf{e}_2 \in \mathbb{Z}_q^n$, $\mathbf{e}_1 \neq \mathbf{e}_2$, $\mathcal{H}(\mathbf{e}_1) - \mathcal{H}(\mathbf{e}_2) \in \mathbb{Z}_q^{n \times n}$ *is full-rank.*
2. $\mathcal{H}$ *can be computed in a polynomial time, i.e.,* $\mathcal{O}(n \log q)$.

Two following facts will be used in the security proofs of this work.

Lemma 8 ([1]). *Let* $n \geq 1$, *prime* $q > 2$, $m > (n+1) \log q + \omega(\log n)$, $\mathbf{A}, \mathbf{B} \xleftarrow{\$} \mathbb{Z}_q^{n \times m}$, *and* $\mathbf{R} \xleftarrow{\$} \{-1, 1\}^{m \times m}$ mod q. *Then, for all* $\mathbf{w} \in \mathbb{Z}_q^m$, $(\mathbf{A}, \mathbf{AR}, \mathbf{R}^\top \mathbf{w})$ *is statistically close to* $(\mathbf{A}, \mathbf{B}, \mathbf{R}^\top \mathbf{w})$.

3   Our Lattice-Based CA-RIBE-CU Scheme

Our lattice-based CA-RIBE-CU is a combination of a two-level lattice-based HIBE and an RIBE [7] from which the PKG issues a long-term private key to each user id. This private key consists of an HIBE trapdoor and a series of short vectors, not a single trapdoor matrix as in Zhang et al. [32]. In addition, we also adopt a classical BT revocation mechanism [19] to alleviate the workload of the PKG.

As a preparation, we need to explain our treatment of the identity space $\mathcal{I} \subseteq \mathbb{Z}_q^n \backslash \{\mathbf{0}_n\}$ and time space $\mathcal{T} \subseteq \mathbb{Z}_q^n \backslash \{\mathbf{0}_n\}$, which was recently introduced by Wang et al. [31] in the context of simplified lattice-based RHIBE. Because an identity id $= (1, id_1, \cdots, id_n) \in \mathcal{I}$, we define $\mathcal{I} = \{1\} \times \mathbb{Z}_q^{n-1}$. In addition, we define a new space $\widetilde{\mathcal{I}} = \{-1\} \times \mathbb{Z}_q^{n-1}$ which satisfies $\mathcal{I} \cap \widetilde{\mathcal{I}} = \emptyset$ and $|\mathcal{I}| = |\widetilde{\mathcal{I}}| = q^{n-1}$. Thus, there is a one-to-one correspondence between a real identity $\mathsf{id} \in \mathcal{I}$ and a virtual identity $\widetilde{\mathsf{id}} \in \widetilde{\mathcal{I}}$. The time period space is treated as discrete, i.e., $\mathcal{T} = \{0, 1, \cdots, \mathsf{t_{max}} - 1\}$, and is encoded into the set $\{2\} \times \mathbb{Z}_q^{n-1}$.

3.1   Description of the Scheme

As in Wang et al., our lattice-based CA-RIBE-CU scheme also consists of eight pt algorithms: Setup, PriKeyGen, KeyUpd, DecKeyGen, Encrypt, Update, Decrypt and Revoke. The main algorithms are described as follows:

- Setup(1^n, N): On input a security parameter n and the maximal number of users $N = 2^n$, set prime modulus $q = \widetilde{\mathcal{O}}(n^3)$, dimension $m = 2nk$ where $k = \lceil \log q \rceil$, Gaussian parameter $s = \widetilde{\mathcal{O}}(m)$ and norm bound $\beta = \widetilde{\mathcal{O}}(\sqrt{n})$ for a distribution χ. The PKG specifies the following steps:
  1. Let the identity space $\mathcal{I} = \{1\} \times \mathbb{Z}_q^{n-1}$, time space $\mathcal{T} = \{2\} \times \mathbb{Z}_q^{n-1}$, and message space $\mathcal{M} = \{0, 1\}$.
  2. Run TrapGen(q, n, m) to get $\mathbf{A} \in \mathbb{Z}_q^{n \times m}$ with a trapdoor $\mathbf{R_A}$.
  3. Set an FRD function $\mathcal{H} : \mathbb{Z}_q^n \to \mathbb{Z}_q^{n \times n}$ as described in Definition 5.
  4. Sample $\mathbf{A_0}, \mathbf{A_1}, \mathbf{B} \xleftarrow{\$} \mathbb{Z}_q^{n \times m}$, and $\mathbf{u} \xleftarrow{\$} \mathbb{Z}_q^n$.
  5. Set the sate $\mathsf{st} = \mathsf{BT}$ that BT is with at least N leaf nodes, and the initial revocation list $\mathsf{RL} = \emptyset$.
  6. Set $\mathsf{pp} = (\mathbf{A}, \mathbf{A_0}, \mathbf{A_1}, \mathbf{B}, \mathbf{u}, \mathcal{H})$, and the master secret key $\mathsf{msk} = \mathbf{R_A}$.
  7. Output ($\mathsf{pp}, \mathsf{msk}, \mathsf{RL}, \mathsf{st}$), where msk is kept in secret by the PKG, and pp is made public and as an implicit input of all other algorithms.
- PriKeyGen($\mathsf{msk}, \mathsf{id}, \mathsf{st}$): On input an identity $\mathsf{id} \in \mathcal{I}$, the master secret key msk and the state st. The PKG specifies the following steps:
  1. Set id to an unassigned leaf node of BT, and for each $\theta \in \mathsf{path(id)}$, if $\mathbf{u}_{1,\theta}$, $\mathbf{u}_{2,\theta}$ are undefined, then sample $\mathbf{u}_{1,\theta} \xleftarrow{\$} \mathbb{Z}_q^n$, set $\mathbf{u}_{2,\theta} = \mathbf{u} - \mathbf{u}_{1,\theta}$, and store ($\mathbf{u}_{1,\theta}, \mathbf{u}_{2,\theta}$) in node θ.
  2. Define $\mathbf{A_{id}} = [\mathbf{A}|\mathbf{A_0} + \mathcal{H}(\mathsf{id})\mathbf{B}]$, and $\mathbf{A_{\widetilde{id}}} = [\mathbf{A}|\mathbf{A_0} + \mathcal{H}(\widetilde{\mathsf{id}})\mathbf{B}] \in \mathbb{Z}_q^{n \times 2m}$.
  3. Run SampleLeft($\mathbf{A_{id}}, \mathbf{R_A}, \mathbf{u}_{1,\theta}, s$) to generate $\mathbf{e}_{\mathsf{id},\theta} \in \mathbb{Z}^{2m}$ satisfying $\mathbf{A_{id}}\mathbf{e}_{\mathsf{id},\theta} = \mathbf{u}_{1,\theta} \bmod q$.
  4. Run RandBasis(ExtBasis($\mathbf{R_A}, \mathbf{A_{\widetilde{id}}}$), s) to generate a trapdoor $\mathbf{R_{A_{\widetilde{id}}}}$ for $\Lambda_q^{\perp}(\mathbf{A_{\widetilde{id}}})$.
  5. Output an updated st, and $\mathsf{sk_{id}} = ((\theta, \mathbf{e}_{\mathsf{id},\theta})_{\theta \in \mathsf{path(id)}}, \mathbf{R_{A_{\widetilde{id}}}})$. *Note:* $\mathsf{sk_{id}}$ is sent via a secret channel.
- KeyUpd($\mathsf{RL}, \mathsf{t}, \mathsf{msk}, \mathsf{st}$): On input a time $\mathsf{t} \in \mathcal{T}$, the master secret key msk, a revocation list RL and the state st. The PKG specifies the following steps:
  1. Define $\mathbf{A_t} = [\mathbf{A}|\mathbf{A_1} + \mathcal{H}(\mathsf{t})\mathbf{B}] \in \mathbb{Z}_q^{n \times 2m}$, and for each $\theta \in \mathsf{KUNodes(BT, RL, t)}$, retrieve $\mathbf{u}_{2,\theta}$.
  2. Run SampleLeft($\mathbf{A_t}, \mathbf{R_A}, \mathbf{u}_{2,\theta}, s$) to generate $\mathbf{e}_{\mathsf{t},\theta} \in \mathbb{Z}^{2m}$ satisfying $\mathbf{A_t}\mathbf{e}_{\mathsf{t},\theta} = \mathbf{u}_{2,\theta} = \mathbf{u} - \mathbf{u}_{1,\theta} \bmod q$.
  3. Output $\mathsf{uk_t} = (\theta, \mathbf{e}_{\mathsf{t},\theta})_{\theta \in \mathsf{KUNodes(BT, RL, t)}}$.

- DecKeyGen($\mathsf{sk_{id}}$, $\mathsf{uk_t}$, t): On input a private key $\mathsf{sk_{id}} = ((\theta, \mathbf{e}_{\mathsf{id},\theta})_{\theta \in \mathsf{path}(\mathsf{id})}, \mathbf{R}_{\mathbf{A}_{\widetilde{\mathsf{id}}}})$, a time t and the current update key $\mathsf{uk_t} = (\theta, \mathbf{e}_{t,\theta})_{\theta \in \mathsf{KUNodes}(\mathsf{BT},\mathsf{RL},t)}$. The receiver id specifies the following steps:

  1. If $\mathsf{path}(\mathsf{id}) \cap \mathsf{KUNodes}(\mathsf{BT}, \mathsf{RL}, t) = \emptyset$, return $\perp$ and abort.
  2. Otherwise, define $\mathbf{A}_{\widetilde{\mathsf{id}},t} = [\mathbf{A}_{\widetilde{\mathsf{id}}} | \mathbf{A}_1 + \mathcal{H}(t)\mathbf{B}] \in \mathbb{Z}_q^{n \times 3m}$.
  3. Run $\mathsf{SampleLeft}(\mathbf{A}_{\widetilde{\mathsf{id}},t}, \mathbf{R}_{\mathbf{A}_{\widetilde{\mathsf{id}}}}, \mathbf{u}, s)$ to generate $\mathbf{e}_{\widetilde{\mathsf{id}},t} \in \mathbb{Z}^{3m}$ satisfying $\mathbf{A}_{\widetilde{\mathsf{id}},t}\mathbf{e}_{\widetilde{\mathsf{id}},t} = \mathbf{u} \bmod q$.
  4. Pick $\theta \in (\mathsf{path}(\mathsf{id}) \cap \mathsf{KUNodes}(\mathsf{BT}, \mathsf{RL}, t))$ (only one θ exists), and return $\mathsf{dk_{id,t}} = (\mathbf{e}_{\mathsf{id},\theta}, \mathbf{e}_{t,\theta}, \mathbf{e}_{\widetilde{\mathsf{id}},t})$.

- Encrypt(id, $\mathsf{t_0}$, m): On input an identity $\mathsf{id} \in \mathcal{I}$, a time $\mathsf{t_0} \in \mathcal{T}$, and a message $m \in \{0,1\}$. The sender specifies the following steps:

  1. Define $\mathbf{A}_{\mathsf{id},\mathsf{t_0}} = [\mathbf{A} | \mathbf{A}_0 + \mathcal{H}(\mathsf{id})\mathbf{B} | \mathbf{A}_1 + \mathcal{H}(\mathsf{t_0})\mathbf{B}]$, and $\mathbf{A}_{\widetilde{\mathsf{id}},\mathsf{t_0}} = [\mathbf{A} | \mathbf{A}_0 + \mathcal{H}(\widetilde{\mathsf{id}})\mathbf{B} | \mathbf{A}_1 + \mathcal{H}(\mathsf{t_0})\mathbf{B}] \in \mathbb{Z}_q^{n \times 3m}$.
  2. Sample $\mathbf{s}_{00}, \mathbf{s}_{01} \xleftarrow{\$} \mathbb{Z}_q^n$, $e_0 \xleftarrow{\$} \chi$, $\mathbf{e}_{00}, \mathbf{e}_{01} \xleftarrow{\$} \chi^m$, $\mathbf{R}_{0,00}, \mathbf{R}_{0,01}$, $\mathbf{R}_{0,10}, \mathbf{R}_{0,11} \xleftarrow{\$} \{1,-1\}^{m \times m}$.
  3. Set $\mathbf{c}_{00} = \mathbf{A}_{\mathsf{id},\mathsf{t_0}}^{\mathrm{T}}\mathbf{s}_{00} + \begin{bmatrix} \mathbf{e}_{00} \\ \mathbf{R}_{0,00}^{\mathrm{T}}\mathbf{e}_{00} \\ \mathbf{R}_{0,01}^{\mathrm{T}}\mathbf{e}_{00} \end{bmatrix} \bmod q$, $\mathbf{c}_{01} = \mathbf{A}_{\widetilde{\mathsf{id}},\mathsf{t_0}}^{\mathrm{T}}\mathbf{s}_{01} + \begin{bmatrix} \mathbf{e}_{01} \\ \mathbf{R}_{0,10}^{\mathrm{T}}\mathbf{e}_{01} \\ \mathbf{R}_{0,11}^{\mathrm{T}}\mathbf{e}_{01} \end{bmatrix} \bmod q$.
  4. Compute $c_0 = \mathbf{u}^{\mathrm{T}}(\mathbf{s}_{00} + \mathbf{s}_{01}) + e_0 + m\lfloor\frac{q}{2}\rfloor \bmod q \in \mathbb{Z}_q$.
  5. Output $\mathsf{ct_{id,t_0}} = (\mathsf{id}, \mathsf{t_0}, c_0, \mathbf{c}_{00}, \mathbf{c}_{01}) \in (\{1\} \times \mathbb{Z}_q^{n-1}) \times (\{2\} \times \mathbb{Z}_q^{n-1}) \times \mathbb{Z}_q \times (\mathbb{Z}_q^{3m})^2$.

- Update($\mathsf{ct_{id,t}}$, t'): Two cases need to be considered according to $\mathsf{ct_{id,t}}$.

  1. On input an original ciphertext $\mathsf{ct_{id,t}} = \mathsf{ct_{id,t_0}} = (\mathsf{id}, \mathsf{t_0}, c_0, \mathbf{c}_{00}, \mathbf{c}_{01})$ and a new time $t' = t_1 > t_0$. The CSP specifies the following steps:

    1.1. Define $\mathbf{A}_{\mathsf{id},t'=t_1} = [\mathbf{A} | \mathbf{A}_0 + \mathcal{H}(\mathsf{id})\mathbf{B} | \mathbf{A}_1 + \mathcal{H}(t_1)\mathbf{B}]$, and $\mathbf{A}_{\widetilde{\mathsf{id}},t'=t_1} = [\mathbf{A} | \mathbf{A}_0 + \mathcal{H}(\widetilde{\mathsf{id}})\mathbf{B} | \mathbf{A}_1 + \mathcal{H}(t_1)\mathbf{B}]$.

    1.2. Sample $\mathbf{s}_{10}, \mathbf{s}_{11} \xleftarrow{\$} \mathbb{Z}_q^n$, $\mathbf{e}_{10}, \mathbf{e}_{11} \xleftarrow{\$} \chi^m$, $\mathbf{R}_{1,00}, \mathbf{R}_{1,01}, \mathbf{R}_{1,10}$, $\mathbf{R}_{1,11} \xleftarrow{\$} \{1,-1\}^{m \times m}$.

    1.3. Set $\mathbf{c}_{10} = \mathbf{A}_{\mathsf{id},t'}^{\mathrm{T}}\mathbf{s}_{10} + \begin{bmatrix} \mathbf{e}_{10} \\ \mathbf{R}_{1,00}^{\mathrm{T}}\mathbf{e}_{10} \\ \mathbf{R}_{1,01}^{\mathrm{T}}\mathbf{e}_{10} \end{bmatrix}$, $\mathbf{c}_{11} = \mathbf{A}_{\widetilde{\mathsf{id}},t'}^{\mathrm{T}}\mathbf{s}_{11} + \begin{bmatrix} \mathbf{e}_{11} \\ \mathbf{R}_{1,10}^{\mathrm{T}}\mathbf{e}_{11} \\ \mathbf{R}_{1,11}^{\mathrm{T}}\mathbf{e}_{11} \end{bmatrix} \bmod q$.

    1.4. Compute $c_1 = c_0 + \mathbf{u}^{\mathrm{T}}(\mathbf{s}_{10} + \mathbf{s}_{11}) \bmod q \in \mathbb{Z}_q$.

    1.5. Output $\mathsf{ct_{id,t'=t_1}} = (\mathsf{id}, \mathsf{t_0}, \mathsf{t_1}, c_1, \mathbf{c}_{00}, \mathbf{c}_{01}, \mathbf{c}_{10}, \mathbf{c}_{11}) \in (\{1\} \times \mathbb{Z}_q^{n-1}) \times (\{2\} \times \mathbb{Z}_q^{n-1})^2 \times \mathbb{Z}_q \times (\mathbb{Z}_q^{3m})^4$. *Note*: $(\mathbf{s}_{10}, \mathbf{s}_{11})$ should be stored in secret by the CSP.

  2. On input a $k-1$ ($k \geq 2$) times re-encrypted ciphertext $\mathsf{ct_{id,t}} = \mathsf{ct_{id,t_{k-1}}} = (\mathsf{id}, \mathsf{t_0}, \mathsf{t_{k-1}}, c_{k-1}, \mathbf{c}_{00}, \mathbf{c}_{01}, \mathbf{c}_{(k-1)0}, \mathbf{c}_{(k-1)1})$ and a new time $t' = t_k > t$. The CSP specifies the following steps:

    2.1. Define $\mathbf{A}_{\mathsf{id},t'=t_k} = [\mathbf{A}_{\mathsf{id}} | \mathbf{A}_1 + \mathcal{H}(t_k)\mathbf{B}]$, $\mathbf{A}_{\widetilde{\mathsf{id}},t'=t_k} = [\mathbf{A}_{\widetilde{\mathsf{id}}} | \mathbf{A}_1 + \mathcal{H}(t_k)\mathbf{B}]$.

2.2. Sample $\mathbf{s}_{k0}, \mathbf{s}_{k1} \xleftarrow{\$} \mathbb{Z}_q^n$, $\mathbf{e}_{k0}, \mathbf{e}_{k1} \xleftarrow{\$} \chi^m$, $\mathbf{R}_{k,00}, \mathbf{R}_{k,01}, \mathbf{R}_{k,10}$, $\mathbf{R}_{k,11} \xleftarrow{\$} \{1, -1\}^{m \times m}$.

2.3. Set $\mathbf{c}_{k0} = \mathbf{A}_{\mathsf{id},t'}^{\mathrm{T}} \mathbf{s}_{k0} + \begin{bmatrix} \mathbf{e}_{k0} \\ \mathbf{R}_{k,00}^{\mathrm{T}} \mathbf{e}_{k0} \\ \mathbf{R}_{k,01}^{\mathrm{T}} \mathbf{e}_{k0} \end{bmatrix} \bmod q$, $\mathbf{c}_{k1} = \mathbf{A}_{\widetilde{\mathsf{id}},t'}^{\mathrm{T}} \mathbf{s}_{k1} + \begin{bmatrix} \mathbf{e}_{k1} \\ \mathbf{R}_{k,10}^{\mathrm{T}} \mathbf{e}_{k1} \\ \mathbf{R}_{k,11}^{\mathrm{T}} \mathbf{e}_{k1} \end{bmatrix} \bmod q$.

2.4. Retrieve $(\mathbf{s}_{(k-1)0}, \mathbf{s}_{(k-1)1})$ (it is always pre-defined in the re-encrypted time t_{k-1}), and compute $c_k = c_{k-1} + \mathbf{u}^{\mathrm{T}}((\mathbf{s}_{k0} - \mathbf{s}_{(k-1)0}) + (\mathbf{s}_{k1} - \mathbf{s}_{(k-1)1})) = c_0 + \mathbf{u}^{\mathrm{T}}(\mathbf{s}_{k0} + \mathbf{s}_{k1}) \bmod q \in \mathbb{Z}_q$.

2.5. Output $\mathsf{ct}_{\mathsf{id},t'} = (\mathsf{id}, t_0, t_k, c_1, \mathbf{c}_{00}, \mathbf{c}_{01}, \mathbf{c}_{k0}, \mathbf{c}_{k1}) \in (\{1\} \times \mathbb{Z}_q^{n-1}) \times (\{2\} \times \mathbb{Z}_q^{n-1})^2 \times \mathbb{Z}_q \times (\mathbb{Z}_q^{3m})^4$. *Note:* $(\mathbf{s}_{k0}, \mathbf{s}_{k1})$ is stored in secret by the CSP.

- Decrypt($\mathsf{dk}_{\mathsf{id}',t'}, \mathsf{ct}_{\mathsf{id},t}$): Two cases need to be considered according to $\mathsf{ct}_{\mathsf{id},t}$.
1. On input an original ciphertext $\mathsf{ct}_{\mathsf{id},t} = \mathsf{ct}_{\mathsf{id},t_0} = (\mathsf{id}, t_0, c_0, \mathbf{c}_{00}, \mathbf{c}_{01})$, and a short-term decryption key $\mathsf{dk}_{\mathsf{id}',t'} = (\mathbf{e}_{\mathsf{id}',\theta}, \mathbf{e}_{t',\theta}, \mathbf{e}_{\widetilde{\mathsf{id}}',t'})$. Here, $\theta \in (\mathsf{path}(\mathsf{id}') \cap \mathsf{KUNodes}(\mathsf{BT}, \mathsf{RL}, t'))$. The receiver id' specifies the following steps:
   1.1. If $(\mathsf{id} \neq \mathsf{id}') \vee (t \neq t')$, return $\perp$ and abort.
   1.2. Otherwise, parse $\mathbf{c}_{00} = \begin{bmatrix} \mathbf{c}_{00,0} \\ \mathbf{c}_{00,1} \\ \mathbf{c}_{00,2} \end{bmatrix}$ where $\mathbf{c}_{00,i} \in \mathbb{Z}_q^m$, for $i = 0, 1, 2$.
   1.3. Compute $w_0 = c_0 - \mathbf{e}_{\mathsf{id},\theta}^{\mathrm{T}} \begin{bmatrix} \mathbf{c}_{00,0} \\ \mathbf{c}_{00,1} \end{bmatrix} - \mathbf{e}_{t',\theta}^{\mathrm{T}} \begin{bmatrix} \mathbf{c}_{00,0} \\ \mathbf{c}_{00,2} \end{bmatrix} - \mathbf{e}_{\widetilde{\mathsf{id}},t}^{\mathrm{T}} \mathbf{c}_{01} \bmod q$.
   1.4. Output $\lfloor \frac{2}{q} w_0 \rceil \in \{0, 1\}$.
2. On input a k (≥ 1) times re-encrypted ciphertext $\mathsf{ct}_{\mathsf{id},t} = \mathsf{ct}_{\mathsf{id},t_k} = (\mathsf{id}, t_0, t_k, c_k, \mathbf{c}_{00}, \mathbf{c}_{01}, \mathbf{c}_{k0}, \mathbf{c}_{k1})$, and a short-term decryption key $\mathsf{dk}_{\mathsf{id}',t'} = (\mathbf{e}_{\mathsf{id}',\theta_k}, \mathbf{e}_{t',\theta_k}, \mathbf{e}_{\widetilde{\mathsf{id}}',t'})$. Here, $\theta_k \in (\mathsf{path}(\mathsf{id}') \cap \mathsf{KUNodes}(\mathsf{BT}, \mathsf{RL}, t'))$. id' specifies the following steps:
   2.1. If $(\mathsf{id} \neq \mathsf{id}') \vee (t = t_k \neq t')$, return $\perp$ and abort.
   2.2. Otherwise, parse $\mathbf{c}_{00} = \begin{bmatrix} \mathbf{c}_{00,0} \\ \mathbf{c}_{00,1} \\ \mathbf{c}_{00,2} \end{bmatrix}$, $\mathbf{c}_{k0} = \begin{bmatrix} \mathbf{c}_{k0,0} \\ \mathbf{c}_{k0,1} \\ \mathbf{c}_{k0,2} \end{bmatrix}$ where $\mathbf{c}_{00,i}, \mathbf{c}_{k0,i} \in \mathbb{Z}_q^m$, for $i = 0, 1, 2$.
   2.3. Retrieve uk_{t_0} (it is always sent to all users publicly by the PKG)
   2.4. Define $\mathbf{A}_{\widetilde{\mathsf{id}},t_0} = [\mathbf{A}_{\widetilde{\mathsf{id}}} | \mathbf{A}_1 + \mathcal{H}(t_0)\mathbf{B}]$, and run SampleLeft($\mathbf{A}_{\widetilde{\mathsf{id}},t_0}, \mathbf{R}_{\mathbf{A}_{\widetilde{\mathsf{id}}}}, \mathbf{u}, s$) to generate $\mathbf{e}_{\widetilde{\mathsf{id}},t_0} \in \mathbb{Z}^{3m}$ satisfying $\mathbf{A}_{\widetilde{\mathsf{id}},t_0} \mathbf{e}_{\widetilde{\mathsf{id}},t_0} = \mathbf{u} \bmod q$.
   2.5. Pick $\theta_0 \in (\mathsf{path}(\mathsf{id}) \cap \mathsf{KUNodes}(\mathsf{BT}, \mathsf{RL}, t_0))$, and return a new short-term decryption key $\mathsf{dk}_{\mathsf{id},t_0} = (\mathbf{e}_{\mathsf{id},\theta_0}, \mathbf{e}_{t_0,\theta_0}, \mathbf{e}_{\widetilde{\mathsf{id}},t_0})$.
   2.6. Compute

$$w_0 = c_k - \mathbf{e}_{\mathsf{id},\theta_0}^{\mathrm{T}} \begin{bmatrix} \mathbf{c}_{00,0} \\ \mathbf{c}_{00,1} \end{bmatrix} - \mathbf{e}_{t_0,\theta_0}^{\mathrm{T}} \begin{bmatrix} \mathbf{c}_{00,0} \\ \mathbf{c}_{00,2} \end{bmatrix} - \mathbf{e}_{\widetilde{\mathsf{id}},t_0}^{\mathrm{T}} \mathbf{c}_{01} - \mathbf{e}_{\mathsf{id},\theta_k}^{\mathrm{T}} \begin{bmatrix} \mathbf{c}_{k0,0} \\ \mathbf{c}_{k0,1} \end{bmatrix} - \mathbf{e}_{t,\theta_k}^{\mathrm{T}} \begin{bmatrix} \mathbf{c}_{k0,0} \\ \mathbf{c}_{k0,2} \end{bmatrix} - \mathbf{e}_{\widetilde{\mathsf{id}},t}^{\mathrm{T}} \mathbf{c}_{k1}.$$

2.7. Output $\lfloor \frac{2}{q} w_0 \rceil \in \{0,1\}$.

- Revoke(id, t, RL, st): On input the current revocation list RL, an identity id, a time t, and a state st = BT. The PKG specifies the following steps:
  1. Add (id, t) to RL for all nodes associated with id.
  2. Output an updated RL = RL $\cup$ {(id, t)}.

3.2 Analysis

In this subsection, we will analysis the efficiency, correctness and security of our lattice-based CA-RIBE-CU in the standard model.

Efficiency: The efficiency aspect of our scheme with $N = 2^n$ is as follows:

- The bit-size of public parameters pp is $(4nm + n + n) \log q = \widetilde{\mathcal{O}}(n^2)$.
- The long-term private key sk_{id} consists of a trapdoor matrix of bit-size $\widetilde{\mathcal{O}}(n^2)$, and a series of short vectors of bit-size $\widetilde{\mathcal{O}}(n^2)$.
- The time update key uk_t has bit-size $\mathcal{O}(r \log \frac{N}{r}) \cdot \widetilde{\mathcal{O}}(n)$ where r is the number of revoked users.
- The ciphertext $ct_{id,t}$ has bit-size $(3(n-1) + 1 + 12m) \log q = \widetilde{\mathcal{O}}(n)$ at most.
- The short-term decryption key $dk_{id,t}$ has bit-size $\widetilde{\mathcal{O}}(n)$.

By the above analysis, though as in the lattice-based RIBE-CE scheme [32], our lattice-based CA-RIBE-CU enjoys the same asymptotic efficiency for public parameters pp and master secret key msk, in our scheme, three random matrices over $\mathbb{Z}_q^{n \times m}$, a random matrix over $\mathbb{Z}_q^{n \times \lceil \log q \rceil}$, a hash function have been removed from pp, and only one (not two in [32]) trapdoor matrix over $\mathbb{Z}^{2m \times 2m}$ in msk. Encouragingly, our final ciphertext (including an original ciphertext and a re-encrypted ciphertext) enjoys constant size, and the encryptions and ciphertexts update processing are simple, i.e., not linear in the length of identity and without a burdensome double encryption mechanism.

Correctness: If our first lattice-based CA-RIBE-CU in the standard model is operated correctly as specified, and a receiver id is not revoked at time $t \in \mathcal{T}$, then $dk_{id,t} = (e_{id,\theta}, e_{t,\theta}, e_{\widetilde{id},t})$ satisfies $\mathbf{A}_{id}e_{id,\theta} = u_{1,\theta} \bmod q$, $\mathbf{A}_t e_{t,\theta} = u - u_{1,\theta} \bmod q$, and $\mathbf{A}_{\widetilde{id},t} e_{\widetilde{id},t} = u \bmod q$. In the decryption algorithm, the non-revoked id tries to derive m by using $dk_{id,t} = (e_{id,\theta}, e_{t,\theta}, e_{\widetilde{id},t})$ (and $dk_{id,t_0} = (e_{id,\theta_0}, e_{t_0,\theta_0}, e_{\widetilde{id},t_0})$).

- If the given ciphertext is an original ciphertext, that is, $ct_{id,t} = ct_{id,t_0} = (id, t_0, c_0, c_{00}, c_{01})$.

  1. Parse $c_{00} = \begin{bmatrix} c_{00,0} \\ c_{00,1} \\ c_{00,2} \end{bmatrix}$ where $c_{00,i} \in \mathbb{Z}_q^m$, for $i = 0, 1, 2$.

2. Compute

$$w_0 = c_0 - \mathbf{e}_{\mathsf{id},\theta}^{\mathrm{T}} \begin{bmatrix} \mathbf{c}_{00,0} \\ \mathbf{c}_{00,1} \end{bmatrix} - \mathbf{e}_{\mathsf{t},\theta}^{\mathrm{T}} \begin{bmatrix} \mathbf{c}_{00,0} \\ \mathbf{c}_{00,2} \end{bmatrix} - \mathbf{e}_{\widetilde{\mathsf{id}},\mathsf{t}}^{\mathrm{T}} \mathbf{c}_{01} = \mathbf{u}^{\mathrm{T}}(\mathbf{s}_{00} + \mathbf{s}_{01}) + e_0 + m\lfloor \tfrac{q}{2} \rfloor$$

$$- \underbrace{(\mathbf{A}_{\mathsf{id}} \mathbf{e}_{\mathsf{id},\theta} + \mathbf{A}_{\mathsf{t}} \mathbf{e}_{\mathsf{t},\theta})^{\mathrm{T}} \mathbf{s}_{00}}_{=\mathbf{u}^{\mathrm{T}} \mathbf{s}_{00}} - \mathbf{e}_{\mathsf{id},\theta}^{\mathrm{T}} \begin{bmatrix} \mathbf{e}_{00} \\ \mathbf{R}_{0,00}^{\mathrm{T}} \mathbf{e}_{00} \end{bmatrix} - \mathbf{e}_{\mathsf{t},\theta}^{\mathrm{T}} \begin{bmatrix} \mathbf{e}_{00} \\ \mathbf{R}_{0,10}^{\mathrm{T}} \mathbf{e}_{00} \end{bmatrix} - \underbrace{(\mathbf{A}_{\widetilde{\mathsf{id}}} \mathbf{e}_{\widetilde{\mathsf{id}},\mathsf{t}})^{\mathrm{T}} \mathbf{s}_{01}}_{=\mathbf{u}^{\mathrm{T}} \mathbf{s}_{01}} - \mathbf{e}_{\widetilde{\mathsf{id}},\mathsf{t}}^{\mathrm{T}} \begin{bmatrix} \mathbf{e}_{01} \\ \mathbf{R}_{0,10}^{\mathrm{T}} \mathbf{e}_{01} \\ \mathbf{R}_{0,11}^{\mathrm{T}} \mathbf{e}_{01} \end{bmatrix}$$

$$= m\lfloor \tfrac{q}{2} \rfloor + e_0 \underbrace{- \mathbf{e}_{\mathsf{id},\theta}^{\mathrm{T}} \begin{bmatrix} \mathbf{e}_{00} \\ \mathbf{R}_{0,00}^{\mathrm{T}} \mathbf{e}_{00} \end{bmatrix} - \mathbf{e}_{\mathsf{t},\theta}^{\mathrm{T}} \begin{bmatrix} \mathbf{e}_{00} \\ \mathbf{R}_{0,10}^{\mathrm{T}} \mathbf{e}_{00} \end{bmatrix} - \mathbf{e}_{\widetilde{\mathsf{id}},\mathsf{t}}^{\mathrm{T}} \begin{bmatrix} \mathbf{e}_{01} \\ \mathbf{R}_{0,10}^{\mathrm{T}} \mathbf{e}_{01} \\ \mathbf{R}_{0,11}^{\mathrm{T}} \mathbf{e}_{01} \end{bmatrix}}_{\text{error}}$$

According to our parameters settings, it can be checked that the error term error is bounded by $q/5$ (i.e., $\|\text{error}\|_\infty < q/5$), thus, we have the conclusion $\lfloor \tfrac{2}{q} w_0 \rceil = m$ with overwhelming probability.

- If the given ciphertext is a k (≥ 1) times re-encrypted ciphertext, that is, $\mathsf{ct}_{\mathsf{id},\mathsf{t}} = \mathsf{ct}_{\mathsf{id},\mathsf{t}_k} = (\mathsf{id}, \mathsf{t}_0, \mathsf{t}_k, c_k, \mathbf{c}_{00}, \mathbf{c}_{01}, \mathbf{c}_{k0}, \mathbf{c}_{k1})$.

  1. Parse $\mathbf{c}_{00} = \begin{bmatrix} \mathbf{c}_{00,0} \\ \mathbf{c}_{00,1} \\ \mathbf{c}_{00,2} \end{bmatrix}$, $\mathbf{c}_{k0} = \begin{bmatrix} \mathbf{c}_{k0,0} \\ \mathbf{c}_{k0,1} \\ \mathbf{c}_{k0,2} \end{bmatrix}$ where $\mathbf{c}_{00,i}, \mathbf{c}_{k0,i} \in \mathbb{Z}_q^m$, for $i = 0, 1, 2$.

  2. Compute

$$w_k = c_k - \mathbf{e}_{\mathsf{id},\theta_k}^{\mathrm{T}} \begin{bmatrix} \mathbf{c}_{k0,0} \\ \mathbf{c}_{k0,1} \end{bmatrix} - \mathbf{e}_{\mathsf{t},\theta_k}^{\mathrm{T}} \begin{bmatrix} \mathbf{c}_{k0,0} \\ \mathbf{c}_{k0,2} \end{bmatrix} - \mathbf{e}_{\widetilde{\mathsf{id}},\mathsf{t}}^{\mathrm{T}} \mathbf{c}_{k1} = c_0 + \mathbf{u}^{\mathrm{T}}(\mathbf{s}_{k0} + \mathbf{s}_{k1})$$

$$- \underbrace{(\mathbf{A}_{\mathsf{id}} \mathbf{e}_{\mathsf{id},\theta_k} + \mathbf{A}_{\mathsf{t}} \mathbf{e}_{\mathsf{t},\theta_k})^{\mathrm{T}} \mathbf{s}_{k0}}_{=\mathbf{u}^{\mathrm{T}} \mathbf{s}_{k0}} - \mathbf{e}_{\mathsf{id},\theta_k}^{\mathrm{T}} \begin{bmatrix} \mathbf{e}_{k0} \\ \mathbf{R}_{k,00}^{\mathrm{T}} \mathbf{e}_{k0} \end{bmatrix} - \mathbf{e}_{\mathsf{t},\theta_k}^{\mathrm{T}} \begin{bmatrix} \mathbf{e}_{k0} \\ \mathbf{R}_{k,10}^{\mathrm{T}} \mathbf{e}_{k0} \end{bmatrix} - \underbrace{(\mathbf{A}_{\widetilde{\mathsf{id}}} \mathbf{e}_{\widetilde{\mathsf{id}},\mathsf{t}})^{\mathrm{T}} \mathbf{s}_{k1}}_{=\mathbf{u}^{\mathrm{T}} \mathbf{s}_{k1}} - \mathbf{e}_{\widetilde{\mathsf{id}},\mathsf{t}}^{\mathrm{T}} \begin{bmatrix} \mathbf{e}_{k1} \\ \mathbf{R}_{k,10}^{\mathrm{T}} \mathbf{e}_{k1} \\ \mathbf{R}_{k,11}^{\mathrm{T}} \mathbf{e}_{k1} \end{bmatrix}$$

$$= \mathbf{u}^{\mathrm{T}}(\mathbf{s}_{00} + \mathbf{s}_{01}) + e_0 + m\lfloor \tfrac{q}{2} \rfloor \underbrace{- \mathbf{e}_{\mathsf{id},\theta_k}^{\mathrm{T}} \begin{bmatrix} \mathbf{e}_{k0} \\ \mathbf{R}_{k,00}^{\mathrm{T}} \mathbf{e}_{k0} \end{bmatrix} - \mathbf{e}_{\mathsf{t},\theta_k}^{\mathrm{T}} \begin{bmatrix} \mathbf{e}_{k0} \\ \mathbf{R}_{k,10}^{\mathrm{T}} \mathbf{e}_{k0} \end{bmatrix} - \mathbf{e}_{\widetilde{\mathsf{id}},\mathsf{t}}^{\mathrm{T}} \begin{bmatrix} \mathbf{e}_{k1} \\ \mathbf{R}_{k,10}^{\mathrm{T}} \mathbf{e}_{k1} \\ \mathbf{R}_{k,11}^{\mathrm{T}} \mathbf{e}_{k1} \end{bmatrix}}_{\text{error}'}$$

  3. Retrieve the key $\mathsf{uk}_{\mathsf{t}_0}$, define $\mathbf{A}_{\widetilde{\mathsf{id}},\mathsf{t}} = [\mathbf{A}_{\widetilde{\mathsf{id}}} | \mathbf{A}_1 + \mathcal{H}(\mathsf{t}_0)\mathbf{B}]$, and run $\mathsf{SampleLeft}(\mathbf{A}_{\widetilde{\mathsf{id}},\mathsf{t}_0}, \mathbf{R}_{\mathbf{A}_{\widetilde{\mathsf{id}}}}, \mathbf{u}, s)$ to generate $\mathbf{e}_{\widetilde{\mathsf{id}},\mathsf{t}_0} \in \mathbb{Z}^{3m}$ satisfying $\mathbf{A}_{\widetilde{\mathsf{id}},\mathsf{t}} \mathbf{e}_{\widetilde{\mathsf{id}},\mathsf{t}_0} = \mathbf{u} \bmod q$.
  4. Return a new short-term decryption key $\mathsf{dk}_{\mathsf{id},\mathsf{t}_0} = (\mathbf{e}_{\mathsf{id},\theta_0}, \mathbf{e}_{\mathsf{t}_0,\theta_0}, \mathbf{e}_{\widetilde{\mathsf{id}},\mathsf{t}_0})$ where $\theta_0 \in (\mathsf{path}(\mathsf{id}) \cap \mathsf{KUNodes}(\mathsf{BT}, \mathsf{RL}, \mathsf{t}_0))$.
  5. Compute

$$w_0 = c_k - \mathbf{e}_{\mathsf{id},\theta_0}^{\mathrm{T}} \begin{bmatrix} \mathbf{c}_{00,0} \\ \mathbf{c}_{00,1} \end{bmatrix} - \mathbf{e}_{\mathsf{t}_0,\theta_0}^{\mathrm{T}} \begin{bmatrix} \mathbf{c}_{00,0} \\ \mathbf{c}_{00,2} \end{bmatrix} - \mathbf{e}_{\widetilde{\mathsf{id}},\mathsf{t}_0}^{\mathrm{T}} \mathbf{c}_{01} = \mathbf{u}^{\mathrm{T}}(\mathbf{s}_{00} + \mathbf{s}_{01}) + e_0 + m\lfloor \tfrac{q}{2} \rfloor + \text{error}'$$

$$- \underbrace{(\mathbf{A}_{\mathsf{id}} \mathbf{e}_{\mathsf{id},\theta_0} + \mathbf{A}_{\mathsf{t}} \mathbf{e}_{\mathsf{t}_0,\theta_0})^{\mathrm{T}} \mathbf{s}_{00}}_{=\mathbf{u}^{\mathrm{T}} \mathbf{s}_{00}} - \mathbf{e}_{\mathsf{id},\theta_0}^{\mathrm{T}} \begin{bmatrix} \mathbf{e}_{00} \\ \mathbf{R}_{0,00}^{\mathrm{T}} \mathbf{e}_{00} \end{bmatrix} - \mathbf{e}_{\mathsf{t}_0,\theta_0}^{\mathrm{T}} \begin{bmatrix} \mathbf{e}_{00} \\ \mathbf{R}_{0,10}^{\mathrm{T}} \mathbf{e}_{00} \end{bmatrix} - \underbrace{(\mathbf{A}_{\widetilde{\mathsf{id}},\mathsf{t}_0} \mathbf{e}_{\widetilde{\mathsf{id}},\mathsf{t}_0})^{\mathrm{T}} \mathbf{s}_{01}}_{=\mathbf{u}^{\mathrm{T}} \mathbf{s}_{01}} - \mathbf{e}_{\widetilde{\mathsf{id}},\mathsf{t}_0}^{\mathrm{T}} \begin{bmatrix} \mathbf{e}_{01} \\ \mathbf{R}_{0,10}^{\mathrm{T}} \mathbf{e}_{01} \\ \mathbf{R}_{0,11}^{\mathrm{T}} \mathbf{e}_{01} \end{bmatrix}$$

$$= m\lfloor \tfrac{q}{2} \rfloor + e_0 + \text{error}' \underbrace{- \mathbf{e}_{\mathsf{id},\theta_0}^{\mathrm{T}} \begin{bmatrix} \mathbf{e}_{00} \\ \mathbf{R}_{0,00}^{\mathrm{T}} \mathbf{e}_{00} \end{bmatrix} - \mathbf{e}_{\mathsf{t}_0,\theta_0}^{\mathrm{T}} \begin{bmatrix} \mathbf{e}_{00} \\ \mathbf{R}_{0,10}^{\mathrm{T}} \mathbf{e}_{00} \end{bmatrix} - \mathbf{e}_{\widetilde{\mathsf{id}},\mathsf{t}_0}^{\mathrm{T}} \begin{bmatrix} \mathbf{e}_{01} \\ \mathbf{R}_{0,10}^{\mathrm{T}} \mathbf{e}_{01} \\ \mathbf{R}_{0,11}^{\mathrm{T}} \mathbf{e}_{01} \end{bmatrix}}_{\text{error}}$$

According to our parameters settings, it can be checked that error is bounded by $q/5$ (i.e., $\|\text{error}\|_\infty < q/5$), thus, we have the conclusion $\lfloor \frac{2}{q} w_0 \rceil = \mathsf{m}$ with overwhelming probability.

Security: For the ind-cpa security of our scheme, we show the following theorem.

Theorem 1. *Our lattice-based* CA-RIBE-CU *scheme in the standard model is* ind-cpa *secure if the* LWE *assumption holds.*

Proof. To proof this theorem, we define a list of games where the first one is identical to the original ind-cpa game as in Definition 2 and show that a ppt adversary $\mathcal{A}$ has advantage zero in the last game. We show that $\mathcal{A}$ cannot distinguish between these games, and thus, $\mathcal{A}$ has negligible advantage in winning the original ind-cpa game.

Let id^* be a challenge identity and t^* be a challenge time, we consider two types of adversaries:

- Type-0: An inside adversary $\mathcal{A}_0$ (e.g., a revoked user) who queries a long-term private key on the challenge identity id^*. Thus, id^* must be revoked at $\mathsf{t} \leq \mathsf{t}^*$.
- Type-1: An outside adversary $\mathcal{A}_1$ (e.g., the CSP) who only queries a long-term private key on $\mathsf{id} \neq \mathsf{id}^*$.

By adopting the same proof strategy of Chen et al. [7], we select a bit $ty \xleftarrow{\$} \{0,1\}$ as a guess for the different types of $\mathcal{A}$, and thus, we have a probability $1/2$ to simulate the game correctly.

Due to the limited space, we omit the detailed proofs of Theorem 1, if any necessary, please contact the corresponding author for the full version.

4 Conclusion

In this paper, we propose the first lattice-based cloud-aided scalable revocable identity-based encryption with ciphertext update. In comparison with previous lattice-based constructions of RIBE, our scheme enjoys a significant advantage in terms of ciphertext security when considering the scenario of a secure data sharing in the cloud setting, and the revoked users cannot access to both the previously and subsequently shared data. Two tools called "hybrid ciphertexts" and "hybrid short-term decryption keys" are adopted to enable constant ciphertext and simplified ciphertext update, that is, not linear in the length of identity and without a burdensome double encryption mechanism, which serves as one startlingly solution to the challenges posed by Zhang et al.. In particular, our lattice-based CA-RIBE-CU scheme is selectively secure in the standard model.

Acknowledgments. The authors thank the anonymous reviewers of FCS 2021 for their helpful comments and this research was supported by Key Scientific Research Projects of Colleges and Universities of Henan Province (No. 22A520047), Guangxi key Laboratory of Cryptography and Information Security (Grant No. GCIS201907) and Natural Science Foundation of Henan Province (Grant No. 202300410508).

References

1. Agrawal, S., Boneh, D., Boyen, X.: Efficient Lattice (H)IBE in the standard model. In: Gilbert, H. (ed.) EUROCRYPT 2010. LNCS, vol. 6110, pp. 553–572. Springer, Heidelberg (2010). https://doi.org/10.1007/978-3-642-13190-5_28
2. Ajtai, M.: Generating hard instances of lattice problems (extended abstract). In: STOC, pp. 99–108. ACM (1996). https://doi.org/10.1145/237814.237838
3. Alwen, J., Peikert, C.: Generating shorter bases for hard random lattices. Theor. Comput. Syst. **48**(3), 535–553 (2011). https://doi.org/10.1007/s00224-010-9278-3
4. Boneh, D., Franklin, M.: Identity-based encryption from the Weil pairing. In: Kilian, J. (ed.) CRYPTO 2001. LNCS, vol. 2139, pp. 213–229. Springer, Heidelberg (2001). https://doi.org/10.1007/3-540-44647-8_13
5. Boldyreva, A., Goyal, V., Kumar, V.: Identity-based encryption with efficient revocation. In: CCS, pp. 417–426. ACM (2008). https://doi.org/10.1145/1455770.1455823
6. Cash, D., Hofheinz, D., Kiltz, E., Peikert, C.: Bonsai trees, or how to delegate a lattice basis. In: Gilbert, H. (ed.) EUROCRYPT 2010. LNCS, vol. 6110, pp. 523–552. Springer, Heidelberg (2010). https://doi.org/10.1007/978-3-642-13190-5_27
7. Chen, J., Lim, H.W., Ling, S., Wang, H., Nguyen, K.: Revocable identity-based encryption from lattices. In: Susilo, W., Mu, Y., Seberry, J. (eds.) ACISP 2012. LNCS, vol. 7372, pp. 390–403. Springer, Heidelberg (2012). https://doi.org/10.1007/978-3-642-31448-3_29
8. Dong, C., Yang, K., Qiu, J., et al.: Outsouraced revocable identity-based encryption from lattices. Trans. Emerging Tel. Tech. **30**, e3529 (2018). https://doi.org/10.1002/ett.3529
9. Gentry, C., Peikert, C., Vaikuntanathan, V.: Trapdoor for hard lattices and new cryptographic constructions. In: STOC, pp. 197–206. ACM (2008). https://doi.org/10.1145/1374376.1374407
10. Katsumata, S., Matsuda, T., Takayasu, A.: Lattice-based revocable (hierarchical) IBE with decryption key exposure resistance. In: Lin, D., Sako, K. (eds.) PKC 2019. LNCS, vol. 11443, pp. 441–471. Springer, Cham (2019). https://doi.org/10.1007/978-3-030-17259-6_15
11. Lee, K.: A generic construction for revocable identity-based encryption with subset difference methods. PLoS ONE **15**(9), (2020). https://doi.org/10.1371/journal.pone.o239053
12. Li, J., Li, J., Chen, X., et al.: Identity-based encryption with outsourced revocation in cloud computing. IEEE Trans. Comput. **64**(2), 426–437 (2015). https://doi.org/10.1109/TC.2013.208
13. Yang, C., Xu, Z., Gu, G., Yegneswaran, V., Porras, P.: DroidMiner: automated mining and characterization of fine-grained malicious behaviors in android applications. In: Kutyłowski, M., Vaidya, J. (eds.) ESORICS 2014. LNCS, vol. 8712, pp. 163–182. Springer, Cham (2014). https://doi.org/10.1007/978-3-319-11203-9_10
14. Libert, B., Vergnaud, D.: Adaptive-ID secure revocable identity-based encryption. In: Fischlin, M. (ed.) CT-RSA 2009. LNCS, vol. 5473, pp. 1–15. Springer, Heidelberg (2009). https://doi.org/10.1007/978-3-642-00862-7_1
15. Liu, Y., Sun, Y.: Generic construction of server-aided revocable hierarchical identity-based encryption. In: Wu, Y., Yung, M. (eds.) Inscrypt 2020. LNCS, vol. 12612, pp. 73–82. Springer, Cham (2021). https://doi.org/10.1007/978-3-030-71852-7_5

16. Ma, X., Lin, D.: Generic constructions of revocable identity-based encryption. In: Liu, Z., Yung, M. (eds.) Inscrypt 2019. LNCS, vol. 12020, pp. 381–396. Springer, Cham (2020). https://doi.org/10.1007/978-3-030-42921-8_22

17. Micciancio, D., Peikert, C.: Hardness of SIS and LWE with small parameters. In: Canetti, R., Garay, J.A. (eds.) CRYPTO 2013. LNCS, vol. 8042, pp. 21–39. Springer, Heidelberg (2013). https://doi.org/10.1007/978-3-642-40041-4_2

18. Micciancio, D., Peikert, C.: Trapdoors for lattices: simpler, tighter, faster, smaller. In: Pointcheval, D., Johansson, T. (eds.) EUROCRYPT 2012. LNCS, vol. 7237, pp. 700–718. Springer, Heidelberg (2012). https://doi.org/10.1007/978-3-642-29011-4_41

19. Naor, D., Naor, M., Lotspiech, J.: Revocation and tracing schemes for stateless receivers. In: Kilian, J. (ed.) CRYPTO 2001. LNCS, vol. 2139, pp. 41–62. Springer, Heidelberg (2001). https://doi.org/10.1007/3-540-44647-8_3

20. Nguyen, K., Wang, H., Zhang, J.: Server-aided revocable identity-based encryption from lattices. In: Foresti, S., Persiano, G. (eds.) CANS 2016. LNCS, vol. 10052, pp. 107–123. Springer, Cham (2016). https://doi.org/10.1007/978-3-319-48965-0_7

21. Qin, B., Deng, R.H., Li, Y., Liu, S.: Server-aided revocable identity-based encryption. In: Pernul, G., Ryan, P.Y.A., Weippl, E. (eds.) ESORICS 2015. LNCS, vol. 9326, pp. 286–304. Springer, Cham (2015). https://doi.org/10.1007/978-3-319-24174-6_15

22. Regev, O.: On Lattices, learning with errors, random linear codes, and cryptography. In: STOC, pp. 84–93. ACM (2005). https://doi.org/10.1145/1060590.1060603

23. Sahai, A., Waters, B.: Fuzzy identity-based encryption. In: Cramer, R. (ed.) EUROCRYPT 2005. LNCS, vol. 3494, pp. 457–473. Springer, Heidelberg (2005). https://doi.org/10.1007/11426639_27

24. Seo, J.H., Emura, K.: Revocable identity-based encryption revisited: security model and construction. In: Kurosawa, K., Hanaoka, G. (eds.) PKC 2013. LNCS, vol. 7778, pp. 216–234. Springer, Heidelberg (2013). https://doi.org/10.1007/978-3-642-36362-7_14

25. Shamir, A.: Identity-based cryptosystems and signature schemes. In: Blakley, G.R., Chaum, D. (eds.) CRYPTO 1984. LNCS, vol. 196, pp. 47–53. Springer, Heidelberg (1985). https://doi.org/10.1007/3-540-39568-7_5

26. Shor, P.: Polynomial-time algorithms for prime factorization and dislogarithms on a quantum computer. SIAM Rev. **41**(2), 303–332 (1999). https://doi.org/10.1137/S0036144598347011

27. Sun, Y., Mu, Y., Susilo, W., et al.: Revocable identity-based encryption with server-aided ciphertext evolution. Theor. Comput. Sci. **2020**(815), 11–24 (2020). https://doi.org/10.1016/j.tcs.2020.02.03

28. Takayasu, A.: Adaptively secure lattice-based revocable IBE in the QROM: compact parameters, tight security, and anonymity. Des. Codes Crypt. **89**(8), 1965–1992 (2021). https://doi.org/10.1007/s10623-021-00895-3

29. Takayasu, A., Watanabe, Y.: Lattice-based revocable identity-based encryption with bounded decryption key exposure resistance. In: Pieprzyk, J., Suriadi, S. (eds.) ACISP 2017. LNCS, vol. 10342, pp. 184–204. Springer, Cham (2017). https://doi.org/10.1007/978-3-319-60055-0_10

30. Wang, C., Li, Y., Fang, J., et al.: Cloud-aided scalable revocable identity-based encryption scheme with ciphertext update. Concurrency Computat. Pract. Exper. **29**, e4035 (2017). https://doi.org/10.1002/cpe.4035

31. Wang, S., Zhang, J., He, J., Wang, H., Li, C.: Simplified revocable hierarchical identity-based encryption from lattices. In: Mu, Y., Deng, R.H., Huang, X. (eds.)

CANS 2019. LNCS, vol. 11829, pp. 99–119. Springer, Cham (2019). https://doi.org/10.1007/978-3-030-31578-8_6

32. Zhang, Y., Liu, X., Hu, Y., Jia, H.: Revocable identity-based encryption with server-aided ciphertext evolution from lattices. In: Yu, Yu., Yung, M. (eds.) Inscrypt 2021. LNCS, vol. 13007, pp. 442–465. Springer, Cham (2021). https://doi.org/10.1007/978-3-030-88323-2_24

A Privacy-Preserving Medical Image Scheme Based on Secret Sharing and Reversible Data Hiding

Ming Cheng[1], Yang Yang[1,2]($\boxtimes$) (iD), Yingqiu Ding[1], and Weiming Zhang[3] (iD)

[1] The School of Electronics and Information Engineering, Anhui University, Hefei 230601, China
sky_yang@ahu.edu.cn

[2] Institute of Artificial Intelligence, Hefei Comprehensive National Science Center, Hefei 230601, China

[3] The School of Cyber Science and Engineering, University of Science and Technology of China, Hefei 230026, China

Abstract. With the development of online medical care, the security of patients' private medical data in the cloud has aroused widespread concern. Currently, the security issues for medical images have been researched by some scholars, but these medical images which stored in single server may be destroyed if the server is maliciously attacked. In addition, the patient privacy information which included patients' electronic medical records and personal information are not be protected. Therefore, in order to protect patients' privacy information and secure storage of medical images, this paper proposed a privacy-preserving medical image scheme based on secret sharing and reversible data hiding. The medical image is encrypted at firstly, and the encrypted medical image and private information are shared by (t, n) threshold secret sharing scheme respectively. Then marked encrypted medical image shares are generated by embedding the privacy information share into the encrypted medical image share reversibly. Finally, they are sent to multiple servers for distributed storage. The receiver can combine and recover original medical images and private information after collecting no less than t shares, which greatly improves the security of medical image storage and effectively protects patients' privacy information. Experimental results show that the proposed scheme is superior to other schemes in terms of encryption performance, embedding capacity and visual quality of decrypted medical image.

Keywords: Reversible data hiding in encrypted image · Secret image sharing · Medical image · Privacy protection

1 Introduction

With the development of medical services and the popularity of cloud applications, due to the limited local storage space, a large number of medical institutions begin to store medical data such as medical images and patients' privacy

C. Cao et al. (Eds.): FCS 2021, CCIS 1558, pp. 288–307, 2022.
https://doi.org/10.1007/978-981-19-0523-0_19

information in cloud [14,20]. Because of the patient's medical data contains a lot of sensitive information, they are easy to attract the attention of attackers. In addition, due to the semi-honest characteristics of cloud servers, medical data leakage happens occasionally [17,29].

At present, the security issues for medical images often encrypt the medical image and stored it in single server, but these medical images may be destroyed if the server is maliciously attacked [8,16,28]. Kong et al. proposed reversible information hiding in encrypted medical image (RDH-EI) [13], in which content owner encrypt image before uploading it to one server in the cloud; Cloud manager act as data hider to embed secret information in encrypted image; At the receiving end, only authorized user can extract secret information and decrypt the image [19,24,25]. Due to encrypted medical image is stored in a single server, when the server is attacked, medical image will be completely destroyed. Therefore, some researchers began to consider the distributed storage. Shamir proposed (t, n) threshold secret sharing scheme based on LaGrange polynomial interpolation [3]. Then Blakely proposed a secret sharing scheme based on projective space [15]. In both schemes, the encrypted images and its shared size are the same.

In fact, patient's medical data contains not only medical image but also patients' private information, where patients' private information also includes patients' electronic medical records and personal information. However, the existing papers almost all research the security of medical images, and do not discuss the security of patient's privacy information [27]. This paper researches how to match patients' privacy information with medical images and protect patient privacy information while ensuring the security of medical images.

Based on the above analysis, we aim at the protection of patients' privacy information and the security of medical images. This paper proposed a privacy-preserving medical image scheme based on secret sharing and reversible data hiding. Firstly, the content owner encrypts the plain image (medical image) by means of block scrambling, rotation and image filtering, so that the content of the medical image is not leaked during transmission and storage. Considering the confidentiality of patients' privacy information transmitted in public channels, we use (t, n) threshold secret sharing method to share encrypted medical images and private information respectively, and then embed the private information shares into the respective encrypted image shares by reversible data hiding (RDH) scheme. Finally, the content owner sends these marked encrypted medical image shares to multiple servers in the cloud. Depending on the needs of the server manager, they can also embed additional information into the marked encrypted medical image share through difference expansion (DE) scheme [18]. Finally, according to the different degree of authorization, if doctor act as the receiver of full authorization, after downloading the marked encrypted image shares in different servers. When the number of collected shares is not less than t, the embedding secret key can be used to extract and combine the secret information shares, and then the decryption secret key to reconstruct medical images. It is worth noting that if the doctor, as an unauthorized receiver, receive only the decryption secret key, they can make a preliminary judgment about the patient's condition based on the decrypted medical images without extracting the patients' privacy information. Experiment shows that there is almost no visual difference between the decrypted image and plain image.

The innovations of the proposed algorithm are summarized as follows.

1. **Distributed storage.** The fault tolerance rate of the algorithm is improved. If no more than $(n-t)$ servers are attacked and the storage data is destroyed, the remaining t copies of the data can be restored to the plain medical image content.
2. **Protection of privacy information.** By embedding private information share in the high frequency region of encrypted image share reversibly. Not only can patients' private information be matched with their medical images, but also the privacy information is not leaked.
3. **Integrity of shares.** By extracting additional information, the receiver can determine whether the share has been tampered with and can find out which server was attacked. The overall security of the algorithm is improved.

The rest of this paper is organized as follows. Section 2 describes the proposed RDH-EI algorithm based on (t,n) threshold secret sharing. Section 3 is the simulation and performance analysis of the new scheme. In Sect. 4, we summarize our work.

2   Proposed Method

In order to protect the contents of patients' privacy information and enhance the security of medical image(plain image), this paper proposed a privacy-preserving medical image scheme based on secret sharing and reversible data hiding. As shown in Fig. 1, the overall proposed scheme is divided into three parts: **the content owner's side, the cloud's side** and **receiver's side**. First, the content owner encrypts the medical image to generate a ciphertext image to enhance the security of the medical image. Through the (t,n) secret sharing mechanism, both the encrypted image and the private information are shared, and the private information shars are embedded in the high frequency region of the encrypted image shares. Then, the marked encrypted image shares are uploaded to n servers in the cloud to achieve the purpose of distributed storage. In the cloud, according to different requirements, the servers can also embed additional information (for integrity verification, identity authentication) into the marked encrypted image shares. At the receiver's side, doctor as receiver download the marked encrypted image shares and corresponding secret keys from different servers respectively. When the number of shared copies collected is not less than t, the receivers can use these shares and secret keys to extract patients' privacy information (secret information) and combine them, and reconstruct the plain medical image for consultation.

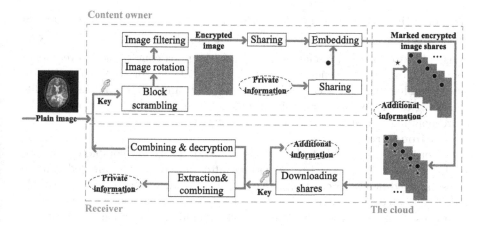

Fig. 1. The schematic of the proposed scheme.

2.1 Content Owner's Side

In order to ensure the security of medical images content, we need to encrypt it. Since the cloud servers are semi-honest, in order to ensure the security of the uploaded content in the stored process, we will upload the marked encrypted image to multiple servers in the form of shares and wait for the servers to embed additional information. The following is a detailed introduction.

2.1.1 Medical Image Encryption

In order to improve the security of image transmission, we need to encrypt the image. Due to scrambling and filtering can quickly disrupt the correlation between adjacent pixels and have a high security level. Therefore, we use the following algorithm to encrypt the medical image. As shown in Fig. 2, the specific steps are as follows.

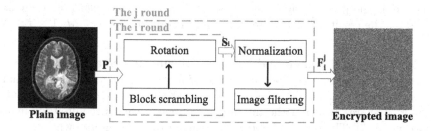

Fig. 2. The schematic of the proposed encryption scheme.

(1) Image block scrambling

In order to reduce the correlation between adjacent pixels of the medical image, adjacent pixels need to be arranged into different rows and columns.

Assuming that the size of the plain image is $M \times N$, the partition principle of block B is $L = min\left\{\lfloor\sqrt{M}\rfloor, \lfloor\sqrt{N}\rfloor\right\}$ and the plain image is divided into $L^2 \times L^2$ image blocks of size $L \times L$. Generates a scrambling box containing two vectors of length L based on the generated secret key key_1. Then, sort the two vectors in the scrambling box to get two indexes, namely row and column indexes. Finally, according to the two row and column indexes, the image block is moved to the corresponding row and column position of the index.

(2) Image rotation

In order to ensure that the positions of all pixels are completely scrambled, the image blocks need to be rotated after the block is scrambled. Rotate the scrambled image block clockwise or counterclockwise according to the angle index generated by the secret key key_1. In order to make the encryption algorithm resistant to differential attack, block scrambling and image rotation can be constructed into a linear combination [11,26], as shown in Fig. 2. In this combination, block scrambling and image rotation can be performed alternately to prevent the image block from returning to its original position when rotated in four separate turns, each 90 °C. Where $i = 1, 2, 3, 4; j = 1, 2, 3$.

(3) Image filtering

In order to apply subtle changes of medical image to the entire encrypted image and realize diffusion, image filtering is introduced to randomly change the pixel value. Firstly, the matrix Q randomly generated by the secret key key_1 is used to realize the normalization of image pixels, as shown in Eq. 1, in order to balance the number of pixels with different pixel intensity.

$$S'_{i,j} = (S_{i,j} + Q_{i,j}) \quad mod \ 256 \tag{1}$$

Where $S_{i,j}$ is the result of block scrambling and rotation combined with disturbance. $S'_{i,j}$ is the result after normalization. In addition, $1 \leq i \leq M, 1 \leq j \leq N$.

Then, the mask M randomly generated by the secret key key_1 is used as shown in Eq. 2 to separate the normalized results and carry out image filtering.

$$F_{i,j} = \left(\sum B \times M + S'_{i,j}\right) mod \ 256 \tag{2}$$

Where B is the divided image block, M is the weight coefficient of the mask, and $F_{i,j}$ is the result obtained after filtering. In addition, $1 \leq i \leq M, 1 \leq j \leq N$.

2.1.2 Encrypted Image and Private Information Sharing

In order to realize the distributed storage of medical images, we need to share the encrypted images, using the (t, n) secret sharing method, where the total number of shares is n and the minimum number of shares required for image recovery is t [7]. The two parameters are defined by the content owner.

First of all, we need to build a sharing matrix K [5]. The constructed sharing matrix K needs to meet the following two conditions:

– The matrix K is an $n \times m$ binary matrix. The matrix K contains at least one '1' in each row;

– The binary matrix K' of the new matrix $h \times m$ is formed by arbitrarily selecting h rows in matrix K. When $h \geq t$, the matrix K' contains at least one '1'
in each column; When $h < t$, the matrix K' contains at least one '0' in each
column.

The construction method of the sharing matrix K is as follows:
First, we construct the column vector K_1 of $n \times 1$. K_1 is made up of $(t - 1)$
zeros and $(n - t + 1)$ ones. Then, each combination that satisfies the above
number of 0,1 becomes a new column vector. So $K = [K_1, K_2, ..., K_m]$, where
$m = C_n^{t-1} = \frac{n!}{(t-1)!(n-t+1)!}$.

Assuming that the encrypted image E is composed of m image blocks, thus
the size of the constructed sharing matrix K is $n \times m$. Then we reshape the
encrypted image into a 1-D matrix of size $1 \times m$, where each element is a 2×2
encrypted image block. The encrypted image is shared into n copies through
Eq. 3. Where each share is a 1-D matrix and the number of image blocks in it is
the same as the number of '1' in the row corresponding to the sharing matrix.

$$Z_i = E \cdot K(i) \quad i = 1, 2, \cdots, n \tag{3}$$

Where Z represents the encrypted image shares and the i-th share Z_i is generated
by the i-th row of the sharing matrix K. '·' indicates the point multiplication.

The recovery shares can be carried out by Eq. 4 to reconstruct the encrypted
image, and 2×2 encrypted blocks in an encrypted image can be recovered by
each row of the sharing matrix.

$$E(j) = Z_{[t]}(1, j) \| Z_{[t]}(2, j) \|, \cdots, \| Z_{[t]}(t, j) \quad j = 1, 2, \cdots, m \tag{4}$$

Where t represents the number of shares used, $E(j)$ represents a 2×2 encrypted
image block and "$\|$" represent bitwise or.

In addition, in order to completely extract private information and accurately
recover the medical image, we need to record the size of the medical image, the
parameters t and n of the sharing matrix and the row index i of the sharing
matrix. Since the rows of the sharing matrix are the same as the plain image of
the values, only the column values of the sharing matrix need to be recorded.
We use the traditional RDH method: difference expansion(DE) [18]. The secret
key key_2 is generated and some pixels are randomly selected for embedding.

Next, the patients' privacy information (secret information) is generated into
n shares by using the same (t, n) secret sharing method.

2.1.3 Private Information Embedding
In order to ensure the security of private information and the matching of private
information and medical image. The content owner need to embed the private
information share into the high-frequency area of the encrypted image share
to generate the marked encrypted image share. In order to improve the attack
resistance of the algorithm, a dynamic embedding method is adopted. Due to
each server will embed the corresponding private information share into the
encrypted image share steps are the same. We will introduce the image share

E and the private information share X as a example. The private information embedding process is shown in Fig. 3. The specific steps are as follows:

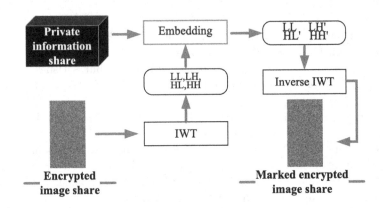

Fig. 3. The schematic of image embedding process.

- **Avoid embedding overflow:** Perform the operation of Eq. 5 on encrypted image share E_i and quantize the pixel value of E_i to between $[\alpha, \beta]$.

$$\mathrm{E}' = \lceil \alpha + \frac{\beta - \alpha}{255} \mathrm{E} \rceil \tag{5}$$

Where the value of α is $(0,10]$ and the value of β is $[240,255)$, which is the most reasonable.
- **Obtaining the wavelet coefficient matrix:** Use integer wavelet transform (IWT) [6] to perform wavelet decomposition on the encrypted image share to obtain the detail coefficient matrix HH, HL and LH and the approximate coefficient matrix LL.
- **Reshaping:** Reshape each of the above detail coefficient matrix into a 1-D array E_1, E_2 and E_3 with the length of mn.
- **Chaotic sequence generation:** Use the key Key_2 to generate three sets of chaotic sequences $A = \{a_i\}_{i=1}^{mn}$, $B = \{b_i\}_{i=1}^{mn}$ and $C = \{c_i\}_{i=1}^{mn}$.
- **Permutation:** Assume that O_1, O_2 and O_3 are the operations of sorting A, B and C, and sorting and permuting A, B and C. Obtain $H = \{h_i\}_{i=1}^{mn}$, $V = \{v_i\}_{i=1}^{mn}$ and $D = \{d_i\}_{i=1}^{mn}$ separately.
- **Stretching:** Stretch private information X into a 1-D array $X = \{X_i\}_{i=1}^{mn}$ whose length is mn.
- **Embedding:** Starting from X_1, they are converted into binary, which are represented as $x_0, x_1, \ldots, x_7$. x_0, x_1 and x_2 are filled in the three least significant bits of h_i; x_3, x_4 and x_5 are filled in the three least significant bits of v_i; x_6 and x_7 are filled in the two least significant bits of d_i. Repeat the above steps until X_{mn} is executed. Three embedded matrices H', V' and D' are obtained.
- **Reverse permutation:** By using O_1, O_2 and O_3 to reverse permutation of H', V' and D' obtain HH, HL and LH.

- **Shaping:** Reshape the HH,HL and LH matrices into HH',HL' and LH' matrices, the size of which is $m \times n$.
- **Generation of marked encrypted image share:** Perform inverse IWT transformation on the aforementioned matrices HH',HL',LH' and LL to obtain a marked encrypted image share.

The content owner then sends n marked encrypted image shares to different servers in the cloud.

2.2 The Cloud's Side

Depending on the needs of each server, the servers can embed additional information needed for shared integrity authentication, copyright protection, and authentication operations. Since the medical image is encrypted in blocks, there is redundancy in the image blocks. Therefore, the server can be embedded using the traditional RDH method. In the subsequent experiments, the Difference Expansion (DE) [18] is used for embedding, so we will not focus on describing this approach in this article.

2.3 Receiver's Side

When the receiver obtains the dense image sharing, the additional information is extracted by the inverse operation of DE method. The next step is to extract the private information and decrypt the image operation, which is the reverse operation of the whole encryption and secret sharing. Firstly, we extract the private information share from the marked encrypted image share. Then, we combine the two kinds of shares respectively to generate the complete private information and encrypted image. Finally, we decrypt the encrypted image. Since the whole process is completely reversible, the initial plain medical image can be completely recovered.

2.3.1 Secret Information Shares Extraction and Combining
(1) Extraction
Assuming that the receiving end has received the secret keys (a_0,b_0 and c_0), we are about to extract the private information share from the marked encrypted image share. The specific steps are as follows:

- **The frequency domain decomposition:** Perform the IWT operation on marked encrypted image share to obtain the LL matrix and the modified HH',HL' and LH'.
- **Stretching:** Stretch the HH',HL' and LH' matrices into 1-D arrays respectively.
- **Generation and permutation of chaotic sequences:** Repeat steps (4) and (5) in Sect. 2.1.3 using the key key_2 received by the receiver. Thus, three sequences $H = \{h_i\}_{i=1}^{mn}, V = \{v_i\}_{i=1}^{mn}$ and $D = \{d_i\}_{i=1}^{mn}$ are obtained.

– **Extraction:** The three least significant bits extracted from h_i are denoted as x_0, x_1 and x_2. The three least significant bits extracted from v_i are denoted as x_3, x_4 and x_5. The two least significant bits extracted from d_i are denoted as x_6 and x_7. Repeat the above steps until X'_{mn} is executed.
– **Reshaping:** Reshape the array $(X'_1, X'_2, \ldots, X'_{mn})$ into private information X.

(2) Combining

Next, we do a combination of private information shares. When the receivers collect not less than t shares of private information, it can start to combinate the shares, that is, recover the complete private information. The following is a detailed description of shares combinating.

First, by obtaining the secret key_2, we can find the matrix elements that store the sharing matrix parameters t, n, row index, and column values of the private information matrix and extract these parameters. We can use these parameters to generate the sharing matrix K as described in Sect. 2.2. By row index and inverse calculation of Eq. 4, we can recover each row of the sharing matrix to its corresponding image share. Among them, one row of the sharing matrix represents a 2×2 block in the image sharing. We scan the sharing matrix in raster order. If the bit is scanned as "0", a 2×2 all-zero matrix block is added to the corresponding restored image share block. If the bit is scanned as "1", the restored image share block remains unchanged. Then repeat the above steps to restore all the images not less than t shares collected. Finally, we can reconstruct the complete private information through Eq. 6.

2.3.2 Encrypted Image Shares Combining and Decryption

(1) Combining

The receiver recovers the encrypted image share to a complete encrypted image by the same method as in Sect. 2.3.1(2). The next step is to decrypt the encrypted image.

(2) Decryption

The following is the process of restoring an encrypted image to plain medical image. If the receiving end receives the secret key key_1. A detailed description of the decryption process is shown below.

– **Image block division:** Calculate the size of image block B*B according to $L = min \left\{ \left\lfloor \sqrt{M} \right\rfloor, \left\lfloor \sqrt{N} \right\rfloor \right\}$.
– **Generation of parameters:** According to the secret key key_1, generate a scrambling box which contains two vectors of row and column, linear combination coefficient i, j, rotation angle, matrix Q and mask weight coefficient M.
– **Inverse filtering:** According to the inverse calculation of Eq. 8, the inverse filtering calculation is carried out in the order from right to left and from bottom to top, which is opposite to the order of filtering operation.
– **Inverse normalization:** According to matrix Q and the inverse calculation of matrix Q and Eq. 6, the inverse normalization calculation is carried out.

Repeat the steps 3 and 4 for j times to obtain the result S_i of the i times of block scrambling and rotation.

- **Inverse rotation:** Rotate the image blocks in the opposite direction to the corresponding angle.
- **Inverse crambling:** Place the image block back to the original position according to the row and column vectors in the scrambling box. Repeat steps 5 and 6 for i times to obtain the plain medical image.

3   Experimental Results and Analysis

In the experiment, we use Matlab2016b platform to simulate the encryption and decryption process of the algorithm on a 3.7 GHz desktop computer with 4 GB memory and Microsoft Windows 10 operating system. The test pictures of the experiment are 10 standard grayscale images. In order to demonstrate the universality of our algorithm, we selected 5 pairs of medical images and 5 pairs of conventional images: CT-abdomen (512×512), CT-brain (512×512), Xray-chest (512×512), MRI-knee (512×512), CT-head (512×512), Lena (512×512), Jetplane (512×512), Baboon (512×512), Barbara (512×512) and Peppers (512×512). All the images used in the experiment are listed in [1,2]. The effectiveness of the scheme will be analyzed from two aspects of security analysis and performance analysis.

In the security performance analysis, we will analyze from three aspects: statistical analysis, sharing scheme analysis and secret key test. (1) Statistical analysis is used to show how effective the encryption algorithm is. The experiments include pixel difference analysis, correlation coefficient analysis and imperceptibility analysis. (2) Sharing scheme analysis is used to demonstrate the security and reversibility of the shareing scheme. (3) Secret key test is used to indicate the security level of the encryption algorithm. The experiments include the calculation of secret key space and sensitivity test.

In the performance analysis, we will use PSNR and SSIM indicators, embedding rate analysis and embedding capacity analysis to show the efficiency of encryption, decryption and embedding private information. (1) PSNR and SSIM can indicate the degree of similarity between the encrypted image and the marked encrypted image, as well as their image quality. In addition, the decryption in this paper is separable. The two indexes of PSNR and SSIM can be used to indicate the degree of similarity and image quality between decrypted image and plain image without extracting private information. (2) The embedding rate analysis and embedding capacity analysis are used to show the embedding effect of high frequency region embedding method.

In order to show the overall process and visual effect of the experiment, we used the "CT-abdomen" image to complete the experiment. As shown in Fig. 4, (a) is plain medical image; (b) is its corresponding encrypted result, called encrypted image. (c) is the encrypted image shares. (d) is the encrypted image shares after embedding the secret information shares, called marked encrypted image shares; (e) is the fully recovered image.

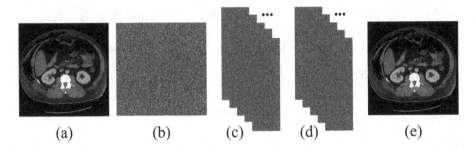

Fig. 4. The simulation results of the proposed algorithm: (a) plain medical image; (b) encrypted image; (c) encrypted image shares; (d) marked encrypted image shares; (e) full recovered image.

3.1 Security Analysis

In this part, we will explain the encryption performance of the proposed algorithm. We will verify the proposed algorithm from two aspects of statistical analysis and the secret key test. Statistical analysis includes pixel difference analysis, correlation coefficient analysis and imperceptibility analysis. Sharing scheme analysis is the influence of share authenticity on share combining. The secret key analysis includes the calculation of the secret key space and sensitivity testing.

3.1.1 Statistical Analysis

(1) Pixel difference analysis

To determine the difference between the images before and after encryption. We introduce the Number of Pixels Change Rate (NPCR) in Eq. 6 and the Unified Average Changing Intensity (UACI) [23] in Eq. 8.

$$\text{NPCR} = \frac{\sum_{i,j} D(i,j)}{W \times H} \times 100\%, \qquad (6)$$

where $NPCR$ calculates the number of pixel differences between two images to determine the difference between the two. $D(i,j)$ represents the difference between the corresponding pixels of the two images, and $D(i,j)$ is defined as:

$$D(i,j) = \begin{cases} 0 & S_1(i,j) \neq S_2(i,j) \\ 1 & S_1(i,j) = S_2(i,j) \end{cases} \qquad (7)$$

where $S_1(i,j)$ and $S_2(i,j)$ are plain image and corresponding encrypted image, respectively.

$$\text{UACI} = \frac{1}{W \times H} \left| \sum_{i,j} \frac{|S_1(i,j) - S_2(i,j)|}{255} \right| \times 100\%. \qquad (8)$$

where $UACI$ judges the difference between the two images by evaluating the visual effects of the two images.

The results are shown in Table 1. Both NCPR and UACI are very close to their ideal values of 99.6094% and 33.4635%. This indicates that the encrypted image obtained by the proposed method has a great difference in both the difference of the corresponding original pixel and the visual effect. In addition, different plain images generate different encrypted images. Since the valid information depends on the plain image, an attacker cannot obtain the valid information for decryption by encrypting some special images.

Table 1. Pixel difference analysis between plain image and encrypted image.

Image	[16]		Proposed	
	NPCR (%)	UACI (%)	**NPCR(%)**	**UACI(%)**
Lena	99.6122	30.2145	**99.7141**	**33.4810**
Jetplane	99.5961	29.7220	**99.7081**	**33.5636**
Baboon	99.6078	31.4212	**99.6200**	**33.4527**
Peppers	99.6022	30.1487	**99.6125**	**33.1592**
Barbara	99.6031	32.1046	**99.6257**	**33.5338**
CT-brain	99.4736	30.8489	**99.6413**	**33.6521**

(2) Correlation coefficient analysis

In order to test the effect of the encryption algorithm adopted in our scheme and the similarity between medical image, encrypted image share and marked encrypted image share, we adopted correlation analysis. In addition, objectively, we introduced the similarity coefficient in Eq. 9 to evaluate the above performance as follows. As an image file, image correlation is an important feature to distinguish an image from other files. There is a strong correlation between adjacent pixels of image data. An excellent encryption algorithm can effectively destroy the strong correlation between adjacent pixels of an image, thus enhancing the ability to resist statistical analysis.

$$C_{xy} = \frac{N\sum_{i=1}^{N}(x_iy_i) - \left(\sum_{i=1}^{N}x_i\right)\left(\sum_{i=1}^{N}y_i\right)}{\left(N\sum_{i=1}^{N}x_i^2 - \left(\sum_{i=1}^{N}x_i\right)^2\right)\left(N\sum_{i=1}^{N}y_i^2 - \left(\sum_{i=1}^{N}y_i\right)^2\right)} \tag{9}$$

where N is the total number of pixels, and x_i and y_i represent the grayscale value of two adjacent pixels.

The specific correlation performance of horizontal, vertical and diagonal directions of each image is shown in Fig. 6, and the corresponding correlation coefficient is shown in Table 2. The absolute value of correlation coefficient is [0,1]. The smaller the similarity coefficient is, the more chaotic the image is.

As shown in Fig. 5, it can be seen that the adjacent pixels of the encrypted image share are all scattered compared to the pixel distribution of the medical image in all three directions. In addition, as shown in Table 2, the correlation coefficient of the medical image of the proposed method is close to 1, and the correlation coefficient of the encrypted image share and the marked encrypted image share is close to 0, which indicates that our encryption algorithm has a good effect of eliminating the correlation between adjacent pixels of the image. Encrypted image share and marked encrypted image share have excellent imperceptibility, which will be analyzed in depth in the next section.

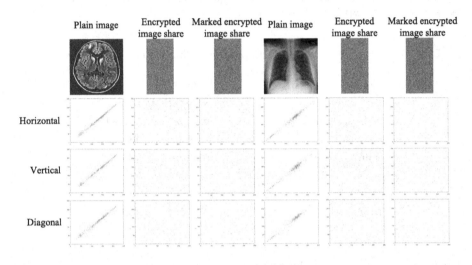

Fig. 5. Correlation analysis: The first line is plain medical image, encrypted image and marked encrypted image. Each column is its corresponding horizontal, vertical and diagonal correlation plots.

Table 2. Correlation coefficients of plain image, encrypted image share and marked encrypted image share.

Image	CT-brain			Xray-chest		
	Plain image	Encrypted image share	Marked encrypted image share	Plain image	Encrypted image share	Marked encrypted image share
Horizontal	0.9756	0.0018	0.0046	0.9767	0.0108	0.0139
Vertical	0.9813	0.0036	0.0029	0.9543	−0.022	−0.0087
Diagonal	0.9658	0.0017	0.0081	0.9356	0.0088	−0.0181

(3) Imperceptibility analysis

In order to further test the security of the proposed method, two indexes, SSIM and PSNR, are introduced to test the similarity between the encrypted image share, marked encrypted image share and plain image, respectively. It can be seen from Table 3 that the PSNR value of both the encrypted image share and the marked encrypted image share is very low, and the SSIM value is close to 0, both of which are lower than the value of the relevant method [10]. The encrypted image share and the marked encrypted image share have visual imperceptibility and have no connection with either plain image. It is difficult to find out the plain image information from them.

Table 3. Comparison of PSNR and SSIM values between encrypted image share, marked encrypted image share and plain image.

Plain image	Encrypted image share				Marked encrypted image share			
	[10]		Proposed		[10]		Proposed	
	PSNR	SSIM	**PSNR**	**SSIM**	PSNR	SSIM	**PSNR**	**SSIM**
Lena	9.2255	0.0341	**9.0158**	**0.0325**	9.2222	0.0351	**9.0042**	**0.0326**
Jetplane	8.0077	0.0346	**7.0150**	**0.0245**	7.9941	0.0359	**6.9981**	**0.0254**
Baboon	9.5108	0.0299	**9.1217**	**0.0126**	9.5182	0.0325	**9.1394**	**0.0250**
CT-head	7.9937	0.0681	**7.2952**	**0.0264**	8.0176	0.0694	**7.3192**	**0.0283**
Xray-chest	6.8839	0.0389	**6.0829**	**0.0267**	6.8838	0.0375	**6.0856**	**0.0201**

Through the above three statistical analysis, it is shown that our proposed scheme has good encryption performance and high security level. There is no risk of privacy disclosure in the process of transmission of encrypted images and marked encrypted images, that is, the possibility of disclosure of patients' medical images and privacy information is greatly reduced.

3.1.2   Sharing Scheme Analysis

In the RDH-EI method based on (t, n) secret sharing, the lossless recovery of plain medical image is established under three conditions: (1) No less than t shares have been collected. (2) Each share used for combining is not maliciously tampered with or faked. (3) The correct secret key. Next, we will prove that the first two conditions are true. The following experiment will be based on the secret sharing mechanism of $(6,8)$. As shown in Fig. 6(b), when we combine five correct shares and one forged share, we combine them. Even if a sufficient number of shares are collected, the result of the reconstructed image is still a failure. At this point, if the medical image cannot be recoverd in the actual application scenario, the receiver will know that the collected share may have been tampered with or information missing. The receiver can then use the extracted additional information to determine the integrity of the share and find the specific attacked server. Finally, find other servers to download the corresponding number of shares according to the number of faulty shares to combine and recover the plain medical image. As shown in Fig. 6(c), when we use six pairs of correct encrypted image shares to combine, then decrypt. The reconstructed image is the same as the plain medical image. It is proved that the (t, n) sharing scheme we use is completely reversible and has high parameter sensitivity. The proposed algorithm has high tamper-proof property and good security performance. The third condition is proved in Sect. 3.1.3(2).

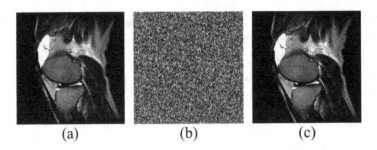

(a)   (b)   (c)

Fig. 6. Sharing scheme analysis: (a) plain medical image; (b) decrypted images generated by sufficient number of shares containing a fake share; (c) decrypted images generated by real and sufficient number of shares.

3.1.3   Secret Key Test

(1)Key space

For a great encryption algorithm, the key space provided should be large enough to make the algorithm resistant to exhaustive attacks. The proposed encryption scheme contains a total of four real numbers and stores them with 64-bit double precision. The secret key space is $24 \times 64 = 2^{256}$, which is larger than the secret key space 2^{100} that an effective encryption system should have as mentioned in literature [4]. Therefore, the secret key space provided by our scheme is large enough to resist all kinds of violent attacks.

(2) Sensitivity test

In order to test the influence degree of the error secret key on the proposed algorithm in the recovery process. An excellent encryption algorithm should be highly sensitive to the secret key in the process of encryption and decryption. A slight change in the secret key will make a huge difference to the result of decryption.

We verify the correctness of the decryption results by a slight change of the secret key by 1-bit. As shown in Fig. 7, the decryption result of the wrong secret key is not correct. Figure 7(a) represents plain medical image; (b) is the result of decryption by randomly changing the encrypted secret keykey_1 by 1-bit; (c) is the result of decryption by randomly changing the embedding secret keykey_2 by 1-bit; (d) is the result of correct decryption. This indicates that the decrypted image has no visual similarity to the plain medical image. Therefore, it is proved that the proposed scheme is sensitive to secret keys and the sharing method has high security.

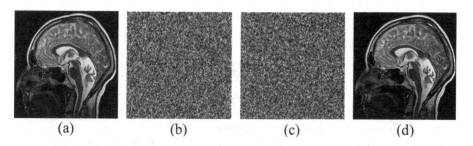

Fig. 7. Key sensitivity analysis: (a) plain medical image; (b)decrypted image obtained by modifying 1-bit key_1; (c) decrypted image obtained by modifying 1-bit key_2; (d) decrypted image with the correct secret key.

3.2 Performance Analysis

The following experiments are still carried out under the setting of sharing mechanism (6,8).

Next, to illustrate the performance of the proposed algorithm. We will verify the proposed algorithm from the following two aspects, including embedding efficiency calculation and visual quality evaluation.

3.2.1 Embedding Efficiency Analysis

Due to the smoothness of each image is different, their embedding rates can vary greatly. The embeddable capacity of a complex textured image is much smaller than that of a smooth textured image. The calculation method of embedding rate is as follows.

$$ER = EC/(M \times N) \qquad (10)$$

Where EC represents the number of bits that can be embedded in pixels and M, N are the length and height of the plain image.

Due to the proposed scheme is that the content owner embed n private information shares into n encrypted image shares respectively. The embedding method is the same, and there is no essential difference between image shares. Therefore, when we calculate the embedding capacity, we only measure the results of one group, and then multiply by n to obtain the embedding capacity of the whole encrypted image. Compared with relevant methods [9,12,22], under the same parameter setting, the embedding capacity and embedding rate of the proposed scheme are both higher than those of other methods. Among them, the maximum embedding capacity is 520251bits, and the corresponding embedding rate is 1.9846 bpp. The results in Table 4 show that the proposed method achieves high embedding capacity and embedding rate without embedding overflow. This allows the medical image to be embedded with a large amount of information about patients' privacy information and other additional information.

Table 4. The value of embedding capacity (bits) and embedding rates(bpp).

Image	EC (bits)				ER(bpp)			
	[12]	[22]	[9]	**Proposed**	[12]	[22]	[9]	**Proposed**
Lena	266286	243348	431148	**440087**	1.0158	0.9283	1.6447	**1.6788**
Jetplane	264818	328755	438462	**460089**	1.0102	1.2541	1.6726	**1.7551**
Baboon	120429	125908	254070	**280573**	0.4594	0.4803	0.9692	**1.0703**
CT-abdomen	207277	186280	387711	**520251**	0.7907	0.7106	1.479	**1.9846**
MRI-knee	296485	371825	432931	**458831**	1.1310	1.4184	1.6515	**1.7503**

3.2.2 Visual Quality Assessment

Since our RDH-EI method is separable, the image can be recovered without extracting the private information. Two indexes, PSNR and SSIM, were introduced to evaluate the visual quality of restored images. We set different embedding rates to compare the visual quality of six images, which were directly restored without extracting the private information. As can be seen from Table 5, the overall PSNR and SSIM are both larger in value than relevant methods [16,21,28]. This indicates that, without extracting private information, the restored image is very similar to the plain medical image visually with almost no discernible difference and is readable by the proposed method. It also makes it easier for the doctor, as the receiver, to see the medical image of the patient without having to extract the privacy information. Thus have some preliminary judgment to the patient's condition.

Table 5. Comparison of plain image with decrypted image without extracting the secret information.

Image	Embedding rate	[21]		[28]		[16]		Proposed	
		PSNR	SSIM	PSNR	SSIM	PSNR	SSIM	**PSNR**	SSIM
Lena	0.0192	55.17	0.9845	58.4300	0.9951	61.28	0.9976	**64.11**	0.9968
	0.0347	55.07	0.9830	56.5800	0.9914	59.24	0.9921	**63.02**	**0.9926**
	0.0964	51.47	0.9773	49.4100	0.9810	52.71	0.9835	**55.97**	**0.9871**
	0.1539	40.31	0.9514	45.8800	0.9709	49.18	0.9749	**53.92**	**0.9896**
Jetplane	0.0183	56.17	0.9759	57.3400	0.9859	59.87	0.9867	**66.09**	**0.9817**
	0.0324	52.37	0.9751	55.2900	0.9844	57.61	0.9844	**64.91**	**0.9893**
	0.0747	51.03	0.9734	51.1700	0.9835	52.42	0.9835	**61.03**	**0.9872**
	0.1369	47.23	0.9714	46.0500	0.9811	47.25	0.9811	**55.62**	**0.9909**
Baboon	0.0153	54.59	0.9825	55.2700	0.9654	57.62	0.9831	**63.67**	**0.9895**
	0.0321	52.82	0.9806	52.4500	0.9611	55.17	0.9810	**62.80**	**0.9849**
	0.0478	50.46	0.9797	50.4700	0.9581	51.97	0.9581	**57.84**	**0.9859**
	0.0644	48.47	0.9785	48.6500	0.9522	49.04	0.9522	**52.13**	0.9778

(continued)

Table 5. (*continued*)

Image	Embedding rate	[21] PSNR	[21] SSIM	[28] PSNR	[28] SSIM	[16] PSNR	[16] SSIM	Proposed PSNR	Proposed SSIM
Peppers	0.0190	54.35	0.9831	57.8700	0.9862	60.75	0.9859	**64.49**	0.9846
	0.0337	53.54	0.9825	55.7300	0.9857	58.41	0.9857	**62.41**	**0.9871**
	0.0952	49.71	0.9754	49.6500	0.9813	51.75	0.9834	**60.95**	**0.9867**
	0.1514	45.26	0.9647	47.2000	0.9798	48.94	0.9798	**58.42**	**0.9883**
Barbara	0.0196	56.41	0.9845	58.1700	0.9854	60.74	0.9895	**64.37**	0.9883
	0.0487	53.51	0.9814	54.3100	0.9812	56.57	0.9887	**62.35**	**0.9940**
	0.1035	51.74	0.9792	49.0300	0.9787	49.03	0.9848	**60.85**	0.9842
	0.1639	48.91	0.9762	46.2700	0.9758	46.27	0.9821	**54.49**	**0.9864**
CT-abdomen	0.0167	57.78	0.9822	57.7400	0.9747	59.94	0.9845	**64.31**	**0.9875**
	0.0393	56.26	0.9786	56.2500	0.9733	57.84	0.9824	**61.95**	**0.9881**
	0.1159	48.45	0.9771	48.6700	0.9658	50.04	0.9793	**57.14**	**0.9808**
	0.1541	47.88	0.9744	46.4100	0.9647	46.41	0.9647	**54.75**	**0.9893**

4   Conclusion

This paper proposed a privacy-preserving medical image scheme based on secret sharing and reversible data hiding. It can be seen from the experimental results that (1) compared with single server storage, the security of medical image and patients' privacy information storage is greatly improved. Even if $(n - t)$ servers are attacked, plain medical images and private information can still be recovered. (2) The scheme successfully protects privacy information. There is almost no correlation between the marked encrypted image containing privacy information and the medical image, and it cannot reveal any privacy information from the appearance. (3) The sharing scheme is highly tamper-proof. When a share is modified or corrupted, additional information can be used to verify the integrity of the share and identify the specific server that was attacked. In the future, we aim to improve the embedding method to improve the embedding capacity and visual quality.

References

1. Related Medical Images of the Experiments. https://openi.nlm.nih.gov/
2. Related Images of the Experiments. https://decsai.ugr.es/cvg/dbimagenes/
3. How to share a secret. Commun. ACM **22**(11), 612–613 (1979)
4. Gonzalo, A., Li, S: Some basic cryptographic requirements for chaos-based cryptosystems. Int. J. Bifurc. Chaos Appl. Sci. Eng. **16**, 2129–2151 (2006)
5. Bao, L., Yi, S., Zhou, Y.: Combination of sharing matrix and image encryption for lossless (k, n)-secret image sharing. IEEE Trans. Image Proces. **26**(12), 5618–5631 (2017). https://doi.org/10.1109/TIP.2017.2738561
6. Calderbank, A., Daubechies, I., Sweldens, W., Yeo, B.L.: Wavelet transforms that map integers to integers. Appl. Comput. Harmon. Anal. **5**(3), 332–369 (1998). https://doi.org/10.1006/acha.1997.0238

7. Chao, K.Y., Lin, J.C.: Secret image sharing: a Boolean-operations-based approach combining benefits of polynomial-based and fast approaches. Int. J. Pattern Recogn. Artif. Intell. **23**, 263–285 (2009)
8. Chen, F., Yuan, Y., He, H., Tian, M., Tai, H.M.: Multi-MSB compression based reversible data hiding scheme in encrypted images. IEEE Trans. Circ. Syst. Video Technol. **31**(3), 905–916 (2021). https://doi.org/10.1109/TCSVT.2020.2992817
9. Chen, Y.C., Hung, T.H., Hsieh, S.H., Shiu, C.W.: A new reversible data hiding in encrypted image based on multi-secret sharing and lightweight cryptographic algorithms. IEEE Trans. Inf. Forensics Secur. **14**(12), 3332–3343 (2019). https://doi.org/10.1109/TIFS.2019.2914557
10. Ghebleh, M., Kanso, A.: A novel secret image sharing scheme using large primes. Multimedia Tools and Applications **77**(10), 11903–11923 (2017). https://doi.org/10.1007/s11042-017-4841-4
11. Hua, Z., Zhou, Y.: Design of image cipher using block-based scrambling and image filtering. Inf. Sci. **396**, 97–113 (2017). https://doi.org/10.1016/j.ins.2017.02.036
12. Kanso, A., Ghebleh, M.: An efficient (t, n)-threshold secret image sharing scheme. Multim. Tools Appl. **76**(15) (2017)
13. Kong, P., Fu, D., Li, X., Qin, C.: Reversible data hiding in encrypted medical DICOM image. Multim. Syst. **2**, 1–13 (2021)
14. Lebre, R., Bastio, L., Costa, C.: A cloud-ready architecture for shared medical imaging repository. J. Digit. Imaging **33**, 1487–1498 (2020)
15. Li, P., Liu, Z., Yang, C.N.: A construction method of (t, k, n)-essential secret image sharing scheme. Symmetry **11**(1), 69 (2019)
16. Long, M., Zhao, Y., Zhang, X., Peng, F.: A separable reversible data hiding scheme for encrypted images based on Tromino scrambling and adaptive pixel value ordering. Signal Process. **176** (2020). https://doi.org/10.1016/j.sigpro.2020.107703
17. Purohit, B., Singh, P.P.: Data leakage analysis on cloud computing. Int. J. Eng. Res. Appl. 3, 1311–1316 (2013)
18. Tian, J.: Reversible data embedding using a difference expansion. IEEE Trans. Circ. Syst. Video Technol. **13**(8), 890–896 (2003). https://doi.org/10.1109/TCSVT.2003.815962
19. Vincent, J., Pan, W., Coatrieux, G.: Privacy protection and security in ehealth cloud platform for medical image sharing. In: 2016 2nd International Conference on Advanced Technologies for Signal and Image Processing (ATSIP), pp. 93–96 (2016). https://doi.org/10.1109/ATSIP.2016.7523054
20. Wang, X., Jin, Z.: An overview of mobile cloud computing for pervasive healthcare. IEEE Access **7**, 66774–66791 (2019). https://doi.org/10.1109/ACCESS.2019.2917701
21. Wu, K.S., Lo, T.M.: An efficient secret image sharing scheme. Appl. Mech. Mater. **284–287**, 3025–3029 (2013)
22. Wu, X., Weng, J., Yan, W.: Adopting secret sharing for reversible data hiding in encrypted images. Signal Process. **143**, 269–281 (2018). https://doi.org/10.1016/j.sigpro.2017.09.017
23. Wu, Y., Noonan, J.P., Agaian, S.: NPCR and UACI randomness tests for image encryption. Cyber J. Multidipl. Sci. Technol. Select. Areas in Telecommun. (2011)
24. Yang, Y., Xiao, X., Cai, X., Zhang, W.: A secure and high visual-quality framework for medical images by contrast-enhancement reversible data hiding and homomorphic encryption. IEEE Access **7**, 96900–96911 (2019). https://doi.org/10.1109/ACCESS.2019.2929298

25. Yang, Y., Xiao, X., Cai, X., Zhang, W.: A secure and privacy-preserving technique based on contrast-enhancement reversible data hiding and plaintext encryption for medical images. IEEE Signal Process. Lett. **27**, 256–260 (2020). https://doi.org/10.1109/LSP.2020.2965826
26. Yu, F., Gong, X., Li, H., Wang, S.: Differential cryptanalysis of image cipher using block-based scrambling and image filtering. Inform. Sci. **554**, 145–156 (2021). https://doi.org/10.1016/j.ins.2020.12.037
27. Yu, K., Tan, L., Shang, X., Huang, J., Srivastava, G., Chatterjee, P.: Efficient and privacy-preserving medical research support platform against covid-19: A blockchain-based approach. IEEE Consum. Electr. Mag. **10**(2), 111–120 (2021). https://doi.org/10.1109/MCE.2020.3035520
28. Zhou, J., Sun, W., Dong, L., Liu, X., Au, O.C., Tang, Y.Y.: Secure reversible image data hiding over encrypted domain via key modulation. IEEE Trans. Circ. Syst. Video Technol. **26**(3), 441–452 (2016). https://doi.org/10.1109/TCSVT.2015.2416591
29. Zhou, L., Varadharajan, V., Hitchens, M.: Achieving secure role-based access control on encrypted data in cloud storage. IEEE Trans. Inf. Forensics Secur. **8**(12), 1947–1960 (2013). https://doi.org/10.1109/TIFS.2013.2286456

Correlation Power Analysis and Protected Implementation on Block Cipher RainDrop

Zhixuan Gao[1], Shuang Wang[2], Yaoling Ding[3], An Wang[3(✉)], and Qingjun Yuan[4(✉)]

[1] School of Cyber Science and Technology, Shandong University, Shandong, China
[2] School of Computer Science, Beijing Institute of Technology, Beijing, China
[3] School of Cyberspace Science and Technology,
Beijing Institute of Technology, Beijing 100081, China
`{dyl19,wanganl}@bit.edu.cn`
[4] Henan Key Laboratory of Network Cryptography Technology, Zhengzhou 450001, China

Abstract. RainDrop is a lightweight block cipher algorithm proposed in 2019. Even though RainDrop proved to be resistant to classical cipher analysis such as differential analysis and liner analysis, little effort has been made to assess its implementation security of side-channel analysis. In this paper, we first give correlation power analysis on RainDrop and a method to recover the main key by using the round key. And we validate their effect via experiments. Then, we propose a masking scheme against correlation power analysis for RainDrop. The experiment result shows that the protected RainDrop only costs 1.1%, 20.8%, 136.8% of extra time, code and RAM.

Keywords: Lightweight block cipher algorithm · RainDrop · Side-channel analysis · Correlation power analysis · Mask

1 Introduction

The study of block cipher began in the mid-1970s, and has a history of more than 40 years till now. The National Institute of Standards and Technology (NIST) adopted the DES algorithm as a federal information processing standard in 1977. With in-depth research on the DES algorithm, differential analysis and liner analysis have been proposed one after another. The security of the DES was greatly reduced, and new cryptographic algorithms were terribly needed. Until 1997, NIST publicly solicited cryptographic algorithm which set off a new upsurge in block cipher algorithms' research once again. Ultimately, NIST published the advanced encryption standard AES, which has become one of the main cryptographic algorithms today, in 2021.

Up to now, block cipher algorithms have been constantly improving and many innovative and more secure algorithms have been proposed one after another, like Simon [1], Midori [2], etc. This also makes block cipher algorithms still widely used in today's society [3]. There are three main structures of common block cipher algorithms: Feistel, SPN and Lai-Massey. Each of them has its unique properties. For instance, Feistel has

C. Cao et al. (Eds.): FCS 2021, CCIS 1558, pp. 308–323, 2022.
https://doi.org/10.1007/978-981-19-0523-0_20

the characteristics of consistent encryption and decryption so it can simplify procedures and reduce the number of codes and transmission routes by almost half.

In recent years, with the rapid development of mobile devices, the application of microcomputing equipment is becoming more widespread [4]. While bringing convenience to our life, how to ensure the security of information has also become a hot topic [5]. Because of the limit of microcomputing equipment, traditional block cipher algorithm can't meet the needs of these equipment well. Thus, lightweight cipher algorithms that pursue both efficiency and security have emerged. Compared with traditional block cipher algorithms, lightweight cipher algorithms have less data, simpler implementation and lower power consumption. Representatives of these cryptography algorithms are SKINNY [6], SPECK [1], etc.

However, the development of technology brings not only the advancement of cryptography algorithms, but also the improvement of attack methods. Side-channel analysis is the product of technology. Nowadays, a lot of commercial cryptographic products are being threatened by side-channel analysis [7], especially for lightweight block cipher algorithms which are limited in resources such as SKINNY [8]. Therefore, the lightweight implementation of side-channel analysis protection has become a hot topic in the industry [9].

RainDrop is a lightweight block cipher algorithm which was just proposed in 2019 [10]. Its structure adopts the Feistel to keep the encryption and decryption consistent and reduce the resource consumption of hardware. In the encryption process, it uses a relatively simple round function to ensure the efficiency of implementation on hardware. Though RainDrop can resist differential analysis [11], liner analysis [12] and impossible differential analysis [13] effectively, it cannot resist side-channel analysis.

In this paper, we propose a correlation power analysis method on RainDrop and give experiments to verify its efficiency [14]. Correspondingly, we propose a countermeasure against this analysis on RainDrop.

The organization of this paper is as follows. Section 2 gives a specification of RainDrop and Correlation Power Analysis (CPA); Sect. 3 introduces the method of CPA on RainDrop; Sect. 4 we implement RainDrop on STC89C52 MCU and show our experimental process and results about CPA on RainDrop; Sect. 5 we present a mask countermeasure against CPA on RainDrop and show our experimental results on protected RainDrop; Sect. 6 concludes the whole paper.

2 Preliminaries

2.1 Specification of RainDrop

Encryption Process. RainDrop has three versions, i.e., RainDrop-128/128/60, RainDrop-128/256/80, and RainDrop-256/256/100. Among them, the front number represents the block length, the middle number represents the length of the main key, and the last number represents the number of encryption rounds. In this paper, we choose RainDrop-128/128/60 as example.

RainDrop adopts Feistel and its round function includes S-Box, MixRows and ShiftColumns. The round function and encryption process are shown in Fig. 1.

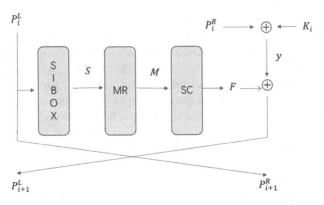

Fig. 1. The round function and intermediate encryption process

During encryption, the input P_i^L of round function is 64 bits. We use a 4 × 4 state matrix IN to represent the 64-bit input. When receiving a 64-bit plaintext $p = p_0 \| p_1 \| \ldots \| p_{14} \| p_{15}$, we set $IN_i = p_i$ for $0 \le i \le 15$:

$$IN = \begin{pmatrix} p_0 & p_4 & p_8 & p_{12} \\ p_1 & p_5 & p_9 & p_{13} \\ p_2 & p_6 & p_{10} & p_{14} \\ p_3 & p_7 & p_{11} & p_{15} \end{pmatrix}.$$

Among them, the length of p_i is specified as follows: $|p_i| = 3$ when i is even and $|p_i| = 5$ when i is odd.

The structure of S-Box uses the Boolean expression of the non-liner operation in the Keccak function and the length of output depends on the length of the input. Suppose that S-box inputs are $(x_0, x_1 \ldots \ldots x_k)$, and outputs are $(y_0, y_1 \ldots \ldots y_k)$. Then the input x_i and output y_i satisfy the following relationship:

$$y_i = x_i \oplus \left(\sim x_{(i-1) \bmod k} \right) \& x_{(i-2) \bmod k}.$$

According to this relationship, we can build a 256-byte S-Box input and output table: use the 8-bit data consist of $p_i \| p_{i+1} (0 \le i \le 14, i$ is even$)$ as the input of this table. The corresponding output of this table is 8-bit y_i. The first three bits of y_i are the output of p_i through S-Box. And the last five bits are the output of p_{i+1} through S-Box. Because the input length of the table is 8 bits, so there are 256 kinds of inputs. So, the size of the S-Box table is 256 bytes.

RainDrop uses a matrix M in MixRows as follows:

$$M = \begin{pmatrix} 0 & 0 & 1 & 1 \\ 1 & 0 & 0 & 1 \\ 0 & 1 & 0 & 0 \\ 1 & 1 & 0 & 0 \end{pmatrix}.$$

Right multiply the internal state matrix by matrix M and get a result:

$$\begin{pmatrix} p_0 & p_4 & p_8 & p_{12} \\ p_1 & p_5 & p_9 & p_{13} \\ p_2 & p_6 & p_{10} & p_{14} \\ p_3 & p_7 & p_{11} & p_{15} \end{pmatrix} \times \begin{pmatrix} 0 & 0 & 1 & 1 \\ 1 & 0 & 0 & 1 \\ 0 & 1 & 0 & 0 \\ 1 & 1 & 0 & 0 \end{pmatrix} = \begin{pmatrix} p_4 \oplus p_{12} & p_8 \oplus p_{12} & p_0 & p_0 \oplus p_4 \\ p_5 \oplus p_{13} & p_9 \oplus p_{13} & p_1 & p_1 \oplus p_5 \\ p_6 \oplus p_{14} & p_{10} \oplus p_{14} & p_2 & p_2 \oplus p_6 \\ p_7 \oplus p_{15} & p_{11} \oplus p_{15} & p_3 & p_3 \oplus p_7 \end{pmatrix}.$$

We denote the cascade value of the i-th column in state matrix $Col_i = p_{4i}\|p_{4i+1}\|p_{4i+2}\|p_{4i+3}$ $(0 \le i \le 3)$. In ShiftColumns, Col_0 don't move, Col_1 left cyclic shift 6 bits, Col_2 left cyclic shift 7 bits and Col_3 left cyclic shift 12 bits.

Key Generation Algorithm. The length of the main key of RainDrop is 128 bits. The length of round keys that each round of encryption uses is 64 bits. For RainDrop-128/128, we need to generate 60 round keys. First, we assign the 128-bit main key MK to the key state TK_1. Then, generate each key state TK_r using the method shown in Fig. 2. R represents the round number for $2 \le R \le 60$.

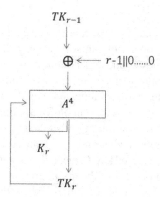

Fig. 2. The key generation algorithm of RainDrop-128/128

In Fig. 2, $r - 1\|0......0$ is the round constant used in the key generation algorithm. $0......0$ represents 64-bit '0'. A^4 represents executing function A four times. Before executing function A, divide the 128-bit key state TK_r into eight groups and the length of each group is 16 bits.

$$TK_r = TK_r^0 \left\| TK_r^1 \right\| TK_r^2 \left\| TK_r^3 \right\| TK_r^4 \left\| TK_r^5 \right\| TK_r^6 \left\| TK_r^7 \right. .$$

The specific execution process of function A is shown in Fig. 3.

The last step of function A is to let the 128-bit temporary state do left cyclic shift 5 bits. The 64-bit round key K_r of the r-th round is the first 64 bits of TK_r, which is denoted by $TK [0:63]$.

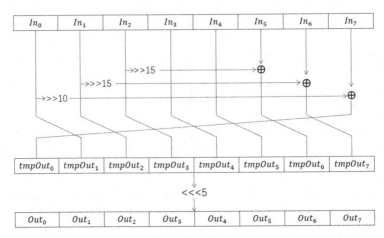

Fig. 3. Function A

2.2 Correlation Power Analysis

The core idea of side-channel analysis is to capture and analyze various physical leakage emitted during cryptographic operations in software and hardware, so as to crack the key [15]. This leakage includes sounds, radiation, power consumption, etc. Because this leakage is related to the intermediate process involving the key, so we can use this information to recover the intermediate value and then derive the main key. This paper mainly discusses CPA and its implementation on RainDrop.

CPA is generally divided into two stages: trace acquisition and key recovery. First, choose an appropriate point as the analysis point. Let the cryptographic device encrypt N times with different plaintext and fixed key. Collect the instantaneous power consumption emitted during the encryption process of the cryptographic device to plot power traces.

Afterwards, iterate over all possible key values and use these guessed keys to encrypt those plaintexts mentioned above. Then we can get a list of intermediate values. At last, calculate the correlation coefficient of the Hamming weight of intermediate value and real power consumption. The larger the correlation coefficient, the more likely the key is to be the correct key. Find whose correlation coefficient is the biggest and that is the fixed key in the device.

3 Correlation Power Analysis on RainDrop

3.1 Recover the Subkey of Round 1

Before introducing CPA, we must first introduce an important concept: Hamming weight (HW). The definition of Hamming weight is the number of bits 1 in a string of data. Hamming weight has a certain degree of relationship with the real power consumption emitted during encryption. Collect the power consumption of the cryptographic device during encryption and plot the power trace. The value of the power trace at the designated abscissa position x and the Hamming weight $HW(x)$ of x have the following liner relationship:

$$T = aHW(x) + b.$$

According to this property, we can calculate the correlation coefficient of any data's Hamming weight and its value in the power trace. When the correlation coefficient is high, it means data x has something to do with the calculation at this point in the power trace.

Now, we can introduce our strategy for the correlation power analysis. We choose the point where plaintext P_i^R is XORed to the round key K_i, shown in in Fig. 4, $y = P_i^R \oplus K_i$.

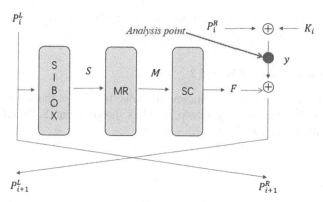

Fig. 4. The point that we use to analyze in the encryption process of RainDrop

Due to the design of RainDrop, the round key K_0 is the left half of the main key MK, which is MK [0:63]. So, if we recover the round key K_0, then we recover half of the main key. The reason why we choose this point is that it involves the XOR operation of the round key. So, the leakage information here is directly related to the round key. Considering the implementation of correlation power analysis in reality, we should reduce the time and resources we spent. So, our analysis is implemented in bytes. Now we take the first byte of the round key (set to k) as an example to describe our analysis procedures as follows:

(1) First, we select n groups of plaintexts randomly.
(2) Secondly, we use the device to execute RainDrop with its fixed key and plaintexts we selected in procedure (1). The encryption process of n groups of plaintexts will generate n power traces, denoted as $P_1, P_2 ...... P_n$.
(3) Afterwards, guess the secret key k from 0 to 255:

a. Execute RainDrop with the guessed key to encrypt n groups of plaintexts and get n groups of y, denote as $y_0', y_1', ... y_n'$.. Record their Hamming weight as $HW(y_i')$.

b. For the power trace i, record the value of its point whose abscissa is x as T_i^x. For every abscissa x of n groups of traces, there are n groups of T_i^x. Use n groups of $HW(y_i')$ and n groups of trace points T_i^x to compute correlation coefficient, denoted as C_i:

$$C_i = \frac{\sum_1^n \left[(HW_i - \overline{HW})(T_i^x - \overline{T^x}) \right]}{\sqrt{\sum_1^n (HW_i - \overline{HW})^2} \sqrt{\sum_1^n (T_i^x - \overline{T^x})^2}}.$$

c. Calculate the average value of C_i, denoted as $\overline{C_k}$.

(4) Finally, the key whose correlation coefficient is the biggest one is regarded as the correct key.

After performing the above operations on the 8 bytes of the round key K_0, we can recover K_0.

3.2 Recover the Subkey of Round 2

Then, we can use the strategy we introduced above to analyze the same point in the second round of encryption of RainDrop, which is shown in Fig. 5. Therefore, we can recover the 8 bytes of the round key K_1.

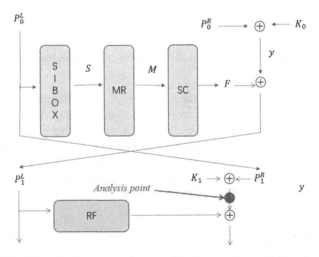

Fig. 5. The point that we use to analyze in the second round of encryption

This intermediate value of the point that we use to analyze is also set to y_i. Because the right half of the input P_1^R in the second round of encryption is the left half of the input P_0^L in the first round of encryption. So, we can use P_0^L as the plaintext of our analysis. The analysis strategy we use in the second round is the same with that in the first round. But the key we use to encrypt is K_1 and the plaintext is P_0^L.

3.3   Recover the Main Key of RainDrop

After recovering the round key K_0, we have recovered the first 8 bytes of the main key MK. The round key K_1 is the first half of the key state TK_2. Use function A to push back the key state TK_2. After performing A^{-1} four times, we can derive partial information of the key state TK_1, which is the information of MK. The reverse derivation process is shown in Fig. 6. Those bits in the red lines are the known part.

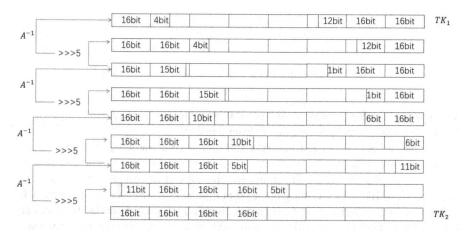

Fig. 6. The process of deriving key state TK_1 from the key state TK_2

It is shown in Fig. 6 that we can use the round key K_1 to derive the last 44 bits of the main key reversely. Then, the unknown part of MK is only 20 bits left. We can use exhaustive attack method for these 20 bits and then the main key MK is retrieved.

4   Experimental Process and Result

We use the MathMagic side-channel analyzer as our experimental device and implement RainDrop as C codes on its STC89C52 MCU.

Before we started our experiment, we selected a fixed key:

$$key = 0x112233445566778899AABBCCDDEEFF00.$$

This key is seen as the key device carried, which is the main key MK. In real analysis, the main key is unknown. This key was just to verify the result of our experiment. So, we assumed that the real key is unknown.

We chose the point we mentioned in Sect. 3.3 to analyze and set the trigger signal in front of this point (see Fig. 7). Because there are 8-byte plaintext P_0^R and key K_0 doing XOR operation in this point, so we collected power traces of 8-byte data separately. Because each byte of the key uses the same operation to recover, so we take the experiment of recovering the first byte of K_0 (set to k_0) as an example to introduce our experiment. We first selected 100 groups of plaintexts randomly. Then we used the

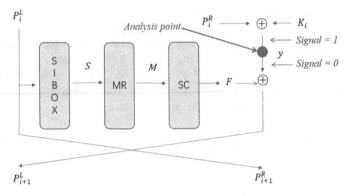

Fig. 7. The position of the trigger signal to open and close

device to encrypt these plaintexts and get 100 power traces, denoted as $P_1, P_2 \ldots \ldots P_{100}$. Then, we guessed every possible key k_i from 0 to 255.

Use every guessed key k_i to encrypt 100 groups of plaintexts and get 100 groups of intermediate values y_i. Use the method we introduced in Sect. 3.1 to calculate the correlation coefficients of the Hamming weight $HW(y_i)$ of 100 groups of y_i and 100 groups of T_i in 100 traces. If the leakage point is already known, we can use mean CPA to analyze: Find 100 groups of T_i whose abscissa is the leakage point in 100 traces and calculate their correlation coefficients with 100 groups of y_i and then get the mean C_j which is the correlation coefficient of the key we used to encrypt; If the leakage point is not known, then we need to use direct CPA: Use 100 groups of y_i to calculate correlation coefficients with each groups of T_i in 100 traces and get the mean C_j. Then we choose the biggest one as the correlation coefficient of the key we used to encrypt.

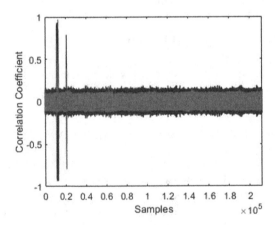

Fig. 8. Direct CPA result

After every guessed key doing the operation above, choose the key whose correlation coefficient is the biggest as the result of our analysis. For k_0, the result of direct CPA is presented in Fig. 8. The horizontal axis is the number of sampling points, the vertical axis is the correlation coefficient, the red line represents the correlation coefficient of the correct key, and the blue line represents the correlation coefficient of the wrong key.

In our experiment, we successfully recovered all 8 bytes of K_0 by mean CPA (see Fig. 9). The horizontal axis is the guessed key, the vertical axis is the correlation coefficient, and the correct key is shown in the figure.

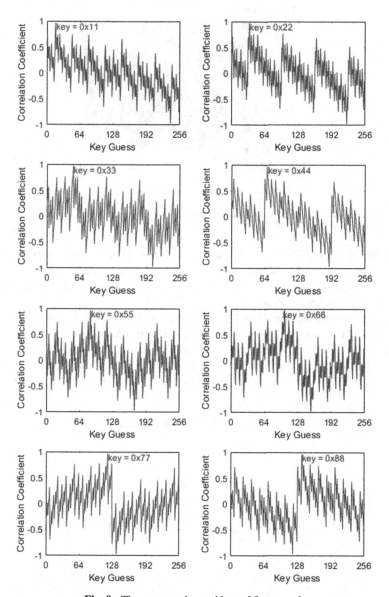

Fig. 9. The recovered round key of first round

Besides, we got the efficiency of CPA. It can let us know how many traces we need to recover the key. The efficiency of recovering the first byte of K_0 is shown in Fig. 10. The horizontal axis is the trace number, the vertical axis is the correlation coefficient, the red line represents the correlation coefficient of the correct key, and the blue line represents the correlation coefficient of the wrong key.

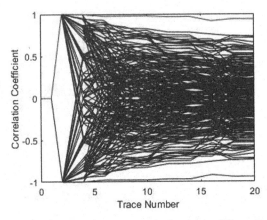

Fig. 10. The efficiency of recovering the first byte of K_0 on RainDrop

According to Fig. 10 we can see that when we select six or more traces to analyze, the correlation coefficients between the correct key and the wrong keys have significant difference. Through the CPA efficiency analysis, we can accurately assess the difficulty of key recovery under this platform.

After recovering the round key K_0, we used mean CPA to recover the round key K_1 of RainDrop. The first two bytes of the recovered round key K_1 and the efficiency of recovering the first byte of the round key K_1 are shown in Fig. 11 and Fig. 12.

After recovering the round keys of the first and second round, use the method we introduced in Sect. 3.3 to recover the main key. The main key MK we recovered is as follows:

$$MK = 0x112233445566778899AABBCCDDEEFF00.$$

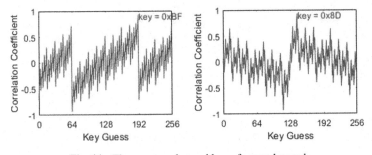

Fig. 11. The recovered round key of second round

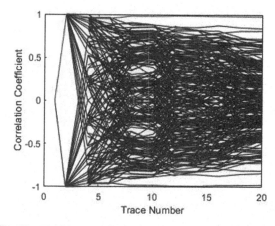

Fig. 12. The efficiency of CPA in second round on RainDrop

5 RainDrop Countermeasure Against Correlation Power Analysis

We have talked about the implementation of the correlation power analysis in the above sections. In this section, we introduce the countermeasure against correlation power analysis using mask.

If we want to protect algorithms from side-channel analysis, we need to make the energy consumed by encryption devices don't depend on the intermediate value y of the algorithm. The masking method can achieve this goal very well. Mask is a random sting of 0 or 1 which has the same length with the data we want to hide. Masking method can hide the true value of the intermediate value y by doing operation like XOR to randomize y during encryption process.

Mask is generated by the random number generator in the device. Normally, the entire encryption process only generates two masks m and w. These masks will be used repeatedly in every round. We can save a lot of space by doing this. The operations used in the masking scheme are mostly XOR, modulo, or modular multiplication. And the data used to calculate with the mask are usually the round keys, the inputs and outputs of the round function, and the intermediate values performed by the device. Because these data are directly related to the ciphertext, so the ciphertext generated by the masked algorithm is also masked. After finishing the last round of encryption, we need to XOR the masked ciphertext with the mask to recover the original ciphertext. Thus, we can simplify the process of recovering the ciphertext by using the same masks.

The masking scheme used on RainDrop is to add masks for plaintexts and the inputs and outputs of S-Box (see Fig. 13).

First of all, we have to build a masked input and output table of S-Box according to the original input and output table of S-Box. The original input of S-Box is $p_i \| p_{i+1} (0 \le i \le 14, i$ is even) and the relationship between it and the output y_i is:

$$p_i \| p_{i+1} \rightarrow y_i.$$

Now, the relationship between the input and the output of S-Box is changed to:

$$((p_i \| p_{i+1}) \oplus m) \rightarrow (y_i \oplus w).$$

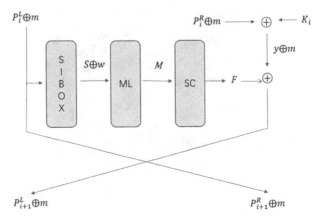

Fig. 13. The round function and encryption process of masked RainDrop

In MixRows, because the input plaintexts will be XORed with each other, and every pair (p_i, p_j) of them are masked with the same masks. So, when they are XORed with each other, the mask will disappear and that will make the plaintexts exposed. Therefore, we take a small measure to make part of the plaintexts $p_i\|p_{i+1}$ (i is even) do the operation as follows:

$$(p_i\|p_{i+1} \oplus m) \oplus w.$$

Then, we change some of those masks from w to m. So, when they calculate with other plaintexts masked with w, the masks won't disappear.

After each round of encryption, we expect that both right and left parts of the input of the next round of encryption still be the plaintexts at the same position in the original algorithm masked with m. Suppose that the intermediate value y is generated by the right part of the input P_i^R and the key K_i using XOR operation and the output of the round function is F. In order to achieve this goal, we need to get $F \oplus y \oplus m$ after the new output F' of the round function calculating with the new intermediate value ($y \oplus m$) using XOR operation. So, we can make the output of the round function become $F \oplus y \oplus m$ by removing the masks of $F' \oplus y \oplus m$. The output of the round function adding masks is:

$$F' = f_0 | f_1 | f_2 | f_3 | f_4 | f_5 | f_6 | f_7.$$

The process of removing the masks is as follows:

$$f_i \oplus m \oplus w(i = 0, 1),$$

$$f_i \oplus ((m \oplus w) <<< 6)(i = 2, 3),$$

$$f_i \oplus ((m \oplus w) <<< 7)(i = 4, 5),$$

$$f_i \oplus ((m \oplus w) <<< 12)(i = 6, 7),$$

Through the above improvements to the round function, we just need to let plaintexts P_0^L, P_0^R XORed with mask m. Then the outputs of the round function are $P_i^L \oplus m$, $P_i^R \oplus m$. After finishing the last round of encryption, we only need to let the outputs C_L, C_R XORed with mask m again and then we can get the correct ciphertext M.

We have implemented the masked RainDrop on STC89C52 MCU and compared the difference between the naive hardware implementation of RainDrop and the hardware implementation of masked RainDrop (see Table 1).

Table 1. Hardware implementation of RainDrop and masked RainDrop

	Unmasked RainDrop	Masked RainDrop	Extra cost
Code	3463B	4403B	20.8%
Time	0.396 s	0.373 s	1.1%
RAM	198 B	483 B	136.8%

In order to test the effectiveness of the masking scheme, we did an experiment using correlation power analysis on masked RainDrop. And its efficiency is shown in Fig. 14.

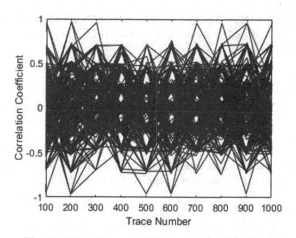

Fig. 14. The efficiency of CPA on masked RainDrop

It can be seen from the figure that traces have been taken to 1000 but the correct key still cannot be separated from the wrong keys, and the correlation coefficient of the correct key changes irregularly. In this way, the masking scheme achieves our expected effect.

6 Conclusion

In this paper, we show that a naive hardware implementation of RainDrop is vulnerable and we give experimental results on correlation power analysis on this implementation of RainDrop. It can be seen that the efficiency of correlation power analysis is very high. Furthermore, we propose a countermeasure against correlation power analysis in which the inputs of the round function are masked. Using this masking scheme, RainDrop can effectively resist correlation power analysis.

Acknowledgement. This work is supported by National Natural Science Foundation of China (Nos. 61872040, 62002021), Beijing Natural Science Foundation (No. 4202070), Henan Key Laboratory of Network Cryptography Technology (No. LNCT2019-A02).

References

1. Beaulieu, R., Shor, D., Smith, J., et al.: The SIMON and SPECK lightweight block ciphers. In: Proceedings of the 52nd Annual Design Automation Conference. ACM. Article No. 175. IEEE, San Francisco (2015)
2. Banik, S., et al.: Midori: a block cipher for low energy. In: Iwata, T., Cheon, J.H. (eds.) ASIACRYPT 2015. LNCS, vol. 9453, pp. 411–436. Springer, Heidelberg (2015). https://doi.org/10.1007/978-3-662-48800-3_17
3. Qu Y., Xiong N.: RFH: a resilient, fault-tolerant and high-efficient replication algorithm for distributed cloud storage. In: the 41st International Conference on Parallel Processing, pp. 520–529 (2012)
4. Fang, W., Yao, X., Zhao, X., Yin, J.: A stochastic control approach to maximize profit on service provisioning for mobile cloudlet platforms. IEEE Trans. Syst. Man Cybern. Syst. **48**(4), 522–534 (2016)
5. Zhang, Q., Zhou, C., Tian, Y.C., Qin, Y., Hu, B.: A fuzzy probability Bayesian network approach for dynamic cybersecurity risk assessment in industrial control systems. IEEE Trans. Ind. Inform. **14**(6), 2497–2506 (2017)
6. Beierle, C., et al.: The SKINNY family of block ciphers and its low-latency variant MANTIS. In: Robshaw, M., Katz, J. (eds.) CRYPTO 2016. LNCS, vol. 9815, pp. 123–153. Springer, Heidelberg (2016). https://doi.org/10.1007/978-3-662-53008-5_5
7. Lisovets, O., Knichel, D., Moos, T., Moradi, A.: Let's take it offline: boosting brute-force attacks on iPhone's user authentication through SCA. In: CHES 2021, Beijing, China (2021)
8. Ge, J., Xu, Y., Liu, R., Si, E., Shang, N., Wang, A.: Power attack and protected implementation on lightweight block cipher SKINNY. In: 13th Asia Joint Conference on Information Security. IEEE, Guilin, China (2018)
9. Shahmirzadi, A.R., Božilov, D., Moradi, A.: New first-order secure AES performance records. In: CHES 2021, Beijing, China (2021)
10. Li, Y.Q., Li, M.Z., Fu, Y., Fan, Y.H., Huang, L.N., Wang, M.Q.: Raindrop: a block cipher designed for hardware. J. Cryptol. Res. **6**(6), 803–814 (2019)
11. Biham, E., Shamir, A.: Differential cryptanalysis of DES-like cryptosystems. In: Menezes, A.J., Vanstone, S.A. (eds.) CRYPTO 1990. LNCS, vol. 537, pp. 2–21. Springer, Heidelberg (1991). https://doi.org/10.1007/3-540-38424-3_1
12. Matsui, M.: Linear cryptanalysis method for DES Cipher. In: Helleseth, T. (ed.) EUROCRYPT 1993. LNCS, vol. 765, pp. 386–397. Springer, Heidelberg (1994). https://doi.org/10.1007/3-540-48285-7_33
13. Biham, E., Biryukov, A., Shamir, A.: Cryptanalysis of skipjack reduced to 31 rounds using impossible differentials. In: Stern, J. (ed.) EUROCRYPT 1999. LNCS, vol. 1592, pp. 12–23. Springer, Heidelberg (1999). https://doi.org/10.1007/3-540-48910-X_2

14. Huang, S., Liu, A., Zhang, S., Wang, T.: BD-VTE: a novel baseline data based verifiable trust evaluation scheme for smart network systems. IEEE Trans. Network Sci. Eng. **8**(3), 2087–2105 (2020)
15. Mangard, S., Oswald, E., Popp, T.: Power Analysis Attacks: Revealing the Secrets of Smart Cards. Springer, Heidelberg (2007). https://doi.org/10.1007/978-0-387-38162-6

Data and Application Security

Research on Security Assessment of Cross Border Data Flow

Wang Na[1,5], Wu Gaofei[2,6], Yue Qiuling[3], Hu Jinglu[4], and Yuqing Zhang[1,3,5(✉)]

[1] Guangzhou Research Institute of Technology, Xidian University, Xi'an, China
zhangyq@nipc.org.cn
[2] Guangxi Key Laboratory of Cryptography and Information Security, Guilin, China
[3] School of Cyberspace Security, Hainan University, Haikou, China
[4] Graduate School of Information, Production and Systems, Waseda University, Honjo, China
[5] National Computer Network Intrusion Prevention Center, University of Chinese Academy of Sciences, Beijing, China
[6] School of Cyber Engineering, Xidian University, Xi'an, China

Abstract. At present, the trend of cross-border data flow is inevitable. Therefore, as the liquidity demand for cross-border data increases, the issues related to national security and the protection of personal data are gradually exposed. Due to the demand and cost problems, the domestic risk assessment only stays in the business scope of the company or enterprise. Even if the data processing process involves the data subject and data controller, the evaluation object is only for the data controller. In order to avoid risks, enterprises will conduct multiple risk assessments on data during the business execution cycle. Therefore, the domestic risk assessment model has the characteristics of a single process and multiple cycles. However, there are differences in use, scope, and characteristics between cross-border data risk assessment and domestic risk assessment. That's why the general evaluation model can't be directly applied to the cross-border process. Therefore, the purpose of this paper is to propose a multi process and multi cycle data security risk assessment model applicable to cross-border data. The two processes of domestic risk assessment and foreign cross-border process assessment are integrated in this article. Therefore, the analysis of risk factors is also based on these two perspectives. In addition, common risk assessment methods such as comprehensive analytic hierarchy process will be used to assess and describe the risk level of data cross-border operations. Then, the risk threshold is calculated, and the wavelet neural network is used to simulate the evaluation process. Ultimately, the prospect of cross-border data can provide references for the development and research of cross-border data in the future.

Keywords: Cross-border data · Risk assessment · Wavelet theory · BP neural network

1 Introduction

1.1 Cross-Border Data Status

The Internet and high-tech information technology are developing rapidly around the world. This not only makes cross-border flow of information possible, but also makes it

© Springer Nature Singapore Pte Ltd. 2022
C. Cao et al. (Eds.): FCS 2021, CCIS 1558, pp. 327–341, 2022.
https://doi.org/10.1007/978-981-19-0523-0_21

the new international normality in the worldwide communication. While cross-border data brings new development opportunities, it also brings new challenges to data security issues. For example, there is no comprehensive method and workflow for the classification and security assessment of personal cross-border data.

Towards cross-border data, there are different attitudes in different countries. Data localization policy is strictly pursued in Russia. The United States minimizes data cross-border restrictions to develop economy and technology. Other countries such as the European Union, Australia, China, and Japan have adopted intermediate methods to restrict cross-border data. It is precisely the rapid development of economy, science and technology that promoted the process of globalization. Due to the rapid increase in demand, the field of cross-border data has gradually become the focus of attention, which has attracted heated discussion from all walks of life.

The risk factors of cross-border data are complex and it involve multiple subjects, so most countries, including China, are on the sidelines. Internet data contains a large amount of sensitive information. Therefore, refusing to allow important data to exit the country can prevent the risk of leakage in the data circulation process. It is also beneficial to prevent events and accidents that threaten social stability and national security. However, banning cross-border data will limit or even stifle the development potential of countries or enterprises. It has a far-reaching impact on important fields such as economy, politics, science and technology.

1.2 Significance of Risk Assessment

As an essential link in the process of maintaining information security, information security risk management covers the whole life cycle of information system from construction to abandonment, which undertakes the work of prediction, identification, analysis, assessment, management and control of risks. It determines the risk factors that may exist in the system and define the degree of harm to the system by the risk through scientific and reasonable analysis methods. Then, the assessor can take appropriate protective measures for the system based on the severity of the risk obtained from the analysis. In addition, improving the level of technology, organization and management can also minimize risks. Certainly, the assessor can control the risk within an acceptable range through security deployment measures, which is beneficial to conduct business more smoothly.

2 Cross-Border Data Risk Influencing Factors Analysis and Evaluation Index System Construction

2.1 Cross-Border Data Risk Assessment Needs and Feasibility Analysis

Unlike ordinary businesses involving data collection and use, the cross-border flow of data involves multiple subjects. The general cross-border process is shown in Fig. 1 [1], including data subjects which is the original owner of data, the initiator and receiver involved in each cross-border. That means the cross-border data flow involves at least three subjects. If data is transmitted across borders among multiple countries, the situation will be more complex and the resulting risks will increase significantly.

The traditional risk management model cannot fully consider all the risk factors of large-scale data transmission and collection. As the key segment of the existing risk management system, risk assessment plays an important role in identifying and controlling risks.

Based on the simplest one-way data cross-border scenario between two countries, this paper systematically analyzes the necessity and feasibility of data cross-border risk assessment. The assessment flow chart is shown in Fig. 2.

First of all, before the cross-border implementation of data (the first stage), companies or organizations may face security issues in every aspect. The collection and storage of massive amounts of data may lead to risk accidents such as information leakage, destruction of information integrity, and informal authorized access. Most companies take information security risk assessment as an important means to avoid the above risks although cross-border processes are not yet involved. They are committed to providing users with the greatest security of personal information through the identification and analysis of assets, threats and related technical vulnerabilities.

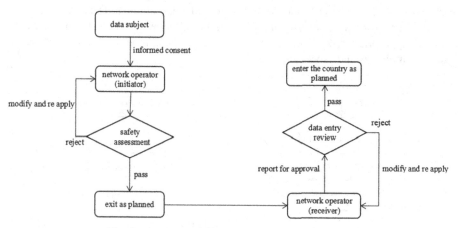

Fig. 1. General flow chart of cross border data flow

However, once data is transferred or accessed across borders, the scope of risk factors will be evidently expanded and complicated compared with the first stage. The importance of data is self-evident under the trend of expanding competition between domestic and foreign companies. This is also the origin of security risks. For example, data is more likely to face the risks of transmission interruption, data interception, tampering and forgery due to long-distance and uncontrollable transmission media in the transmission process. On the other hand, weak links such as diverse bearing media, scattered storage territories and numerous visitors may cause data leakage and other problems in the storage process. Therefore, these are factors that we need to carefully consider before implementing data cross-border. Of course, it is significant to determine the integrity of security measures of data recipients and investigate the purpose of data reception, technical vulnerabilities and management vulnerabilities comprehensively as well. In addition, the differences in the attitudes of countries towards cross-border data will lead to differences in the enforcement of policies and regulations. Therefore, there may be great diversities in the degree of data protection and the accountability mechanism after risk, which must also be included in our investigation. Only by considering the risk factors comprehensively can we reduce the possibility of risk as much as possible.

As for feasibility, in order to achieve cooperation without revealing important and sensitive business information of the company, the two parties can first reach a consensus on the evaluation model through negotiation, and then determine whether the data cross-border activities can be implemented by analyzing the comprehensive evaluation results. If the risk value exceeds the expected value, targeted strategic deployment can be carried out based on the assessment results. What's more, effective practical measures must be taken to control the risk until the risk value is within an acceptable range. Therefore, risk assessment is an indispensable and feasible data information security solution in cross-border data preparation for relevant enterprises or operators.

2.2   Risk Assessment Stage 1-Local Data Collection and Storage

Risk assessment elements include assets, threats and vulnerabilities. The risk assessment elements for information security are shown in Fig. 3 below. We need to consider how to select appropriate risk elements for analysis and calculation according to different assessment objects and processes.

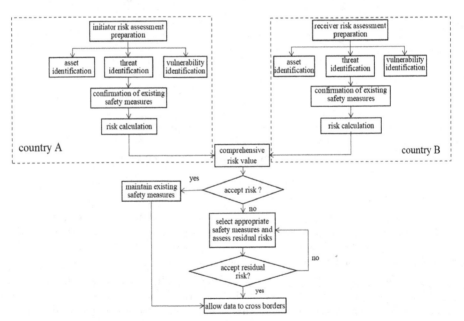

Fig. 2. Flow chart of cross border risk assessment of data

2.2.1   Data Collection Information Security Risk Factor Analysis

The collection and use of personal information of data subjects by operators is the first stage of cross-border data assessment. As an information provider, the data subject obviously does not bear the responsibility for passive disclosure of information in the process of interaction with enterprises or operators. Under the premise of cooperation between the two sides, the enterprise must ensure the accuracy, availability and confidentiality of the data in order to maintain the value of the data and the interests of the data subject. Therefore, besides the security attributes of the data itself, the enterprise's data management level must also be included in the risk assessment.

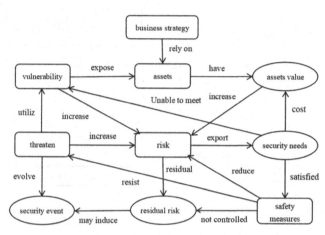

Fig. 3. Risk assessment elements chart

Environmental conditions and employee capabilities are extremely significant in all aspects of data collection, local storage, classification, use, and analysis. This means that both technical and human factors are important causes of threats. Therefore, in the assessment process of first stage, besides evaluating the important security attributes reflecting the value of data assets, the most important thing is to make relevant judgments for the enterprise itself. In short, the technical level, management level, environmental and human factors of the data exporter should be considered at the same time in the risk assessment.

2.2.2   Construction of Risk Assessment Index System

For the analysis of risk factors, based on GB/T 20984–2007 "*Information Security Technology – Information Security Risk Assessment Specification*", we select three basic elements of information security assessment: assets, threats, and vulnerabilities as the evaluation indicators for the first stage, as shown in Fig. 4 below.

2.3   Risk Assessment Stage 2 - Cross-Border Data Use Process

2.3.1   Analysis on Risk Factors of Cross-Border Data Information Security

There is no doubt that the first thing to consider is cross-border data sensitivity. Data from the national government and other important agencies are prohibited from leaving the country according to Chinese current policy. Moreover, different information fields also have different sensitivity levels. For example, ID card numbers and email addresses also have different sensitivity levels within the scope of personal information. Therefore, the sensitivity of data fields must be analyzed and determined before data cross-border.

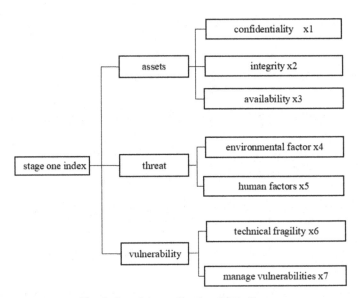

Fig. 4. Local data collection risk indicators

The maturity of big data technology and the increase in data volume are conducive to the analysis of user behavior and habits. On the other hand, it can also help companies improve their technology and data processing capabilities. In addition, when the risk occurs, the larger amount of data is bound to cause wider losses, affect more users, and the enterprise will bear more responsibilities and penalties. Therefore, data magnitude is also a risk factor that cannot be ignored. Besides the value of data assets, cross-border parties need to formulate a plan, which must include the cross-border purpose and the future use of the data (for example, the data will be transmitted to a third party) according to the *"Measures for the Security Evaluation of Personal Information Exiting Borders"* (draft for comments). It is also necessary to judge potential risks based on a series of measures taken on cross-border data. As in the first stage, we still need to investigate the technical and management capabilities of overseas operators. In addition, national policies and laws must also be taken into consideration due to the particularity of cross-border data operations in the current era. The policy intensity and degree of data protection vary among different countries, and the higher the intensity, the risk will be relatively smaller. Finally, for data security incidents that have occurred, rules and systems on how to take corresponding remedial measures must be formulated and perfected. Therefore, risk response capability is also an important reference basis for risk assessment.

2.3.2 Construction of Risk Assessment Index System

Based on the analysis of risk factors, the risk assessment indicators in the data cross-border process stage are established, as shown in Fig. 5.

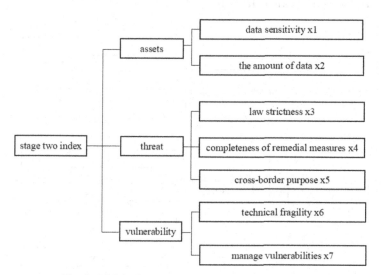

Fig. 5. Risk indicators of data cross border use process

3 Cross-Border Data Security Risk Assessment Model Based on Fuzzy Neural Network

3.1 Analytic Hierarchy Process

Analytic hierarchy process (AHP) is a multi-level objective strategic decision-making analysis method integrating qualitative analysis and quantitative analysis. Its main advantage is that it can comprehensively consider the relationship between various key factors involved in complex decision-making problems in real life [3].

The establishment of risk assessment model by analytic hierarchy process can be generally carried out according to the following steps [3]:

(1) Clarify the evaluation problems, determine the scheme to be evaluated and the evaluation objectives.

(2) Establish the hierarchical structure model of the system after depth analysis of various influencing factors of the system to be evaluated. The structure is shown in Fig. 6 below.

After establishing the hierarchical structure as shown in Fig. 6 below, the membership relationship between the upper and lower layers can be determined. Therefore, the judgment matrix can be constructed through the membership relationship. The purpose is to assign the weight to the factors of the lower layer according to the relative importance under the same determined factor. Normally, the 9-point method proposed by Santy is adopted. The scale is shown in Table 1.

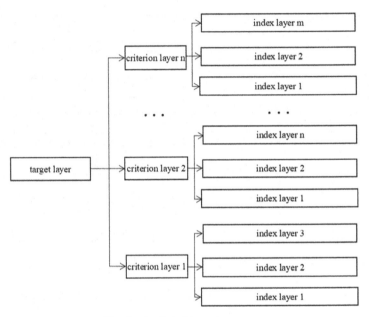

Fig. 6. Analytic hierarchy process

The judgment matrix is shown in the following formula, in which the value of each factor is the value obtained by comparing two elements according to the nine-point method.

$$A = \begin{bmatrix} a11 & a12 & \dots & a1j \\ a21 & a22 & \dots & a2j \\ \dots & \dots & \dots & \dots \\ ai1 & ai2 & \dots & aij \end{bmatrix} \tag{1}$$

(3) Hierarchical ranking and consistency test

The specific operation process is shown in the Table 2.

Table 1. Scale

Importance scale	Meaning
1	Two elements are equally important
3	The former is more important than the latter (slightly)
5	The former is more important than the latter (evidently)
7	The former is more important than the latter (strongly)
9	The former is more important than the latter (extremely)
2, 4, 6, 8	Indicates an intermediate value between the corresponding 1–9 scales
$1/k, k = 1, \cdots 9$	If the relative importance ratio of element X_i to element X_J is A_{ij}, the relative importance ratio of element X_j to element X_i is $A_{ji} = 1 / A_{ij}$

The steps to check the consistency are as follows:

① Calculate the CI value with maximum eigenvalue λ_{max} and order n according to the following formula.

$$CI = (\lambda \, max - n)/(n - 1) \tag{2}$$

② When $n = 1$ or $n = 2$, the judgment matrix has complete consistency; when $n > 2$, the CR value needs to be calculated according to the CI value and the RI value corresponding to the order in Table 3 below. The calculation formula is as follows:

$$CR = CI/RI \tag{3}$$

Table 2. Sorting operation flow

Operation steps	Formula
The elements in judgment matrix A are normalized by column	$\bar{a} = aij / \sum_{i=1}^{n} aij$
The elements in judgment matrix A are added by row	$\overline{wi} = \sum_{j=1}^{n} \overline{aij}(i, j = 1, 2, ..., n)$
The judgment matrix A is normalized again	$wi = \overline{wi} / \sum_{j=1}^{n} \overline{wi}(i, j = 1, 2, ..., n)$
Maximum eigenvalue of judgment matrix A λ_{max}	$\lambda max = \sum_{i=1}^{n} \frac{(Aw)i}{nwi}(i, j = 1, 2, ..., n)$

Then make a judgement according to the CR value. If $CR < 0.10$, the consistency is acceptable, but when $CR > 0.10$, we need to reconstruct a new and more reasonable judgment matrix.

Table 3. RI value table of order judgment matrix

Matrix order	1	2	3	4	5	6	7	8	9
RI value	0	0	0.58	0.90	1.12	1.24	1.32	1.41	1.45

3.2 Fuzzy Evaluation Method

The fuzzy comprehensive evaluation modeling based on analytic hierarchy process can be carried out in the following steps [3].

(1) Determine the domain of influencing factors of the evaluated object, n evaluation factors, $U = \{U_1, U_2,..., U_n\}$.
(2) Establish the evaluation level domain of the evaluated object, $V = \{V1, V2,..., Vm\}$, that is, the evaluation level set. Each set of comment levels is equivalent to a fuzzy subset.
(3) Generate single factor evaluation fuzzy relation matrix R.

We have a single factor evaluation.
$f : U \rightarrow F(V)$, $ui \rightarrow f(ui) = (ri1, ri2, \ldots, rim) \in F(V)$, according to the fuzzy mapping f, we can induce the fuzzy relationship $Rf \in F(U \times V)$, that is, $Rf(ui, vj) = f(ui)(vj) = rij$, it can be expressed by the fuzzy matrix $R \in \mu n \times m$:

$$R = \begin{bmatrix} r11 & r12 & \cdots & r1m \\ r21 & r22 & \cdots & r2m \\ \cdots & \cdots & \cdots & \cdots \\ rn1 & rn2 & \cdots & rnm \end{bmatrix} \tag{4}$$

(4) Determine the weight of the influencing factors of the evaluated object.

In this paper, we use analytic hierarchy process to determine the normalized weight of the factors of the evaluated object.

$$A = (a_1, a_2, ..., a_n), \sum_{i=1}^{n} a_i = 1, a_i \geq 0 \tag{5}$$

(5) Synthetic fuzzy comprehensive evaluation index.

Using appropriate fuzzy operators to synthesize factor weight a and fuzzy matrix R of each evaluated object, the fuzzy comprehensive evaluation index B of each evaluated object is obtained:

$$B = A \circ R = (a_1, a_2, ..., a_n) \begin{bmatrix} r_{11} & r_{12} & \cdots & r_{1m} \\ \cdots & \cdots & \cdots & \cdots \\ r_{n1} & r_{n2} & \cdots & r_{nm} \end{bmatrix} = (b_1, b_2, ..., b_n) \tag{6}$$

Where b_i represents the membership degree of the evaluated object to the fuzzy subset of level v_i as a whole.

(6) Analyze the result vector of fuzzy comprehensive evaluation.

The calculation method of using weighted average to calculate the membership level can effectively use all the evaluation information. So that it can overcome the shortcomings of the "maximum membership principle".

B reflects the evaluation value of the risk factor. Its value is between (0, 1), which can be used as the input of BP neural network.

3.3 The Structure of Wavelet Neural Network

Wavelet neural network mainly refers to the fusion of wavelet theory and BP neural network [4]. The basic structure of wavelet neural network in this paper is shown in the Fig. 7.

The nonlinear function y(t) can be fitted by wavelet functions y, a, b (t) as follows:

$$\hat{y}(t) = \sum_{k=1}^{K} w_k \Psi\left(\frac{t - b_k}{a_k}\right) \qquad (7)$$

In the formula: $\hat{y}(t)$ is the fitting value sequence of nonlinear function y(t); w_k is the connection weight of the kth node of the output layer and the middle layer; K is the number of wavelet bases; b_k and a_k are translation factors and contraction expansion factors.

Wavelet is used as the activation function of hidden layer.

$$\psi(t) = \cos(1.75t)\exp(-\frac{t^2}{2}) \qquad (8)$$

3.4 Training Algorithm of Wavelet Neural Network

BP algorithm is used to train the network in the batch processing mode, and the weight coefficient of wavelet is adjusted in the adopted mode [4].

The training algorithm of wavelet neural network is as follows:

(1) Initialization of network parameters: translation factor b_k, contraction expansion factor a_k, weight w_{ik}, w_k are assigned as random initial values;
(2) Input training sample $x_l(i)$ and expected output y_l, where $l = 1, 2, \ldots\ldots, L$, L is the number of input samples;
(3) Network self-learning: calculate the output of the network $\hat{y}_l$ through the current coefficient;
(4) Forward propagation:

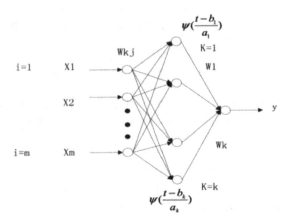

Fig. 7. Wavelet neural network structure

Suppose the number of input layer nodes is m; the number of output layer nodes is 1; w_{ki} is the connection weight between the kth middle layer node and the ith input layer node; w_k is the connection weight between the kth middle layer node and the output layer node.

The input of the kth middle layer is

$$hi_k^l = \sum_{i=1}^{m} w_{ki} x_l(i) \tag{9}$$

The output of the kth middle layer is

$$ho_k^l = \psi\left(\frac{hi_k^l - b_k}{a_k}\right) \tag{10}$$

The input of the lth output layer is

$$oi^l = \sum_{i=1}^{K} w_k ho_k^l \tag{11}$$

The output of the output layer is

$$\hat{y}_l = \frac{1}{1 + \exp(-oi^l)} \tag{12}$$

(The excitation function of the output layer is S-type function).

Assuming that the expected output of sample data L is y_l, the network coefficients can be optimized through the following minimum mean square error energy function [5] to minimize the error of fitting sequence.

$$E = \frac{1}{2} \sum_{l=1}^{L} [y_l - \hat{y}_l]^2 \tag{13}$$

In BP algorithm, the gradient descent method is used to calculate the instantaneous gradient vector.

$$\frac{\partial E}{\partial w_k} = -\sum_{i=1}^{L}(y_l - \hat{y}_l)\hat{y}_l(1 - \hat{y}_l)ho_k^l \tag{14}$$

$$\frac{\partial E}{\partial w_{ki}} = (-\sum_{i=1}^{L}\hat{y}_l w_k x_l(i)(y_l - \hat{y}_l)(1 - \hat{y}_l)(ho_k^l)')/a_k \tag{15}$$

$$\frac{\partial E}{\partial a_k} = (-\sum_{i=1}^{L}\hat{y}_l w_k(y_l - \hat{y}_l)(1 - \hat{y}_l)(ho_k^l)'\frac{hi_k^l - b_k}{a_k})/a_k \tag{16}$$

$$\frac{\partial E}{\partial b_k} = (\sum_{i=1}^{L}\hat{y}_l w_k(y_l - \hat{y}_l)(1 - \hat{y}_l)(ho_k^l)')/a_k \tag{17}$$

(5) Back propagation:

Adjust the learning rate of the weight η, the introduced momentum factor α is less than η in order to avoid the vibration error index function and speed up the convergence of the network.

The calculation and optimization steps of the coefficient are as follows:

$$w_k(n + 1) = w_k(n) - \eta\frac{\partial E}{\partial w_k} + \alpha\Delta w_k(n) \tag{18}$$

$$w_{ki}(n + 1) = w_{ki}(n) - \eta\frac{\partial E}{\partial w_{ki}} + \alpha\Delta w_{ki}(n) \tag{19}$$

$$a_k(n + 1) = a_k(n) - \eta\frac{\partial E}{\partial a_k} + \alpha\Delta a_k(n) \tag{20}$$

$$b_k(n + 1) = b_k(n) - \eta\frac{\partial E}{\partial b_k} + \alpha\Delta b_k(n) \tag{21}$$

In the formula: n is the number of iterations in the network learning process, $\Delta w_k(n)$, $\Delta w_{ki}(n)$, $\Delta a_k(n)$ and $\Delta b_k(n)$ are the changes of iteration weights respectively.

The network learning will stop if the error function value is less than the present value of the model, otherwise go to step 2 until the error value reaches the standard.

4 Summary

Cross-border data is gradually irreplaceable under the trend of globalization. However, the risk problem cannot be easily ignored. The problem of how to better ensure data security in the cross-border data process and achieve a win-win situation among enterprises needs to be solved urgently. The construction and continuous improvement of the entire cross-border data management system is the foundation for ensuring the healthy and stable development of future cross-border data operations. Risk assessment plays an important role in the practical link of predicting and avoiding risks. Combined with the characteristics of data cross-border scenarios, the assessment process is improved on the basis of existing risk assessment research to make it more suitable for the current situation of data cross-border. However, the data cross-border operation is so complex that there are far more factors to be considered than mentioned in the article. Analyzing the cross-border risk of data from a simpler perspective and greatly simplifying the details involved in the cross-border process are just to provide ideas and reference solutions for data cross-border risk assessment. The evaluation methods actually applied in the future need to be improved and supplemented on this basis.

References

1. Yuanshan, W.: On the connotation and principle of cross-border data flow. J. Political Sci. Law **38**(01), 110–122 (2011)
2. Kun, Z.: Research on information security risk assessment based on AHP and BP. Hebei University of Technology, Hebei Province (2016)
3. Xuewei, F.: Research and application of Fuzzy comprehensive Evaluation based on Analytic Hierarchy Process. Harbin Institute of Technology, Heilongjiang (2011). 10.7666/ D.D262385
4. Dongmei, Z., Jinxing, L., Jianfeng, M.: Risk assessment of information security using fuzzy wavelet neural network. J. Huazhong Univ. Sci. Technol. **37**(11), 43–49 (2009)
5. Shuo, D.: The enlightenment of eu legislation on cross-border flow of personal Data to China. Shandong University, Shandong (2018)
6. Monan, Z.: Cross-border data flow: global situation and china's countermeasures. Open Guide **2**, 44–50 (2020)
7. Wenhua, H., Huafeng, K.: Computer applications and software **36**(8), 306–310 (2019) https://doi.org/10.3969/j.issn.1000-386x.2019.08.051
8. Zhang, Y.A.: The enlightenment of foreign cross-border data flow security management measures to China. World Telecom **3**, 76–80 (2016). https://doi.org/10.3969/j.issn.1001-4802.2016.03.013
9. Xiaolei, Z.: Research on governance of cross-border data flow in Japan. Japan J. **4**, 85–108 (2020)
10. Shin, Y.J.: A study on privacy protection tasks for cross-border data transfers. In: 2014 International Conference on IT Convergence and Security, ICITCS 2014, January 23 (2014)
11. Khorev, P., Chernetsov, A.: The problem of ensuring cross-border personal data transfer and methods for its solving. In: 2020 5th International Conference on Information Technologies in Engineering Education, April (2020)
12. Ram, S., Liu, J.: Understanding the Semantics of Data Provenance to Support Active Conceptual Modeling. In: Chen, P.P., Wong, L.Y. (eds) Active Conceptual Modeling of Learning. ACM-L 2006. LNCS, vol. 4512. Springer, Berlin (2007). https://doi.org/10.1007/978-3-540-77503-4_3
13. Luo, Y., Xie, C.: Traceability system construction of agricultural products cross-border e-commerce logistics from the perspective of Blockchain technology. In: Sugumaran, V., Xu, Z., Zhou, H. (eds) Application of Intelligent Systems in Multi-modal Information Analytics. MMIA 2020. AISC, vol. 1233. Springer, Cham (2021). https://doi.org/10.1007/978-3-030-51431-0_16
14. Deng, Q.: Application analysis on Blockchain technology in cross-border payment. In: 5th International Conference on Financial Innovation and Economic Development (2020)

15. Yan, S., Bingzhi, W.: Legislative protection of personal information security in the era of cross-border data flow. Cyberspace Secur. **10**(5), 29–33 (2019)
16. Sibo, F.: Personal data protection in cross-border data Flow. Electr. Intellectual Property **6**, 85–97 (2020)
17. Wenge, Z.: Regulation of Cross-border Flow of Personal Data. Dalian Maritime University, Liaoning (2019)
18. Yanhua, L.: The regulatory path of global cross-border data flow and China's choice. Times law Sci. **17**(5), 106–116 (2019)
19. Yao, X.: Korean path and EU path in cross-border data flow governance. Collection Korean Stud. **2**, 237–249 (2017)
20. Senyu, L.: Research on Information security Risk Assessment Method based on improved Neural Network. China University of Mining and Technology (2018)
21. Standard, B., Standard, N.Z.: Risk Management - Principles and guidelines BS ISO, 31000 (2009)
22. Purdy, G.: ISO 31000:2009—setting a new standard for risk management. Risk Anal. Int. J. **30**(6), 881–886 (2010)
23. Shu-ning, P., Sha, F.: Telecommunication Network Technology 8, 59–63 (2011)
24. Xiaonan, G., Yutang, L., Zhenbo, H., Yan, W.: Application of OCTAVE risk assessment method in e-government extranet. Inf. Secur. Res. **4**(10), 922–927 (2018)
25. Qingyun, G.: A review of the information security risk assessment standards. J. Inf. Secur. **12**(1), 11–25 (2018)

A Review of Data Representation Methods for Vulnerability Mining Using Deep Learning

Ying Li[1,2], Mianxue Gu[1,2], Hongyu Sun[2,3], Yuhao Lin[1,2], Qiuling Yue[1], Zhen Guo[1], Jinglu Hu[4], He Wang[2,3], and Yuqing Zhang[1,2,3(✉)]

[1] School of Cyberspace Security (School of Cryptography), Hainan University, Haikou Hainan 570100, China
zhangyq@nipc.org.cn
[2] National Computer Network Intrusion Protection Center, University of Academy of Sciences, Beijing 101408, China
[3] School of Cyber Engineering, Xidian University, Xi'an 710126, Shaanxi, China
[4] Graduate School of Information, Production and Systems, Waseda University, Shinjuku-ku, Tokyo 169-8050, Japan

Abstract. The rapid development of software has brought unprecedented severe challenges to software security vulnerabilities. Traditional vulnerability mining methods are difficult to apply to large-scale software systems due to drawbacks such as manual inspection, low efficiency, high false positives and high false negatives. Recent research works have attempted to apply deep learning models to vulnerability mining, and have made a good progress in vulnerability mining filed. In this paper, we analyze the deep learning model framework applied to vulnerability mining and summarize its overall workflow and technology. Then, we give a detailed analysis on five feature extraction methods for vulnerability mining, including sequence characterization-based method, abstract syntax tree-based method, graph-based method, text-based method and mixed characterization-based method. In addition, we summarize their advantages and disadvantages from the angles of single and mixed feature extraction method. Finally, we point out the future research trends and prospects.

Keywords: Deep learning · Vulnerability mining · Data representation

1 Introduction

In recent years, with the rapid development of the Internet, the functions of software has brought greater influence. However, the popularization of modern

This work was supported by the Key Research and Development Science and Technology of Hainan Province(ZDYF202012), the National Key Research and Development Program of China(2018YFB0804701), and the National Natural Science Foundation of China (U1836210).

C. Cao et al. (Eds.): FCS 2021, CCIS 1558, pp. 342–351, 2022.
https://doi.org/10.1007/978-981-19-0523-0_22

cutting-edge technology has caused more and more complex security problems while providing the convenience for peoples' life and work [1]. In the process of software development by modules, there are a large number of security. Security vulnerabilities threaten everyone's personal and property security, and may cause serious consequences such as information disclosure [4]. Even experienced programmers can't guarantee the absolute security in the process of software development. In the process of vulnerability mining, many aspects need to be considered and studied. Therefore, how to effectively extract the information of vulnerability features is also a topic worthy of in-depth research and discussion.

Compared with other technologies, deep learning performs better in vulnerability mining [6]. Although the application of deep learning in the field of vulnerability mining has achieved a certain number of representative achievements, but the development at this stage is not yet mature. The current research has conducted in-depth research and analysis on the application of deep learning in the field of security vulnerability mining. By summarizing the existing research results of software vulnerability mining based on deep learning [3], we find that there is still a long way to go to realize automatic and intelligent vulnerability mining due to the wide variety of vulnerabilities [8]. Therefore, it can be seen that it is imperative to optimize the design of software vulnerability detection methods. The vulnerability mining model based on mixed representation is applied in the design of software vulnerability detection methods, which is committed to fundamentally improving the efficiency of software vulnerability detection.

This paper is summarized as follows. The second section briefly introduces the working model framework of deep learning applied to data mining. The third section focuses on combing and analyzing the existing feature extraction model methods. The fourth section summarizes and prospects the above work. The main contributions of this paper are as follows: summarize the general framework of deep learning applied to vulnerability mining, classify and describe feature extraction, and look forward to the construction direction of model framework in the future.

2 Relevant Knowledge

In this section, we will give a briefly introduction about the general framework of deep learning-based vulnerability mining. This framework consists of three phases, including data collecting, learning stage and detection phase [2]. The framework of deep learning-based vulnerability mining process is illustrated in Fig. 1. Next, we will give a detailed description about these three phases.

2.1 Data Collecting

A good deep learning model needs a large number of training samples. However, when collected training data is insufficient, the obtained model has a shortcoming of over fitting, which is not suitable for validating other data samples [24]. At present, in the existing work, the sample objects collected for different application scenarios and learning tasks include binary programs, PDF files, C/C++

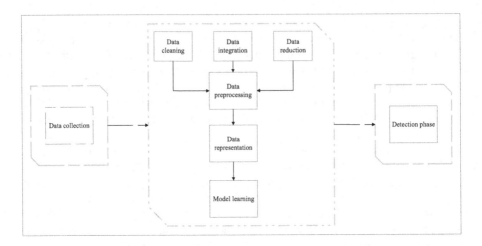

Fig. 1. The framework of deep learning-based vulnerability mining.

source code, IOT, etc. The collecting models of these data are uneven, such as fuzzy test generation, etc. For many file formats such as DOC, PDF, SWF, etc., it is a common model to obtain the test input set by using web crawler [14]. At this stage of data collecting, we need to collect a large amount of vulnerability data, most of which come from major open source websites [21].

2.2 Learning Stage

Most of the collected data have more or less problems. It can not be used directly, so the data should be continuously processed and expressed as vector input to ensure the effect of vulnerability detection. Generally speaking, the learning stage consists of three parts, including data pre-processing, data representation and model learning. Detailed descriptions are discussed in the following.

Data Pre-processing. Data pre-processing refers to some data processing before main processing. The collected data in the real world are generally incomplete or inconsistent [13], which can not be directly used, easily lead to unsatisfactory mining results. It can be divided into three parts: data cleaning, data integration and data reduction [15].

Data cleaning "cleans" missing values, smoothing noise data, error data, etc. Data integration [24] refers to the process of combining and storing data from multiple data sources to establish a data warehouse. Data reduction [18] is a kind of data mining, the reduction representation of the data set is obtained by using data specification technology.

Data Representation. Security researchers mainly investigate the performance of various aspects of security vulnerabilities and use different methods to build models, but the extraction process is difficult for the diversity of data. In this paper, we divide existing data representation methods into five categories. We respectively review these five methods and briefly summarize their advantages and disadvantages in Sect. 3. This is the key issue to be discussed in this paper.

Model Learning. As an essential factor of vlunerability mining, a good learning model is important. By combing the existing software vulnerability mining literature based on deep learning, this paper finds that most of the works mainly put forward to new vulnerability mining models from the improvement of data representation. It mainly focuses on the classification based on deep feature representation.

2.3   Detection Phase

The process of the detection phase is similar to data pre-processing and data representation. Firstly, we abstract the extracted data representation module and determine the key points of software vulnerability detection. Then we extract the key points in software vulnerabilities and process the software vulnerability detection data. We also eliminate the detection data irrelevant to the key points of software vulnerabilities and learn the model to quantitatively express the characteristics of software vulnerabilities. Finally, input the results to get the vulnerability mining model. So we realize the software vulnerability detection based on the hybrid deep learning model.

3   Data Representation Methods

In this section, we give a detailed analysis on data representation methods, including sequence characterization-based method, abstract syntax tree-based method, graph-based method, text-based method and mixed characterization-based method. Moreover, we divide the above methods into two categories, named single feature extraction method and mixed feature extraction method.

3.1   Single Feature Extraction Model

Work [28] describes the process of distinguishing outliers in data preprocessing. However, researchers found that these data still have defects in the process of work, so more accurate data feature extraction methods are needed for more accurate classification.

Sequence Characterization-Based Method. This method mostly informs by lexical analysis of source codes or binary files. In work [23], the library API function is divided into forward and backward calls, generating one or more slices respectively. But only part of the code can be detected and the exact location

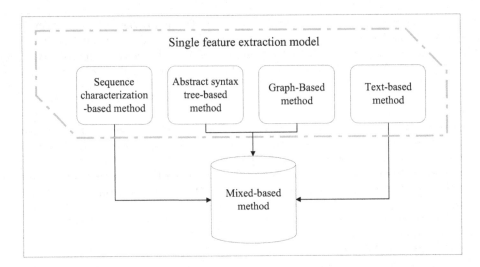

Fig. 2. Five data representation methods for deep learning-based vulnerability mining.

information of the vulnerability can not be known. In work [22], the deep neural network technology is used to train the rectifier linear unit by random gradient descent method and batch normalization method. It also predicts the vulnerable software components. In addition, the statistical feature selection algorithm is used to reduce the feature and search space. The evaluation results show that the proposed technology can predict vulnerable classes with high precision and recall rate, and has good vulnerability detection ability.

Abstract Syntax Tree (AST) Method. This method is a tree representation of the abstract syntax structure of source code in the process of program compilation. A Novel Neural Source Code Representation based on Abstract Syntax Tree (ASTNN) is proposed in work [9]. Different from the existing processing methods, ASTNN divides the whole AST into a series of small syntax trees. The data in the grammar book is vectorized in a series of ways. Then the RNN model is used to generate the vector representation of the code.

Graph-Based Method. This method mainly mines security vulnerabilities from different program source codes or binary files [19]. Work [5] attempts to represent the program graphically. They use the syntax and semantic information between PDG edges and use GNN to build a vulnerability mining model. The comparison with the model using less structured program representation shows the advantages of modeling known structures. Work [7] expressed the program structure, syntax and semantics in the form of graph, and analyzed the corresponding structure of the program on this basis.

In work [29], improvements are mainly made in face image extraction. After preprocessing with HSV, hierarchical HMAX was used to extract features, which extracts more features than previous work. In work [30], based on the famous Hessian affine feature extraction algorithm, a new local feature descriptor is proposed. This method is used to adapt automatic remote sensing image, which can resist local distortion and greatly improve robustness. In work [31], they mainly study the feature extraction method for quality classification. Based on Support Vector Machine (SVM), SVM-RFE with filter is constructed for experiment and made good progress.

Text-Based Method. This method is to extract the main information of text content, then we vectorize it and convert it into data information that can be used directly [20]. The combination of text mining and deep learning technology is used to realize vulnerability mining, and deep learning is applied to program analysis, which has achieved good detection performance. Work [5] proposes a coding standard for constructing program vector representation, and builds a word frequency statistical model to describe the Java source file disclosure mode. In the program classification task, they further feed back the representation into the deep neural network, and obtain higher accuracy than the "shallow" models (such as logistic regression and SVM). In fact, they only extract rough syntax and semantic information from program source code information, which limits the performance of vulnerability mining model.

In work [26], we proposed to use the attention mechanism algorithm to adaptively perceive the context information and extract the text features from readers' emotional changes in the reading process. And the convolution threshold recurrent neural network is used to predict readers' emotions. Work [32] proposed a feature extraction method based on Bag-of-Matrix-Word (BOMW). It extracts from a matrix dictionary and finally counts the frequency of the matrix words to obtain the middle-layer feature of the MFL data matrixes. This improves the effectiveness of features and recognition speed. The advantage of the proposed method not only improves the effectiveness of the features, but also increases the speed.

3.2 Mixed Characterization-Based Method

The major way of data extraction in recent years is close to the mixed characterization-based model. This model refers to the combination of at least two feature representation methods mentioned above, which has higher performance than the four single feature representation methods. It can be seen from work [17] that the prediction accuracy of the deep learning model constructed by CNN and LSTM is higher than the traditional method in the experiment. But there is still a certain gap compared with the mixed characterization-based model constructed by CNN-LSTM. In work [11], using the intermediate representation technology of low-level virtual machine and CNN-RNN to extract the key information of the source code. The results show that the effect is better than the previous experiments. In Work [7], the features in the candidate set samples are abstracted by combining CNN and NLP for vulnerability mining. Therefore, how to integrate multiple features to realize automation and fine-grained vulnerability mining is a research topic worthy of exploration.

In work [25], a two-channel-network model prediction method is proposed. The processed data are put into two parallel convolutional neural networks for feature extraction, and the combination of CNN and LSTM algorithm is used for prediction. The results are the same as work [17] and the mining performance of mixed characterization-based model is better. Work [27] combines work [25] and work [26]. The attention mechanism, CNN and LSTM are used to build a model for photovoltaic prediction.

3.3   Method Comparison

Table 1 is obtained by comparing models of single feature extraction and Mixed characterization-based method. Among them, the sequence characterization-based method mainly extracts features such as identifiers and operators. However, in practical application, due to the large amount of code, only part of the code can be detected, and the extraction effect is not perfect. The abstract syntax tree-based method is to read the source code, merge them into identification tokens according to the regulations, remove blank symbols, comments, etc., and then perform syntax analysis, convert the analyzed array into a tree, and verify the syntax. In this way, data information can be obtained more deeply through node traversal. But the process involves the whole code base, the detection speed is slow, and some identifiers will be deleted when generating the tree, which does not completely match the source code. The graph-based method is to extract features by generating graph structure, which mainly focuses on the logical relationship between data to ensure the integrity of source code to a certain extent, but the detection speed is slow. The text-based method refers to extracting keywords from the text to replace the text information, but it only extracts the semantics roughly. It is easy to ignore the context structure. In contrast, the mixed characterization-based method combines any two or more of the above methods. They can make up for the shortcomings of each other. It also makes the extracted information richer and more complete. How to integrate multiple methods is a problem worthy of further research.

4   Discussion

Traditional machine learning technology needs to extract vulnerability features manually. Then they convert the features into vectors as the input of machine learning algorithm. The technology does not have the ability to automatically extract features from the original data. It heavily depends on expert knowledge for manual work [21]. In the process of combining deep learning with vulnerability mining in the future, I think there are two aspects can be deeply studied.

One is the efficiency and accuracy of vulnerability mining. Firstly, the process of vulnerability mining depends on computing, which is closely related to software scale, hardware system and analysis technology. In the research process, according to different factors, the corresponding countermeasures should be adjusted better to meet the needs and improve efficiency. The other is the

Table 1. Comparison of single feature extraction model and mixed characterization-based method.

Method name	Advantages	Disadvantages
Sequence characterization-based method	Extract identifiers, operators, etc.	Detect part code, the effect is not perfect
Abstract Syntax Tree (AST) method	Get more in-depth data information	Slow speed, mismatched the source code
Graph-based method	Ensure source code integrity	The detection speed is also slow
Text-based method	Replace keywords with text information	Its logic is not strong
Mixed characterization-based method	Extract richer feature information	How to integrate needs further research

automation and intelligence of vulnerability mining. At present, the depth of many studies depends on the experts to solve problems. Automatic vulnerability mining is the Key points and difficulties of current technology research. It plays an important role in realizing automatic vulnerability mining and even network attack and defense.

5 Conclusion

In this paper, we review some representative deep learning-based works of vulnerbaility mining. These methods can be generally divided into five categories: sequence characterization-based method, abstract syntax tree-based method, graph-based method, text-based method and mixed characterization -based method. Meanwhile, we summarize their advantages and disadvantages from the angles of single and mixed feature extraction. Compared to traditional vulnerability mining approaches, deep learning-based methods can realize automatical vulnerability detection without security experts to pre-define mining rules.

Therefore, this paper believes that for different types of problems, we should construct a vulnerability mining model in line with the actual situation. The mixed characterization-based model can extract data information to the greatest extent. In the future, it is an inevitable trend to add deep learning algorithm into the process of vulnerability mining. Automatic and intelligent vulnerability extraction is of far-reaching significance to all aspects of learning and research. More and more accurate information extraction is the premise and foundation of all this. Vulnerability mining based on deep learning is a topic worthy of in-depth discussion.

References

1. Zhao, H., Li, X., Tan, J., Gai, K.: Smart contract security issues and research status. Inf. Technol. Netw. Secur. **40**(05), 1–6 (2021)
2. Gu, M., et al.: Software secure vulnerability mining based on deep learning. Comput. Res. Dev. **58**(10), 2073–2095 (2021)
3. Li, Y., Huang, C., Wang, Z., Yuan, L., Wang, X.: Overview of software vulnerability mining methods based on machine learning. J. Softw. **31**(07), 2040–2061 (2020)
4. Tao, Y., Jia, X., Wu, Y.: A research method of industrial Internet security vulnerabilities based on knowledge map. Inf. Technol. Netw. Secur. **39**(01), 6–13 (2020)
5. Peng, H., Mou, L., Li, G., et al.: Building program vector representations for deep learning. In: 8th International Conference on Knowledge Science, Engineering and Management, pp. 547–553 (2015)
6. He, Y., Li, B.: Learning rate strategy of a combined deep learning model. J. Autom. **42**(06), 953–958 (2016)
7. Allamanis, M., Brockschmidt, M., Khademi, M.: Learning to represent programs with graphs. In: International Conference on Learning Presentations, pp. 1–17 (2017)
8. Wang, L., Li, X., Wang, R., et al.: PreNNsem: A heterogeneous ensemble learning framework for vulnerability detection in software. Appl. Sci. **10**(22), 7954 (2020)
9. Zhang, J., Wang, X., Zhang, H., et al.: A novel neural source code representation based on abstract syntax tree. In: 41st International Conference on Software Engineering, pp. 783–794 (2019)
10. Wang, H., Li, Han., Li, H.: Research on ontology relation extraction method in the field of civil aviation emergencies. Comput. Sci. Explor. **04**(02), 285–293 (2020)
11. Li, X., Wang, L., Xin, Y., et al.: Automated software vulnerability detection based on hybrid neural network. Appl. Sci. **11**(07), 3201 (2021)
12. Yang, H., Shen, S., Xiong, J., et al.: Modulation recognition of underwater acoustic communication signals based on denoting and deep sparse autoencoder. In: INTER-NOISE and NOISE-CON Congress and Conference Proceedings, pp. 5506–5511 (2016)
13. Wang, X.: Application of hierarchical clustering based on matrix transformation in gene expression data analysis. Comput. CD Softw. Appl. **15**(24), 46–47 (2012)
14. Zhu, X.: Deep learning analysis based on data collection. Jun. Mid. Sch. World: Jun. Mid. Sch. Teach. Res. **04**, 66 (2021)
15. Liu, M., Wang, X., Huang, Y.: Data preprocessing in data mining. Comput. Sci. **04**, 56–59 (2000)
16. Mohamed, A., Sainath, T., Dahl, G., et al.: Deep belief network for telephone recognition u sing discriminant features. In: IEEE International Conference on acoustics, pp. 5060–5063 (2015)
17. Wu, F., Wang, J., Liu, J., et al.: Vulnerability detection with deep learning. In: 3rd IEEE International Conference on Computer and Communications, pp. 1298–1302 (2017)
18. Yu, X., Chen, W., Chen, R.: Implementation of an approximate mining method for data protocol. J. Huaqiao Univ. (NATURAL SCIENCE EDITION) **29**(03)29, 370–374 (2008)
19. Jaafor, O., Birregah, B.: Multi-layered graph-based model for social engineering vulnerability assessment. In: International Conference on Advances in Social Networks Analysis and Mining, pp. 1480–1488 (2015)

20. Gao, R., Zhou, C., Zhu, R.: Research on vulnerability mining technology of network application program. Mod. Electron. Tech. **41**(03), 15–19 (2018)

21. Lin, Z., Xiang, L., Kuang, X.: Machine Learning in Vulnerability Databases. In: 10th International Symposium on Computational Intelligence and Design (ISCID), pp. 108–113 (2018)

22. Pang, Y., Xue, X., Wang, H.: Predicting vulnerable software components through deep neural network. In: 12th International Conference on Advanced Computational Intelligence (ICACI), pp. 6–10 (2017)

23. Zou, Q., et al.: From automation to intelligence: progress in software vulnerability mining technology. J. Tsinghua Univ. (NATURAL SCIENCE EDITION) **58**(12), 1079–1094 (2018)

24. Li, Z., Zou, D., Xu, S., et al. VulDeePecker: A deep learning-based system for vulnerability detection. In: 25th Annual Network and Distributed System Security Symposium(NDSS), pp. 1–15 (2018)

25. Jian, X., Gu, H., Wang, R.: A short-term photovoltaic power prediction model based on dual-channel CNN and LSTM. Electr. Power Sci. Eng. **35**(5), 7–11 (2019)

26. Zhang, Q., Peng, Z.: Attention-based convolutionalgated recurrent neural network for reader's emotion prediction. Comput. Eng. Appl. **54**(13), 168–174 (2018)

27. Liu, Q., Hu, Q., Yang, L., Zhou, H.: Research on deep learning photovoltaic power generation model based on time series. Power Syst. Protect. Control **49**(19), 87–98 (2021)

28. Jiang, L., Liu, J., Zhang, H.: Discrimination and compensation of abnormal values of magnetic flux leakage in oil pipeline based on BP neural network. In: Chinese Control and Decision Conference (CCDC), pp. 3714–3718 (2017)

29. Pisal, A., Sor, R., Kinage, K., Facial feature extraction using hierarchical MAX(HMAX) method. In: International Conference on Computing, Communication, Control and Automation (ICCUBEA), pp. 1–5 (2017)

30. Sedaghat, A., Ebadi, H.: Remote sensing image matching based on adaptive binning SIFT descriptor. IEEE Trans. Geosci. Remote Sens. **53**(10), 5283–5293 (2015)

31. Liu, X., Tang, J.: Mass classification in mammograms using selected geometry and texture features. New SVM-Bas. Feature Select. Meth. **8**(3), 910–920 (2014)

32. Jiang, L., Liu, J., Zhang, H., Xu, K.: MFL data feature extraction based on KPCA-BOMW Model. In: 31st Chinese Control and Decision Conference (CCDC), pp. 1025–1029 (2019)

Author Index

Ali, Ikram 181

Cao, Chunjie 3, 30, 103
Cheng, Ming 288
Chu, Juan 120

Deng, Jiezhen 14
Ding, Yaoling 308
Ding, Yingqiu 288
Dong, Linxiao 120
Duan, Qiang 63

Feng, Liwen 197
Feng, Mengyue 163
Feng, Tao 163
Fu, Yongkang 245

Gao, Zhixuan 308
Gaofei, Wu 327
Gong, Yongkang 257
Gu, Mianxue 342
Guo, Zhen 342

Han, Jianming 230
Haruna, Charles Roland 181
He, Hua 214
Hu, Jinglu 78, 342
Hu, Yongyang 63
Hu, Yupu 269
Huang, Yuhang 163
Huang, Zhicheng 14

Ji, Xin 120
Jia, Huiwen 269
Jiang, Xinrui 197
Jiao, Xiang 63
Jinglu, Hu 327

Kpiebaareh, Michael Y. 181

Lei, Liao 78
Li, Fagen 134, 181
Li, Jian 152, 245
Li, Jie 152
Li, Lin 214

Li, Xuejun 78
Li, Ying 342
Lin, Yuhao 342
Liu, Cong 214
Liu, Ximeng 269
Luo, Xi 103
Luo, Xiangyang 49
Lv, Xinjian 152

Ma, Bin 49, 245
Mao, Terui 257
Mu, Jieru 214
Mwitende, Gervais 134

Na, Wang 327
Nkurunziza, Egide 134

Ou, Guoliang 78

Pang, Shanchen 214
Peng, Hao 230

Qian, Zhen 230
Qiu, Tingyu 14
Qiuling, Yue 327

Ren, Hansong 78

Shi, Nan 152
Shu, Xiang 30
Sun, Hongyu 78, 342

Tandoh, Christopher 181
Tandoh, Lawrence 134, 181
Tao, Fangjian 3, 30
Tian, Xiao 78
Tian, Yuan 152

Wang, An 308
Wang, Chao 63
Wang, Chunpeng 245
Wang, He 163, 342
Wang, Jinwei 49
Wang, Longjuan 3, 30, 103
Wang, Randing 257
Wang, Shuang 308
Wang, Wenjie 163

Wang, Xiaoming   14
Wang, Yuli   245
Wei, Jing   152
Wei, Xianglin   63
Wen, Wenjian   14
Wu, Congyun   14
Wu, Gaofei   78
Wu, Hongwen   14
Wu, Songyang   230

Xiong, Naixue   49
Xu, Guangquan   230

Yan, Diqun   257
Yang, Chengyue   120
Yang, Yang   288
Yu, Xinying   197

Yuan, Qingjun   308
Yue, Qiuling   342

Zhang, Haifeng   120
Zhang, Han   163
Zhang, Jiawei   49
Zhang, Jiayuan   163
Zhang, Kejun   197
Zhang, Weiming   288
Zhang, Yanhua   269
Zhang, Yuqing   78, 327, 342
Zhao, Dandan   230
Zhong, Ming   230
Zhou, Ke   14
Zou, Binghui   3
Zou, Jianming   14

Printed in the United States
by Baker & Taylor Publisher Services